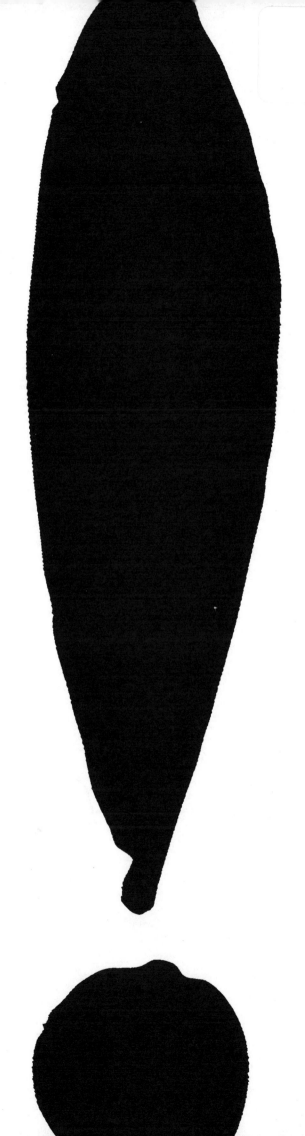

ONUS

Perspecta 53
The Yale Architectural Journal

Foreword

In architecture, ethics are malleable. In theory, the terms are rigid, yet the reality is elastic. Although much of the built environment is ostensibly designed for an individual client's needs, architecture's effects reverberate politically, environmentally and culturally, often in unexpected ways and far beyond the limits of any parcel or project. This issue of Perspecta considers the ethical questions and moral tensions that arise during the ideation, development, completion and aftermath of the design process.

Architecture operates on a temporal scale largely disconnected from social shifts. While architectural projects are often funded by those who are most powerful, the practice still has implicit obligations to those most vulnerable. By making abstract concepts concrete, architecture's manifest nature can work to either reinforce or disrupt political, environmental and social structures.

This issue delves into multi-faceted conversations around the idea of responsibility in architecture, grounded in the historic trajectory of the topic while recognizing more speculative positions. Contributors from a diverse span of geographies and practices offer insights, provocations and questions about the dilemmas that architects encounter at every stage of designing the built environment: Whose architectural ideas get to become reality? What ethical role does form play in design? What moral burdens must architects shoulder in the act of building? Lastly, what is the future cost of today's actions?

Through arguments, essays and projects that examine the issue at a range of scales — from the intimacy of a single material to the reach of global typology — Perspecta 53 explores the complex dynamics of architectural onus and the ways in which designers navigate conflicting agendas to pose new possibilities.

Notes on
the Activist
Tradition
in Architecture

Lola Sheppard
and
Mason White

The activist tradition is the power house of architecture, the most dynamic of all the traditions, because of its continual insistence on transcending realities as they exist.
— Charles Jencks, *Architecture 2000*, p. 88

There has been no shortage of attempts to make taxonomic claims and stylistic labels on architecture throughout history. However, none has been more impactful, yet contentious, than architectural historian Charles Jencks' 1971 "Evolutionary Tree."[1] Critical of Modernism, Jencks was probably best known as an early theorist of Post-Modernism, and this diagram fit well within his singular interest to chronicle movements. Jencks' diagrammatic drawing identifies and charts six "traditions" within architecture from 1920-2000. Comparing Jencks' original drawing from 1971 with the re-drawn version of 2000, a series of important differences appear. The first version ambitiously attempted to be both historical, 1920-1971, and predictive, 1971-2000. The diagram charted and projected six traditions in architecture: logical, idealist, self-conscious, intuitive, activist and unselfconscious. Especially relevant to the disciplinary question of ethics and social impact of the architect, is the so-called "activist" tradition. Jencks argues that the "activist tradition contains the strongest critics of the present system and its apologists."[2] While this characterization fits in with a general understanding of activism, Jencks' diagram is primarily intended to orient this -ism within and among other -isms. The diagram suggests the modern origin of the activist tradition is a utopian, Futurist, Constructivist and Communist strain during the 1920s, as advocated by Ivan Leonidov, Hannes Meyer, El Lissitzky and others.

It is true that these architects and thinkers made considerable contributions to architecture's political claims as Modernism was forming. However, he does not emphasize that the activist tradition is representative of the discipline's most social and political intentions. The diagram also identifies a 1960s-70s interest in various sub-themes of activism including: "revolutionist," "interest community advocacy," "workers-councils," "student-activist tendencies," and it includes significant figures, such as architect Cedric Price and urban activist Jane Jacobs. He then predicts a "revolutionist" strain in the 1970s-80s that includes, without much elaboration, "minority group" and "black riots." When Jencks re-visited the diagram for Architectural Review in a July 2000 issue, he updated the original to include actual events and figures from the ensuing years 1971-1999 across all the traditions. These additions were identified with a gray background to distinguish them from the black background of the 1971 drawing. The 2000 edition expands the activist tradition in the 1970s with the label "participation in design," and it includes Lucien Kroll and Ralph Erskine, but also surprisingly Charles Moore, Frank Gehry and OMA. It is hard to imagine in what way Moore or Gehry embodied participation or was in any way politically or socially motivated, so these inclusions reveal Jencks' primary interest to identify the emergence of Post-Modernism. What was previously a distinct gap in the 1990s, now shows

1
Charles Jencks's "Evolutionary Tree to the Year 2000" as published in *Architecture 2000: Predictions and Methods* (New York: Praeger, 1971), 46–47.

2
Ibid, 75.

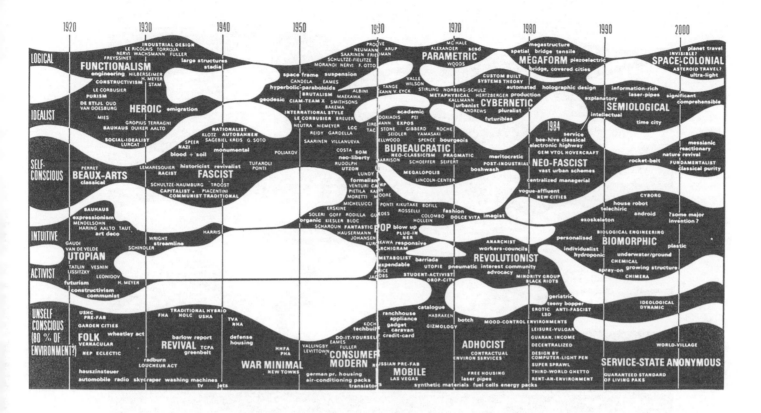

Charles Jencks, "Evolutionary Tree," 1971. Jencks first published
this diagram in *Architecture 2000: Predictions and Methods*
(New York: Praeger, 1971), 46-47.

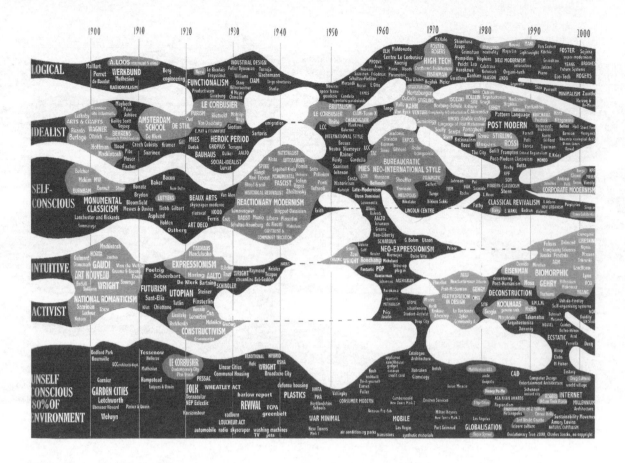

Charles Jencks, "Evolutionary Tree," 2000. Jencks revisited the 1971
diagram in "Jencks's Theory of Evolution, an overview of twentieth-century architecture," *Architectural Review*, July 2000, 76-79.

the encroachment of the "intuitive" thread and its preoccupation with biomorphism and expressionism. In fact, Jencks argued that the "activist" lineage merged with interests found in the "intuitive," embodied by the labels "deconstruction," "ecstatic" and "biomorphic" from 1980-2000. In the 1971 edition, he anticipated that "in the 1990s these two traditions [intuitive and activist] might well coalesce into the Biomorphic School and emerge as the strongest, single movement at the end of the twentieth century, for many of the breakthroughs which are predicted in biology and automation will satisfy the desire of both traditions for more personal autonomy and freedom."[3] This did not come to fruition as such and falsely aligned formal biomorphic ideas with the potential role of environmental thinking. Instead, the activist tradition, by nature of its political and social motivations, should always be distinguished from any formally governed preoccupations. If aspects of any other tradition were to align with activism in architecture, it should maintain social or political intentions as a primary design objective.

Despite the opportunity to revisit the diagram in 2000, and to retrospectively clarify the activist tradition in architecture, Jencks does little to articulate and distinguish the socio-political from the techno-formal motivations, which by 2000 would have been even more evident with hindsight. Although he was not focused singularly on one tradition, and seemed more interested in the distinction and emergence of traditions within the discipline, what exactly Jencks meant by "activist" is made even less clear from the revisions and inclusions in the 2000 edition. In the ensuing 20 years since Jencks' second diagram, the activist tradition has continued to expand and evolve with no proper documentarian.

While Jencks' charting and parsing of activism as one of the six traditions in architecture is noble, he has made it fraught with ambiguity over various notions and intentions. For this reason, his diagram has been both admired and criticized. One strong condemnation came in the form of Anthony Vidler's 1981 essay in *Skyline*, in which he took Jencks to task for focusing disproportionately on stylistic traits, rather than recognizing the social and cultural agendas associated with various movements and factions.[4] According to Vidler, in its attempt to totalize the discipline, Jencks' diagram had generalized and simplified traditions. This is evidenced by the missed opportunity to distinguish the activist tradition as a powerful form of practice that engages society and politics in real time. It seems opportune, 20 years later, to re-examine in greater detail the impact and contributions within the activist tradition, in isolation from other traditions, and how it has realigned the discipline. This re-examination begins with a constellation of architects working in the 1960s to early 1980s and another resurgence of activism in the mid to late 1990s and then further in the 2010s.[5] In homage to Jencks' attempt to identify competing agendas for the discipline, the activist tradition has been re-drawn and expanded in isolation from other traditions using his diagrammatic technique over the period 1950-2020. Isolating the activist tradition reveals that it has expanded and bifurcated, showing even more activity

3
Ibid, 89.

4
Anthony Vidler, "Cooking Up the Classics," *Skyline* (October 1981): 18–21.

5
Since parsing current tendencies and developments is sufficiently risky, we will not attempt the challenge of predicting 30, 15, or even 5 years from now.

and development than Jencks had predicted. Revisiting the diagram also creates the opportunity to understand the arc of the activist tradition and the forms of practice within it today. In what way have architects operated as activists in both the past and present? What are their tools and agendas?

Action, Activism and Practice

The activist tradition can be understood as the use of spatial practice to expose injustice and foster socially inclusive and politically motivated design. In an attempt to clarify and articulate the tradition, the criteria for sub-categories within the activist tradition is established according to tools, strategies, methods and intentions of activism. It considers the questions: how is activism in architecture understood and materialized? What modes of practice distinguish it from other traditions? Who has the privilege and the voice in the activist tradition? As the profession expands its gender, cultural and demographic representation, a wider range of voices are participating on behalf of those under-represented in spatial and aesthetic discourse. In politics, activism is understood as the use of direct, often confrontational action in support of a cause, whether social, political, economic or environmental. Embedded in the notion of activism is the assumption that some kind of action is necessary for structural transformation. In architecture, how this action might be practiced is as varied as its motivation. In the reconsideration of practices and agendas within the activist tradition, some have embraced a critique of the discipline's models of practice and have offered counter-points to conventional client-based services; others are driven to redress social or economic inequalities; and still others

use design-based research to reveal political, economic or logistical forces that are surreptitiously shaping our physical environment. This expanded notion offers a wider understanding of the architect as an activist agent.

For philosopher and political theorist Hannah Arendt, who wrote extensively about the politics of public realm, agency is characterized by an action's effect on the world and its ability to disrupt the assumed flow of events. Arendt identifies action as rooted in freedom, and hence inherently unpredictable; no actor has control of the outcome, and each action can set in motion a number of other, unpredictable actions.[6] Arendt argued that the public realm is a precondition of public life and society; it is the space of appearance and the space of action, of being seen and made visible in society.[7] Public space is contingent on the possibility of spontaneous and unforeseeable actions. For Arendt, "to act, in its most general sense, means to take initiative, to begin […], to set something in motion," and action requires an audience or public.[8] Activism is embodied in one's appearance in the public realm, as well as the forms or "tools" of communication used. Forms and tools can range from petitions to boycotts, including strikes, rallies, protests and sit-ins, among others. Each of these forms of action is linked with a spatial venue — the public square, the street, the campus, or today, the digital realm. It is noteworthy that political activism is determined by the mode of action. The notion of "tools" and "actions" is paralleled in architectural

6
Hannah Arendt, *The Human Condition*, 2nd ed. (Chicago: The University of Chicago Press, 1995), 191.

7
Ibid, 199.

8
Ibid, 177.

Re-Defining Landscape: Erbil's Urban-Rural Greenbelt

Jala Makhzoumi

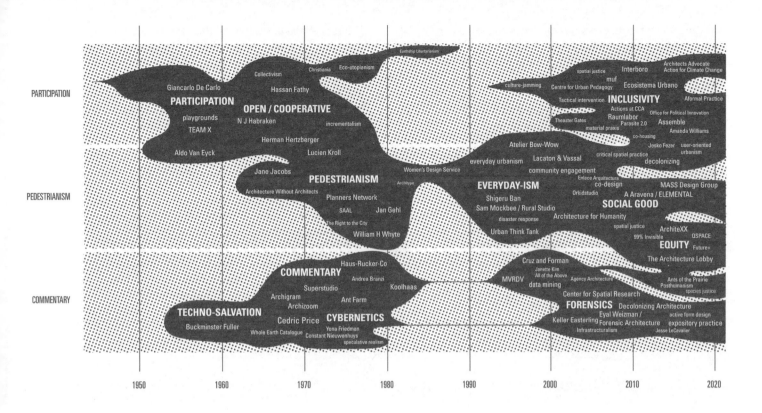

PARTICIPATION

Giancarlo De Carlo
PARTICIPATION
playgrounds
TEAM X
N J Habraken
Aldo Van Eyck
Herman Hertzberger
Jane Jacobs
Architecture Without Architects

Collectivism
Christiania
Hassan Fathy
incrementalism
Lucien Kroll

Earthship Libertarianism
Eco-utopianism

spatial justice   Interboro   Architects Advocate Action for Climate Change
culture-jamming   Centre for Urban Pedagogy   muf   Ecosistema Urbano
Tactical intervention   **INCLUSIVITY**   Aformal Practice
Actions at CCA   Office for Political Innovation
Theaster Gates   **Raumlabor**   Assemble
material praxis   Parasite 2.0
co-housing   Amanda Williams
Atelier Bow-Wow   Jesko Fezer   user-oriented urbanism
everyday urbanism   Lacaton & Vassal   critical spatial practice
community engagement   decolonizing
Enlace Arquitectura

PEDESTRIANISM

PEDESTRIANISM
Planners Network
Women's Design Service
Archtype
SAAL   Jan Gehl
The Right to the City
William H Whyte

EVERYDAY-ISM
Shigeru Ban
Sam Mockbee / Rural Studio
disaster response
Urban Think Tank

co-design   **MASS Design Group**
Orkidstudio   A Aravena / ELEMENTAL
SOCIAL GOOD
Architecture for Humanity
spatial justice   ArchiteXX
99% Invisible   QSPACE
EQUITY   Future+
The Architecture Lobby

COMMENTARY

Haus-Rucker-Co
COMMENTARY
Andrea Branzi
Superstudio   Koolhaas
Archigram   Ant Farm
Archizoom

TECHNO-SALVATION
Buckminster Fuller
Cedric Price   **CYBERNETICS**
Whole Earth Catalogue   Yona Friedman
Constant Nieuwenhuys
speculative realism

Cruz and Forman
Janette Kim
All of the Above
MVRDV   data mining   Agency Architecture
Center for Spatial Research
FORENSICS   Decolonizing Architecture
Eyal Weizman /   active form design
Keller Easterling   Forensic Architecture   expository practice
Infrastructuralism   Jesse LeCavalier

Ants of the Prairie
Posthumanism
species justice

1950   1960   1970   1980   1990   2000   2010   2020

Mason White and Lola Sheppard, "The Activist Tradition," 2020.
This diagram, in the spirit of Jencks's Evolutionary Tree, revisits and
isolates only the activist tradition from 1950-2020.

Traditional conceptions of nationhood usually include a common history, identity, territory, economy and a collective call for a people's sovereignty. Yet until very recently, Kurds have been denied this. Iraqi Kurdistan is a semi-autonomous region in the north of Iraq. It is home to 5.2 million of the world's estimated 30 million Kurds, a stateless people who populate the border regions between Iraq, Turkey, Iran and Syria. The repercussions of sustained, continuous war and displacement have shaped modern Kurdish identity. Like the Kurds themselves, the landscape has been shaped by the struggle for political recognition. Due to the history of turmoil that has cast its shadow over the region, an equitable and comprehensive discussion on the idea of a designed landscape has not had the chance to develop.

As a term, "landscape" defies singular definition. It is dependent on the environmental context within which it is defined and the political and cultural lenses through which it is viewed. Landscape means something tangible and intangible: a physical setting shaped by the people who inhabit it and a mosaic of meanings and values that manifest themselves into a world-view, rooted in a specific culture and place.[1] By exploring the multiple meanings of landscape within the context of both

1
Makhzomi, Jala (2016)
"From urban beautification to a holistic approach: the discourse of 'landscape' in the Arab Middle East".
Landscape Research 2, (10), pp. 1-10.

the nature and culture around the city of Erbil, it becomes possible to understand landscape's potential agency as a force of positive change in a place scarred by both historic colonial occupation and recent ethnic and political conflict.

Here is a case study of a project that never came to pass. It closely follows the design process for the large-scale development of a greenbelt surrounding Erbil, commissioned by the city in 2009. As a landscape architect, my role in the project was to integrate three distinct interpretations of Kurdish landscape into one coherent whole, a task that led to both productive collaboration and sharp contention between the client and the community. Tracing the development and ultimate suspension of the greenbelt design illustrates a key case study in the complexities, challenges and opportunities of working with a local government looking to define its city as both an oasis of modernity and the birthplace of civilization in a region continuously ravaged by war.

The Opportunity

In 2003, Erbil became the capital of the semi-autonomous Kurdistan Regional Government (KRG), offering hope for a new season of prosperity. In the following years, the city evolved into an

and urban practice: actions or tactics can serve a means of circumventing traditional power structures of client-architect, as a means of giving voice and agency to under-represented groups, or simply to catalyze attention and discussion to important urban or environmental issues.[9] For many activists, architecture serves as a form of advocacy, bringing agency to groups or issues often denied the social and political benefits of architectural innovation. The architects and practices highlighted below each embrace diverse "tools" for actions — be it writing, speech, events, installations, exhibitions, drawings and buildings. Equally, there is diversity in the venue and platform that hosts their forms of activism.

This reconsideration of the activist tradition, circa 1950-2020, reveals a few important threads that run concurrently within practices throughout multiple decades and generations. The following three activist agendas emerge or have been undergoing transformation since Jencks' 2001 consideration:

1. From Participation to Inclusion
2. From Pedestrianism to Social Good
3. From Commentary to Forensics

These transformations offer parallel threads of the activist's role in architecture, as well as new tools for practice.

From Participation to Inclusion

One way that activist architects have challenged the discipline is by reconceiving the design process — consultation, design and construction — and public participation in these processes. Team 10, a group of architects working in the 1960s and 70s, in reaction to the *Congrès Internationaux d'Architecture Modern* (CIAM)'s more doctrinaire approach to architecture and planning, represented a critical moment for challenging the hierarchical relationship between architect and user. Born of the political and social upheaval of the late 1960s in Europe, and critical of CIAM's colonizing and universalizing tendency (led by architects such as Le Corbusier, Gropius, Mies van der Rohe, Loos), a younger generation of architects such as Giancarlo de Carlo, Herman Hertzberger, Aldo van Eyck, Ralph Erskine, Lucien Kroll, John Habraken and others, sought to humanize and localize architecture's links to society.[10] The emphasis on participation, a direct critique of CIAM's functionalist orthodoxy, destabilized the traditional power dynamics of the architect.

Italian architect Giancarlo De Carlo (1919-2005) was arguably the strongest advocate for broadening participation in architecture, declaring: "We have participation, in fact, only when everyone takes part equally in the management of the power structure, or when the power structure no longer exists because everyone is directly and equally involved in the process of decision-making."[11] De Carlo

9
The Canadian Centre for Architecture's exhibition and eponymous book *Actions: What You Can Do With the City* documented 99 actions, from the banal, to the marginally legal, that offer new modes of engagement in the city.

10
Amongst others, some of the most defining architects to come out of Team 10 were Giancarlo de Carlo, Herman Hertzberger, Aldo van Eyck, Ralph Erskine, Lucien Kroll and John Habraken.

11
Giancarlo De Carlo, "An Architecture of Participation" in *Perspecta*, V. 17, (MIT Press, 1980): 77.

Landscape means something tangible and intangible: a physical setting shaped by the people who inhabit it and a mosaic of meanings and values that manifest themselves into a world-view, rooted in culture and place. Photo by author.

believed architecture should be a consensus-based activity, and he was critical of Modernism's tendency to decouple design from social behaviors and its disregard for the role of the user in architecture.[12] He argued that participation would introduce "a plurality of objectives and actions whose outcomes cannot be foreseen."[13] In projects, such as *Villagio Matteoti* (1969-74), de Carlo worked directly with the future residents for over a year. The process involved discussions, the production of numerous design models, resulting in 40 variations of housing types. Like De Carlo, Dutch Structuralist architect Herman Hertzberger (1932-) considered architecture as a framework for social behavior, one which could support collectivity. Without eschewing form, but embracing a humanistic understanding of architecture, De Carlo, Hertzberger and van Eyck's work emerged from an anthropological understanding of place, threshold and use, where buildings celebrate and foreground the seemingly banal realities of everyday life.[14]

N. John Habraken (1928-), also linked with the Structuralists, strove more overtly for user participation in design, particularly in housing. Embracing the idea of "open building architecture," he advocated for an architecture of "supports (or fixed components) and infills," developing a structural framework that would enable conditions of flexibility and user customization.[15] Design was centered more on the development of a system of design (of structural systems, bays, components and dimensions) to allow this customization, than it was a specific formal outcome. Belgian architect Lucien Kroll embraced a more radical participatory process, best exemplified in the provocative University of Louvain medical student residence, nicknamed *La MéMé*, completed in 1976. Kroll advocated for diversity,

radical community living and transparency of daily life, rejecting both Modernism and the doctrines of efficiency, industrialization and prefabrication that came with it. While Jencks referred to *La MéMé* as a "totalitarianism of enforced participation," Kroll rejected excessive architectural control and homogeneity, arguing that the building was "a political project, not an aesthetic one" that is "un-geometrical, anti-authoritarian, anarchical, that is to say, human."[16] The legacy of Habraken and Kroll's participatory and inclusive

12
De Carlo noted that architects' photographic documentation of their own buildings was typically devoid of the life that validated its very existence, as though users sullied the integrity of the architectural act.

13
Giancarlo De Carlo, "Architecture's Public," *Parametro*, V. 5 (1970).

14
Both in Hertzberger's analysis of other architects' work and his own, those often overlooked by architecture—the elderly, children, office workers, the working class—are celebrated in the unfolding activities of daily life. This is particularly evident in his housing for the elderly (1974) and his celebrated *Central Beheer* offices in Appeldoorn (1967-79). See Herman Hertzberger, *Lessons for Students in Architecture* (Rotterdam: 010 publishers, 1991).

15
N. John Habraken, *Supports: An Alternative to Mass Housing* (London: The Architectural Press, 1972); and *The Structure of the Ordinary: Form and Control in the Built Environment, rev.* ed. (Cambridge: MIT Press, 2000).

16
Lucien Kroll, "Anarchitecture," in C. Richard Hatch, *The Scope of Social Architecture* (New York: Van Nostrand Reinhold, 1984), 167.

---

economic hub in a fragile region.[2] Today, Erbil offers employment and provides refuge to those forcefully evacuated from the rural periphery and, most recently, to Syrian refugees and Iraqi families displaced from their villages in northern Iraq by ISIS. Because of its relative safety and economic prosperity, Erbil has doubled its population since 2003. Correspondingly, the urban footprint has expanded threefold in a series of concentric zones, with a citadel at its historic core. To address this phenomenal expansion, Erbil's government commissioned the architecture, engineering, and planning office DAR Group in 2007 to prepare a master plan, "Erbil 2030." One of its main tenets was the creation of the Erbil Inner Greenbelt, an urban greening project conceived to deter future sprawl, to improve urban microclimate and to provide chances within the city for people to find respite in nature.[3]

The concept of greenbelts first dates to 19th century Europe, when they were implemented to alleviate the adversity of urban living under the thrall of the Industrial Revolution. Protecting areas of largely undeveloped land around urban areas from industry or large-scale agriculture would improve air quality and ensure land conservation. In Western urban planning, greenbelts were codified in Ebenezer Howard's seminal treatise

Garden Cities of To-Morrow (1898), which extolled the use of green space to separate workers' housing from polluted industrial sites. In this context, greenbelts could be used as a source of fertile land and a common area for recreation and exercise. Today, greenbelts are flexible in terms of their spatial parameters and their programmatic intent, as informed by the science of resource preservation and guided by the global drive for sustainable development. These spaces can be multi-functional, combining productivity, nature conservation, leisure and recreation as a means of sustainable urban greening.[4]

In 2009, the KRG invited the Lebanese architecture and urban planning firm Khatib and Alami to develop the Erbil Greenbelt Master Plan.[5] An interdisciplinary project team was assembled, including architects, planners, hydrologists, agronomists and myself, as the landscape architect.[6] GIS technicians provided support in data collection and mapping. Together, the team sought to re-define the idea of the greenbelt to reflect the Kurdish experience, using three interpretations: landscape as a productive agricultural system; landscape as a site for recreation and enjoyment; and landscape as a space for discovery and ecological restoration. As the landscape architect, my task

2
Kurds fought for recognition and self-rule throughout the twentieth century, confronting British colonial rule, post-colonial state and the Baathist regime. UN Security Council *Resolution 688* following the Gulf War in 1991, gave birth to a "safe haven" following international concern for the safety of Kurdish refugees. The semi-autonomous rule was formalized in 2005, which resulted in Erbil being declared the capital of the Kurdish Regional Government.

3
The Erbil master plan 2030 proposed an "inner" greenbelt and "outer" one, The team leader for the greenbelt project discussed in this article argued there was no need for an outer greenbelt, pointing out that if Erbil followed the growth trend in other Iraqi cities, the area inscribed by the inner greenbelt will be able to host 4 million inhabitants, more than four times Erbil's current population, (*Erbil Green Belt: Master Plan and Design Guidelines*, Volume I, May 2010).

4
Makhzoumi, J. (2015) "The greening discourse: ecological landscape design and city regions in the Mashreq." In R Saliba (ed.) *Reconceptualizing Boundaries: Urban Design in the Arab World*. Ashgate, London, pp. 63-80.

5
Khatib and Alami http://www.khatibalami.com/

6
The design team assembled by K&A for the EGB project include a range of expertise: Edgar Murad: architect/planner, team leader- Hadi Jafar: hydrologist/agricultural engineer- Laurence Cherbel: geologist- Ali Zeidan: environmental scientist- Johny Hajj: GIS- Rami Zurayk: ecologist/sustainable agriculture; Jala Makzouni: architect/ecological landscape planning.

approach can be found in more recent planning projects, such as Balkrishna Doshi's Aranya housing in Indore, India (1989), West 8's *Borneo-Sporenburg* (1993), OMA's *Almere Homeruskwartier* (1994), Alejandro Aravena's *Elemental housing in Chile* (2003), and Lacaton & Vassal's Mulhouse housing (2005).

There is considerable resistance to participation and inclusion within the disciplinary structure of the design process and within the Modernist ethos of authorship. Architecture struggles to enact an activist position in the face of its inherent dependence on systems of financing and patronage — be it public or private capital. The rise of neoliberalism and governments' increasing divestment from social infrastructure have spurred activist practices to react to contemporary financial and patronage structures. Based on collaborative models, which eschew the architect as singular author, practices are developing projects through inclusion with local stewards. Within flattened hierarchies, alternate agencies for architects appear. Arendt identifies agency as having multiple meanings:

1. giving visibility through a public stage
2. establishing the capacity to interact and communicate
3. creating contexts free of outside forces and pressures.[17]

This reading of agency is embodied in several contemporary practices operating across a range of media — from research to urban actions and events to built projects — which seek to create new public platforms for social engagement.

There are several contemporary practices that embody this transition from participation-based advocacy to cooperative agency. The Berlin-based collective Raumlabor ("Space Laboratory"), was established in 1999 in the wake of the dramatic urban transformations occurring in post-reconstruction Berlin. Often relying on temporary interventions, the group galvanizes communities through participatory projects, in which objects, events and spaces become experiments and materializations of collectivity. The British multi-disciplinary collective Assemble is another multi-headed practice functioning in this tradition. Their work operates between activism, community engagement, industry and labor. Many projects, such as Granby Four in Liverpool, involve extensive engagement with a marginalized community, renovating abandoned houses and creating community infrastructure. The use of repurposed materials and self-building is often central to the conceptualization and implementation of their projects. While it may emerge out of financial necessity, it is also a conceptual imperative. There is a Ruskinian belief in the material culture and social engagement of architecture that shapes the philosophy of their work. Interboro Partners, based out of New York, is perhaps the most overtly political of these contemporary practices, negotiating the line between architecture, urban interventions and planning, but always recentering the focus on how people and urban policy shape, in both intentional

17
Andrea Thuma, "Hannah Arendt, Agency, and the Public Space," *Institute for Human Sciences*, Junior Visiting Fellows Conferences, vol. xxix.

was to integrate these variable ideas into a coherent and compelling whole.

The Site

Erbil is located 225 miles north of Baghdad, the capital of Iraq. Its ancient citadel is one of the oldest continually inhabited settlements in the world and a UNESCO Heritage site.[7] The Erbil plain, an area over 3,000 square kilometers is bounded by distinct geographies — mountains to the northeast and desert to the south and west. Circa 800 B.C., Neo-Assyrian kings, went to great lengths to realize their vision of capital cities as a carefully planned space in which imperial power would be expressed through architecture and lush and abundant surroundings. Their engineers redirected the surface hydrology of rivers and wadis into canals that fed city and countryside alike. The fortunes of Erbil waxed and waned in the centuries that followed, a consequence of its location at the border of competing political interests.

In the centuries that followed, Erbil became a battlefield for the Greeks, the Romans, the Persians, and the Arabs. Bloody exchanges of power and the disastrous warfare that followed erased all signs of the prosperous landscape that once defined the region. All that

remained were scattered, impoverished villages and the citadel town, a solitary landmark in an empty plain.

The site of the Erbil greenbelt lies 12 kilometers beyond the citadel town. It is inscribed between two circular roads and encompasses an area of 150 square kilometers. The area was once densely populated, but many villages were destroyed by the Baathist regime in its attempts to "Arabize" the Kurdistan Region between 1986-89. The deportations and mass emigrations that followed wrought dramatic changes in the landscape. Cemeteries perched atop barren hills stand as desolate markers of the villages that once were. Today, the remaining inhabitants are mainly farmers, subsisting on cultivation and herding. They own their home, but they rarely own the land they farm. Living conditions are poor and wages are low, at usually no more than $250 per month. In 2009, at the project outset, the majority of the population was Kurdish, while some villages and farmsteads were home to Arab families.[8]

There are no historical records of forests in Erbil, yet historians generally agree that its plain was stripped of its native landscape centuries ago. The earliest photographs of the Erbil Citadel (circa 1900), reveal bare expanses of land without a single tree in sight. Today,

7
UNESCO inscribed Erbil Citadel on the World Heritage List in 25 June 2014.

8
Since 2013, the share of Arab families has increased with refugees escaping the war in Syria. In 2016, internally displaced families from the Mosul Province whose villages were destroyed by ISIL also moved into the Erbil peripheries, some live in camps, others sought refuge in the villages.

and unintentional ways, the public realm. Their work largely eschews questions of form and style to focus on user engagement, participatory planning processes and community empowerment. Their recent book *The Arsenal of Exclusion & Inclusion* (2016), a documentation of 101 "weapons" used by practitioners to "restrict or promote access to the city," serves as a rejoinder to the complacency of urbanists and policy makers' when it comes to the disenfranchisement of the marginal urban and suburban communities in America.[18]

However, there are also contemporary sceptics of participation in architecture and the presumption that it is an innocent, well-intentioned act. Historian Jeremy Till notes the pitfalls of participatory architecture and the easy slip into token or symbolic models of participation.[19] Similarly, theorist Markus Meissen, has expressed concern about the "nightmare of participation," in which individuality is subsumed, instead of advocating for what he calls "crossbenching," a form of collaboration in which individuals do not lose their autonomy in the process.[20] Miessen argues against consensus, and that "all-inclusive democracy has to be avoided" in the design process.[21] Some skeptics see participation and cooperation as a threat to the autonomy of the discipline, while others see it as tokenism. While these are

worthy concerns, it does not mean that participation should be abandoned as a process, but that vigilance and innovation are important attributes to ensure inclusion. Also, the potential for new techniques and tools in participation allows new models of inclusion. For many of the practices in the participation lineage, design often resists formal figuration, serving more as an armature or support for daily life and the expression of society. In foregrounding inclusive design processes, the architect serves as choreographer of behaviours rather than aesthetic tastemaker.

18
T. Armborst, D. D'Oca, and G. Theodore, *The Arsenal of Exclusion & Inclusion* (Barcelona: Actar, 2017).

19
Peter Blundell Jones, Doina Petrescu, Jeremy Till, eds., *Architecture and Participation* (London: Routledge, 2005).

20
Markus Miessen, *The Nightmare of Participation, Crossbench Praxis as a Mode of Criticality* (Berlin: Sternberg Press, 2010). Miessen borrows crossbench from the term for an independent politician that is able to freely shift from one side of the political spectrum to the other on the basis of a specific issue.

21
Ibid, 13.

Erbil Basemap. Map by author.

These images show the production of bespoke mantlepieces made by Assemble and Will Shannon for the project 10 houses on Cairns Street, Liverpool. The mantelpieces were produced in a temporary workshop situated in the back yard of one of the houses, from pieces of brick and slate salvaged from skips on the street. The mantelpieces were originally commissioned as part of the *Build Your Own Exhibition* at the FACT Gallery in Liverpool 2015 and are now produced for sale by Granby Workshop, the social enterprise based in Liverpool, set up by Assemble as part of their Turner prize show. Courtesy of Assemble.

the land is not lush, but it is not fallow either. Wheat, barley, lentils and chickpea crops cover nearly 50% of the project site. Fruit trees, including pomegranate, fig, mulberry, apricot, walnut and almond trees can be found in and around the few surviving villages, while eucalyptus and pines adorn the main roads and small enclaves.

With expanses of rain-fed arable land, orchards and villages, the landscape embodies the complexities of the ancient yet continuously inhabited spaces. This particular eco-system necessitates a layered, bio-regionalist understanding of the existing site and an articulate, participatory approach to design and community engagement. The city government's aims, however, diverged sharply from such an approach. As with most state funded projects, city officials embraced a top-down approach to planning. Oblivious to the beauty and intricacy of the existing landscape, the government hoped to indiscriminately "re-forest" the entire greenbelt project site. This approach is not uncommon to both state and private clients, partly because of their limited knowledge of natural and human modified ecosystems. From their perspective, the site is empty, a *tabula rasa* waiting to be filled with trees in the case of the greenbelt, or buildings in the case of the city.

The Challenge

By the time our team was hired, officials had already begun to expropriate cultivated lands and to relocate the inhabitants of the villages for the sake of reforestation. The impact of this measure on the Erbil Plain would be devastating ecologically, socially and economically. It would displace close to 5,000 village residents and eradicate agricultural activities in over 25,000 acres.[9] In addition, replacing agricultural lands with newly planted forests would grossly undermine the government's own stated aspiration to rehabilitate the agricultural sector, a key part of Kurdish culture and the backbone of the Kurdish economy.[10] Above all, reforesting the entire greenbelt area would fail to value the uniqueness and diversity of the existing rural landscape as both an ecologically resilient and culturally significant landscape — what should be a prized and precious repository of Kurdish heritage. Although vaguely well-intentioned, this approach lacked nuance. It ignored the social, economic and political particularities of the region in an attempt to create a landscape that has not existed in this area for over six millennia. Projects like these can be challenging for even the most sophisticated client, because, in addition to environmental constraints,

9
The economic cost of the greenbelt was estimated at 900 million USD with an expected running cost of 45 Million USD per year, including expropriation of the entire project site and the reforestation of around 10, 000 hectares. (*Erbil Green Belt: Master Plan and Design Guidelines*, Volume I, May 2010).

10
Speech by KRI Prime Minister Nechirvan Barzani on 27 January 2009 at a Conference on Agriculture Strategic Planning held in Erbil, quoted in the EGB Report on Agriculture.

From Pedestrianism to Social Good

Closely allied with participatory practices of the 1960s was a contingent of urban activists who galvanized a lay-public to protest against technocratic masterplanning and infrastructural projects being proposed in cities across North America. One of the most significant activists of the 20th century, American-Canadian Jane Jacobs fought against urban renewal and its tendency to infringe on citizens' rights. Jacobs offered a form of activism that was both physical, through protests in the street, and intellectual, through publishing. It is no small feat that *The Death and Life of Great American Cities* (1961) is one of the most read and referenced books on urban planning in modern history. Jacobs' leadership at rallies, community meetings and protests arguing for a more pedestrian urbanism helped galvanize a citizenship to confront the top-down forces of urban renewal. Following Jacobs, the work of William H. Whyte, the Planners Network and Lucien Kroll through the 1970s continued the movement to empower and give voice to citizens. Given the rapidly increasing role of automobiles, much of the agendas of 1960s urban activism was to resist large-scale automobile-centered planning and urban design. Since then, agendas for activism have focused on resisting oppressive governments, corporate ownership of public realm and the forces of gentrification, which limit expression and demonstration among citizens. Despite the increasing ubiquity of social media and the role of the Internet as 21st-century "public realm," the importance of physical space as a platform persists. Recent political events and citizen action during the Occupy movement in the United States of 2011, the Egyptian revolution of 2011, the Umbrella Movement in Hong Kong of 2014 and recent protests in that city and among others, are evidence of the impact of a mobilized citizenship that is able to advocate on its own behalf on urban and societal matters. Equally, it is evidence of the enduring power with which the public realm can be claimed by citizens seeking to give voice to a cause.

An influential contemporary figure who continued advocacy in the manner of Jacobs is the Danish urban designer Jan Gehl, considered to be a guru of the contemporary "people-centered urban design."[22] To support his claims of the importance of the public realm to the contemporary city, Gehl articulated three types of outdoor activities — necessary, optional and social — that take place "between buildings."[23] Jacobs and Gehl have been immensely influential on contemporary urban design practice over the past five decades, and it is hard to deny the validity of their calls for more liveable, walkable and cycle-friendly cities. However, Gehl's message, and the application of it in planning documents tends towards merely "good" urban design, which has given it global popularity but also a generic ubiquity. As cities embrace this mantra, and happily partner with private developers, profound questions of power and conflict can be overlooked, as are the attendant forces of gentrification, privatization and displacement of public realm. The risks of unquestioned "good urbanism" are crystallized in the pilot Sidewalk Toronto project in Toronto, Canada. The project, a

22
Gehl's 2010 book *Cities for the People* (Island Press) argues for four human concerns in urban design: lively, safe, sustainable and healthy.

23
Jan Gehl, *Life Between Buildings* (1971).

there is a web of social and political complexities in the wake of war and displacement.

When our project team came on-board, decrees had already been issued to expropriate all privately-owned agricultural lands in the project site, and the government was planning to relocate the inhabitants of the 23 villages. In contrast to other nations, the Iraqi government pays rural farmers and landowners a pittance for land expropriated by force, exacerbating the already precarious lifestyle of farmers by robbing them of their livelihoods. The government's approach was both devastating and disconcerting, raising immediate concerns. Who was the true audience of this "new and improved" Erbil greenbelt? At every turn, it became clear that the plans seem to prioritize urban, often wealthier Kurds at the expense of their rural counterparts.[11]

The difference between the expectations of the local government and our team is familiar to designers. Regardless of the country or the era, municipal projects are often hastily or ill-conceived, developed with inadequate concern for larger environmental or social ramifications and with no attempt to include the wishes, needs, or voices of the people who will actually use these spaces. Thus, our approach needed to be polyvalent. Through extended negotiation

11
The continued focus on cities can be traced to colonial rule, following the First World War, when national boundaries were established in the Middle East and capital cities designated. The focus on capital cities continued through post-colonial governments with default social and economic marginalization of rural peripheries, which, in part, account for the influx to cities from the villages and smaller towns. Conflict is another reason for rural-urban migration.

processes and sustained client discussions, we managed over time to convince the city government that a more sustainable, socially equitable and ultimately more marketable path forward could be forged.

Our holistic concept derived from an in-depth thematic analysis of three design components, which formed the basis for our distinctly Kurdish vision for the greenbelt. First, we examined landscape as a site for agriculture, the vital economy of these local villages. We explored how production could be enhanced and integrated into a more sustainable plan for the region. Second, we considered how the vernacular customs and cultural practices of the Kurds could inform the landscape as a site for recreation and, thereby, creating distinct landmarks. These spaces could introduce tourists to traditional rural practices and festivities while becoming the physical mark of a shared identity in Iraqi Kurdistan. Third, we proposed a non-traditional approach to linking natural reserve spaces along the greenbelt, a network to show landscape as a site for ecology and discovery. These areas could allow both locals and visitors to engage in bird watching, hiking, exploration and a connection with the land, while concurrently allowing the region's native plant and animal communities to

190-acre so-called "idea district" in downtown Toronto conceived by Sidewalk Labs, which shares the parent company of Google, appears to represent the social (and environmental) intentions of Gehl's pedestrianism. However, beneath the appearance of "good" pedestrian urbanism is an agenda of data-harvesting, high-tech infrastructure and potentially surveillance, the first of this scale and scope in North America.

However, the activist focus on the everyday urban conditions found in the work of Jacobs, Whyte, Gehl and others has since assumed higher stakes and shifted into regions previously overlooked. While earlier focus was on the space of the street, contemporary activism has broadened out to more complex and intricate webs of global inequality and injustice, as well as become more inward looking in terms of equity in professional practice. These issues have relocated the primary activist platform from the street to the screen, not only as a communication space, but also as a tool to empower data, computation and image processing.

Although it is safe to assume that architecture has the collective good in mind, how might projects dedicated to "social good" be distinguished? In some cases, the regions in which a firm operates have been traditionally overlooked by main-stream, western architectural media. Practices such as MASS Design Group, Orkid Studio or Basurama operate through a network of collaborators, working closely with local partners that possess a range of skills, from economic development to construction skills or project management. Expanding the traditional role of practice, they build social capacity in the regions in which they work through the project and its process. Contemporary practices, such as Rural Studio, Estudio Teddy Cruz + Fonna Forman, Enlace

"Now What?!" is the first exhibition to examine the little-known history of architects and designers working to further the causes of the civil rights, women's, and LGBTQ movements of the past fifty years. 2018. ArchiteXX, co-curators Lori A. Brown, Andrea J. Merrett, Sarah Rafson, and Roberta Washington.

flourish. Through this tri-partite reading of the landscape, grounded in Kurdish ecologies, economies and traditions, our argument won the client over. As a result, the orders for land expropriation were reversed and the forced depopulation of the villages was halted, pending the implementation of our revised master plan.

Agriculture: Landscape as Production

Agriculture was invented in Kurdistan. Almost all basic grains and livestock, with the notable exceptions of cows and rice, come from this part of the world. Yet over the past century, agricultural vibrance has been stymied by war. Orchards of stone fruit, apples, apricots, pears, grapes, figs and pomegranates have been ravaged by bloody political regimes. This prolonged agricultural downturn is sharply felt. Landscape can be a lasting casualty of war. Today, sustained violence has limited agriculture in the Erbil plain to vast expanses of wheat and barley cultivation and rangelands for sheep and goats.

When the Kurds began to self-rule in 2003, for the first time ever, revitalizing Erbil's agriculture and, thereby, strengthening the area's identity and market economy, was a key tenet of the government's economic plan.[12] Yet despite these good intentions, the effort to restore Erbil's past agricultural heyday faces sharp challenges. War destroyed the notion of stable farmsteads and created an itinerant population, resulting in the unsustainable management and maintenance of farmland. More recently, extreme climate cycles have led to recurrent droughts, making already tenuous new crops even more vulnerable.[13] Against the backdrop of this delicate recovery process, agriculture became the lifeblood for our new conception of the Erbil greenbelt. Our design called for the cultivation of fruit and olive trees, using a type of perennial planting that would make crops less prone to climate change, which could, in turn, provide higher economic return and revive a landscape not seen in Kurdistan for over forty years.[14]

Here, the landscape becomes not just something to be looked at or played upon, but something to be tended, allowing plant and human communities to grow alongside one another. Throughout the design process, the team considered numerous ways to weave agriculture into the greenbelts, including large-scale collaborations with agro-food industries or branding ideas that would market produce as "greenbelt-grown."[15]

12
The Kurdistan Region: Invest in the Future, KRG, 2008.

13
Article "Ministry of Agriculture Announces Strategic Five-year Plan", 19 Jan 09, *Kurdish Globe*.

14
Erbil Green Belt: Master Plan and Design Guidelines, Volume IV, May 2010.

15
Sustainable agriculture integrates environmental stewardship, farm profitability and prosperous farming communities. Two institutional frameworks were proposed for sustainable agriculture in the EGB: International social and Environmental Accreditation and Labelling Alliance (ISEAL), oriented towards non-governmental organizations and smallholders; Global Good Agricultural Practices (GLOBAL GAP) implemented the world industry standards, (Reference: *Erbil Green Belt: Master Plan and Design Guidelines*, Volume IV, May 2010).

Arquitectura or Agency Architecture operate in the social, climatic and cultural challenges of particular places. The charged realities of these contexts generate a range of responses. Rural Studio, based in Hale County, Alabama, is sustained by Auburn University, and it has a long tradition of community engagement through design-build projects for marginalized residents. Cruz and Forman's work is focused on the emergence of what they call a "political equator," a global line of conflict that divides the "functioning core" from the "non-integrating gap," and they conduct design-research on informality at the San Diego-Tijuana border using research-based documentation and visualization as tools of activism.[24] These practices are motivated to address the social gaps of built infrastructure or reveal social or environmental injustice where governments fall short.

Contemporary activist traditions working in the realm of social good has further expanded to include other positions on advocacy and equity. A form of practice has emerged that is reconsidering architecture for underrepresented agents. Embracing a more post-humanist agenda, Ants of the Prairie, an experimental practice directed by Joyce Hwang in Buffalo, New York, advocates for the consideration of new stakeholders, disciplinary agencies and modes of practice that displace our human bias with concerns for species, habitats and plant-life.[25] Utilizing scanning and surveillance technology, her work challenges the normative notion of patronage and client. With similar interests, concerns of disciplinary and professional equity motivate the work of several other groups. The Architecture Lobby, a labor advocacy collective, co-founded by Peggy Deamer, champions the value of architecture in the general public and pushes for greater accountability within the discipline, including the need for improved labor conditions and compensation in practice. Another contemporary advocacy collective is ArchiteXX, founded by architect Lori A. Brown, which champions gender equity and diversity within the profession, as well as academia.[26] These practices and collectives demonstrate the expansion of activist priorities from pedestrianism and public realm (what and where) to equity and social good (who and how). With these widening agendas of architectural agency, it is clear that conventional practice expressed through building for clients is not addressing the perceived shortfall within society. This shift in agenda shows the interest of architects to affect social change within the discipline and practice, as well as within culture and society at large.

24
Teddy Cruz, "Border Tours: Strategies of Surveillance, Tactics of Encroachment," in *Indefensible Space: The Architecture of the National Insecurity State*, ed. Michael Sorkin (New York: Routledge, 2008), 111.

25
Hwang's *Beyond Patronage: Reconsidering Models of Practice* (Barcelona: Actar, 2016) examines new modes of practice that move beyond patronage to various models of self-initiated projects, working for a range of stakeholders.

26
Lori A Brown is the author of *Contested Spaces: Abortion Clinic, Women's Shelters and Hospitals* (New York: Routledge, 2013). The book continues Brown's advocacy for recognizing the relationship between architecture and social justice.

A typical pastoral scene in Iraqi Kurdistan. Photo by author.

From Commentary to Forensics

Architecture as socio-cultural commentary, exemplified by the countercultural movements of the 1960s and 70s, is a third thread of the activist tradition in direct dialogue with cultural transformations and social movements. Architectural activism responding to urgent provocations (rather than conventional practice-based services) expands the mode of communication and the subjects covered to include critical commentary. As commentary, architecture could respond to topics such as rising consumerism, environmentalism, racism, sexism, authoritarianism and many other concerns previously considered peripheral to the discipline. Without the intellectual burden of criticism, commentary afforded a looseness and quickness to action. The 1960s European avant-garde practices Archigram, Archizoom and Superstudio embodied the potential of commentary.[27] Their form of practice brashly critiqued contemporary socio-cultural conditions with brazen, sometimes, ironic, visions. Archigram exposed the mediocrity and conventionality of architecture culture in Britain, while Archizoom revelled in the ubiquity of urban systems, and Superstudio commented on architecture's increasingly complex confrontation with environmentalism. These practices were less interested in the practicality of their vision than a layered criticism of the discipline to a wider cultural audience. This form of the activist tradition used the power of the imaginary to expose and comment upon timely social and political conditions to reflect on architecture's role in society.

The familiar tools of orthographic drawings and perspectives appear staid in the face of cultural urgency. Therefore, unconventional representational tools have become one of the hallmarks of the activist tradition, from comics and postcards to collages and films. This is even more evident in the commentary and forensics thread of activism. Commentary, sometimes through irony or sarcasm, may initially appear flippant, but its impact on the discipline and its dialogue with design culture is considerable and enduring. Following the heady 1960s, and with increased ubiquity of technology and media in everyday life, contemporary activist practices have shifted from commentary and critique toward evidence and data. The looseness of collaged juxtapositions and multi-media of the 1970s has been replaced by statistics and geo-spatial analysis, especially since the 2000s. An example of this transition is the early work of MVRDV, such as *Metacity / Datatown* (1999), which took a matter-of-fact statistical approach to representing the needs of the contemporary city, as extrapolated from Dutch statistics. Using a crude infographic aesthetic, the project portrays "a city that knows no given topography, no prescribed ideology, no representation, no context. Only huge, pure data."[28] Although more subtle than the Utopianists of the 1960s, MVRDV employed data as commentary to convey the scale, scope and almost ridiculous needs of contemporary society. Similarly, their *Pig City* (2001) project was a provocative way to represent the statistical needs of pig farming in the Netherlands, a significant consumer of the nation's limited land. Their work embodies a transition from pure commentary to statistically based evidence, but still with a sense of irony. Following increased access to data and computation, practices in the activist tradition today have shifted toward even more evidentiary means, in order to reveal observations, commentaries or discoveries. Irony has been replaced with social and political realism.

Aesthetics: Landscape as Enjoyment

As we proposed the concept of an agricultural, production-based greenbelt, the governmental rejoinder was resounding: "But how will the greenbelt serve as a recreational landscape with no trees?"

This concern was understandable. Based on the prevailing custom, Kurdish families take every opportunity to leave the city and venture out to the countryside to have picnics under trees in the reforested pockets. On weekends and holidays, the Erbil countryside is peppered with families arrayed on their carpets and pillows; the aroma of grilled meats, boiling rice and roasted vegetables wafts through the air.

As a landscape architect, this concern was my starting point, and it required serious engagement with both civic leaders and neighbors about how public space should look, feel and operate.[16] For many, landscape can only infer a park or municipal garden.[17] To respond to the need for traditional park space, we designed a "green ring" to define the inner periphery of the green belt, replete with flowering trees and lawns. In addition, three large scale city parks were proposed, located at an axis point with roads leading west, east and south.

16
The planning committee spent a lot of time deciding where to locate reforestation sites and how to enrich these sites with native species. We decided to designate two larger watercourses north and south of the city as greenways: multifunctional landscapes that combine environmental, ecological and amenity functions. Instead of foresting hillsides, we decided to crest these waterways with greenery. Forestation would define them as landscapes, protect them from urban encroachment and, with the right choice of species, support wildlife habitat. This was followed through with the use of hardy "standard species," such as pines, cypresses and casuarina, which constituted 70% of greenway reforestation. A second choice of species included "biodiversity species," such as oaks, ash, pistacia, acer, cercis, sumac and rowan.

17
Makhzoumi, J. (2002) "Landscape in the Middle East: An inquiry", *Landscape Research* Vol. 27, No.3, pp. 213-228.

Regionally specific greenways and waterways.
Photo by author.

Forensic Architecture, still from "The Bombing of Rafah" video.

Since the 1990s, the increased role and availability of big data, geographic information systems and ubiquitous computing has fostered evidence-based activism. Access to data has elevated architectural commentary to be more serious and statistical. Rather than imagining and visualizing societal shifts, activist architects since the 2000s produce factual juxtapositions of political and spatial information to expose injustice. Several practices and research centers have been important to the formation of a data-informed activist tradition, employing tools of technology and media to expose power structures, inequalities or injustice. The work of Laura Kurgan at the Spatial Information Design Lab (now the Centre for Spatial Research) at Columbia University, for example, powerfully represented America's incarceration problem with a 2004 study called *Million Dollar Blocks*.[29] This study revealed the concentration of incarcerated individuals from specific neighborhoods in Brooklyn. Another example is the *Trash/Track* (2009) project by Senseable City Lab, founded in 2004 at MIT and directed by architect Carlo Ratti, which shows the geographic footprint of waste cycles in real-time. This work operates as commentary on ecology and consumerism by using GPS-based evidentiary tools, represented with maps, diagrams, animations and assembly drawings.

29
Laura Kurgan initiated the Centre for Spatial Research at Columbia University in 2015. Prior to this Kurgan co-directed the Spatial Information Design Lab since 2004 with Sarah Williams. Williams now runs the Civic Data Design Lab at MIT.

Another large component of this aesthetic approach to landscape had a different function: wayfinding. As a team, we recognized both the client's desire for exotic tree species and Kurdish culture's love of color. Thus, we designated flowering tree species for key locations along the greenbelt. We called these sites "virtual gateways," but they are actually army surveillance points on the roads. We chose the flamboyant *Delonix regia* for those entering the greenbelt from Mosul to the east, the lilac *Jacaranda mimosifolia* with its lilac blossoms for visitors coming from Shaqlawa to the north, and the *Robinia pseudoacacia* with its distinct yellow flowers for those coming from Kirkuk to the south. In combination, the virtual gateways, three city scale parks and the green ring were designed in multiple scales of wayfinding, creating distinct identities and hubs.

Within the greenbelt itself, we designed multiple scales of wayfinding, creating distinct identities and hubs using the landscape trope of a shelterbelt. Shelterbelts are rows of trees that are meant to provide protection from wind and hot weather. In doing so, they also act as landmarks and create marked boundaries. We proposed multiple types of shelterbelts, including rows of trees, denoting the edge of a village. In addition, property shelterbelts utilize rows of trees to denote the edge of a farmer's domain.

Network: Landscape as Ecology

In contrast to the conventional park space of the "green ring," our third approach to landscape looked critically at the surrounding rural context. We synthesized disparate patches of infertile land, such as rangelands, rocky outcrops, waterways and settlements, into a natural reserve network for Kurds to enjoy. To ecologically revitalize these patches further and to help these lands better support plant and wildlife diversity, we also recommended targeted re-forestation and the creation of open meadows.

As we conceptualized different types of terrestrial networks, we also paid specific attention to the flow of water. Water is vital to the ecology of the Erbil region, and water availability heavily determined our approach to land use. Tributaries of the Tigris, networks of smaller streams, wells and the ancient qanat system of irrigation (Kurdish: *karez*) have sustained the land and those who have tilled its loamy soil since Assyrian times. As areas under cultivation expand, water resources in this

Roadside remembrances in Iraqi Kurdistan. Photo by author.

Some activist practices have assumed even greater political responsibilities. The work of Eyal Weizman and his Forensic Architecture group based at Goldsmiths, University of London, produces spatial evidence of acts of war and infringement in war-torn regions. Forensic Architecture utilizes the agency of the architect to offer spatial and representational expertise as evidence in human rights violations. Tools are important for Weizman; novel analytic and representational mediums, including composite animations or virtual reality environments, are key to the production of spatial evidence. In a 2015 project commissioned by Amnesty International, Forensic Architecture constructed a 3-D model of the conditions in which civilians were killed during the 2014 four-day bombing of Rafah in the Gaza strip by using footage from social media. This spatial analysis was incorporated into Amnesty's report and helped identify the munition used as a war crime. Another initiative for activism, established by Weizman with Sandi Hilal and Alessandro Petti, is the Decolonizing Architecture Art Residency (DAAR) in Palestine, a residency program and studio that focuses on visualization of architecture "materialized in both built and political space."[30] These activist practices operate at the front-line of complex and unstable territories by bringing the capacity of the architect to a space of conflict in which architecture is not typically found.

Several other practitioners and thinkers broaden the initiatives of forensics-based architectural activism. For example, theorist Keller Easterling's subtle form of activism demonstrates the power of commentary in forensics, especially as found in her book *Extrastatecraft* (2014), in which she exposes the inequalities of contemporary managerial capitalism, with a particular focus on communication and infrastructural networks.[31] Her representational medium is more narrative than drawing, but its evidence of political action is not diminished. Another example might be Jesse LeCavalier's spatial-logistical unpacking of Walmart in the *The Rule of Logistics* (2016), in which he reveals how capitalism and retailing have scripted an "architecture of fulfillment."[32] LeCavalier's project confronts issues of capitalism and corporate influence through statistical and spatial evidence. With a realignment of research-based practices toward political and social issues, the activist tradition embraces technology and data as forces of resistance.

Conclusion

Upon revisiting Jencks' "evolutionary tree" technique, and by isolating the activist tradition, the three sub-traditions — participation, pedestrianism and commentary — identify not only disciplinary agendas, but they also reveal specific tools and techniques used by architects. This permits a more nuanced understanding of the activist tradition, as discussed here and drawn in the associated diagram to show the parallel realms, in which architects contribute to architecture's political conditions. As in Jencks' diagram, these traditions

30
Decolonizing Architecture Art Residency website: http://www. decolonizing.ps/site/about/. Accessed May 22, 2019.

31
Keller Easterling, *Extrastatecraft: The Power of Infrastructure Space* (London: Verso, 2014).

32
Jesse LeCavalier, *The Rule of Logistics: Walmart and the Architecture of Fulfillment* (University of Minnesota Press, 2016).

Kurdish villages, seen at left and right. Kurds fought for recognition and self-rule throughout the twentieth century, British colonial rule and the Baathist regime. Photos by author.

do not always stay in their lane, there are fascinating cross-overs that blur previously distinct traits. Of interest here might be "everyday-ism," which is identified as equal parts participation and pedestrianism. "Everday-ism" brings architecture out of the realm of exclusivity and acknowledges citizens as participants in activating the public realm. Similarly, the strong interest in advocacy for social equity can be aligned within pedestrianism and commentary and even within participation. Advocacy groups and practices, operating as collectives, continue to have significant influence in terms of disciplinary shifts and public awareness. Observing contemporary activist preoccupations reveals inclusivity, equity, social good and forensics as motivating factors for architects operating at the front-line of architecture as politics.

Comparing Jencks' drawing from 2000 with this updated activist-only version, the gaps are striking. For example, the stagnation of activist practices in the 1980s reflects the hegemony of both Post-Modernist discourse in architecture and the concomitant political conservatism, ushered in by the Reagan and Thatcher era. Referred to as the "decade of greed," the absence of activist architecture during this time underlines the profound connection between practice and politics. If the 1960s offered an ideal incubation for activist architecture because it aligned with a state-led social contract, the late 1990s and 2000s mark an era when architects self-organized to pursue activist interests. The question is how the architect aligns architecture within the spectrum of activism, and how do processes, techniques and tools contribute to disciplinary innovations. The activist tradition is alive, as it is still evolving and shifting within.

It is worth noting that many of the practitioners highlighted here are involved with academia or research labs. In this sense, they use research to foster innovation in activism. If traditional practice responds to questions of client, site and budget, then activist architects operate by verbs: advocate, co-opt, leverage and participate. This begs the question: what might motivate activism in the future? Speculating is a near impossible task. However, as issues, such as climate change, mass human migration and economic disparity continue to increase, environmental activism and social justice will likely continue to shape aspects of disciplinary discourse. Ecological priorities were made manifest in the early 2000s in architecture's interest with infrastructure and ecology. While the ambitions were laudable, the ability to put such large-scale proposals into action have proven difficult. As architecture continues to grapple with its relevancy in the public imagination and in government priorities, it must expand its agency. The questions raised by architecture, the stakeholders it engages, the realms in which it operates and the tools of advocacy it employs will shape architectural education, the profession and the society it serves.

---

region, threatened by desertification, are variable and scarce. Excessive rates of pumping are diminishing ground water reserves and exceeding the aquifer safe yield.[18] As a result, the surface water and the plant and animal communities that depend on it have become compromised. While sustainable management of rivers as living ecosystems and ecological corridors is favored elsewhere, many countries in the Middle East still implement antiquated engineering solutions that have long been abandoned elsewhere, such as channeling smaller streams and covering seasonal water courses to deleterious effect.

Our fragile but resilient watercourses are linear lifelines, helping to infiltrate and replenish aquifers while providing crucial shelter for the region's wildlife. Despite the sparse vegetation, the Erbil area is home to a considerable diversity of animal life, including amphibians and reptiles, badgers, bats, foxes, porcupine and rabbits. A rich swath of birds dots the skies over Erbil, both native and migratory species on their way to warmer climates in the fall. The white stork is common, as their exceptionally large nest have been known to crown the domes of the city's many mosques and shrines. Gaggles of geese, favored for their eggs and delicious meat, have long been a common sight in villages,

[18]
Some reports state that the water table in the Green Belt zone has dropped from 100m depth in 1999 to 200m in 2009 due to over-pumping, and that the flow of the Great Zab river has been reduced by Turkish control upstream (Reference: *Erbil Green Belt: Master Plan and Design Guidelines*, Volume III, May 2010).

where they roam freely. To create a fluid and traversable terrain for these species, the two largest watercourses that are located north and south of Erbil City were designated as greenways to ensure landscape connectivity. To prevent real estate development, these spaces were densely planted with trees. We also proposed demarcating green corridors as seasonal watercourses and sourcing supplementary irrigation from treated sewage.

Moving Forward

In March 2010, the greenbelt master plan report was submitted to the KRG. Although the project was approved almost immediately by its council of ministers, the semi-autonomous government body responsible for implementation, *Istithmar*, became besotted with the site as a venue only for future development, completely failing to appreciate the greenbelt's value or complexity. Meanwhile, the Department of Urban Planning, who had been following the greenbelt project from its inception, raised its own concerns about *Istithmar's* market-driven approach. In the midst of this discord, a new spate of political and fiscal woes suddenly appeared in the region, signaling the death knell for the project.

In 2012, funding for most projects in Kurdistan began to evaporate. Tensions rose between the KRG and the Iraqi central government on key issues around power sharing, oil production and territorial control. In 2014, just as this pressure began to ease, militia fighters from the Islamic State of Iraq and the Levant (ISIL) crossed the Syrian border, invading northern Iraq.[19] ISIL fighters occupied Mosul, and their fighters made camp in the greenbelt project site. Although eventually warded off by Kurdish *peshmerga* forces, the impact of the fighting devastated Iraq's northern region . Already precarious villages were looted, their inhabitants captured and tortured. Ancient buildings were destroyed, and archaeological sites were robbed.[20]

Invariably, development projects like the Erbil Greenbelt were forgotten, no longer a priority as the KRG grappled with displaced families, refugees and fiscal restrictions from the Iraqi central government. Even now, the region is only now slowly recovering from the aftereffects of the conflict, and just starting to replenish its empty coffers.

What room is there for design in countries where civil strife and displacement are the norm? When lives are disrupted, ideas about development and equitable progress ebb away in the grim face of survival. Constant political instability diverts the energies and resources of both people and their governments away from developing infrastructure that could improve both livelihoods and living conditions. At the institutional level, chronic conflict deters local and regional governments from staying current with global trends. Not only is there no sustainable development, the idea of even involving citizens in a participatory planning process is non-existent. Instead, the needs and wishes of the citizens are, at best, assumed by the state on their behalf. And yet, autocratic approaches to planning indelibly damage rural communities, exemplified in the government's original plan for the Erbil Greenbelt in which the livelihoods and well-being of the area's farmers were constantly undermined. As a result of this process, the rich and diverse heritage of our rural landscapes rapidly fades away. Rural peripheries are becoming threatened by real-estate speculations, reduced to land available for quick development schemes radiating out from capital cities. In Erbil, as in Baghdad and Basrah, an amoebic, advancing urban footprint consumes villages, destroys fertile agricultural lands and homogenizes the landscape. In theory, there are bylaws that safeguard environmental resources and protect rural ecologies, but their

19
Also known as the Islamic State of Iraq and Syria (ISIS).

20
As of August 2019, there are 1.5 million internally displaced persons (IDPs), as a result of the conflict caused by ISIL in Iraqi Kurdistan (see UNHCR https://data2.unhcr.org/en/documents/download/72619).

A scene on the village periphery. Photo by author.

The Anacoluthic City: *Urbs Oeconomica* and the Dissolution of Urban Ground

Elisa Iturbe

enforcement is rare, due to the perpetual conflicts engulfing the region and the lack of human and financial resources.

For the time being, I realized that in its current form, it was difficult to imagine that our proposed greenbelt project would be implemented. Since late 2019, the civil uprisings that have engulfed central and southern Iraq have paralyzed the central government in Baghdad. Even if there was no political conflict from this point forward, much has changed about the project site since the master plan was finalized. The villages of the Erbil Greenbelt are now filled with refugees, predominantly ethnic Arabs, with social and cultural practices that differ from the indigenous Kurdish culture but also Kurds from villages raided by ISIL.

In October of 2019, when I visited the site, the change was palpable. The village of Gazna was no longer a rural community but a suburb of Erbil. Warehouses, industrial compounds and large neighborhoods housing the displaced families had totally transformed society and morphology of a traditional Kurdish village. I couldn't help but wonder about the impact of recent political events on Kurdish rural heritage and on the lives of farmers and rural inhabitants.

Yet even though the project was not implemented, the conversation it sparked, between officials, community leaders and between Kurdish and Iraqi architects and engineers was enduring. Until recently, this community has never encountered projects like the Erbil Greenbelt, that offer an alternate but urgently needed understanding of "sustainability," as proposed by the greenbelt design, informed by ideas of both ecology and indigeneity. The mainstream conversation around "sustainability" in the region is narrowly defined to address natural resource use and abuse, not more nuanced social and economic dimensions. Although the client demanded "sustainable" development, their understanding of the concept was superficial, grounded in technical quick fixes about solar-powered street lighting and efficient water usage. In this unique context, forestation ran the risk of replacing the rich and resilient mosaic of ecosystems that form the project site with a non-regionally specific solution prone to fire and pests. Instead, our project aimed to shift the discussion from prescriptive notions of greenwashing to true bio-cultural diversity, in which environmental conservation can work in tandem with the practice of preserving cultural rituals and landscape heritage.

During the engagement process with both the city and the community, watching the Kurdish community realize that the landscape could play a key role in the preservation of identity was incredibly gratifying. In the Middle East, rural landscapes, especially those in the shadow of large cities, are not seen as sites deemed worthy of cultural protection.[21] There is a limited understanding of cultural heritage, especially in rural areas, as a concept. Although it was not implemented, our plan broadened the discussion around Kurdish heritage by expanding the scope of the project beyond archaeological sites and historic buildings, including the parts of our ancient landscape that were shaped not by human hands but by the ineffable forces of nature.[22] Our revised master plan illustrates how the aspects of our landscape shaped by human hands and those shaped by natural causes are intrinsically bound together.

Yet even given these dilemmas, I found it impossible to abandon this project. Here is when I found that academia can be not just a refuge but a stimulus. Collaborating with scholars from around the world, I am now working to advocate for a new approach to the social, economic and cultural complexities of the rural heritage in the Erbil Greenbelt site and as a still necessary model for participatory post-conflict development.[23] Through research and development, we hope to not only

In the 20th century, architecture grappled with Classicism, from the Modernists who declared the beginning of modernity and the end of the Classical to the Postmodernists who responded by experimenting with the meaning of the Classical in a modern century. Throughout this trajectory, the Classical was not just a style but a mode of thought, one which drew to a close with the recognition of its own fictions.[1]

In the 21st century, a different specter looms over architecture, one which no longer holds the language of architecture as a central concern, instead demanding architecture's compliance to global economic production. The evolution of Late Capitalism has cast a shadow deep into the architectural discipline—not only because real estate has become a foundational economic engine of the global capitalist city, but because, like Classicism, it generates architectural fictions.

Homo Oeconomicus: An Introduction

To understand capitalism's architectural fictions, it is first necessary to understand one of its own central myths: *homo oeconomicus.* This term emerged as an economic concept that theorized human individuals as rational, self-interested, yet efficient beings—a portrayal of humanity that emerged in order to reconcile the individual and the market. First conceived by John Stuart Mill, *homo oeconomicus* is a human archetype characterized by an ability to optimize between choices presented by the market. In such a conception of human behavior, the market precedes and shapes the subjective condition of *homo oeconomicus,* who, as a result, can only

1
In the wake of Postmodernism, architecture theory moved away from reactionary critique towards an interro-gation of the common threads across the purported historical breaks of both Modernity and Postmodernity. For examples of this approach, see Colin Rowe's famous essay "The Mathematics of an Ideal Villa" from 1947 and Peter Eisenman's "The End of the Classical: The End of the Beginning, the End of the End" from 1984. Both works attempted to identify the underlying fictions of both classical and modern thought, moving the focus of architectural theory away from a crisis of historicism and, instead, toward theorizing the way in which meaning is produced in architecture. As such, Classicism ceased to be a central focus of theoretical discourse towards the end of the twentieth century. See Colin Rowe, "Mathematics of an Ideal Villa," *Mathematics of an Ideal Villa and Other Essays.* MIT Press, Cambridge: 1976, pp. 2-26 and Peter Eisenman, "The End of the Classical: The End of the Beginning, the End of the End," *Perspecta* 21 (1984), pp 154-173.

address the complexities and concerns emerging from the greenbelt project but to build on it further, thereby engendering context sensitive approaches that reframe the way in which we think about our shared heritage. Sometimes, the most powerful transformations must begin by recognizing what is already there.

21
Makhzoumi, J., (2014) "Is rural heritage relevant in an urbanizing Mashreq? Exploring the discourse of landscape heritage in Lebanon". In I Maffi and R Daher (eds) The Politics and Practices of Cultural Heritage in the Middle East. Positioning the material past in contemporary societies I.B. Tauris, London, 233-252.

22
Lowenthal argues that the concept of "heritage" can imply "virtually anything by which some kind of link, however, tenuous or false, may be forged with the past" (quoted in Harvey, 2001, p. 319). Traditional rural landscapes in Erbil's periphery serve as a venue for recognizing Kurdish "heritage."

23
I proposed the Erbil Greenbelt project site to Howayda Al Harithy, Chairperson, Department of Architecture and Design, American University of Beirut, as an alternative to the focus on Erbil's built heritage. She agreed to adopt the theme of rural-urban heritage to frame postwar recovery in northern Iraq and proceeded to apply for funding. The project proposal was submitted by the Urban Lab, American University of Beirut, to the Nahrein Network, Arts and Humanities Research Council, United Kingdom, and it was approved for funding in June 2019. Al Harithy is lead investigator, myself, Camillo Boano (University College London) and Salahaddin Baper (University of Salahaddin, Erbil), co-investigators, Joanna Dabaj instructor, Najmeh Viki instructor and project coordinator.

operate within the logic of economic exchange.[2] *Homo oeconomicus*, thus, becomes the ideal capitalist subject, reifying the market by extending its logic into previously non-economic realms of life. Michel Foucault calls this process by which social and political dynamics become embedded into economic processes, "the generalization of the economic form of the market."[3] The dynamics of the market become a framework, an "*economic grid*," by which to interpret "non-economic processes, relations, and behavior…a sort of economic analysis of the non-economic."[4] It is the way of seeing of *homo oeconomicus*, and it naturalizes the use of economic exchange as an interpretive framework. In so doing, the economy, rather than an outgrowth of social dynamics or a single aspect of human relations, becomes a new origin story. Peter Eisenman stated that the early twentieth-century Modernists "were ideologically trapped in the illu-sion of the eternity of their own time."[5] Today, we are trapped in the illusion of the eternity of capitalism.[6] This collective disposition cannot but affect the city, for a city built by *homo oeconomicus* will be inevitably subjected to the same dynamics, producing an architecture that embodies and materializes a system of economic value. No longer striving to signify cultural value or produce meaning, as it did before the twenty-first century, the city of *homo oeconomicus* assumes instead that the truth has already been constructed by the facts of economic exchange. In this sense, we have entered into a new phase in the history of the city. The city of *homo oeconomicus*—which we might, perhaps, call *urbs oeconomica*—requires a different theorization, one that makes visible these dynamics.

2
Homo oeconomicus first emerged in the writings of John Stuart Mill as a "hypothetical subject whose well-defined motives made him a useful abstraction in economic analysis." (Persky, 222-223). In other words, *homo oeconomicus* as a category of *homo sapiens* is not taxonomical, biological or empirical. Rather, this term is an interpretation of human behavior used, first by Mill and then many others, to explain how humans relate to the market and the dynamics of economic exchange. In other words, to conceive of man as *homo oeconomicus* in the first place, market dynamics must already be in place. In this specific context, the question in play is: how do individuals operate as market actors? To answer this question, economic theorists constructed the ideal cap-italist subject, modeling them according to market forces. See Joseph Persky, "Retrospectives: The Ethology of *Homo Oeconomicus*," *Journal of Economic Perspectives*, Vol 9 No. 2, Spring 1995, pp 221-231 and Michel Foucault, *Birth of Biopolitics: Lectures at the College de France, 1978-1979*, ed. Michel Senellart. Palgrave Macmillan, New York: 2004.

3
The example Foucault gives is of a mother who sees the care and rearing of her child as an investment: a better childhood education will lead to better colleges, which will lead to better salaries for the child. Here, well-being is framed as relative to salary numbers. Yet, even if the "profit" can be construed as the personal satis-fac-tion that a mother feels in seeing her child succeed, the neoliberal mindset uses economic terminology to make sense of the work of caregiving. See Foucault, *Birth of Biopolitics*, pp. 240-248.

4
Ibid.

5
Eisenman, "The End of the Classical." pp. 163.

6
Of course, I am not the first person to argue this. For example, see the quote attributed to Frederic Jameson: "it is easier to imagine end of the world than the end of capitalism." Fredric Jameson, *The Seeds of Time* (New York: Columbia University Press, 1994); this phrase also appears in the writings of Slavoj Žižek, "The Spectre of Ideology." in *Mapping Ideology*, ed. Slavoj Žižek (New York: Verso, 1994).

This journal is the product of myriad terms and currents of capital. Yale School of Architecture, the publisher, has a contract with MIT Press, the distributor who, in turn, contracts with Penguin Random House to sell the volumes. The authors have signed agreements with Yale for the right to print their words. The copyright for the images has been negotiated or purchased. The fonts used here are under license. These terms dictate what is included in the colophon, where the barcode is printed, when the magazine needs to be shipped and where the issue will be available. This network of regulations, agreements and terms are the underlying setting for our work as designers, editors, writers and for you the reader. They influence the form of the journal, in ways direct and indirect, visible and invisible, knowing and inadvertent.

Dispersed throughout the magazine, *Document as Form* is a collection of artistic projects that operate in this field of regulation and law. The works take the form of codes, protocols and legal documents, gathered from the practices of artists, curators and art institutions. They range from the prototypical to the paralegal to the esoteric.

To use the expression of a former teacher Keller Easterling, the authors in this collection are "flipping the footnotes into the main text." In other words, they are looking towards less-visible areas of production in written documents like laws, conventions and protocols. Rather than representing, translating or materializing the effects of these legal instruments, they participate directly in their production in order to uncover and influence structural issues of inequality, power and discrimination.

In 1971, curator Seth Siegelabub and lawyer Robert Projansky published the *Artists Rights Resale and Transfer Agreement*. The document is a template agreement to be signed by collector and artist upon the sale of an artwork. The terms require future collectors to pay 15% of any profit to the artist upon resale of the work. In addition, this document established the right of the artist to be consulted about their work's inclusion in public exhibitions and to borrow the work (at no cost to the collector) for a variety of usages.

Like the other projects included here, the *Artists Rights Resale and Transfer Agreement* operates as a regulatory measure in a variety of ways. As a symbolic gesture, it claims rights previously unacknowledged or ignored: notably, the right of the artist to economically benefit from the secondary market. As an actionable code of conduct, it reconstructs how the systems of artistic production proceed, relocating power in the hands of the artist. As the contract itself affirms, "the artist is more right than anyone else." In the case of this contract and others in the collection — many of which reach beyond art to highlight the legacy of slavery in financial structures or propose new ways to provide access to people with disabilities — the art resides both in the act of writing the text and in its playing out over time.

These projects can't stop the ideological systems that produce inequality. They operate locally and are not all legally binding. Some set unrealistic or even absurd expectations. Yet, by participating directly in the production of regulation, their makers complicate these systems, add friction and write a way forward. They offer new models for art and design to engage with justice. What happens, practically and parabolically, when designers consider the regulatory setting of their work, their ingrained ideologies and the relationships implied therein as part of their theater of operations?

Introduction

The *economic grid* outlined by Foucault is not meant to be understood as a spatial or geometric concept but as an analytic and interpretive lens. As such, the economic dynamics upon which the grid depends are not to be scrutinized in themselves. Rather, the economic grid can be used as a "principle of intelligibility and a principle of decipherment of social relationships and individual behavior."[7] In other words, one does not *see* the grid, one *looks through* the grid in order to judge one's surroundings and predict the outcome of particular social and economic interactions.[8]

An *urban grid* can also operate as an analytic and interpretive lens for understanding the city. However, unlike the economic grid, it is both spatial and material, providing formal readings of the city and indexing the history of politics and economics in its structure. As such, the urban grid cannot claim to predict human behavior nor promulgate any single truth. For, due to its scale and material reality, the structure of the city—whether a perfect Euclidean grid or an irregular network of streets and buildings—reflects both the informal negotiations of urban existence and the formal agreements of our social contracts. The urban grid is both *de facto* and *de jure*, meaning it constitutes both what is negotiated on the ground and what is premeditated and designed—it is both what *is* and what is *made to be*.

Despite the differences between the economic grid and the urban grid, Pier Vittorio Aureli argues in *The Possibility of an Absolute Architecture* that the economic aims of the capitalist engine are enacted by urbanization and the corresponding expansion of the urban grid. In other words, the deployment of an economic grid is manifested in the urban grid itself, as the form of the city begins to mirror the capitalist demand for totality.[9] However, underlying this thought is the idea that spatial management and economic management are part of the same machinations of power. This approach is evident not only in Aureli's argumentation but also in Foucault's examination of spatial management as a means to theorize power. Throughout his writings, he analyzes the practice of quarantine in medieval cities during the Black Plague, arguing that the spatial management of the city is an early example of biopower, one that reveals the way in which urban form itself can directly serve the ends of power.[10] I would like to argue that in today's neoliberal paradigm, the concern for space shown by contemporary forms of

7
Foucault, *Birth of Biopolitics: Lectures at the College de France, 1978–1979*, ed. Michel Senellart. Palgrave Macmillan, New York: 2004, pp. 243.

8
This concept is not only attributable to Foucault, but it can also be traced to the very definition of *homo oeconomicus*, whose subjective condition is fully defined by the idea of market opportunity.

9
Pier Vittorio Aureli, *The Possibility of an Absolute Architecture*, MIT Press: Cambridge, 2011.

10
Foucault discusses the plague and its management throughout his writings. See Foucault, *Security, Territory, Population: Lectures at the College de France, 1977–1978*, ed. Michel Senellart. Palgrave Macmillan, New York: 2007, pp 1–28, 55–86; *Discipline and Punish: The Birth of the Prison*, trans. Alan Sheridan, Vintage Books, New York: 1995, pp 195–198; *Abnormal: Lectures at the College de France, 1974–1975*, trans. Graham Burchell. Pic-ador, New York: 1999, pp 44–48.

power has shifted away from management and organization in order to fully focus on commodification. Through the extreme commodification of space and the increasing power of real estate, the contemporary city has undergone the same process that created *homo oeconomicus*, as all operations—social and spatial—are pulled under the umbrella of economics. If Aureli is concerned about the totalization of the urban grid, I am concerned about the totalization of the economic grid *at the expense of* the urban grid, for the economic grid can subsume any urban structure no matter its form, as long as land is made available on the market. In this context, the urban grid ceases to serve as a conceptual framework for the city. This, then, is *urbs oeconomica*: an urban paradigm in which real estate processes are indifferent to form; they have, though the commodification of space, found the means to lay claim to formal differentiation within the city. As a result, *urbs oeconomica* is neither whole nor fragmented, and it is not characterized by its density or form but rather by its voraciousness for space, which it consumes (buys), digests (renovates) and spits out in commodity form (sells). The fallow gaps in the city are folded into its logic of profit, rendered productive via the extreme difference in value before and after revitalization.

Detroit might serve as an example of the indifference of *urbs oeconomica* towards urban form. In this regard, the extreme condition of depopulation makes the mechanisms of the economic grid glaringly visible.

As one of the largest cities in the United States, it is striking that Detroit's urban grid is more or less continuous throughout its metropolitan area.[Fig. 1] Yet, despite this continuity,

there are two significant differentiations between the core and periphery. Morphologically, the core is dense, while the periphery consists of vast neighborhoods of single-family homes—a differentiation that can be traced back to the early planning of the city. More recently, the periphery and core are distinguished by the pace of investment and revitalization. The core of the city, consisting of 7.2 square miles is being gentrified at a rapid rate. This economic zone has no formal boundaries. It is separated from the city by invisible legislative boundaries and by the city's decision to create defined zones of investment. There are no spatial markers or infrastructural barriers that designate why revitalization should be focused in one central area.[Fig. 2] Rather, the differentiation comes from a decision made in the 1990s by business leaders and local foundations to encourage investment specifically in that area.[11] The result is that private investment has re-no-vated abandoned buildings, built sports venues and added a new transit line that operates only between downtown and midtown.[12] This financial

11
For example, Quicken Loans got a $50 million tax break simply to move their operations downtown. Peter Moskowitz, *How to Kill a City: Gentrification, Inequality, and the Fight for the Neighborhood*, Nation Books: New York, 2018, pp 94. See chapter 5 for more examples.

12
For more on this, see Moskowitz, who not only describes the development projects themselves but their in-fluence on real estate and gentrification as well. "The M-1, its supporters freely admit, is no longer public transit, but a real estate development tool." Moskowitz, *How to Kill a City: Gentrification, Inequality, and the Fight for the Neighborhood*, Nation Books: New York, 2018, pp 87.

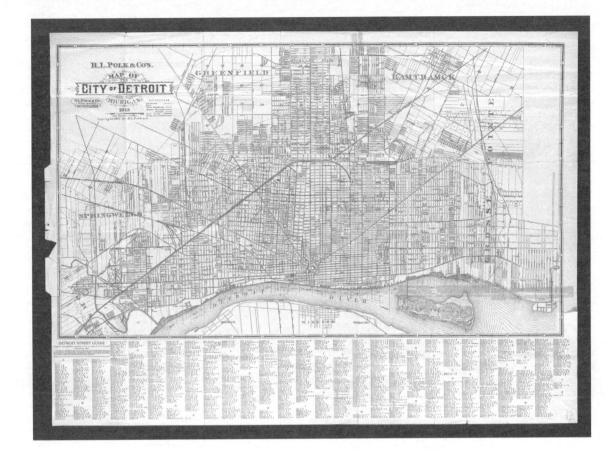

Fig. 1. Map of Detroit, Michigan, 1913.

model of redevelopment is praised for bringing a renaissance to downtown Detroit while explicitly causing wealth segregation and exacerbating class difference in the core at the expense of the continued disintegration of the residential fabric on the periphery, even though the urban grid is continuous through both zones[(fig. 3)]. While this *does* produce a change in urban morphology in one sense, as the core gets denser and the periphery grows more sparse, the formal differentiation within *urbs oeconomica* is less important or likely insignificant, relative to the economic differentiation that this produces. As such, the formal differentiation lacks political potential. Instead, this legible spatial condition is transformed into a rent gap: the differentiation in value that is necessary for the reproduction of the economic grid (buy cheap, sell at a profit). Any gap in the urban fabric here, thereby, provides little resistance to the economization of the city, but rather it becomes an engine for the economic process itself. In the past few years, these investment-driven plans for resettlement were accelerated.[13] Eventually, the economic grid will function throughout the periphery, integrating the city into a single economic mode, *indifferent to its current spatial conditions*.

This is not unique to Detroit. The discourse around redevelopment is pervasive, presenting urban change as a series of economic strategies for revitalization that not only use the economic success of developers to conceal increasing inequality but that also make conversations about space (and the discipline and profession of architecture as well) seem irrelevant. As urban planning departments continue to dwindle, cities put forward economic plans for revitalization.

Meanwhile, there seem to be few architectural or spatial boundaries that can halt the process of total economic integration.

And yet, the decoupling of spatial management from economic management does not mean that the ex-pression of this phenomenon is not spatial. On the contrary, the root of the problem is deeply spatial, due to the fact that the entire system is rooted in the commodification of space.

Urban Ground & the Public/Private Dichotomy

The questioning of spatial commodification would seem to point towards a critique of privatization, since private real estate development is one of the principal means by which *urbs oeconomica* claims land. However, this attitude would

13
Maurice Cox, former head of the planning department, called his revitalization projects "inclusive recovery" and centered the role of design in the gentrification process. This accelerated the process of resettlement but not without strengthening private development. For examples of projects, as well as insight into the language often used to mystify the project of gentrification, see Matt Shaw, "Five Years After Detroit's Bankruptcy, De-sign Fuels Recovery," *The Architect's Newspaper*, Feb 15, 2019. https://archpaper.com/2019/02/five-years-after-detroit-bankruptcy-de-sign-fuels-recovery.

Fig. 2. The dotted white line here indicates the boundary of the greater downtown area of Detroit, now commonly referred to as "the 7.2" due to its land area of 7.2 square miles. Despite the lack of morphological or spatial differentiation at this line, it remains a stark divider of economic and racial inequality.

Fig. 3. Detroit, disintegration of residential fabric.

A Common Occupation: John Dewey, Hannah Arendt, and the Aesthetics of Public Encounter

M. Surry Schlabs

take for granted the public/private dichotomy as fundamental to the distribution of space in the city. Within a contemporary neoliberal paradigm, the public sphere is reconfigured as a framework that supports the market, and, as such, it has lost much of its ability to counter the discourse of privatization.[14] With the public sphere significantly weakened, looking past the public/private dichotomy has never been so urgent. Yet, even if the public sphere were in a robust state, the idea that private ownership and public management are opposites that define each other would still be an obstacle to subverting the logic of privatization. This is not to argue for the death of the public realm but to argue for the need to conceive of the public realm as something that can *precede* the dichotomy of public management vs. private ownership.

In *The Architecture of the City*, Aldo Rossi argues that all growth and change in the city require expropriation, stating that plans for urban expansion and development "are closely linked to expropriations, with-out which they would not be possible and through which they are manifested."[15] In this passage, he underscores expropriation as a fundamental urban process determined through a process of economically moti-vated territorialization in which both public and private interests participate, demonstrating "the primary importance of the economic facts of expropriation in relation to the architectural artifacts of form."[16]

By highlighting the act of expropriation or territorialization as fundamental to all land use—whether specified by zoning or determined through the purchase of a parcel—we are left with an important question: is it possible to conceptualize the city before it has been territorialized by public and private interests and subdivided into public and private realms? If so, perhaps this condition could be called an urban ground: the raw space that is taken up in any act of space-making and any act of politics; the precondition for territorialization.[17] Perhaps, this idea can be pushed even further. If it is possible to conceive of a spatial condition that *precedes* the dichotomy of public/private ownership and management, then it could also be possible to imagine a space in the city that is outside of the public/private dichotomy, even *after* territorialization occurs. In other words, the notion of urban ground not only speaks to the nature of spaces that are yet to be occupied, but it changes the idea of what the given condition of an existing space would be if somehow the act of territorialization were to be left incomplete. The concept of the urban ground, then, acknowledges the possibility

14
David Harvey, *A Brief History of Neoliberalism*. Oxford University Press, 2007.

15
Aldo Rossi, *The Architecture of the City*, MIT Press: Cambridge, 1982, pp 144.

16
ibid.

17
Here, "urban" does not have to refer to the density of a settlement but rather to the condition of negotiation that is inevitable when groups of people must share a territory. In this case, "urban" refers to a basic condition of coexistence best embodied by the city but also present and perceptible in any population. In other words, an "urban ground" can also exist in a rural context, as it is the pre-condition of a negotiated or contested space. Thus, it exceeds the dichotomy between urban and rural.

On the morning of September 17, 2011, a small group of political activists loosely associated with the journal *Adbusters* descended on Lower Manhattan's Zuccotti Park, a so-called "privately owned public space," operated by Brookfield Properties. By afternoon, their gathering had grown to include more than a thousand people, many of whom brought tents, sleeping bags and other camping supplies in preparation to spend the night. Over the course of the next two months, the occupation of Zuccotti Park would emerge as something of a global phenomenon, spawning an arcane system of collective communication and decision making: a loose network of communally supported social services, including health clinics, kitchens, the "People's Library" and hundreds of similarly motivated encampments around the world.

Interestingly, and perhaps ironically, a loophole in New York City's political and statutory regime of public park administration allowed Occupy Wall Street's encampment in Zuccotti Park to endure as long as it did. In 1961, the New York City Planning Commission had instituted a policy allowing developers to construct some 20 million extra square feet of leasable space in exchange for the development of roughly 500 "privately owned public spaces" or "P.O.P.S.'s." While the city imposes curfews in all of its municipally owned "public" parks, most of these privately owned public spaces were still statutorily required in 2011 to remain accessible for "passive recreation"

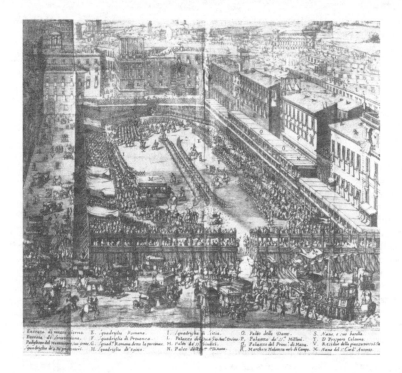

Fig. 4. As a paradigmatic example of baroque urban scenography, Genevieve Warwick cites the festival held by Cardinal Antonio Barberini in Piazza Navona in honor of the arrival of the Prince of Poland to Rome. The event consisted of elaborate performances which in turn required the construction of elaborate scaffolding, seating, and stages. Warwick argues that once these temporary structures were taken down, the material fabric of the city continued to resemble the ritual within the form of the Piazza, whose form at the time was loosely adhering to the footprint of the remains of an antique stadium, but was still relatively in flux. The ritualization hosted by the powerful allowed the form of the piazza to remain, and that space was ultimately returned to the people once the festival was over.

The People's Library at Occupy Wall Street, 2011. Photograph by David Shankbone.

of that incompleteness, of a political interstice that is manifested as an active spatial condition in the city.

The development of public plazas in early modern Rome can serve as an example of how the dynamics of an active urban ground can play out. Genevieve Warwick, in her study of public space in Baroque Rome, notes that before the Renaissance common spaces in the city tended to be interstices, intersections and hubs for the distribution of good and resources.[18] The claiming of space for public use was done through negotiation and improvisation in the gaps between territorialized space. Throughout the Renaissance, the investment in architecture and sculpture by the Papacy instigated massive building projects, resulting in the "scenographic transformation of urban space."[Fig. 4][19] However, Warwick argues that, despite the explicit performance of power that was hosted by these Papal projects, the alliance between power and space never became absolute due to the fact that the space remained public—not in the sense of being managed by public agencies, but rather the space remained accessible to all. Even as the new architectural scenography afforded power a place to parade and exert pressure, the public space of the city was not *taken*; it was merely *shaped*. Within those forms, the urban ground remained active. The alliance between power and space never became absolute, and the space itself was returned to the people after the papal spectacles ended.[20]

The baroque piazzas, then, not only formalized power, but they also inevitably framed and preserved the urban ground, allowing for the simultaneity of the *de facto* use of space as well as its *de jure* embodiment of power. In other words, the urban ground is the site that affords an

oscillation between different forms of power—a possibility that makes evident the need to conceptualize public space as something other than zones of public and private management. The urban ground is an area of the city where territorialization is incomplete, allowing for the contestation or inversion of social hierarchy, however fleeting it might be.

In contrast, *urbs oeconomica* obstructs the dynamics of the urban ground through mechanisms of spatial commodification. Once a space is owned, its use is no longer negotiated but managed, instituting the *de jure* dynamics of ownership to intervene upon or regulate social interaction and suppressing *de facto* use, thereby eliminating the above-mentioned oscillation of power that characterizes an urban ground. An example of this can be readily found in the fate of the Occupy Wall Street movement, where protestors directly faced this conflict between the de facto and de jure during their occupation of Zuccotti Park.[Fig. 5] Although privately owned, the park falls under the category of a privately-owned public space, where private actors develop an urban space for public use in exchange for zoning concessions. In this

18
Genevieve Warwick, "Ritual Form and Urban Space in Early Modern Rome," *Late Medieval and Early Modern Ritual: Studies in Italian Urban Culture*, ed. Samuel Cohen Jr, et al., Brepolis Publishers, 2013, pp 297-328.

19
Warwick, 297-328.

20
Warwick cites in particular the 1634 carnival celebrations thrown by Cardinal Antonio Barberini in honor of the Prince of Poland, held in Piazza Navona. Warwick, pp 297-300.

Occupy Wall Street Poster, 2011.
Designed by Will Brown for *Adbusters*.

Fig. 5. Aerial view of Zuccotti Park.

case, the definition of "public" is inherently ambiguous—an ambiguity that first made Zuccotti Park an ideal site for the Occupation. However, when protesters began their months-long nonviolent occupation, the ensuing struggle between protesters, private actors and city government resulted in a series of court orders that ultimately restricted unregulated occupation of the space. Several court rulings, both during and after the Occupation, limited the legal parameters of free speech to ban encampment and overnight sleepins, slowly erod-ing the ambiguity of privately-owned public space to make these spaces increasingly similar to private property.[21] These rulings increased the ability of private actors to legally regulate the use of public space in New York City, preventing any oscillation between different modes of power, further entrenching the *de jure* management of space as the urban status quo.

While the Occupy Movement is perhaps an extreme example of spatial contestation, the outcome underscores how the initial act of commodification is never neutral. Even when private actors are forced to make concessions to the public, through the mechanisms of ownership they are predisposed to leverage property rights to achieve their ends, opening up new avenues of control over public space. Independent of its form, through

21
Hao Cao, "A Noneventful Social Movement: The Occupy Wall Street Movement's Struggle Over Privately Owned Public Space." *International Journal of Communication* 11 (2017), 3162-3181.

twenty-four hours a day.[1] In New Haven, Connecticut, home to the country's longest-lasting Occupy encampment, the occupiers used a similar loophole, the Town Green being owned and administered, not by the city itself but by a self-selecting group of five prominent citizens, an arrangement dating back to 1641. While the city parks department is generally responsible for maintaining the grounds of the New Haven Green, all decisions regarding its use and care—its occupation, as it were—are made by this "Committee of the Proprietors of Common and Undivided Lands at New Haven," whose members resisted early pushes on the part of city government to oust the occupiers before winter.[2]

The occupation of public parks and the disruption of municipal infrastructure, of course, have been tools of public protest in America since at least the 1960s, when the Freedom Riders "occupied" segregated buses throughout the South, and Martin Luther King Jr. led his march down U.S. Route 80 from Selma to Montgomery. The times, however, have long since changed, and today we confront a new reality, one in which physical and material space have become progressively divorced from the patterns of human social life, reflecting what art historian Jonathan Crary has characterized as a widespread "depreciation

1
Kayden, Jerold S., "Meet Me at the Plaza," *New York Times*, October 19, 2011. (http://www.nytimes.com/2011/10/20/opinion/zuccotti-park-and-the-private-plaza-problem.html) accessed 1/28/2018; and Mattathias Schwarz, "Map: How Occupy Wall Street Chose Zuccotti Park," *The New Yorker*, (https://www.newyorker.com/news/news-desk/map-how-occupy-wall-street-chose-zuccotti-park) accessed 1/28/2018.

2
O'Leary, Mary E., "Occupy New Haven court case leads to question: who is in charge of the Green?" (http://www.nhregister.com/news/article/Occupy-New-Haven-court-case-leads-to-question-11466425.php) accessed 1/28/2018.

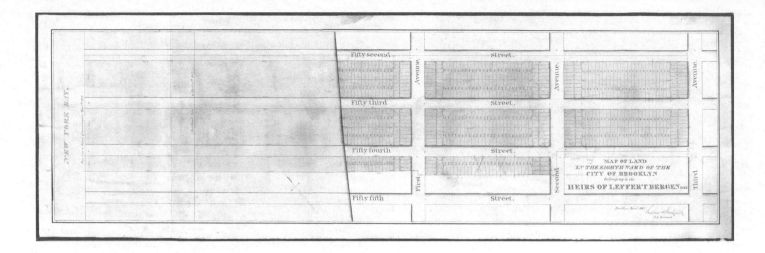

Fig. 6. This map shows land owned by the Bergen family,
one of the first groups of Dutch settlers to arrive
in Brooklyn. At first the land was used to farm field
crops, but as New York City grew, leasing the land
to tenant farmers became more profitable. This map
indicates the platting of land for sale in 1882, by
which point the land had been subdivided into valuable
city blocks. Of particular interest is the fact that
half of the seaside property was below the high water
mark. Despite difficult access, piers could be built to
receive ships, and as such, the land continued to be
platted below the water mark.

and disparagement of [the] 'brick and mortar' world."[3] In such light,
this short article positions itself as a plea for the return of aesthetic values to the discussion of what it means for a space or place to be
considered "public."

Primary to this effort will be a discussion of certain issues
surrounding the New Civil Rights Movement's[4] fraught relationship to
public space, in terms of both John Dewey's only focused work of
political philosophy, *The Public and Its Problems*[5] — which, like most of
his work, may be read in distinctly aesthetic terms — and the political
and social criticism found in Hannah Arendt's *Human Condition*, a text
that rejects modernist notions of the "atomic individual" in favor of a
view of humanity as manifestly and inextricably *plural* in nature. Dewey,
in his day, was a fierce advocate of broad-based, participatory democracy, which he understood to be less a form of government
than a mode of communal life, an approach to building community and
achieving political ends, of which the voting booth is but a minor and
relatively inconsequential part. Arendt, likewise, developed a vision of
political endeavor based in a culture of civic engagement, collective
deliberation and active citizenship. In these terms, democracy proceeds
slowly and deliberately by way of personal interaction with a wide
variety of essentially different others. These interactions facilitate the
construction of community, built up through close association with
other individuals to whom we are held personally accountable.

commodification, the space is *taken*—an act that is naturalized when private ownership becomes the dominant mode by which development occurs. The urban ground is dissolved by default and the economic grid becomes the primary way to interpret and experience space. In turn, the terms by which one can engage with urban space become increasingly homogenized and limited. In this context, the concept of urban ground becomes increasingly necessary. Otherwise, it becomes impossible to imagine the city as anything other than a fully territorialized zone, making *urbs oeconomica* the dominant architectural fiction of the late capitalist city.

The Development Parcel & the Dissolution of Urban Ground

It is argued above that *urbs oeconomica* is indifferent to form. However, the city of *homo oeconomicus* does have a formal logic in itself, and it is perhaps through identifying this formal logic that we might further recognize its fictions and even disturb or weaken its processes.

In the capitalist city, urban growth is conducted via the buying and selling of parcels. While this process is driven by the abstraction of economic exchange, it does have material consequences: the parcel becomes the primary organizer for the city.(Fig. 6) In other words, the parcel becomes the spatial expression of the economic grid. This is in contrast to the totalizing urban grid, critiqued by Aureli, which operates by producing an overall organization within which subdivision occurs. For *urbs oeconomica*, subdivision itself is the primary organizational logic, since the city grows according to a series of closed perimeters within which individual architectural

objects are bound.(Fig. 7) Roads and infrastructure may run between parcels, but their relevance lies in providing access to the parcel, rather than in structuring an overarching formal logic for the city. Such a logic becomes unnecessary, since a parcel can be of any shape or size. As long as one can draw a property line around it, it is part of the economic grid. The city, then, becomes continuous via an aggregative system—both spatial and economic—rather than by a pre-existing logic of geometric continuity.

There are three archetypes of development that are characteristic of *urbs oeconomica*, all of which rely on the logic of the parcel. Although all have existed in some form in other times and places, through the dynamics of *urbs oeconomica*, they have become major avenues for the propagation of the economic grid.

The first is the subdivision, particularly in a suburban context—a model that became dominant in United States urban planning in the twentieth century. While it may seem that a suburb is out of place in a discussion of the late capitalist city, the birth of the subdivision marks an important moment in the economic integration of urban growth. The suburbs came into being first and foremost as a business model rather than as the product of demographic change or other such catalysts of urban growth. A shift in the concept of development and of urban settlement was required for the built environment to grow in this new way.[22] Before the prevalence of platting land for the sale of

22
Marc A. Weiss, *The Rise of Community Builders*, Beard Books, 2002.

Though *The Public and Its Problems*, more than anything else, is a work on politics, unlike other superficially similar projects of political, social and cultural criticism, Dewey's approach is unique in its development of an essentially *aesthetic* model. Of course, Dewey's conception of the "aesthetic" is something quite different from that of many other modern thinkers. Simply stated, Dewey's broader project is built on an expanded understanding of the term "aesthetic" to include implications of the related, if not wholly equivalent, term "artistic." Thus, he relates his aesthetics not only to passive perception, enjoyment or judgment, but also to an active mode of productive engagement in the world, to the creative act of *making*, generously understood.[6]

3
Crary, Jonathan, "Untitled Remarks," *The Pragmatist Imagination: Thinking About "Things in the Making,"* Joan Ockman, ed. (Princeton: Princeton Architectural Press, 2000) p. 142 Crary notes: "For the first time in history, there has been a delinking of economic circulation from physical space, as abstracted forms of wealth have a mobility and fluidity unrelated to what we used to think of as location." This is not to suggest that the various abstractions associated with the "flow" of capital or the "liquidity" of wealth don't, in and of themselves, possess either spatial or temporal characteristics – they do. Yet they exist, necessarily, outside of those "tangible, worldly" places which Hannah Arendt understood to constitute both the private and the public realms of human experience. Indeed, the array of evocative metaphors conventionally deployed to describe the nature and movement of wealth, as opposed to property (in the Arendtian sense), become necessary precisely because of this disconnect. Our common understanding of the term "public" has likewise been reduced, in the popular imagination, to denote little beyond abstract notions of state ownership or, in the case of parks, generally unfettered physical or visual access, regardless of ownership. See Hannah Arendt, *The Human Condition* (Chicago: University of Chicago Press, 1998 [1958]) p. 70.

4
The term "New Civil Rights Movement" refers here to a loose network of grassroots political movements and organizations centered on the experiences of historically marginalized groups in American society. The term was originally intended to imply a connection to the 1960s American Civil Rights Movement. It has since expanded to reflect "a broader agenda that includes LGBTQ issues and immigration reform." See: Gene Demby, "The Birth of a New Civil Rights Movement," *Politico*, December 31, 2014 (http://politico.com/magazine/story/2014/12/ferguson-new-civil-rights-movement-113906) accessed 12/15/2019.

5
Conceived as a critical retort to Walter Lippmann's Phantom Public (1925), in which Lippmann appeared to advocate technocracy over democracy, Dewey's book refutes Lippman's description of the democratic public as little more than nostalgic abstraction- the "phantom" of his title facilitated the manipulation of mass consciousness by authority through a process he dubbed "manufactured consent." Sixty years later, the term was resuscitated and developed by Noam Chomsky and Edward S. Herman in *Manufacturing Consent: The Political Economy of the Mass Media* (New York: Pantheon Books, 1988).

6
Jay, Martin, *Songs of Experience*, University of California Press (Berkeley: 2005) p. 138-139.

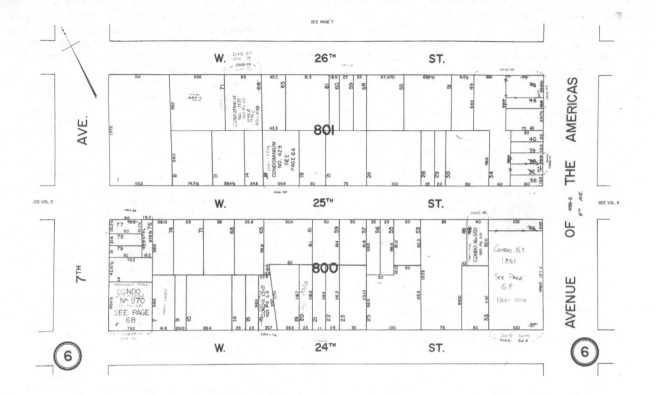

Fig. 7. Although we think the gridiron plan of
Manhattan is highly rigid, a look at the ca-
dastral map shows that internal to each block,
there is irregularity between parcels. In the
end, it is the parcel structure that allows for
extreme difference between buildings, not the
block structure, and the parcels can be of any
shape or size.

Free Speech Zone. Photo by Mustafa and Aziza, 2004.

residential parcels, land in the United States was primarily carved into building lots and sold to new owners, who would afterwards determine the use of the land. In contrast, the planning and development of new low-density residential districts conceived growth as the process of creating and selling a specific product: high-income suburban communities. The execution of this business plan necessitated substantial planning in terms of landscape, infrastructure and deed restrictions, all of which required new levels of control over investment and regulatory processes.[23] As the economic model gained traction, the subdivision began to proliferate, creating patterns of growth that were no longer reliant on a geometric grid, or even a plan. Growth, then, could occur without a conception of overarching form, allowing the economic grid to countervail the need for any organizational geometry.

Despite the formal indeterminacy of the subdivision as an archetype, parcelization is first and foremost an imposition of an economic grid by means of explicit spatial delineations. The process often begins with a single act of territorialization. The moment in which the land gets platted, a large tract of land is created that operates essentially as one large parcel or territory that is then managed and sold off by the developer. The individual lots come into being afterwards, replicating the initial logic of the first parcelization. At both scales, the economic logic is made fully determinate by means of rigid spatial delineation. Unlike a heterogeneous urban condition in which space can be contested, the logic of subdivision leaves no possibility for an active urban ground.

The second archetype of *urbs oeconomica* is the privately-owned public space, which is an open space in the city that, although owned by a private entity, is required by the municipality to allow access to the public under certain conditions. This spatial designation has become increasingly common in municipalities subject to—or responsible for—austerity measures under which the city can no longer afford the care and management of open urban space. Private actors take on the management of these spaces, often in exchange for zoning concessions. Zuccotti Park, mentioned above, is one such example.

The physical edges of publicly-owned private spaces tend to be unmarked, as the space is explicitly meant to seem public or at least evoke a sense of accessibility. However, despite this ambiguity, the parcel that delineates a privately-owned public space actively creates a new zone of authority, one in which the corporate owners of the space can impose and enforce supra-legal regulations. For example, the site of London's City Hall is now owned by the St. Martins Property Corporation, a real estate company which is, in turn, owned by the sovereign wealth fund of Kuwait.[24] Outside the seat of London's government, the real estate corporation that owns the land no longer allows the public to congregate,

23
Weiss, 146.

24
"Revealed: The Insidious Creep of Pseudo-Public Space in London," *The Guardian*, July 24, 2017. https://www.theguardian.com/cities/2017/jul/24/revealed-pseudo-public-space-pops-london-investigation-map.

With that said, in this book, Dewey concerns himself primarily with the *making* of community, which he equates, more or less, with democracy. The public, in Dewey's view, may only be brought about through "the lasting, extensive and serious consequences of associated activity. In itself, it is unorganized and formless." The functions and scope of the state, he insists, are "something to be critically and experimentally determined," in an open, public forum.[7] Lamenting the rise of individualism in modern democratic societies, Dewey notes the fallacy of ignoring the reciprocal relationship between admittedly individual thoughts and actions and those of others, between what we think and how we act, and the consequences those actions have outside our immediate selves.[8] Individualism, for Dewey, far from the benign or even noble celebration of humanity's "natural rights," represents a subversion of such rights acquired by individuals in their capacity as members of a community. He attributes this subversion, in part, to a false segregation of freedom of expression from freedom of thought, seeing its origins in "the idea of a mind complete in itself, apart from action and from objects" and rejecting the notion that "men may [somehow] be free in their thought even when they are not in its expression or dissemination."[9]

7
Dewey, John, *The Public and its Problems* (Athens: Ohio University Press, 1988 [1927]) p. 74.

8
ibid, p. 24.

9
ibid, p. 167.

Fig. 8. Photograph by author.

employing private security to prevent assembly and protest. Publicly-owned private spaces create new pseudo-juridical zones, and anyone moving through these spaces would be subject to the enforcement of privately-written rules. The result is the regulation of open space within the city but without the consent of the public.

In opposition to this erosion of public space, some activists have begun to demand a return to public management of these spaces. In London, the response to the public discontent around this issue has been to draw up a charter by which these pseudo-public spaces can be subject to municipal oversight. In other words, the city will impose an additional juridical overlay by which the municipality places specific constraints on the power of private actors who manage the space. However, this not only leaves the economic grid fully intact but it further justifies its continued growth by reducing the friction between private actors and the public while allowing the erosion of the public sphere to continue at a fundamental level.

The way in which pseudo-juridical zones in the city impose a specific kind of social and behavioral order within a designated space may seem in contradiction to the above argument that economic management becomes more important than spatial management within the context of *urbs oeconomica*. However in Foucault's argumentation, the *aim* of spatial management was power itself; its end was to control the population. In these projects, the *aim* of spatial management is real estate; its end is simply capital. Corporate owners agree to manage a public space in exchange for the ability to leverage that space for capital accumulation—the inviolate mandate of *urbs oeconomica*. Control over its usage is a means, not

Noting a tendency among political and legal theorists to define freedom as such, in terms of the loosening of existing restrictions on individual behavior as opposed to the assertion of rights as a populace, Dewey remarks that, "no man and no mind was ever emancipated merely by being left alone," the removal of formal limitations being "but a negative condition." "Positive freedom," he insists, "is not a state, but an act," one "which involves methods and instrumentalities for control of conditions."[10]

In 1958's *The Human Condition*, Hannah Arendt echoes and occasionally amplifies a number of positions laid out by Dewey in *The Public and its Problems*, emphasizing the importance of shared experience to the construction of a "common human world," a material environment occupied by a host of others who see that world from an infinitely variable range of differing perspectives, thereby granting us a collective image of "reality in the round." Without the "shared common sense," developed through intimate and sustained engagement with difference, she suggests, we "are each driven back on our own subjective experience, in which only our feelings, wants, and desires have reality."[11] However, Arendt, like Dewey, hardly views this condition as essential or inescapable. Indeed, her critique leaves ample room for agency, if not outright revolution; her model of political experience, built on an understanding of human society, is characterized, above all, by its plurality.

an end, serving primarily to prevent any disturbance to the creation of value. Despite the spatial aspect of a publicly-owned private space, as
long as this mechanism of ownership is in place,
it is the economic grid that remains most active.

The strength of the economic grid is further
evidenced by the fact that these sites are
often designated by discreet plaques in the side-
walks and walls, or, at times, they are left
unmarked. The transition from public to private
management of a space is hardly perceptible to the
average person. (Fig. 8) Aside from the obvious difficulties this presents for a democratic use of
space, with no physical indicators of a juridical
transition, the economic grid can easily spread
and move across the urban grid, thereby conforming
and adjusting to economic opportunity while indifferent to the contours, limits and delineations
of the urban grid itself. In other words, with the
space of the city becoming abstracted into pure
value, the urban grid becomes increasingly inactive
as a political force within the city. The economic grid can easily gain ground, indifferent, once
again, to form.

The third archetype typical of *urbs oeconomica*
is the unique architectural object that has come
to serve as an icon for the globalized city.
As noted by Emmanuel Petit in his analysis of
postmodern space, these architectural icons do
not operate as parts to an urban whole but as
terminals characterized by their involutedness
and an overall tendency to curve and turn in on
themselves.[25] Due to this formal disposition, it is
easy for these projects to become urban enclaves,
often reconfiguring the city to align with the
desires of the wealthy by hosting entertainment
hubs, performance centers and commercial zones.[26]

Examples of these kinds of spaces abound, as contemporary architecture has rushed to satisfy the
demand for these projects from Bilbao to Shenzen.

The unique architectural object embodies
economic power—spatially, by serving as spatial
markers for consumption sites, and financially,
by functioning as nodes within the economic grid.
Their physical edges are less important than the
edges of their economic domain, which, in turn,
need not be spatialized or materialized (hence
their involutedness), because they are maintained
by economic regulation. As such, like privately-owned public spaces, the edge of the parcel
that hosts the project tends not to provide any
legible spatial differentiation—and, in fact, it
is often invisible or intentionally obscured by
the architecture itself, such as the Norwegian
National Opera and Ballet by Snøhetta, which
seamlessly folds into the ground. Without architectural demarcation, the parcel serves purely
as an abstract boundary of ownership, which, in

25
Emmanuel Petit. "Grids,
Labyrinths, Orbits,"
lecture at UIC School of
Architecture, March 17,
2014, https://www.youtube.
com/watch?v=oLLwQtr4N38

26
Erik Swyngedouw, "The
Zero-Ground of Politics:
Musings on the Post-
Political City" *Urban
Asymmetries: Studies and
Projects on Neoliberal
Urbanization*, ed. Tahl
Kaminer, Miguel Robles-
Duran, and Heidi Sohn, 010
Publishers, 2011.

This sense of plurality, Arendt insists, "assures us of the reality
of the world" around us.[12] Though she stops short of entirely collapsing
the distinction between "public" and "private," as Dewey sought
to do, the two realms remain, in her thinking, mutually and inextricably
dependent upon one another. The term "public," in this view, signifies nothing less than "the world itself." It is the "world of things...
between" — between us "who have it in common, as a table is located
between those who sit around it; the world, like every in-between,
relates and separates men at the same time."[13]

Though Arendt's take on the notion of the individual is decidedly
less critical than Dewey's had been, she shares his advocacy for a
public space where people may be seen and heard by others in face-to-
face contact, a condition, she writes, which:

10
ibid, p. 168. The philosophical distinction between positive and negative freedom, or
liberty, dates back to at least Kant, though its most well-known modern theorist is
probably Isaiah Berlin, whose "Two Concepts of Liberty" (1958) engaged and elaborated
upon the decidedly negative conception of freedom espoused by John Stuart Mill in *On
Liberty* (1859). Perhaps because Dewey never made this distinction the focus of any
specific book or essay, addressing the problem of freedom in democracies in a variety of
contexts across a range of different works, his account here – which predates Berlin's by
over thirty years – tends to be ignored in most historical accounts of the issue.

11
Canovan, Margaret, "Introduction," *The Human Condition*, by Hannah Arendt (Chicago:
University of Chicago Press, 1998 [1958]) p. xiii-xiv.

12
Arendt, p. 50.

13
ibid, p. 52 Due in part to the widely acknowledged intimacy of Arendt's relationship with
her one-time teacher and mentor, Martin Heidegger, accounts of Arendt's intellectual
development have a tendency to overemphasize those aspects of her thought most
readily described as *Heideggerian*. Not only do such accounts tend to ignore the
indisputably more productive, decidedly less sensational or controversial, relationship
Arendt enjoyed with Karl Jaspers, her dissertation advisor, but they obscure other,
equally productive and potentially revelatory relationships and affinities linking Arendt
to a range of thinkers with whom she is otherwise not widely associated. These include
both Dewey, discussed here, and Martin Buber, whose dialogical theory of communication and intersubjective relations prioritized "the 'lived concrete, the everyday reality'
of human existence." See Maurice S. Friedman, *Martin Buber: The Life of Dialogue*,
(New York: Harper & Row, 1960) p. v. With that said, certain aspects of Heideggerian
existentialism do appear generally operative in Arendt's critique of "the public" in
The Human Condition. These include a phenomenological emphasis on the essentially
experiential character of human life in common, an account of the objective characteristics of political being-in-the-world as distinct from other forms of being – and a general
privileging of common experience over and above other theoretical forms of knowledge.

turn, creates differentiations of value that are generated by the economic activity on the site. Therefore, the main function of the parcel in this context is not to delineate space but to serve as a tool for the designation of value. This function is essential to the proper functioning of *urbs oeconomica*, because speculative real estate development relies on the premise of value differentiation to function. As Reinhold Martin highlights, without inequality in income or wealth, incentives for speculation would disappear and the real estate system as we know it would collapse. As such, a process of urban growth and development reliant on the real estate market must maintain inequality as a necessary condition of their own perpetuation.[27] The parcel is an indispensable device for producing those differences in value. Through the parcel, spatial juxtapositions within an urban grid become less important than changes in relative value within the economic grid, making the economic system a more powerful source of differentiation in the city than architecture itself. The preeminence of the economic over the spatial enables the architectural object to turn in on itself and disassociate from its immediate context. In this light, the autonomy of the parcel portrayed in Koolhaas' *The City of the Captive Globe*, can only ever be a fiction in that the architectural and consumerist excess on each urban block can only be produced through the economic mechanisms of relative value. What Koolhaas shows, however, is that architecture has the capacity to materialize the otherwise abstract economic grid. When this occurs, architectural projects no longer operate as *urban artifacts* in the Rossian sense but rather as nodes within an economic network of value. Thus, while Koolhaas would like to suggest that the urban grid releases architectural form from any constraints, he confuses the economic possibility of the parcel with the formal autonomy of architecture, producing an architectural fiction that readily serves the ends of capitalist processes. *Urbs oeconomica* has, over and again, proven its ability to create extreme juxtapositions of discrete architectural objects, with or without the Manhattan grid—from Las Vegas to London to Singapore. It is not the geometric clarity of the grid itself that releases the urban block from any obligation to its context. Rather, the mechanism of the parcel isolates the architectural object within a set of bounded monetary flows and disassociates it from its spatial and material context. Within the resulting spectacle of architectural delirium, the economic grid reigns, even when the legibility of the urban grid remains strong, as it

27
Reinhold Martin writes, "governing is an art; it derives from techniques, not agents. Inequality is one such technique. It is designed, built into the system...Inequaltiy in housing is an intentional consequence of the real estate system, rather than a historical accident." Reinhold Martin, "Real Estate Agency," *The Art of Inequality: Architecture, Housing, and Real Estate: A Provisional Report*, The Temple Hoyne Buell Center for the Study of American Architecture, 2015, pp 92-131. See also Jason Moore and Susanne Schindler, "Defining Inequality," pp. 18-34.

derive[s] [its] significance from the fact that everybody sees and hears from a different perspective.... Only where things can be seen by many in a variety of aspects without changing their identity, so that those who are gathered around them know they see sameness in utter diversity, can worldly reality truly and reliably appear.[14]

Whereas in Dewey, the loss of this "worldly reality," of a public forum where individuals come together to construct community, results in cultural, social and political stasis—which he referred to as "eclipse"—in Arendt, the same loss results in tyranny. "The end of the common world," she writes, "has come when it is seen only under one aspect, and is permitted to present itself in only one perspective."[15] Whether "under conditions of radical isolation, where nobody can any longer agree with anybody else" or "under conditions of mass society or mass hysteria, where we see all people suddenly behave as though they were members of one family, each multiplying and prolonging the perspective of his neighbor," the resulting condition is the same. In both cases,

men have become entirely private, that is, they have been deprived of seeing and hearing others, of being seen and heard by them. They are all imprisoned in the subjectivity of their own singular experience, which does not cease to be singular [even] if the same experience is multiplied innumerable times.[16]

Writing in 1927, clearly prefiguring current debates on the role of digital technology in public social life, John Dewey describes advancements in communication and information technology on human society as

does in Manhattan. In other words, in *urbs oeco-nomica*, architecture is subordinate to the spatial delineations of property rather than active in shaping the formal logic of the city.

So tamed, the exuberant and expressive forms of unique architectural objects operate in a para-doxical mode. On one hand, they embody and announce the economic processes that make them possible. On the other hand, through the production of spec-tacle, they perform what Roland Barthes called *exnomination*—society's tendency to naturalize its own values to the point in which they are taken for granted and go unnamed. According to Barthes, the unnamed is easily appropriated by ideology, then made to seem self-evident.[28] The unique archi-tectural object exnominates real estate processes through the spectacularity of its own form. As such, exuberance in architectural form both embod-ies and exnominates *urbs oeconomica*, a city where the victory of free form over the forces of archi-tectural conservatism has been captured, leading to the victory of economic conservatism over urban and architectural form.

Beyond the Anacoluthic City

In all three archetypes of *urbs oeconomica*, the scales and morphology differ. This is not only a symptom of *urbs oeconomica's* indifference to form but also an opportunity to understand the plight of architecture in the neoliberal city. In each example, the production of architecture exnominates processes of territorialization, which, in turn, deny the possibility of an active urban ground in the city. As a result, the for-mal expression of architecture becomes secondary to the economic dynamics of territorialization,

which, in *urbs oeconomica*, are defined by par-cel-by-parcel growth. In the early modern period, debates over urban form were often framed by a dichotomy between organic form (pre-modern) and geometric form (modern). Throughout the mid- and late twentieth century and the beginning of the twenty-first, *urbs oeconomica* has rendered this debate obsolete. The parcel, operating as the basic spatial unit of the city, establishes and reifies the economic grid within either formal structure. However, the dissolution of this di-chotomy does not mean that *urbs oeconomica* lacks a distinct formal logic of its own. In the words of Lewis Mumford, "the form of the metropolis, then, is its formlessness, even as its aim is its own aimless expansion."[29] Similarly, one can iden-tify the non-syntactical nature of urban form as a formal disposition in itself and thus refer to *urbs oeconomica* not only by its economic dynamics but also by its non-syntactical formal logic. *Urbs oeconomica*, then, is an anacoluthic city.

The anacoluthic city provides unlimited possi-bilities for territorialization for two reasons. First, its aggregatory logic can easily subsume irregularities of form and terrain. Second, when possibilities of urban change are always framed

28
Roland Barthes, *Mythologies*, trans. Annette Lavers, Hill and Wang: New York, 1972.

29
Lewis Mumford, *The City in History: Its Origins, Its Transformations, and Its Prospects* (1961; San Diego: Harcourt Brace & Co., 1989), 544.

contributing to precisely this sort of fragmentation and alienation.[17] The external means of collecting, abstracting and transmitting information had, in Dewey's mind, far outstripped our collective capacity for "inquiry and organization" of its consequences.[18] The "older forms" of associ-ation, through which human communities are brought into being, have ceased to satisfy the needs of our increasingly technologically driven society, he insists, while the new forms of association we rely on to keep those communities together are increasingly "remote and indirect,"[19] leaving society open to manipulation and exploitation. For Dewey, this condition was neither inevitable nor necessary, and could in fact be mitigated through the rehabilitation and reconstruction of community. In his view, the idea of restoring true community represented the best pos-sible means of reconciling the loss of humanity's organic relationship to

14
ibid, p. 57.

15
ibid, p. 57-58.

16
ibid This is not to say that Arendt advocated, in any sense, the abolition or dissolution of the private realm (or of private property, for that matter) altogether. Indeed, the public and the private realms, in her view, are equally vital to the general health and continuity of human life in common. In a passage concerning "The Location of Human Activities," she writes: "Although the distinction between private and public coincides with the opposition of necessity and freedom, of futility and permanence, and, finally, of shame and honor, it is by no means true that only the necessary, the futile, and the shameful have their proper place in the private realm. The most elementary meaning of the two realms indicates that there are things that need to be hidden and others that need to be displayed publicly..." See Arendt, p. 73.

17
ibid p. 142.

18
ibid, p. 179-80 Dewey, of course, was writing in his day of the impact had by radio and telephone on the social character of public life in America, but his words apply just as clearly, I think, to the rise of web-based "social media" in today's world. Social networks, like Twitter and Facebook, receive regular accolades on the nightly news for their instrumental role in facilitating the organization of large-scale public protests among dissidents in places like Tehran and Cairo, even as their susceptibility to—perhaps even culpability in—government surveillance goes unquestioned and, more-or-less, unchecked. What is more, the implication that such tools might even serve as appropriate substitutes for the sort of organization and assembly previously tied to the *"public square,"* or *"commons"*—that is, to the real spaces of contemporary urban life—speaks to the continued relevance of Dewey's critique today.

19
ibid, p. 212-213.

within the logic of buying and selling land, the parcel becomes the given condition of the city. Access to space becomes dependent on access to capital, a quality that predetermines the politics of the site and neutralizes the act of territorialization. Other modes of claiming space are precluded and the urban ground is erased, producing a fiction that serves the economic order.

In light of this, I would like to propose two alternatives that could begin to resist the totality of urbs oecono-mica.

The first is for architecture to attempt to materialize the boundary between public and private in order to reactivate the dynamics of urban ground. The goal would not be to reify the public/private divide but rather to ask whether architecture can, through its own processes, make the process of territorialization visible so that it can be contested. Precedents of this do exist in architectural history. As Aureli notes in his analysis of the *Palazzo Rucellai* by Alberti, the facade both holds the boundary between public and private, and simultaneously uses the grid to extend the ordering logic of the building past the boundaries of the singular architectural object and towards the city itself. Though its explicit flatness and repetition of a measurable order, the project mediates the relationship between public and private through architecture.[30] Of course, because the spatial conditions of the city have so radically changed since then, it is no longer possible to repeat these architectural devices. Today, facades are conceived as skins or wrappers for exuberant architectural form, exemplified by the commodified architectural object. However, by studying the spatial diagram of *urbs oeconomica*, architecture can, perhaps, discover new means by which to make this divide visible. Architecture itself might still become a way to locate the urban ground or identify sites for its re-emergence.

The second approach would be to work towards the dissolution of the lot line, subverting the parcel through alternative land ownership structures that produce a different spatial diagram for the city. For example, community land trusts are a model of collective ownership in which land is held in trust, i.e. removed entirely from the real estate market and owned in perpetuity by a collective entity, usually a non-profit organization. The community land trust may still make individual buildings on that land available for private ownership, but the building and the land beneath it have been decoupled. Thereby, the land itself is no longer private property. This strategy was developed in order to separate the value of the building from the value of the land, thus creating a new mechanism for the creation of affordable housing. When framed purely as an economic idea, the spatial implications can be difficult to see. Most community land trusts today are adapted to existing built environments, and pre-existing parcels continue to dictate the use of space. After all, occupants are often granted use of the land beneath their house as though it were part of the property. However, a community land trust

30
Pier Vittorio Aureli, "Introduction: Means to an End: The Rise and Fall of the Architectural Project of the City," *The City as a Project*, ed. Pier Vittorio Aureli, Ruby Press: Berlin, 2013. pp 26.

Philando Castile Shooting Protest at the Minnesota Governor's Mansion, 2016. Photo by Fibonacci Blue.

nonetheless has the capacity to create a new zone in the city within which the parcel is significantly weakened due to its unconventional treatment of ownership. For example, if a home on a community land trust becomes unoccupied, due to an occupant's financial hardship, the community land trust retains control over the house rather than it returning directly to the market or it going into the hands of a bank. In *urbs oeconomica*, the economic autonomy of the parcel relies on its conception as a discrete commodified spatial unit, one whose value and exchange is regulated by an abstract monetary system far outside of its spatial and material context. This discreteness is the precondition for the formal and spatial disassociation that occurs between parcels, and that, in turn, enables the extreme fragmentation of the anacoluthic city. In contrast, a community land trust creates social and political bonds across properties, subverting the fictional "autonomy" of the individual parcel that currently drives both the ideology of ownership and the mechanisms of the market itself. By reducing the parcel's ability to separate itself, this alternative ownership structure binds a space socially and spatially to the conditions of its context, dissolving the economic logic of the parcel and disturbing the dynamics of *urbs oeconomica* at a fundamental level.

The transformative potential of this ownership paradigm has yet to be realized in the contemporary city. Most land trusts use this ownership mechanism to produce affordability while maintaining the outward appearance of conventional built form. However, if a legible common ground within a specific zone of the city were to be deployed as a new constitutive urban element, a systemic challenge to *urbs oeconomica* could emerge. Within that zone, relationships between occupants can be rewritten. The land held in common would become a critical interstice—the use of which would be constantly negotiated by residents—as well as a source of connection between them, since the land would still have to be stewarded and cared for. Furthermore, the collective governing body of the land trust is well poised to support alternative uses of the land, such as energy production, food production and shared social reproduction. In an urban context, this model has a particularly radical potential, because public and private might both take on new mean-ing as communal spaces transcend the typical dichotomy between public and/or private management of the city. In other words, the shared land operates as a *de facto* urban ground, while also emerging as the product of political cooperation and local organization—it is what *is* and what is *made to be*. With this re-activation of the space between properties, new urban forms can emerge. Perhaps then, the urban grid will be able to rival the economic grid once more, reclaiming the ground lost to *urbs oeconomica*.

the broader environment, which, as in all of Dewey's work, was understood to include other people as integral parts of that environment.[20] To that end, Dewey writes, "community must always remain a matter of face to face intercourse.... Vital and thorough attachments are bred only in the intimacy of [such] an intercourse which is, of necessity, restricted in range.... There is no substitute for the vitality and depth of close and direct... attachment."[21] In Dewey's view, the work of art-making prepares the individual for the responsibility of choice and accountability in a socially intensive setting. By demonstrating the multiplicity of

20
For a detailed and critical account of the implications of Dewey's broader body of work in the context of 21st-century "technological culture" and the role of philosophy in clarifying questions raised by the impact of advanced technology on the nature and quality of modern society and community, see Larry Hickman, *Philosophical Tools for a Technological Culture*, (Bloomington: Indiana University Press, 2001). For an equally thorough analysis of Dewey's critique of technology and his account of its history, see Hickman, *John Dewey's Pragmatic Technology* (Bloomington: Indiana University Press, 1992).

21
Dewey, *The Public and Its Problems*, p. 211-213.

22
Mattern, Mark, "John Dewey, Art, and Public Life," *The Journal of Politics*, vol. 61, no. 1 (Feb. 1999) p. 54.

meanings inherent in any object of human inquiry, art positions the individual in relation to a broader community, in which common concerns, considered from a range of individual perspectives, may be transformed into common goals through a socially engaged exchange of ideas with other community members.[23] Dewey, one of few modern political theorists who didn't equate communication with speech, held art, in fact, to be the "the only media of complete and unhindered communication between man and man... in a world full of gulfs and walls...."[24]

    This suggests a capacity inherent in art, as well as architecture, to open up novel "social and public spaces within which communicative interactions, necessary for the creation and sharing of meaning and the development of commonalities of identity and orientation, [can] occur."[25] It likewise sets Dewey in dialogue with a range of leftist critics of art and culture, whose reductionist view of culture's relationship to capital finds popular and public art capable of little beyond kitsch narrative, merely "reflecting, not determining, the course of history."[26] However, for Dewey, whose main work on aesthetics, *Art as Experience*, privileged the creative act of making by framing art as a locus for the construction of meaning, thought and knowledge, art is more than a mere reflection of conditions beyond the reach of social control; it is a means of engaging and altering those conditions, a mode of active human agency.

In this model, the type of direct, engaged experience made manifest in art, and necessary to the construction of shared meaning and common purpose in Dewey's vision for democracy, depends strongly for its effectiveness, however, on proximity, visibility and tangibility. For Dewey, *all* experience may be viewed as aesthetic. Therefore, for experience to be effective and for community to thrive, a site, place or physical form is required. The revolution, in other words, will not be televised.[27]

The fragmentation, segregation and individualization of the public which Dewey and Arendt speak of has, over the past few decades, given way to an increasing privatization and bureaucratization of our

23
ibid, p. 56.

24
Dewey, John, *Art as Experience*, (New York: Perigree, 1980 [1934]) p. 105.

25
ibid, p. 59

26
ibid, p. 59 (footnote #5) Though Theodor Adorno's position on popular music, specifically – that it constituted the "dregs of musical history"– is more widely familiar outside of art historical circles, I refer here, too, to the work of art critic Clement Greenberg, whose essays in the late 1930s and early 1940s married an ostensibly Marxist critique of bourgeois culture to a neo-Kantian understanding of human subjectivity and aesthetic judgment. His work for *Partisan Review* and The Nation during these years laid the groundwork for the American school of formalist art criticism, which both privileged and encouraged a highly objective mode of visual abstraction and "medium-specificity" in Modernist painting and sculpture. In his landmark essay, "Avant-Garde and Kitsch," Greenberg rejects the cultural sphere as a viable site for the evaluation and interpretation of aesthetic production, noting the glaring "disparity" between ostensibly similar forms of both "high" and "low" culture and the insurmountable challenge inherent in seeking to situate those forms "in enlightening relation to one another" within the same critical frame. See Theodor Adorno, *Introduction to the Sociology of Music*, transl. E. B. Ashton (New York: The Seabury Press, 1976), p. 29; and Clement Greenberg, "Avant-Garde and Kitsch," *The Collected Essays and Criticism, vol. 1.* (Chicago: University of Chicago Press, 1988) p. 6.

27
ibid, p. 71-72.

cities' public spaces, as an alliance of government officials, real estate developers and militarized law enforcement has colluded in effectively closing the *public square*, transforming protest — a "lawful form of politics enshrined in the constitution" — into a dangerous, potentially criminal act.[28] Historically, the notion of assembly in the United States has long exemplified a certain mode of public life, characterized by collectivity and close spatial proximity, clearly conceived as a means of challenging prevailing political and social conditions. Yet, over the past half century, the Supreme Court has "shifted from defending the right of assembly to defending the 'right of association,' a phrase that does not appear in the constitution." This alteration has resulted in both a radical narrowing of what qualifies as "political expression" and the erosion of what constitutional law scholar Timothy Zick has dubbed America's "expressive topography": the actual, material spaces where citizens are able to congregate and exercise their first amendment rights. The essential fallacy at the heart of this position is explored and interrogated by Arendt, constituting a central element of her broader critique of the public. "...[W]hatever men do or know or experience can make sense only to the extent that it can be spoken about...Men in the plural, that is men in so far as they live and move and act in the world, can experience meaningfulness only because they can talk with and make sense to each other and to themselves."[29]

On the afternoon of July 9, 2016, a group of citizen activists gathered at the governor's mansion in St. Paul, Minnesota, to do just that, to protest the killing of Philando Castile, whose recent shooting death at the hands of police officer Jeronimo Yanez during a routine traffic stop had sparked nationwide protests, calling further attention to the problem of police violence against African Americans and other people of color. Frustrated and angry, at 10:30 pm, the protesters departed the governor's mansion, marching in unison up the Lexington Parkway and onto Interstate 94, where they proceeded to block all eight lanes of traffic in a controversial act of civil disobedience, the sort of action now widely associated with Black Lives Matter and other factions of the New Civil Rights Movement. Among the most common criticisms of that movement — whether of Occupy's months-long, highly conspicuous assemblies in public parks across the country or of *Black Lives Matters'* penchant for literally stopping traffic as a means of forcing real encounters with others — is the charge that neither group has been especially articulate in sketching out operable "demands," that their sole purpose must, therefore, be disruption, that their grievances might

28
Kessler, Jeremy, "The Closing of the Public Square," *The New Republic*, January 12, 2012. (https://newrepublic.com/article/97901/the-closing-the-public-square-john-inazu-timothy-zick) accessed 1/15/2018 p. 3

29
Arendt, p. 3-4.

be more productively aired some place else, some place out of sight, some place more *private*. Such charges take for granted, however, that the sort of community capable of making and delivering such demands even exists anymore. As I hope this brief attempt to theorize and emphasize the aesthetic dimension of public action and occupation in recent political protest movements begins to make clear, it doesn't.[30]

As artists and architects—invested both personally and professionally in the betterment and sustenance of the city, the neighborhood and the community—this should give us pause. One aspect of contemporary political life set in stark relief by Occupy Wall Street was the reality that very little of what we consider public space in this country actually qualifies as "public" at all, at least not by any reasonable, historically grounded metric. Zuccotti Park, the "privately-owned public space" where *Occupy* made its initial stand, is hardly unique in this respect. True public spaces, as understood by both Arendt and Dewey, are places where people can assemble, not just to exercise their constitutional right to protest, but to participate in the construction of common meaning and community through real engagement with others. Thus, it should come as no surprise that the disappearance of these spaces has spurred movements, such as Black Lives Matter, to commandeer interstate highways and other major roadways to stage their actions. In many parts of the country, these are arguably the last real public spaces left. Despite their effective inaccessibility and

The Unbearable Lightness of "Complexity"

Maroš Krivý

the essential danger inherent in occupying them as pedestrians, they are particularly well suited as places of encounter between individuals who might otherwise have little in common. But the highway is no public square. The interstate is no common. If the public, as Dewey put it nearly a century ago, now finds itself in "eclipse," should architects not take stock of their work's potential to help bring it back to light, back into being? If, as Hannah Arendt insisted, "there are things... that need to be displayed publicly *if they are to exist at all*,"[31] is the onus not on us — as stewards of the built environment — to help make visible and, thereby, to empower otherwise illegible public formations?

30
In his landmark essay on contemporary Californian architecture and urbanism, "You Have to Pay for the Public Life," first published in *Perspecta* in 1965, Charles Moore predicted – or perhaps merely observed – the urban conditions demanding precisely this sort of strategy on the part of American protest movements. Often considered an opening salvo in the gradual rise and eventual theorization of architectural postmodernism, Moore's "Public Life" is commonly remembered as an apology for the sort of ersatz-urbanism exemplified by Disneyland, though it would be more productively read, I believe, as a lament. Indeed, the replacement of California's "vanished" public realm with Disney's *Main Street USA*, a hollow simulacrum of 1910's middle-American urbanism, is hardly cause for celebration, in Moore's view, its total exclusion of "political experience" being an area of particular concern. But then Moore sees the lack of a public realm where the politics of democracy might take shape as being more-or-less characteristic of Los Angeles in general. In one especially prescient passage, he writes:
　　"It is interesting, if not useful, to consider where one would go in Los Angeles to
　　have an effective revolution of the Latin American sort: presumably, that place
　　would be the heart of the city. If one took over some public square, some urban
　　open space in Los Angeles, who would know? A march on City Hall would be equally
　　inconclusive. The heart of the city would have to be sought elsewhere. The only
　　hope would seem to be to take over the freeways...."
See: Moore, Charles W. "You Have to Pay for the Public Life," *Perspecta* 9/10 (1965) p. 58.

31
Arendt, p. 73 [my emphasis].

It is now a dictum that we live in an age of complexity. Ours is an age of complex transformations in economy, politics and architecture, one in which boundaries between these fields of human practice have become blurred, where human and non-human agencies have become entangled. The notion of a complex world reveals the limits of modern techno-science and anthropocentric hubris when it attempts to serve as a discursive platform on which to pin hopes for a more equitable and environmentally sound future.

Yet, as I argue in this essay, we live in an age not of complexity but one permeated by the unbearable lightness of complexity thinking. As a pivot of new forms of power-knowledge — a term that Michel Foucault used to interrogate power relations built on specific patterns of intelligibility — "complexity" does a subtle and potentially insidious ideological work.[1] Its cunning, evident in Friedrich Hayek's argument for neoliberalism and contemporary Silicon Valley-style design thinking, consists in appearing anti-elitist while instituting new forms of elite power.[2] My objective here is to avoid contrasting complexity to simplicity. I ask, instead, what kinds of epistemic violence are concealed behind roll-off-the-tongue statements, such as "the world is complex"?

1
Michel Foucault, *The History of Sexuality. Volume 1: An Introduction*. (New York: Pantheon Books, 1978); Jacques Bidet, *Foucault With Marx* (London: Zed Books, 2006).

2
William Davies, "Elite Power under Advanced Neoliberalism," *Theory, Culture & Society* 34, 5–6 (2017), 227–250.

3
For canonical accounts of complexity science, see Murray Gell-Mann, *The Quark and the Jaguar: Adventures in the Simple and the Complex* (New York: W. H. Freeman, 1994); Stuart Kauffman, *At Home in the Universe: The Search for Laws of Self-Organization and Complexity* (Oxford: Oxford University Press, 1995). Mitchell M. Waldrop, *Complexity: The Emerging Science at Edge of Order and Chaos* (New York: Simon & Schuster, 1992) is an admiring history of the Santa Fe Institute. Cf. Stefan Helmreich, *Anthropology Inside and Outside the Looking-Glass Worlds of Artificial Life*. Unpublished dissertation (Stanford University, 1995).

How does "complexity" shape the architectural discipline and the urban arena? What forms of agency does it justify? Which power relations does it obscure?

Our contemporary understandings of complexity descend from Northern American theories that, in the 1960s and 70s, challenged cybernetic and other then-dominant scientific theories of systems and control. As opposed to the prevailing view that systems naturally move towards equilibrium, the political scientist Herbert Simon and the ecologist C. S. Holling, as well as other like-minded colleagues, depicted systems as emergent, self-organizing and unpredictable. By the end of the Cold War, "complexity" came to mean less a critique of cybernetic science than a new scientific paradigm. In this view, complexity is a property of systems — so-called "complex systems" — whose behavior cannot be deduced from the behavior of their parts. Instead of providing causal explanations, complexity scientists study behavior patterns across systems, as in the case of the Santa Fe Institute. Founded in 1984, this research center became the self-appointed world headquarters for complexity science, bringing together disparate fields, ranging from physics and biology to economy and history.[3]

On March 25, 2020, a black man named George Floyd was murdered by a white Minneapolis police officer, Derek Chauvin. The act occurred in broad daylight, on a busy street and within public view of bystanders, one of whom recorded the encounter on video and swiftly uploaded it to social media. The public outcry was immediate; the police response, predictably brutal, proving (yet again) the urgent need for radical reform, if not wholesale reconstruction, of American law enforcement. As the preceding article has attempted to make clear, protest and assembly are acts of public formation, and communion, necessary to the maintenance and health of any functioning democracy. While truly public space may be in short supply, as the protests and demonstrations sparked by George Floyd's death remind us, some times the streets will do. As spaces and places where people can come together, to see and be seen by others, whether in acts of loving celebration or mutual antagonism, streets matter. Their form and character and accessibility to members of the public matter.

BLACK LIVES MATTER.

**New Haven
June 13, 2020**

Much has been written about how complexity thinking undermines the hubris of modernist techno-science, while relatively little has been said about its own hubristic, neo-positivist mindset, according to which systemic instability and catastrophes provide, as Isabelle Stengers put it, a reassuring "fresco of cosmic complexification."[4] Today, there is no better arena to examine this issue than urbanism, where the idea that cities are complex and self-organizing systems seems as incontrovertible as it is ubiquitous. This discourse pervades municipal strategies, TED talks and pin-up boards in architecture schools, informing how planners, designers and policy makers frame urban affairs. Complexity thinking is intrinsic to a distinctive political rationality, the aim of which is not to master plan but to govern urban self-organization. The notion of "complexity urbanism" backs up a new kind of expert power that blurs institutional accountability, preempts democratic contestation and contributes to depoliticizing urban change. This power does not adhere to the urban status quo, but it naturalizes the sheer matter-of-factness of urban flux.

To elaborate this premise, I will not dwell on canonical urbanists such as Jane Jacobs and Melvin Webber, those who ardently believed that cities are complex systems and, therefore, cannot be rationally planned. Let us instead examine, through the lens of urbanism, the so-called projective architectural theory popularized in the millennial years by prominent North American academics, such as Robert Somol, Sarah Whiting, Jeffrey Kipnis and Michael Speaks. The aim of this cohort was best expressed in Somol and Whiting's now-classic manifesto essay, published in the 2002 issue of *Perspecta*. They argued that the discipline should disengage from the so-called "critical architecture" associated with architect Peter Eisenman and theorist K. Michael Hays, who believed that capitalism could be challenged through "autonomous" architectural forms.[5] Anxious to steer the discipline toward efficacy and social impact, Somol and Whiting disregarded the fact that Eisenman and Hays's *critical architecture* was already a distorted interpretation of a Marxist and distinctively European *critical architectural history* (associated with the Italian historian Manfredo Tafuri), which emphasized the idea that architecture is embedded in capitalist relations and, therefore, not autonomous. As architectural critic Tahl Kaminer put it, Somol and Whiting called

4
Isabelle Stengers, "Complexity: A Fad?," in *Power and Invention: Situating Science* (Minneapolis: University of Minnesota Press, 1997), 4.

5
Robert Somol and Sarah Whiting, "Notes Around the Doppler Effect and Other Moods of Modernism," *Perspecta* 33 (2002), 72–77. Other contributions include Michael Speaks, "After Theory," *Architectural Record* 6 (2005), 72–75; Jeffrey Kipnis, "Is Resistance Futile?," *Log* 5 (2005), 105–109. The argument is anticipated in Jeffrey Kipnis, "Toward a New Architecture," *Architectural Design* 25 (1995), 40–49.

on architects to engage with "the compromised and 'dirty' world of daily life, economic exploitation, and mass culture," but effectively endorsed "the current social and political conditions, while questioning the need for an alternative vision."[6] The irony was that, while putting the discipline's pragmatic engagement with society on center stage, theorists of the projective assisted in creating a condition in which architecture has been "doubly removed" from the reality of capitalist institutions: powerless to resist them but also forbidden from questioning them.

This short-lived debate is dated, but the covert and often overt "anti-critical" ethos that went with it still lingers in schools of architecture and planning today. I argue that complexity thinking helped to make critical reason appear obsolete, while transforming the meaning of the term "project." Amidst the backdrop of the post-Cold War demise of alternatives to capitalism, "complexity" became the linchpin of innovation and design agency, and the bewildering twenty-first century metropolis became its compelling avatar. This was effectively a call on architects to engage with, not understand or question, contemporary urban change, instilling in them purpose but also unprecedented political and institutional myopia. The questions of society and urbanization were put on the table, while class and the other situated power relations shaping them were ignored.

In what follows, I focus on the architectural theorist, educator and editor Sanford Kwinter, interpreting his work as symptomatic of the limits to complexity urbanism.[7] Kwinter presents an interesting case, because he has written extensively on the urban question and anticipated by a decade the projective debate. Blending an antipathy towards criticality and a complex epistemology in ways that are emblematic of our contemporary predicaments, he described critique as reactionary, neurotic and corrupt. In other words, critique was a reason behind "our atrophied capacities of acting [...] in a world whose scope and complexity have effectively passed beyond grasp or measure."[8] This essay, by contrast, examines the ideological work of "complexity" that goes into naturalizing power relations in the late-capitalist city. It does so through a close reading of Kwinter's lecture-manifesto "Politics of Pastoralism," delivered at a 1994 symposium hosted by the now-discontinued journal *Assemblage*, held at Tulane University.

6
Tahl Kaminer, *The Efficacy of Architecture: Political Contestation and Agency*, p. 51 (London: Routledge, 2017). For critical reading of the "projective" see George Baird, "'Criticality' and Its Discontents," *Harvard Design Magazine* 21 (2004), 1–6; Reinhold Martin, "Critical of What? Toward a Utopian Realism," *Harvard Design Magazine* 22 (2005), 1–5; Daniel Barber, "Militant Architecture: Destabilising Architecture's Disciplinarity," *The Journal of Architecture* 10, 3 (2005), 245–253; Richard Anderson, "Tired of Meaning," *Log* 7 (2006), 11–13; Douglas Spencer, "Architectural Deleuzism. Neoliberal Space, Control and the 'Univer-City'," *Radical Philosophy* 168 (2011), 9–21.

7
Sanford Kwinter and Michel Feher (Eds.), Zone 1|2: *The Contemporary City* (Cambridge, MIT Press: 1987); Sanford Kwinter, "New Babylons: Urbanism at the End of the Millennium," *Assemblage* 25 (1994), 80–81; Sanford Kwinter, "Wildness (Prolegomena to a New Urbanism)," in Sanford Kwinter, *Far from Equilibrium. Essays on Technology and Design Culture*, pp. 186–194 (Barcelona: Actar Press, 2007); Sanford Kwinter, "Notes on the Third Ecology," in Mohsen Mostafavi and Gareth Doherty (Eds.), *Ecological Urbanism*, pp. 94–105 (Zurich: Lars Müller, 2010); Sanford Kwinter, Requiem: *For the City at the End of the Millennium* (Barcelona: Actar Press, 2010).

8
Sanford Kwinter, *Architectures of Time. Toward a Theory of the Event in Modernist* Culture (Cambridge, MA: MIT Press, 2001), 5.

THE ARTIST'S RESERVED RIGHTS TRANSFER AND SALE AGREEMENT

The accompanying 3 page Agreement form has been drafted by Bob Projansky, a New York lawyer, after my extensive discussions and correspondence with over 500 artists, dealers, lawyers, collectors, museum people, critics and other concerned people involved in the day-to-day workings of the international art world.

The Agreement has been designed to remedy some generally acknowledged inequities in the art world, particularly artists' lack of control over the use of their work and participation in its economics after they no longer own it.

The Agreement form has been written with special awareness of the current ordinary practices and economic realities of the art world, particularly its private, cash and informal nature, with careful regard for the interests and motives of all concerned.

It is expected to be the standard form for the transfer and sale of all contemporary art, and has been made as fair, simple and useful as possible. It can be used either as presented here or slightly altered to fit your specific situation.

If the following information does not answer all your questions consult your attorney.

1

Seth Siegelaub and Robert Projansky, *The Artists' Reserved Rights Transfer and Sale Agreement*, 1971

The Artists' Reserved Rights Transfer and Sale Agreement was published in 1971. Its primary authors are Seth Siegelaub, an art dealer, publisher and curator, known for his pioneering exhibitions of dematerialized art, and Robert Projansky, a lawyer. The text was distributed as a free fold-out poster and published in several art magazines including *Art News*, *Studio International* and *Arts Canada*. Licensed under free use, it now circulates as a pdf.

The document has two parts: an introduction, which describes its background and intentions, and a contract template that can be filled out and signed. The contract stipulates that artists get 15% of resale profit (if any) of the work; they reserve the right to know about subsequent exhibitions of the work; and they hold reproduction rights for the work.

The text is widely known if not widely used. Famously, the artist Hans Haacke uses it on all sales of his work. The contract did affect legal discussions on artist resale rights, and it is cited as an influence on the 1990 Visual Artists Rights Act, which reserves certain rights for artists around authorship and the use of the artist's name in connection with a work.[1]

1
Haaften-Schick, Lauren van. "Conceptualizing Artists' Rights," Oxford Handbooks Online: Law, Oxford University Press, 2018. https://doi.org/10.1093/oxfordhb/9780199935352.013.27.

Seth Siegelaub and Robert Projansky, *The Artists' Reserved Rights Transfer and Sale Agreement*, 1971

In the lecture, Kwinter presented a vision for a "new urbanism" that would be "free of the controlling obsession with certainty, predictability, or permanence." His new urbanists would instead, as he mused in a string of metaphors, monitor the city "like tweaking interest rate dials in financial markets," only intervening in it "like a shepherd driving his herd" in order to "relinquish control [of it] to the regime of complexity."[9] Kwinter's metaphor for the city, as a self-organizing, part-computational and part-biological system, was strikingly at odds with the symposium's stated purpose to investigate "the political dimension of scholarly work in architecture," one that was underscored by New Orleans's palpable class and racial tensions.[10]

Centered around the phrase "regime of complexity," which Rem Koolhaas used in the essay "What Ever Happened to Urbanism?" Kwinter's lecture elaborated the dilemma set up for urbanists by the Dutch architect: if you want to reclaim authority, relevance and efficacy, you must relinquish the fantasies of being omnipotent and having the city under control. Kwinter said, "he [Koolhaas] says that we must relinquish control to the regime of complexity," arguing that this shouldn't be understood as surrendering

9
Sanford Kwinter, "Politics and Pastoralism," *Assemblage* 27 (1995), 25–32, 31. See also Sanford Kwinter, "The Building, the Book, and the New Pastoralism," *ANY* 9 (1994), 17–22.

10
From the invitation and announcement by Catherine Ingraham, cited in Robert McAnulty, "Introduction," *Assemblage* 27 (1995): 6–7, 7. The conference report noted that "the deep tensions that sometimes violently mark the urban landscape of New Orleans ... never surfaced in the discussion." (Ibid.)

11
Kwinter, "Politics and Pastoralism," 30.

12
Kwinter, "Politics and Pastoralism," 30.

13
Stuart A. Kauffman, *At Home in the Universe: The Search for the Laws of Self-Organization and Complexity* (New York, Oxford University Press, 1995), vii and 192. Cf. Reinhold Martin, "Complexities," *The Journal of Architecture* 3, 3 (2005), 187–209.

architects' capacity to intervene in the urban.[11] In the geopolitically turbulent early 1990s, "complexity" was for the theorist not a barrier but a defining moment in the process of restoring the systemic agency of urbanism — contra postmodernism and deconstructivism, contra "critical architecture." It was both a condition *of* and a technique *for* governing the city as a large-scale and higher-order system. Lending a veneer of scientific credibility to Koolhaas's intellectual provocations, Kwinter identified ("I have no idea where he [Koolhaas] got it [but] I know where it comes from") the biologist Stuart Kauffmann as the author of the phrase "regime of complexity."[12]

Kauffmann, a long-term faculty member at the Santa Fe Institute and the author of *The Origins of Order* (which Kwinter referenced) and the 1995 bestseller *At Home in the Universe*, is known for generalizing a set of insights on spontaneous biological order as the "laws of self-organization and complexity" that apply across history and in social, cultural and technological realms. His work abounds in sentences, such as "organisms interact with organisms to form ecosystems, economies, societies" and "tissue and terracotta may evolve by deeply similar laws."[13] Kwinter adopts the biology *à la* Santa Fe uncritically as a design toolbox. He draws a link between Kauffmann's "laws" and Koolhaas's speculations, while he eludes concrete social realities obscured by such generalizations.[14]

During the lecture, Kwinter patronized the audience by stating that "swarm[ing] toward a state of pure 'algorithmic computationality'" was a phrase that "may well mean something only to those who study the work of the Santa Fe Institute."[15] This statement is remarkable not because the audience, indeed, might have found the phrase enigmatic, but because Kwinter himself implied that the phrase was enigmatic and, therefore, persuasive to architects. The enigma is predicated on a simple distinction between two kinds of nature-based metaphors: those of various "organicist" architectural theories that center around organic forms (morphologies) and those inspired by complexity science. The latter category centers around the processes of organic formation (morphogeneses), and it sees organisms as if they were self-programming super-computers. However, Kwinter wrongly implies that because morphological approaches to urbanism are naive and conservative, morphogenetic ones are sound and progressive.[16] Reducing

14
On Kwinter's reading of Kauffmann and the Santa Fe Institute, see also Kwinter, *Architectures of Time*, 3–32 (chapter "The Complex and The Singular"); Sanford Kwinter, "Soft Systems," in Brian Boigon (Ed.), *Culture Lab*, pp. 207–228 (Princeton: Princeton Architecture Press, 1993).

15
Kwinter, "Politics and Pastoralism," 30.

16
In his later work, Kwinter further played on this tension. See Sanford Kwinter, "Who's Afraid of Formalism", in Sanford Kwinter et al. (Eds.), *Phylogenesis: Foa's Ark— Foreign Office Architects*, pp. 96–99 (Barcelona: Actar, 2004); Sanford Kwinter, "Confessions of an Organicist," *Log* 5 (2005), 71–75.

17
Kwinter, "Politics and Pastoralism," 31.

the urban question to what he, following Kauffmann, calls "spontaneous formation" is no less tenuous than reducing it to urban morphology.

This brings me to the lecture's key passage, in which Kwinter's urban vision is articulated figuratively. It should be cited at length:

> The shepherd observes the unfolding life of the flock, its movements, its collective affects, the flow of the continually reshaping mass and the flow of the landscape in continuous interaction. Yet his intervention is soft, fluid, indirect, and yet for all this almost precise: he "controls" it like the drummer in a jazz quartet, only by adding to it, using the "fuzzy" dynamism of his dog (no pun intended) and communicating with the dog (who is in perpetual "coasting" movement) by means of an approximate language of whistles, instructing it to press here, push there. This new urbanism — it does not plan, it does not precisely or inflexibly impose, and it does not fetishize the integrity and pristine unfolding of the fixed abstract scheme. This new urbanism is a moving urbanism, a pastoral urbanism of inflection.[17]

To begin with, Kwinter's pastoral metaphor is problematic in the way in which it echoes Heidegger's controversial claim that humans are not lords but shepherds of being—a claim that Anson Rabinbach described as "a gesture of defiance in the cloak of humility."[18] Regardless of his choice of imagery, Kwinter makes three decisive points in this passage: complexity obviates the need for comprehensive city planning; the urban is to be governed through continuous monitoring, detections of potentials and local interventions; the efficacy of the intervention is proportional to its covert character. Limited to a set of procedural rules, inspired by biological metaphors and the "laws" of complexity, Kwinter's pastoral vision for urbanism falls short of addressing substantive political concerns. It fails to ask: whose movements and affects are visible to urbanists? As a result, what goes unnoticed or gets deliberately ignored? In what institutional setting do urbanists intervene… and to what ends? What power relations create, and are created by, an urbanism that "adds to" the city—but does not subtract, "whistles"—but does not speak, and "inflects"—but does not contest?

Delivered a quarter century ago, the lecture belongs to a genealogy of contemporary urbanism, throwing into sharp relief how complexity thinking naturalizes power relations in the late-capitalist city. It brings out vividly what historian Zeynep Çelik Alexander calls "neo-naturalism:" an epistemological regime in which nature is seen as a model for politics, design and other spheres of human practice, such as urbanism, "not because it is the realm of order and necessity […] but because it is the realm of emergence and complexity."[19] Rather than replacing one class of biological metaphors with another, we need to pose questions about the limits to extending biological metaphors—old or new—within the urban field. Considering that the fascination with complexity has become endemic in contemporary design, drawing attention to how it conceals and potentially aggravates urban inequality remains an urgent task.

For example, Koolhaas's study on Lagos portrays the city's infrastructural crisis as a marvelous case of self-organization.[20] Or we can also look to the case of Patrik Schumacher, who recently proposed to eliminate public housing and privatize streets. The architectural community was unsettled, but few commentators noticed that Schumacher's proposals are the logical corollaries of his tangled

18
Martin Heidegger, "Letter on 'Humanism'," in *Pathmarks*, pp. 239–77 (Cambridge: Cambridge University Press, 1998); Anson Rabinbach, "Heidegger's Letter on Humanism as Text and Event," *New German Critique* 62 (1994), 3–38, 23.

19
Zeynep Çelik Alexander, "Neo-Naturalism," *Log* 31 (2014), 23–30, 28. On this view, complexity theory is of a piece with intellectual currents, such as new materialism, neo-vitalism and object-oriented ontology, which theorize nature through ontological, neo-metaphysical lenses and obfuscate questions of epistemology, power and history. For this critique, see Susanne Lettow, "Turning the Turn: New Materialism, Historical Materialism and Critical Theory," *Thesis Eleven* 140, 1 (2017), 106–121; Andres Malm, *The Progress of This Storm: Nature and Society in a Warming World* (London: Verso, 2018).

20
Rem Koolhaas and Harvard Project on the City, "Lagos," in Francine Fort et al. (Eds.), *Mutations*, pp. 651–718 (Barcelona: Actar, 2001). Cf. Matthew Gandy, "Learning from Lagos," *New Left Review* 33 (2005), 37–53.

treatise *The Autopoiesis of Architecture*. This book draws upon the complexity theory of society developed by German sociologist Niklas Luhmann, and it presents the argument that architects should disengage from political debates and address social complexity strictly by means of design.[21] Another example is the politically covert but no less controversial agenda of the "new science of cities," propagated by planner Michael Batty. Informed by complexity science, Batty's scientific urbanism aims not to social-engineer cities but to foster and facilitate their bottom-up self-organization. Behind this egalitarian veneer, Batty disregards institutional contexts and renders urban change natural; his overly simplistic neo-behavioral approaches have been applied in controversial contexts, ranging from Olympic-led urban regeneration to suppressing street riots.[22] Lastly, we can evaluate the overbearing, so-called "urban physics" publicized in journals, such as *Nature*, and propagated by a cohort of ex-Los Alamos physicists at none other than the Santa Fe Institute, celebrated by Kwinter. Having come to the fore in the post-2008 era of austerity and urban competitiveness, they bluntly argue that the job of urban policy-makers worldwide is to adjust municipal policies relative to the laws of complexity—what these are, needless to say, are defined by the physicists themselves.[23]

By obfuscating institutional contexts, foreclosing possibilities for democratic contestation and rendering questions of accountability moot, theories of complexity are symptomatic of the erosion of democratic control in the urban arena and the attendant transformation of urban planning into an adjunct for financialized real estate and digital platforms.[24] Favoring heuristic over critical mindsets, complexity-based explanations have little to say about historical and institutional contexts that determine how urban problems are identified, defined and fought over. As geographer Matthew Gandy put it, "the theoretical novelty of such a perspective sits sharply at odds ... with the capacity for what one might term 'avant-garde urbanism' to actually explicate any substantial dimensions to urban change."[25] The notion of complexity mystifies rather than illuminates the source of increasing economic disparities and the reasons why social discontent is on the rise. It offers few answers to the challenges of late-capitalist urbanization, and provides no viable program for progressive urban politics. Finally, "cosmologies" of complexity eschew politics but they cannot escape

21
Patrik Schumacher, *The Autopoiesis of Architecture* (Hoboken: Wiley, 2011). Cf. Maroš Krivý, "Parametricist Architecture, Smart Cities, and the Politics of Consensus," *Ehituskunst: Investigations in Architecture and Theory*, 57 (2016), 22–45. Compare here the supposedly bias-free flow chart urban model by systems theorist Jay Forrester from half a century ago: steeped in a cybernetic rather than complexity-theory framework, the model justified the same conclusion that public housing programs should be discontinued. Cf. Felicity Scott, *Outlaw Territories. Environments of Insecurity/Architectures of Counterinsurgency* (New York: Zone Books, 2016), 190.

22
Michael Batty, *The New Science of Cities* (Cambridge: MIT Press, 2013). Cf. Kevin Grove et al., "Interventions on Design and Political Geography," *Political Geography* 74 (2019), 102017.

23
Luis Bettencourt, Geoffrey West, "A Unified Theory of Urban Living," *Nature* 467 (2010), 912–13. Cf. Brendan Gleeson, "What Role for Social Science in the 'Urban Age'?," *International Journal of Urban and Regional Research* 37, 5 (2013), 1839–1851.

24
Samuel Stein, *Capital City* (London: Verso, 2019); Sarah Barns, *Platform Urbanism* (London: Palgrave, 2019). On complexity theory and finance, see Bill Maurer, "Complex Subjects: Offshore Finance, Complexity Theory, and the Dispersion of the Modern," *Socialist Review* 25, 3&4 (1995), 113–145; Melinda Cooper, "Complexity Theory after the Financial Crisis," *Journal of Cultural Economy* 4, 4 (2011), 371–385.

25
Matthew Gandy, "Cyborg Urbanization: Complexity and Monstrosity in the Contemporary City," *International Journal of Urban and Regional Research* 29, 1 (2005), 31.

The Onus of Coherence

Nicholas de Monchaux

its ghosts: it may be that they nurture, as their flipside, various conspiracies, racisms, xenophobia and other atavistic theories and desires for an uncomplicated world.[26]

Admittedly, the debate on "complexity" is to be credited with rejecting the Cartesian duality of nature and culture by broaching the questions of non-human agency and the congenital anthropocentrism of the humanities. It challenged the kinds of nature metaphors that likened streets to arteries and parks to lungs. Today, nevertheless, "complexity" perpetuates another kind of naturalism, one that considers unpredictable events as the norm and catastrophic change as inevitable. The point is not to reject "complexity" in the name of simplicity. Rather, we need to be serious about confronting the lightness of complexity thinking and its equivocal role in the urban arena.

Instead of getting lost in reassuring frescos of ever-increasing complexification, architects and urbanists could do at least three things. First, we should put political economy and ecology back on the agenda. This means addressing questions of finance, ownership and regulation. Thus, we need to build alliances with initiatives across geographies and scales, which could be manifested through grassroots housing movements, new municipal initiatives and public infrastructure reforms.[27] Second, more engagement is needed at the level of pedagogy, where critique should be rehabilitated and reinvented as a form of socio-political inquiry. We are now faced with a false dilemma: falling back onto the idea of disciplinary autonomy or embracing interdisciplinarity based on the principle that everything is complex and, therefore, measurable as data. Rather, the challenge is to experiment with "indisciplinary" approaches across education, teaching and research.[28] By doing so, we will be better able to problematize how forms of knowledge and expertise are distributed in (architectural) academia and outside of it. Finally, it is urgent to historicize and question, as I have tried to do above, various forms of power-knowledge deployed in architecture and urbanism around "complexity." Indeed, many salient aspects of late-capitalist urbanization, from rising levels of socio-economic disparity to displacement caused by sea level rise, have been shaped by various complexities of financial markets and climate change. However, this hardly means that inequality, inequity and other forms of political and ethical urgencies are themselves "complex."

26
William Davies, Nervous States: *How Feeling Took Over the World* (London: Verso, 2019).

27
Leonard Ma, "Financialized Intentions," *AA Files 77* (forthcoming); Philip Oltermann, "Berlin's Rental Revolution: Activists Push for Properties to Be Nationalised," *Guardian*, 4 April 2019; Bertie Russell, "Beyond the Local Trap: New Municipalism and the Rise of the Fearless Cities," *Antipode* 51, 3 (2019), 989–1010; Daniel Aldana Cohen, "A Green New Deal for Housing," *Jacobin*, 2 August 2019.

28
I borrow the term from Jacques Rancière, Marie-Aude Baronian, Mireille Rosello, "Jacques Rancière and Indisciplinarity," *Art and Research* 2, 1 (2008), 1–10.

Acknowledgment
This research was supported by an ERC Advanced Grant entitled "Rethinking Urban Nature."

Page 40 of Van Halen's 1982 "Hide Your Sheep" tour concert rider famously qualifies the provision of M&M's in the band's dressing room; "WARNING: ABSOLUTELY NO BROWN ONES."[1] The band's lead singer, David Lee Roth has since acknowledged that the provision—buried deep under complex electrical, logistical and architectural requirements—was far from trivial. The absence of brown M&M's marked the presence of coherence in the venue's understanding and preparation of many more essential but far less visible components of the concert's infrastructure.[2]

Today, we are all enmeshed in a network of cables, wireless connections and digital infrastructure far more complex than a rock show. This includes, in large part, the semiotically insubstantial "cloud" that would, if it were a country, be the 9th-largest electricity user in the world. Given the necessary precision of such systems and the underlying, yes-or-no character of the digital world, the capacity for failure runs far greater than a missed audiovisual cue.

We perceive this massive, modern infrastructure only through a narrow technological window. This interface is designed in a very particular way. Its coherence is not just logical and visible for its own part, but because its miniscule, visible portion so attempts to advertise the precision design and reliability of the enormous and invisible infrastructure upon which it rests. Architecture—as architects know it—has become one more indication—and recipient—of this order.

We all now endure the unexpected effects and predictable unpredictability of complex technological systems; and we both crave and need coherence as we negotiate them alongside physical space. From pixel to portico, this is one of the particular burdens of architecture in our time.

Architecture at Bay

The San Francisco Bay Area, home to a mere seven million of this country's 321 million inhabitants, is usually consigned to the footnotes of architectural history.[3] Yet today, it exists as a global center of the struggle between architectural coherence in two increasingly overlapping realms: technology and the city. We can trace this story most dramatically through two big edifices that loom in our contemporary cultural landscape.

The first of these is Apple, and its ideas and ethics, as embodied in its monumentally circular headquarters, recently constructed in Cupertino, California. The other is George Lucas' technological vision of *Star Wars*, as embodied in the Death Star: the spherical, moon-sized battle station and colossal narrative device of the first and third original *Star Wars* films, as well as recent sequels.

The critical and cultural collusion of these juggernauts was first superficially suggested when images of Apple's planned building first appeared

1
http://www.thesmokinggun.com/documents/crime/van-halens-legendary-mms-rider, accessed June 15, 2019. Permalink at https://web.archive.org/web/20200215220511/http://www.thesmokinggun.com/sites/default/files/imagecache/750x970/documents/1982vanhalen9_0.gif

2
Roth, David Lee. *Crazy from the Heat.* (New York: Hyperion, 1997) pp. 97–98

3
To give two examples, Dell Upton's *Architecture in the United States* mentions only Morgan and Maybeck. William Curtis' Modern Architecture since 1900 mentions Morgan, Maybeck, and Moore; its only other indexical reference to San Francisco is Frank Lloyd Wright's V.C. Morris Gift Shop.

in 2011 — "Apple to Build Death Star HQ" announced, for example, *Stuff Magazine*.[4] However, more than superficial fandom is at stake. Both monumental structures are exemplary of an even larger, coherent but invisible universe, a system of order that they deliberately evoke in their design. As such, they reveal a great deal about the conflict and balance between order and openness, as well as the distribution of power that must be constantly negotiated and renegotiated as we negotiate technology, culture, city and society in the twenty-first century.

User Serviceable Parts

While brilliantly conceived by Steven Wozniak, the very first Apple Computer was not visually coherent. The Apple I consisted of a green circuit board with an assortment of user-serviceable parts, and it could also be assembled and enclosed in a variety of ways by its users. For the more commercial Apple II, Jobs turned to a friend from the Homebrew Computer Club, Jerry Manock, who was paid $1,800 to produce a case design. After much back-and-forth, the computer's innards remained accessible — complete with a pop-off lid revealing the inner circuits. However, every screw attaching the metal case to the circuit board was hidden on the case's underside.

This tension between both a uniform aesthetic and the customizability that characterized personal computing's modular hobbyist origins defined the push-and-pull of Apple's early designs. It was in service of these designs that, starting in 1982, Jobs began a collaboration with Hartmut Essinger and his firm Frog Design, known then chiefly for the sleek and elegantly segmented

shapes it produced for Japanese electronics-maker Sony, including a prototype modular stereo system, white and blocky, nicknamed "Skywalker." Essinger created a design language, referred to internally as "Snow White," — which would shape most of Apple's products until Jobs' first departure in 1985.

By the time the first Macintosh came out in 1984, its outer case was emblazoned, under Job's direction, with a warning that was anathema to personal computing's home-brewed origins: "No user serviceable parts inside."[5] Yet, Apple's corporate board concurrently pushed projects — like the Macintosh II — that adopted a more "PC-like" architecture of open cases and user-swappable parts. Jobs' perfectionism, nonetheless, ensured that the internal arrangement of these modular, white machines remained as resolved as their external shapes, even when closed from view.

After Job's departure from Apple in 1985, this tension — between open modularity and closed coherence, between user-serviceable parts and a uniform aesthetic — was elegantly resolved, perhaps, in an un-built design project, presented to Apple in June 1985, after Jobs' departure (and shortly before frogdesign was, too, fired). Code-named "Jonathan," it was an entirely modular computer in which uniform black or white boxes holding disk drives, hard drives, processors and memory were

---

4

"Apple to Build Death Star HQ", announced, for example, *Stuff Magazine* June 8, 2011, http://www.stuff.tv/apple/apple-makes-plans-death-star-hq/news

5

It should be said that the capacitor of the built-in monitor had the potential to deliver hundreds of volts to any unwary tinkerer.

stacked and assembled in unique configurations. Each purchaser, who could extend and upgrade each component over time.[6] (The unsuccessful proposal was even designed to run Microsoft's DOS and the Mac OS side-by-side from different modules.) Here—as we would often like to imagine as architects—a visual and spatial coherence signals functional and flexible interoperability. Like the diverse facades making up an urban street-wall, things lining up with other things for all our benefit.

The Modular MacGuffin

What of a galaxy far, far away? In the very first *Star Wars*, too, we find the tension between a smoothly uniform look and the under-the-hood jumble of user-serviceable technology. Each is essential to the film's narrative.

Since the 1930s and its reported invention by Alfred Hitchcock, the term "MacGuffin" has been used in the context of film to describe an object that may itself be incomprehensible but which, nevertheless, drives the film's plot forward.[7] In the voiceover commentary that accompanied the 2004 DVD release of *Star Wars Episode IV: A New Hope*, George Lucas describes R2-D2 as "the main driving force of the movie ... what you say in the movie business is the MacGuffin."

---

[6]
The unsuccessful proposal was even designed to run Microsoft's DOS and Mac's OS side-by-side from different modules.

[7]
Examples include *the Maltese Falcon* in The Maltese Falcon, the Holy Grail in *Monty Python and the Holy Grail*, and the Letters of Transit in Casablanca.

The first half of the 1977 film is resolutely
pushed forward by a set of inscrutable, open-
ended artifacts: R2-D2, Anakin Skywalker's hand-
crafted lightsaber and the *Millennium Falcon*.
Together, the form of these establish, more than
anything else, the distinct character of the *Star
Wars* universe. And they move us through it. They
take us from Leia's plea to Obi-Wan, delivered by
R2-D2, to Luke's first physical encounter with
his father's legacy, and finally to Han and
Chewbacca's fallible, fabulous command of the
Millennium Falcon. "What a piece of junk!" Luke
remarks on first sighting the ship in *Star Wars*;
it remains a "bucket of bolts" to Leia in *The
Empire Strikes Back*. Yet, it is also the fastest
spaceship in the galaxy. Lucas, by his own account, drew far more than the aesthetics of armor
from his time devouring Japanese cinema in film
school. More than the shapes of the worlds he
encountered, he was captivated by the experience
of dropping into a foreign yet coherent universe,
where — unlike the mansplaining tradition of heroic
science fiction — nothing was directly explained.

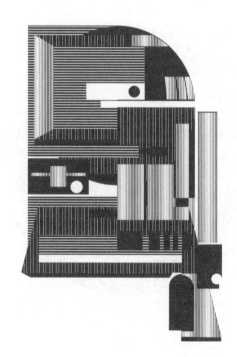

The mastery of finish

By contrast to Mos Eisly or the *Millennium Falcon*,
the aesthetic of the Empire is not of people,
systems, or technology made loosely, strangely
apparent, but rather of infinite complexity, sleekly and powerfully contained. From the deltoid sweep
of the Imperial Star Destroyer sighted in *A New
Hope's* opening frame (its cannons blazing at a
Rebel ship seemingly bolted together from a line
of metal barrels) to the blank faces of stormtroopers and their leader, Darth Vader, the Empire's
control of the galaxy, ineffable and immense, is

made clear by a mastery of architectural finish. Appropriately, the drama of the middle act of the first *Star Wars* revolves around the first pivotal confrontation between these two aesthetics: the elaborate effort by Obi-Wan Kenobi to hack into the closed and desolate architecture of the Death Star's tractor-beam controls. There, in the edifice's deep interior, a vast, manifest coherence masks unexpected vulnerabilities.

Boxes and Balloons

And what of Apple? The instrument of Steve Jobs' return to Apple, after a twelve-year exile, was another computer company, which Apple purchased in 1996. NeXT's machines were also designed by Hartmut Essinger. The computer's case consisted of a single magnesium cube, containing only a single circuit board to which all the computer's components were elaborately affixed. Their design recalled another science-fiction icon: the black, rectangular monoliths of Stanley Kubrick's *2001: A Space Odyssey*. The design also prefigured the sleek "unibody" devices that Jobs would produce in his second act at Apple. Yet the physical perfection and processing power of NeXT came at a high price. Marketed to universities and laboratories only, it cost $6,800 in 1986 dollars (nearly $15,000 today). Jobs expended an enormous amount on an elaborately designed stage-set of a robotized factory. But it, and the company, were a commercial failure.

Ironically, the rigidity and control that epitomized Jobs' vision of NeXT's hardware—complete with custom-made connectors and interfaces—was belied by its software. Instead of building a new operating system from scratch, NeXT's operating kernel was borrowed from a version of AT&T's Unix, refined at Berkeley in the 1970s, in order to better allow robust, "object-oriented" programming. (Most usefully, this allowed parts of the software to fail while others kept on running.) This DNA meant that, unlike the first Macintosh, it was designed from the outset to be networked and connected to other computers. It was in 1989, at the European Physics Laboratory CERN, that Tim Berners-Lee used a NeXT workstation to develop the first version of HTML and the modern web browser. This powerful and flexible system would lead to Apple's purchase of NeXT in 1997, not incidentally acquiring Jobs once more as an adviser, then CEO. The story of the larger corporate turnaround that followed has been told many times elsewhere. But the turnaround was visual as much as it was financial.

Apple and Empire

Apple's resulting shift was not back to the aesthetic of the Rebel Alliance at all—stylish, informal modularity. Rather, it would steadily and thoroughly encompass the reverse: the sleek, sharp and shiny shapes of *Star Wars'* sinister Empire. As in the *Star Wars* Universe, where Lucas explained tirelessly to modelmakers that the Empire should share a visual character with the Republic from which it evolved, it is a contrast not so much of the presence or absence of coherence, but rather in terms of degree.[8]

8
NdeM, Interview with Adam Savage, former ILM model-builder, June 17 2017. Audio recording.

Oratory Bethlehem: Birdville Church & House Wonderful

Justin Duerr

This shift did not happen at once. In a young and heretofore frustrated Apple designer, Jony Ive, Jobs famously found a creative translator and collaborator. Their initial outing, 1998's iMac, featured tight, polycarbonate curves and bright paint-box palettes, departing dramatically from the bleakly beige aesthetic of mid-1990s Apple. This tinted translucency, became for a period of time, the company's signature aesthetic, rendering the new and as-of-yet untamed internet approachable and transparent.[9]

This "see-through" aesthetic of the iMac era lasted until the revised iMac of 2002. With its LCD display and half-sphere base, this design started a trend of slipping computers and monitors into ever-thinner, ever-sharper enclosures. Ads for the first iMac's hemispherical base and articulated arm explicitly echoed the anthropomorphic movements of Luxo Jr. Yet by 2004, the iMac was settling into an ever-thinner slab of plastic, then aluminum, on a single, smoothly curved base. So too with Apple's laptops. While the first model to come out under Jobs' new reign, the iBook, hewed to the translucent, curved-and-colored aesthetic of the iMac, but subsequent designs eschewed extraneous detail and color in favor of ever-thinner, seemingly solid slabs of aluminum. The iPod and iPhone sleekly followed suit; Thinner, flatter, without a crease or joint visible, and ever-fewer accessible openings to inside.

In Gary Hustwit's 2009 survey of industrial design in the millennial age, *Objectified*, Ive appears onscreen to discuss a crucial watershed in this developing design aesthetic. The "unibody" approach was introduced in 2008, in which the main body of the Macbook is made from a single block of aluminum to which the keyboard, battery, boards

[9]
Perhaps not by coincidence, this was the aesthetic of 1990s Pixar as well, exemplified in the NURBS geometry of Woody, Buzz and the uniformed Pizza Planet Aliens from *Toy Story*. The firm, which had started its life as the digital division of Lucasfilm, was Jobs' other mid-career company. In the decade leading up to *Toy Story*, Jobs would ultimately pour more than half of his $100 million Apple severance into the firm, (which he purchased for only $5 million as an artifact of Lucas' 1986 divorce from his wife and creative partner Marcia). The gamble paid off: Pixar's IPO, scheduled for the week after *Toy Story's* opening, valued Jobs' 80% share of the company at more than $1.2 billion or 20 times his investment. By then, this same curve-friendly mathematics of animation software was baked into industrial design packages like McNeel's Rhinoceros and Dassault Systems' Solidworks. As a result, the iMac's shape recalled both the nose of an airplane and an alien clown. The iMacs shared not just their curves with Buzz and Woody but also a common complexion: light greens, blues, pinks and oranges. And the same complex effects of translucency and distortion, so essential to the rendered reality of the frames in *Toy Story*, were also a large part of what made the real iMacs engaging. While not user-serviceable, the internal workings of the first iMacs were, nevertheless, displayed through their translucent cases and celebrated for their well-ordered complexity. (de Monchaux, Interview with Alvy Ray Smith, 2018 –audio recording.)

I don't remember exactly when or where I first heard about Birdville Church, but I do remember that once I heard, I couldn't forget it. Like all good true stories, I didn't know how much was folk-tale and how much was based in fact. The earliest version I remember told that around 1914, a man in New Jersey had built a small church by hand, meant not only to save human souls but to attract and house wild birds. I filed it away in the back of mind as a place to investigate sometime. My wife Mandy, an avid gardener and botanist, enjoys the occasional trip to the New Jersey Pine Barrens to search for rare plant specimens, so on July 2011, we decided to make a day of visiting "Birdsville Church"[1] on the way to the Pine Barrens.

Parking nearby, we approached a structure overgrown with weeds and vines. It looked like some temple built by an ancient monastic sect, plopped down on an obscure corner in an Ocean County, New Jersey neighborhood, otherwise populated by vinyl-sided tract houses. With its fluted concrete columns, Moorish arches, and embellished tile inlay, it looked like a miniature roadside Hagia Sophia. It was being used by a trash removal company for equipment storage. There was something sublimely incongruous

Birdville postcard, n.d. Text on the reverse: *Gateway to Patio and Oratory. [...] The several points of interest here are Oratory Bethlehem and the "House Wonderful," the largest Rustic Birdhouse factory in the U.S.A. and last, The Flower Garden.*

1

This variation is an example of how information slowly changes over time. References to Birdville in local press began to use "Birdsville" at some point in the 1990s. While I don't recall what my first introduction to the story was, I do remember initially hearing it described as "Birdsville." This likely began with the presence of a blue and white hand-painted sign installed on the property (at an unknown date, and removed as of 2015), which read "Est. 1914 Birdsville Church."

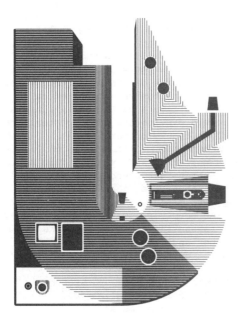

and all the ports are adhered, along with an increasingly confounding set of miniature screws, themselves designed to prevent users accessing the device's shrinking interior.

In Hustwit's film, Ive is introduced just after an extended monologue from Apple style's most obvious historic influence: German design legend Dieter Rams. In the 1960s, Rams, as a Braun Electronics employee, had been asked to collaborate with several faculty members of the *Hochschule für Gestaltung Ulm* (itself a self-conscious re-founding of the Bauhaus) on a cohesive design language for all of Braun's products. From shavers to coffee-makers to coffee-table-sized radios, the clean, white-and-black lines of the Braun devices hewed to Rams' re-take on Bauhaus director Mies Van der Rohe's famous disctum "less is more:" "Good design is as little design as possible."[10]

Yet "as little design as possible" is precisely not the absence of design. It is, rather, the exhaustive application of design until every detail, every offending element, is brought under strict and harmonious arrangement. We notice nothing because everything is under control. And here is where we get to the essence of the relationship and resonance between the artifacts of Apple and that of the Empire of Star Wars: for both express, above all, the exertion of control and power over the complex, messy reality of systems and objects. In technological and aesthetic terms, it makes sense for the contrasting objects of the insurgent Rebel Alliance to be ragtag;

10
Hustwit, Gary, dir. 2009.
Objectified. Plexi Film.

about this wholly unique and weirdly imposing building, designed as a sacred space, now used only to protect sundry tools and a forklift. That afternoon, we spent some time poking around, peering over the fence and taking pictures of the poured concrete structure. It was clearly built using a technique similar to Henry Mercer's Fonthill Castle in Doylestown, Pennsylvania and was decorated copiously with Mercer's Moravian tiles.

Henry Mercer and The Arts and Crafts Movement in the Mid-Atlantic

Located approximately 68 miles from Toms River, Fonthill and its attendant Moravian Pottery and Tile Works are masterpieces of poured-concrete architecture. The two buildings were designed by Harvard educated archaeologist, historian and craftsman Henry Chapman Mercer (1856-1930) and were completed in 1912. Mercer was an American proponent of the Arts and Crafts movement propagated by William Morris and John Ruskin, and many of the "Moravian tiles" manufactured at Mercer's workshop were based on medieval designs, which he encountered during research expeditions in England. The Arts and Crafts movement was a marriage of both political and aesthetic concerns, and many of its advocates looked to the medieval guild system—in the absence of feudal landowners and a monarchy—as a potential way to organize humane labor conditions. One of John Ruskin's most repeated quotes — *"Life without Industry is guilt, and Industry without Art is brutality"[2]* serves well to sum up the spirit with which Mercer approached life and labor.

2
John Ruskin, Lectures on Art
(London: George Allen 1904) p. 112.

3
"Fonthill Castle" Mercer Museum
& Fonthill Castle website.

Built between 1908-1912, Fonthill was the home of Henry Chapman Mercer (1856-1930). Archaeologist, anthropologist, ceramist, scholar and antiquarian, Mercer built Fonthill both as his home and as a showplace for his collection of tiles and prints. Designed by Mercer, the building is an eclectic mix of Medieval, Gothic, and Byzantine architectural styles, and is significant as an early example of poured reinforced concrete.[3]

less Mercedes-Benz, more MacGyver. The only reaction one can imagine Han Solo having towards the sleek touchscreen iPhone is the attitude he takes towards the sleek, all-too-functional internal comm-links of the Death Star—blasting it to bits.

That's no moon

Which brings us back in turn to the Death Star. The great reveal of the *Star Wars* battle-station's introduction is not just its singular form, but the way in which the seemingly sleek sphere slowly comes into view. We see this sequence twice in the first *Star Wars*—first in the *Millennium Falcon*'s tractor-beam approach, and then, even more so in the film's dramatic, dogfight-laden conclusion. A giant, perfect whole resolving into a complex universe of bits, pieces, and well-defined components. As echoed again in *Return of the Jedi*, where we see the scaffolded innards of a new Death Star in mid-construction, the Empire's might is expressed not just in the battle-station's singular shape, but in all the enormous complexity compressed into and controlled beneath its surface.

The idea of all of human complexity brought into the order of a well-set tabletop is, of course, a quintessential architectural dream, particularly at the hands of architects like Le Corbusier, Mies Van der Rohe and Walter Gropius. So it is particularly useful to observe the three iconic modernists' shared background in the consumer electronics of another age. The three worked together (though not overlapping completely) in the studio of architect Peter Behrens during the construction of the iconic AEG Turbinfabrik, itself a small part of the consulting position with the electronics giant that had led Behrens to leave his teaching position and open a full-time studio in 1908. Behrens' pathbreaking work for AEG—encompassing appliances, graphics, factories and showrooms—established design's complicity in negotiation technology's entry into domestic and urban space. In the words of his great chronicler, Stanford Anderson, "Behrens was not hired as an engineer with a sensitive eye. He was retained as an artist who could provide the signs of technical perfection through beauty of form."[11]

With an approach that echoes the techno-optimism of today's Bay Area (and even its fascination with crystals) Behrens was preoccupied with quasi-mystical ideas about the liberating power of both technology and design. Yet, also much like Jobs, he was also deeply pragmatic about the need for flashes of reassuring familiarity—such as in the way the shapes and details of new AEG electric kettles evoked the curves and ornaments of their ceramic, chinese antecedents.

While architecture had harbored systematic ambitions long before industrialization, it was the advent of physical systems and networks of technology and transportation that provided the aesthetic, philosophical and even physical justification for Modernism's grandest claims of coherence. And within these systems, architecture began to play a new role.

11
Anderson, 127

Birdville, Flint Road at Mill Street, South Toms River, Ocean County, NJ. A detail highlighting one of the Birdville architect's own directly-applied pebble designs. The Mercer tile to the right is a design called "Small Swan and Tower" and is based on a sixteenth-century Spanish example in the British Museum, which was acquired by C.H. Read in Spain in 1893 while he was travelling with Henry Chapman Mercer. The Latin inscription, *FLUMINIS IMPETUS LETIFICAT CIVITATEM DEI* translates as Psalm 46:4 - There is a river whose streams make glad the city of God, the holy place where the Most High dwells. Several examples of this tile are found at Birdville. Its reference to a river and a holy place seems very appropriate for Greim's sanctum at Toms River.

Fonthill contains 44 rooms and 18 fireplaces, all encrusted with thousands of Mercer's tiles and mosaics. While Mercer himself participated in the building process, he also relied on an experienced work crew, to aid with both physical labor and engineering quandaries.

While there are striking similarities, the little sanctuary in Toms River has important differences to Fonthill and the Moravian Tile Workshop. Birdville is an improvised structure and the builder clearly lacked the budget or labor force available to Mercer. The ornament is much simpler. Alongside the Moravian tiles are various decorative elements and cross designs composed simply of small stones and pebbles, a technique not employed by Mercer. Our brief visit to this neglected shrine was awe-inspiring. We left fascinated but with little more knowledge than the scraps and rumors available online.

Exploring Birdville

Later, as she was inspecting the photographs of Birdville's facade, Mandy noticed a crucial detail — a phone number for the trash removal business visible on the window of a forklift parked in the lot. To our delight and surprise, the foreman who answered when we called agreed to show us around. We arranged to meet on-site.

There are several photographs of Birdville available online, including several taken for the Library of Congress circa 1991, but none are of the interior. Whatever awaited us would be a complete surprise.

As we arrived, accompanied by a few local New Jersey historians and friends, we were led through a large, newly-installed, out-of-place garage door that led into a damp, dark and musty space that felt like it hadn't seen a full ray of sunlight in a century. The building had the atmosphere

Usually seen in cropped isolation, Walter Gropius' so-called *Fagus Factory* is actually a relatively small building added to a much larger factory complex, designed by factory designer Eduard Werner. Factory owner Carl Benscheidt, however, commissioned Gropius to improve the visual coherence of the vast assembly, or in his own words, "to give the complex a tasteful appearance."[12] The Fagus factory is frequently presented in historical surveys with another building, the AEG Turbinfabrik, which Gropius, Mies and Corbusier were all involved in for Peter Behrens. It served a similar but even more ambitious purpose. Within Behren's larger consulting work for AEG, the building was deliberately designed, far beyond its functional purpose, as a public façade for the network of cables, factories, supply-chains and electromagnetic charges that formed the company's sprawling and often invisible empire.

Apple and Empire, 2

A big building standing in for an enormous empire is hardly a new idea. Rome's empire stretched from Scotland to Persia, but it found its fullest form in the scale-model spans of the Pantheon and ur-colossal Colosseum. Likewise, by the time St. Peter's was completed in 1626, the Catholic Church's dominion stretched from Poland to Patagonia, but it was more palpably signified by the enormous new Basilica.

Steve Jobs biographer Walter Isaacson reports that the Apple CEO was fond of sharing a drawing by Norman Foster & Partners. It showed the new headquarters' vast interior swallowing up St. Peter's as well as its enormous, circular forecourt, completed by Gian Lorenzo Bernini in 1667.

In Isaacson's biography, this appears as one of the last scenes of the book's penultimate chapter, immediately before Jobs' final illness and death.[13]

The implication, is that another job often given to architecture; securing immortality for all involved. One of the most masterful shots in the *Force Awakens* hints at this as well. In it, a great star-destroyer, the sleek, city-sized dreadnought, sits as a ruin on a desert planet. First a single explorer, then a host of ships, and finally even the *Falcon* itself, zoom within.

Yet in real life, the immortality of scale, organization and totalizing coherence can come at the cost of the city's own life. Towards the end *The Death and Life of Great American Cities*, Jane Jacobs recounts the number and diversity of the neighbors in the building where she worked. She reports:

> The floor of the building in which this book is being written is occupied also by a health club with a gym, a firm of ecclesiastical decorators, an insurgent Democratic party reform club, a Liberal party political club, a music society, an accordionists' association, a retired importer who sells maté by mail, a man who sells paper and who also takes care of shipping the maté, a dental laboratory, a studio for watercolor lessons, and a maker of costume jewelry. Among the tenants who were

12
Quoted in Schwartz, 188

13
Isaacson, Walter. *Steve Jobs.* (New York: Simon & Schuster, 2011). p. 536

Birdville, Flint Road at Mill Street, South Toms River, Ocean County, NJ.

here and gone shortly before I came in, were a man who rented out tuxedos, a union local and a Haitian dance troupe. There is no place for the likes of us in new construction. And the last thing we need is new construction." (Added in a forceful footnote:) "No, the last thing we need is some paternalist weighing whether we are sufficiently noncontroversial to be admitted to subsidized quarters in a Utopian dream city.[14]

That there is little room for controversy or discord in the Death Star—amongst its legion of same-suited stormtroopers, say—may go without saying. But what of Apple? Like the products themselves, Apple's core identity relies on keeping disagreement and discord behind a tightly controlled façade. And sometimes even a tightly controlled corporate interior; one of Jobs' least successful management interventions on his return to Apple was a short-lived attempt to have all his many thousand employees wear the same, black, custom-made Issey Miyake clothing. To Jobs' credit, he quickly withdrew the proposal, but its memory survived in the many hundred black turtlenecks Miyake crafted for Jobs' own use.[15]

For all Jobs' imperiousness, if there is something disturbing in the design of Apple's own apparent Death Star, it is not so much in the company's clearly successful internal operations, nor in its beautifully singular product range. Rather, it lies in the runaway result of this success can be measured in the ways in which so many of our interactions with the world are now filtered through a single, handheld interface. This despite the fact that, particularly in the case of Apple, a ubiquitous system of interfaces is not just well-intentioned but essential.

The one thing we all know about technology, something its purveyors never admit, is that it never works like it is supposed to. The first *Star Wars* shoot was so plagued with technical difficulties (and the derisive insults they inspired on the part of the unionized workforce on the Pinewood Studio lot) that more than one cast member concluded that George Lucas appeared much more sympathetic to the authority and order of the Empire than the ragtag Rebel Alliance. Apple has thrived above all in the last two decades by offering the particular beauty in its products' order, organization, simplicity and in the predictable delight that results when something infinitely complex, in the company's own phrase, "just works."

This core truth of technology—that it often doesn't work like it's supposed to—is key to Apple's success. The clean lines on an iPhone's surface or the obsessive typography of its software interface are welcome indications of a much deeper order: a synthesis of software, hardware and supporting infrastructure that turns out to be the best way to make the most ambitious infrastructure work.

The precision of Apple's approach, however, is in making this coherence precisely manifest as well. Like the absence of Van Halen's brown M&M's, the absence of gaps or joints in an iPhone's surface serve an essential purpose far beyond the visual (or gastronomic.) They indicate a thoroughness and coherence not so much in what we can see, but what we cannot.

14
Jane Jacobs, *Death and Life of Great American Cities* (NY: Vintage, 1962) p. 193

15
Isaacson, op cit, 362

of a sacrosanct catacomb, the movie set of a fictional cult or an abandoned funhouse, all while cluttered with trash removal equipment. We meandered through in the dark, finding our way by flashlight, camera flash and the dim glint of the sun that filtered in through the tar-patched pinnacle of the collapsing concrete dome.

The building was modest. The focal point was a central domed chapel with a few smaller rooms off to the side. It was breath-taking, despite, or even perhaps due to, its state of neglect, and above the doorway, the chapel's name was inscribed in tile — Oratory Bethlehem. The marks of the wood used to first form the concrete were still visible, and the entirety of the interior was a constellation not only of Moravian tiles but also pebbles, pieces of broken china and other small decorative elements. There was a rounded fireplace, and an archway beyond that led to what clearly was once an altar, now profaned by use as a shelf. Several painted silhouettes of dancing girls, perhaps added later, adorned one of the walls. Hollowed out of the roof were several niches, which we instinctively assumed to be birdbaths although upon later reflection, we deduced that they could have also been planters. Despite the sagging roof and the dampness, the structure seemed sound. Only the occasional piece of metal rod framing was visible — a testament to the craftsmanship for whomever built what was so clearly a labor of love.

ALBERT P. GREIM
OCCUPATION: BIRD MAN

Birdville was the life's work of Albert P. Greim, also sometimes known as Albert Crescent, as per the name of his business, the Crescent Company. Like its Renaissance man founder, the Crescent Company was many things:

"Oratory Bethlehem" was one of the original names given to Birdville by its architect and builder. The domed arch leads to the small chapel. The Mercer tile in the center is a variant of the Psalm 46:4 tile, found in several locations on both the interior and exterior, indicating it was a favorite of the architect. Photo by the author, 2011.

Ironically, one of the things we cannot see is the means by which this surface coherence is achieved. According to Brian Merchant's 2017 book, *The One Device*, instead of investing in the prohibitively expensive fabrication processes throughout its long supply chain to ensure every surface component fits together, the firm instead produces the parts to a relatively inexpensive and loose engineered tolerance. They then employ legions of workers in their offshore assembly plants to test the fit of many different parts with each other, creating a theater of precision from inexpensive labor instead.[16] The necessary coherence of technology demands and produces a strict coherence in the social and infrastructural systems that create it.

Cities, however, depend on an essentially different balance of order and openness. Where technology is often unexpectedly brittle, cities are often unexpectedly resilient. And their resilience comes from something first noted by Jane Jacobs in 1958 (in a letter seeking funding for *Death and Life of Great American Cities*) that "within the seeming chaos and jumble of the city is a remarkable degree of order, in the form of relationships of all kinds that people have evolved...Where it works at all well, this network of relationships is astonishingly intricate. It requires a staggering diversity of activities and people, very intimately interlocked (although often casually so), and able to make constant adjustments to needs and circumstances."[17]

This is not to say that cities do not depend on coherence and organization. New York without the Commissioner's Plan or Barcelona without Cerdá would be far less flexible, adaptable and extensible. Yet as Rem Koolhaas astutely explained

several decades ago in *Delirious New York*, this is an order that frames and encourages the unpredictability, redundancy and inventiveness of urban life — qualities that often defy prediction or planning.

By contrast, Apple's success has been, quintessentially, in taming the awkward and unpredictable complexity of technology, so it can be predicted, relied upon and taken for granted as a new kind of creative infrastructure. Yet, the scale and ambition of Apple, as well as its Silicon-Valley brethren, are reaching towards a different kind of scale and complexity — that of the city itself. Here such an approach is rarely successful.

This is apparent at an architectural scale in the perimeter of Apple's circular headquarters itself. In the elaborately produced renderings of the building, it rests, like the spaceship Jobs dubbed it, amidst seemingly infinite orchards and woodlands, harkening back to Silicon Valley's rural history. Like the Golden Gate Bridge against the hills of Marin, it is a vision of a massive, technological achievement, confronting its only worthy foil: wilderness.

But zoom out a bit, and a very different picture emerges. Instead of an Arcadian farmland, the building is revealed instead to be set behind its own moat of trees in one of the densest parts of Silicon Valley. This landscape is regularly,

16
Merchant, Brian. *The One Device : The Secret History of the iPhone*. First ed. (New York, NY: Little, Brown and Company, 2017.) p. 267

17
Jane Jacobs to Chadbourne Gilpatric, July 1, 1958, Jane Jacobs Papers, Boston College.

a vaudeville theater, a rustic furniture business, an artisanal birdhouse manufacturer and the entity who administered Birdville. During its heyday, Birdville immediately became an incredibly versatile, multi-use structure and can be interpreted today in a similarly multi-faceted way.

Day to day, the building was used as a home for Greim, a wild bird aviary and a workshop for his theatrical and architectural side projects. Yet, Birdville also served as an important community hub in Toms River. Greim was an active and involved community member; accordingly, Birdville became an active church and meeting place. Because Greim was an Episcopalian minister and vestryman at Christ Church, several weddings were performed within Birdville's walls. Similarly, Greim was a member of the Toms River Borough Council and served as Justice of the Peace. Thus, Birdville became the home of multiple town planning meetings. Architecturally, beyond its personal and community use, Birdville was also notable as an early example of the "roadside attraction" or inventive storefront that emerged as a uniquely American architectural typology during the automobile age. In the years since it fell into disuse, Birdville's significance has become even clearer: an overlooked, materially innovative example of a visionary environment, constructed single-handedly by one self-taught polymath.[3] In this way, Birdville is similar, not in style but in spirit, to Simon Rodia's *Watt's Towers* in South Los Angeles or Ferdinand Cheval's *Le Palais Idéal* in France. It may be humble in comparison to its contemporary poured-concrete structures such as nearby Fonthill, but it was built and designed entirely by Greim with the aid of one assistant.

Greim was born in 1863 and grew up in Pennsylvania. During his twenties, he moved to various locations within Pennsylvania and New Jersey, taking jobs as a "moulder"

and carpenter before establishing his small "rustic furniture" business in Cedar Brook, NJ in 1906.[4] Greim's father was a carpenter; so, it's no surprise that his son would follow this path, though he seems to have gravitated early to an Arts and Crafts aesthetic and not simply layman carpentry. In addition to his aptitude for carpentry, Greim was known from the beginning as an authority on birds, especially chickens.

In the Millbrook Roundtable of Sat. Feb. 25, 1893, he dispensed poultry advice, lovingly recounting:

> [...] I remember well when I was first interested in chickens how I used to warm bricks and bury them deep down in the dust and then, after it was well warmed up, see the fun. [...] It is true, they will make the house very dusty, but it is a great comfort to them.[5]

When he reported for jury duty, *The New Jersey Courier* recorded him as A.P. Greim. Occupation: Bird Man.[6]

[3]
Greim did have the help of one assistant, Stanley "Cap" Grover.

[4]
An 1887 residency listing has him living in Reading, PA., with the occupation of "moulder." The 1900 census has him in Pennsylvania. By 1910, he was in New Jersey. The Industrial Directory of NJ locates Greim in Cedar Brook, noting, Greim, A.V., manufacturer of rustic furniture, employs four persons.

[5]
A.P. Greim, Maple Shade Poultry Papers IX: Hen Houses and Furniture for Same, Millbrook Roundtable, Sat. Feb. 25, 1893.

[6]
NJ Courier, 10/10/1913, p. 5.

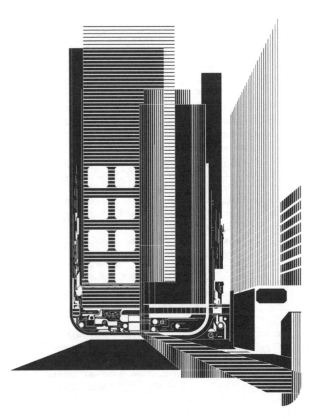

albeit inaccurately, described as "suburban." At 5,200 people per square mile, Cupertino's population density ranks not far behind Seattle's, and its daytime density is much higher, fueled by the many buses-worth of Apple and other tech-company employees carried from San Francisco and elsewhere. While it will never be mistaken for Lower Manhattan or even the San Francisco neighborhoods to which tech-workers now flock, there is, nevertheless, a density of encounter and opportunity in the physical fabric of Silicon Valley that drives much of its unprecedented innovation. What makes Silicon Valley work is not its order and cleanliness but its dense balance between structure and chaos—in which unexpected encounters, like that between Steve Jobs and Steve Wozniak some 40 years ago, can reliably occur.

This friction is, of course, what sparks the city, and fuels the creativity at its core; even if it is sometimes, in the moment, inconvenient. Anyone living in dense urban fabric understands what it is to have to tolerate crazy neighbors. It's a pain, but we do it; for who knows who the eccentric will turn out to be, or might unexpectedly teach you? Yoda himself first appears as ridiculous and embarrassing as the other memorable characters voiced by his puppeteer, Frank Oz (Grover, Miss Piggy, Animal); rooting for food in Luke's backpack, and using addled, backwards grammar crafted by Oz as well. All this before he is revealed to be the universe's most powerful Jedi.

Apple's headquarters respects its founder's singular vision and is presented by Isaacson and others as Steve Jobs' most fitting legacy. But what it respects least of all is the fabric of Silicon Valley that gave rise to such a vision. New York's first zoning code, immortalized by illustrator

Publicity postcard showcasing the birdhouse workshop at Birdville in its initial location. The New Jersey Courier reported on Christmas day of 1914 that Greim's business was thriving: *A.P Greim has nearly doubled his shop room at Birdville, and will put on several new hands to fill his orders. Mr. Greim's business is an example of what advertising does. Last year he spent over $1000 in advertising his bird boxes in the magazines, and in six weeks his orders in November and December amounted to $900. And this is the dull season.[8]*

During his early days in Cedar Brook, *The New Jersey Courier* reliably reported on Greim's business growth and success, noting:

> Oct. 10, 1913:
> The Crescent Company, which builds rustic bird boxes in Berkely, has bought a lot further down the pike and will build a bigger factory.[7]

Construction of what is today called "Birdville" had begun by 1915, but the main feature, reported in the local press as of 1916, was the expansion of the workshop. The unique dynamic of Greim's workshop was fostered by both his own personality (Greim was a musician), as well as his apparent interest in the Arts and Crafts ideal of blurring the lines between the artist and craftsperson and of creating dignified, meaningful work for laborers. Thus, Greim's small "factory" included music and would be:

> Heated by a hot water plant, and has what is seldom found in a factory, a big open fireplace, with benches around it, and an Angelus player piano. For Mr. Greim believes in enjoying life as he goes along, and in having everybody around him enjoy it.[9]

Greim did not write extensively, and the only clues as to his socio-political outlook must be gleaned from scant

7
"Draw Jurors for December Court," New Jersey Courier, December 3, 1915, p. 1

8
New Jersey Courier, 12/25/1914, p. 5

9
New Jersey Courier , 10/10/1913, p. 5.

Hugh Ferris, dictated that the iconic corporate headquarters of the last century, ascending to individual spires at their height, had to respect the street at their base. Apple's headquarters offers no such compromise, affording the prospect of a building as complete, enclosed, and seemingly portable as one of its famed electronic products. (And it is, it turns out, an object: a rigid doughnut floating on massive, seismic base isolators against the bay-area certainties of earthquakes.)

Beyond the manners of the street-edge, why is this a problem?

We might start inside. A rare 2015 interview of Jony Ive in the New Yorker, "The Shape of Things to Come," shifts seamlessly from the discussion of consumer objects to that of architecture. Ive, it is suggested, sees himself as no less than an architect. He finds it, he says, "a curious thing" that in design "we tend to compartmentalize, based on physical scale." He is reported to assert that he has "taught Foster's architects something about the geometry of corners," introducing a seamless, curved detail between wall and floor that now runs throughout the building's interior.[18] The magazine profile, as it is now understood, marked the beginning of Ive's withdrawal from day-to-day design decisions on Apple Hardware in order to focus his attention on the $5 billion headquarters itself as the final and most massive object of his legacy.

Apple's great success, as a consumer-focused company, is rooted in the single power a consumer has above all: choice. Apple's products are ubiquitous, above all, because they are far better than what they compete with a quality that comes precisely from the tight control that Apple exerts on their design. But at the point we don't like our device, we can—and will—buy a different and better one, either from Apple or from some as-of-yet-unimaginable competitor.

Yet, architecture offers no such choice, especially at the scale of the city. We can, if we are lucky, sell a house we don't like, but we can't sell or dispose of the terrible building across the road. And architecture involves many more people than those who design it or pay for it. Myself, I have always wondered about the cleaning staff of the new Apple headquarters; it is for these people, above all, that the usual, clunky detail of wall-meeting-floor exists, with a base molding to catch and disguise the dirt that escapes the polishers. We might think, as well, of Apple's desk-bound employees, who, in order to preserve the clean lines of the building's exterior, are not be able to open windows in their offices. "That would just allow people to screw things up," Jobs reportedly declared—referring to the visual order of the building's façade, not the complex climate control system.

Here is where the difference between the design of products and buildings comes into focus. The particular conundrum solved by the best teams of city-builders and citizens is how to balance a whole set of competing physical, environmental and social demands against each other—including the demands of the powerful against the needs, and rights, of the powerless. And how to balance these needs in a way that frames and supports uses, adaptations, and shifts in purpose that we can never precisely anticipate.

18
Parker, Ian. "Jonathan Ive and the Future of Apple." *The New Yorker.* May 30, 2020.

Crescent Co. advertisement from *The Garden Magazine*, 1919.

texts found in Crescent Company catalogues, as well as the occasional advertisement. He was prolific with the production of his circulars, catalogues and promotional postcards. He patented a sparrow trap, waging a holy war on this specific species. In one particularly florid postcard, he characterized English Sparrows as "Bolsheviki Birds," which would destroy all others if not eliminated:

> All good bird lovers advocate destroying the English sparrow. It is that, or, having no other birds at all in a few years.[10]

Greim also chides the Women's Suffrage movement in a catalogue titled *Bird Architecture:*

> This last summer I read of a woman, who claimed that she assisted, in fact, built most of the nest of a pair of song sparrows that she said did not know how to build their nest. And since she claimed that the male bird was particularly stupid, I judge that the article was written by a Suffragette.[11]

While Greim bristled at the notion of a suspected suffragette coming to the aid of the Bolsheviki Birds, his life's work, intentionally or not, was the very embodiment of the explicitly socio-political credo at the heart of the Arts and Crafts movement. Some of the foundational precepts of the movement share several points of contact with those advanced by Marx and Engels, sparrows notwithstanding.

10
Albert Crescent (Albert P. Greim), *Bird Architecture*, n.d., probably ca. 1915. p. 42.

11
Ibid. p. 23.

As we attempt to design 21st-century cities for an increasing landscape of uncertainty, this is an important lesson to remember. Instead of single, large-scale projects, the staying power of a city depends on a million connections between its inhabitants and the natural and technological systems that sustain them. Cities designed *tabula rasa*, as Jane Jacobs cogently characterized it a generation ago, lack this robust resilience. Instead, their monumental visions of order tend to hide brittleness and fragility, and event catastrophe. Even the most seemingly ordered long-lived city-grid—Manhattan, Barcelona, even San Francisco—simply allows us to better negotiate what is, in reality, a riot of real-world diversity.

Social media, the inevitable hand-maiden to hand-held computing, is particularly relevant here. Appearing to shelter all the diversity and individuality of its hundreds of millions of inhabitants, the edifice of social media is, in fact, a vast machine made to extract value from those relationships—at whatever social cost. The danger for the collision of cities and technology today is not so much a return to visually coherent, high-modernist urban machinery. But rather an ever-"smarter" city that, like an inside-out trojan horse, hides a vast machine inside a façade of people.

The predictable explosion

Yet here it is not actually Apple that is to blame. The revolution in architecture today—one where the world of screens and devices and the common infrastructure of our cities merge, overlap and combine—is much larger than even the enormous, careful company. By convincing regulators, and our larger society, that the insouciant, entrepreneurial enterprises of the Bay Area should be allowed to continuously expand and "innovate" without any restraint, the architects of Silicon Valley have created a world where a series of compromises brokered in the digital world—on privacy, harassment, transparency of motives and accountability of infrastructure—are gushing into the physical spaces of our cities. To turn a phrase on its head, this just doesn't work—particularly in the city, where aesthetic, functional, and moral choices are inextricably combined.

As new empires extend into the city and world, into both the public sphere and the private screen, we should do well to remember the urbane balance that brings true freedom to human environments. This dance between control and openness, hardness and softness, brittleness and resilience is the never-ending choreography of our civic lives. By contrast, the only thing one can say for certain about a Death Star is that it always, unexpectedly, explodes.

Portions of this essay first appeared in Quartz.

Illustrations
Nicholas de Monchaux with
Konstantinos Moustakas and
Ioanna Sotiriou.

The Socio-Political Ideals of the Arts and Crafts Movement

The Arts and Crafts movement was defined by a romantic idealization of Pre-Industrial handcraft traditions. While remembered primarily as an aesthetic movement, it was imbued with and animated by a critique of industrial capitalism. The criticism was akin to that advanced by other contemporary labor movements. The Industrial Revolution, far from improving quality of life through technological innovation, had instead created masses of grossly exploited laborers, alienated from the products they manufactured, benefitting only their bosses and the wealthy factory owners. The appeal of the movement to artists and artisans specifically came from its particular focus on the fact that one of the evils of the industrial system was that it robbed the workers of pride in their work, the sense of a job well done. These beneficial working conditions presumably existed in a Pre-Industrial world when a worker may put a slightly individual "spin" on a handcrafted object or be renowned for a specialized skill. Further, the movement, as articulated by William Morris and John Ruskin, railed against the soulless, uniform factory as itself a dehumanizing force—both of people and of art. The focus of the movement on artistry and the importance of beauty in a healthy society led to its adoption by many members of the affluent classes. While largely ignoring the labor critique, this privileged population could see the appeal of surrounding themselves with handcrafted furniture and goods. In an ironic twist, the mass-produced factory goods became anathema to this elite subset able to indulge in the Arts and Crafts "lifestyle." To illustrate this inherent disconnect between the ideals and the manifestation of the movement, the majority of "Arts and Crafts" houses, which were designed to harmonize with their natural surroundings, included a maid's quarters.

Albert Greim stands as a rare example of a working-class person who fully embraced the handcraft elements of the Arts and Crafts movement, and he organized his entire life in a way that would have been consonant with the movement, as envisioned by its founders. It should be emphasized that he said he never owned a factory but, rather, a "workshop." Furthermore, the descriptions of the workshop, with its player piano and articulated sense of camaraderie, fit well within the Arts and Crafts doctrine of cultivating meaningful, fulfilling labor, while producing objects of beauty, emphasizing the hand of the worker.

Poured Concrete as Ancient and Radical Material

While it is clear that Greim greatly admired Henry Chapman Mercer—and was a collector of his Moravian tiles—the two contemporaries seem not to have been closely acquainted. There is hardly a scrap in Mercer's archival records regarding Greim, and there is no evidence that Greim was an intentional acolyte following Mercer's lead. Instead, Greim was a contemporary who followed a similar path, shaped by the same prevailing zeitgeist as Mercer. Their shared use of poured concrete illustrates this. *Cement Age* magazine featured Greim's early poured concrete work at Cedar Brook in 1908, the same year that Mercer began work on Fonthill. Greim's workshop was not just a commonplace building. Like Mercer, he had become fascinated by the possibilities of poured concrete, and the magazine, which also often reported on the activities of Henry Mercer, gave this report:

The ruins of Greim's residence in Cedar Brook NJ, which was featured in *Concrete-Cement Age* in 1913. Photo by the author, 2020.

The accompanying illustrations show some interesting work in concrete construction and they are presented here because the work is unusual rather than typical. It was done by A.P. Greim, Cedar Brook, N.J., manufacturer of rustic ware. He has been much interested in the ornate possibilities of concrete and has made numerous experiments in that line.

Poured concrete architecture was all the rage during this time — as exemplified by the existence of periodicals such as *Cement Age* itself, which had begun publication in 1902.

Cement was used extensively in antiquity. It was a commonplace material in ancient Rome. Yet by the era of the medieval guilds, so idealized by the Arts and Crafts movement, its use was rare, essentially vanishing from the architectural lexicon. The 18th century saw a rediscovery of cement, and various concrete formulas began to be refined. However, the real breakthrough came later, when people around the world appear to have simultaneously come upon the idea of pouring concrete over iron (and later steel) bars to form "reinforced concrete."[12] This enabled concrete to be formed into almost any shape or design imaginable, leading to a veritable explosion of public excitement and experimentation. There was a belief by many that all buildings of the future would be constructed of poured concrete. There is a slight irony in the technique being adopted heartily by Arts and Crafts adherents, as it was very much seen as part and parcel of the

12
The first (recorded) "rebar" concrete building was the Arctic Oil Company Works warehouse in San Francisco, completed in 1884.

"Oratory Bethlehem" was one of the original names given to Birdville by its architect and builder. The domed arch leads to the small chapel. The Mercer tile in the center is a variant of the Psalm 46:4 tile, found in several locations on both the interior and exterior, indicating it was a favorite of the architect. Photo by the author, 2011.

modernization of contemporary society. That said, its appeal as a medium is easy to see. It offered a way to construct truly unique structures as readily as it lent itself to potential mass-production. On the opposite end of the spectrum from Greim and Mercer, Thomas Edison designed a prototype and proposed the construction of mass-produced "pour to order" homes, securing a patent for this idea in 1908. A 1910 article described the plan:

> The plan which Mr. Edison has been working is, briefly, the completion of a set of steel molds which can be used time after time in pouring houses. [...] Mr. Edison and his engineers claim that such a house can be built for $1200. [...] A common objection to the Edison house is based on artistic grounds. It is said all houses look alike and that a whole row of houses, built by one set of plans, would result in painful monotony.[13]

Edison's plan was a dismal failure, though he did manage to complete several clusters of the houses. The implementation was unworkable, but Edison was ahead of his time in envisioning something similar to what would come to be called "tract housing" during the Levittown projects of the 1940s. It's hard to imagine any architectural style more diametrically opposed to the Arts and Crafts aesthetic. To this day, the "tract" style houses near Birdville offer a study in contrasts. Poured reinforced concrete was a new tool, and it could be used to construct austere, alienating architecture or unique, artistically wrought gems, such as Fonthill, Birdville, or Frank Lloyd Wright's Fallingwater

13
"The Edison Cement House,"
Keith's Magazine, Vol. XXIV, No. 1,
July 1910. p. 309.

(which required extensive renovation after Wright initially failed to employ an adequate amount of steel reinforcement). Albert Greim was a fellow traveler alongside Henry Mercer and Thomas Edison in exploring the possibilities of poured reinforced concrete. When recounting memories of Birdville, Greim's single assistant, C. Stanley "Cap" Grover noted Greim's painstaking attention to detail in concrete.[14] He recalled digging white sugar sand, abundant in the Toms River area, with Greim, because Birdville's creator preferred its color in a concrete mix.

Back to Nature

In addition to the Arts and Crafts ethos and the shared material exploration, there was yet another philosophical connection between Greim and Mercer: their shared connections to the "Back to Nature" movement.

In a 1979 remembrance of Greim and Birdville, a staff writer for the Asbury Park Press wrote that

> In a "back to nature movement" in 1914, Albert F.[sic] Greim selected a site [...] to serve as a bird sanctuary and a workshop for the manufacture of rustic bird houses.[15]

Greim himself, in a Crescent Company catalogue, used this language to describe his mission and the appeal of his birdhouses:

> There are several things to be said in favor of rustic bird houses, particularly of the sweet smelling Jersey cedar, which is a disinfectant in itself. If you are sufficiently interested, nail up a rustic bird house alongside a brightly painted one, and see which they

will select. It is the "back to nature movement" among the birds. Where did they nest before civilized man inhabited this country? In hollow trees, woodpeckers and their kind boring their own [sic] in dead trees. Now such suitable places are fast disappearing under the pruning and slashing axe of man.[16]

As for the Back to Nature movement among humans, its origins are usually traced to German youth groups collectively called *Wandervögel*, which translates to "wandering bird" or "bird of passage." These groups began spontaneously around 1896, rising to the height of their popularity in Germany between 1901 and 1914. There was an apparent influence on worldwide "scouting" movements, as well as quasi-political organizations, such as the Kindred of the Kibbo Kift—a UK based Back to Nature sect founded in 1920 with a focus on hand-craftsmanship and an Arts and Crafts aesthetic. While some Back to Nature groups emphasized nationalism or espoused right-wing political views, there emerged no clear consensus among them. Strains of anarchistic individualism permeated even the nationalist groups, while others were overtly anti-authoritarian and lacked any emphasis on nationalism or "traditional" values. Across socio-political lines, the movement emphasized individual autonomy and often what would today be called "countercultural" values. Urban living was

14
Stanley Grover later became Ocean County Surrogate.

15
James F. Lowney, "Birdville Flutters Into Oblivion in South Toms River," Asbury Park Press, Sun. March 4, 1979, p. G6.

16
Albert Crescent (Albert P. Greim), Bird Architecture, n.d., probably ca. 1915. p. 27.

viewed as morally corrupting and spiritually corrosive. A retreat to a "simpler" time and an abstract "re-connection" with nature, believed to have been lost in the rise of industrialization, were also unifying themes. The ideological connections to the Arts and Crafts movement are apparent.

The movement also emphasized environmental preservation, and this sentiment was especially pronounced among ornithologists and birdwatchers. Activists within these communities became involved in crusades against feather merchants, poachers and wild bird hunters. Aside from their mutual fascination with the possibilities of poured concrete and a love of ornate tilework, Henry Mercer shared with Greim a passion for birds. He was an outspoken opponent of the plume trade, railing against it in an 1897 article titled *Fashion's Holocaust, the Destruction of Birds by Women's Hat Fashion.*[17]

Greim's Invisible Legacy

Greim can be situated neatly in a historic context, but he was, above all, a unique and singular personality. Unfortunately, while Birdville has remained as a roadside curiosity in Toms River, most of the distinctive history of its creator has been lost. None of Greim's trademark birdhouses, which were widely acclaimed and showcased at the Panama-Pacific Exposition of 1915 in San Francisco, are known to survive. Greim donated two examples to the "Decorative Arts Department" at the Newark Museum of Newark, NJ, in 1915 but they were apparently deaccessioned and lost in the ensuing years.[18] There is a strange sadness in the fact that not one of Greim's thousands of birdhouses—not one of the many mail-ordered all over the globe or collected by Japanese Emperor Taishō—is known

to have survived the passage of time.[19] Even archival photographs were discarded at some point, treated as ephemera and weeded away.

During his lifetime, Greim combined his various interests into a body of work that offered him fulfillment on multiple levels—his business was his art was his church was his home. An October 1916 edition of the *New Jersey Courier* may have put it best:

> [...] Now he has a much bigger and fireproof shop, and has planned it so that it can be extended if need be. Mr. Greims [sic] is more than a workman, he is an artist. He has a pride and joy in his work, and is continually working up new designs.[20]

Greim's ambition was that Birdville would outlive him as a monument to his work and as a functioning church. A 1926 article conveyed his hopes:

> Behind all this interesting detail of the house and the masterly skill in its construction there is a deeper story. It is the story of Mr. Greim's heart and soul. He has pledged to go on with the house and the chapel and Stanley [his sole helper in the construction] has pledged to carry them on after him. Without fail the early morning mass on Sundays will continue for interminable years. Who knows but what Stanley will not

17
"The Mercer Tiles and Other Matters," House Beautiful, Vol. 14, June – Nov. 1913 p. 79.

18
According to an email correspondence with archivists there in 2017.

19
Several newspaper articles mention the Japanese Emperor as a collector of Greim's birdhouses.

20
"Big New Shop at Birdville," New Jersey Courier, Oct. 10, 1916 p. 1.

leave successors to hand the traditions down to, and they in turn hand them over to others? And so on for ages to come with the solemnity and reverence of a crowdd [sic] parish. No one could wish for a better memorial than this to which Mr. Greim can look forward. It pleases him and makes him happy. It is in his own words, "As I wish it."[21]

Three years after Greim's death in 1930, a local paper ran what remains probably the fullest account of his life:[22]

[...] When Mr. Greim first came to Toms River, his factory consisted of one small building [...] Instead of building a home connected with the factory, in which to sleep Mr. Greim built a one room structure on stilts, up among the branches of a magnificent oak tree.

[...] Up in the branches of this big tree, he spent his nights, to be awakened at the first gray streaks of dawn by the singing of the birds he loved.

Albert P. Greim was never married and had no children. Greim's heir and assistant, Stanley Grover, kept Birdville, and the business afloat for a number of years after Greim passed, but the Great Depression forced Grover to cut his losses. In 1938, he sold Birdville to Joseph Gerue who continued a modest birdhouse business. In 1949, the property changed hands again; it was sold to Harry Duckworth, a former mayor of Island Heights. Duckworth remembered this as the time when the property began to seem more like a ruin:

Soon after I took it over, the organ was stripped apart by vandals. Then I had the chapel deconsecrated by

a minister. It had been the scene of several weddings years before but there was no longer a need for it.[23]

By 1979, Birdville was left much as it is today, becoming a storage space for a construction company. Jane Homer, the wife of the owner of the construction business, described it as an empty and intimidating:

It's an eerie place. I've only spent five minutes in there. Except for a thing which looks like a sacrificial altar, there is very little there.[24]

As with many things in life, what remains or matters at Birdville is a question of perception, dependent on personal knowledge and what has been transcribed into history. Yet our built environment is largely shaped by people who can often mobilize large amounts of time, capital and manpower to make their architectural ideas a reality.

Birdville stands in defiance of this. Seen through the arc of history, Birdville is an important work of self-taught architecture with unexamined yet important lessons about material exploration and radical ideals in architecture, buried in the vinyl-sided morass of suburban New Jersey. Many revered architects within the traditional historical canon rose to recognition because their work was their manifesto. It showed what they believed in and the ideas

21
"The 'Bird House King' Builds," Chillicothe Gazette, May 15 1926 (page unknown).

22
Oddly enough, it appeared in the context of an article about a school field trip.

23
"Birdville Flutters Into Oblivion in South Toms River, " Asbury Park Press, Sun. March 4, 1979, p. G6

24
Ibid.

Truths of Fraudacre City

Jae Shin and Damon Rich

that they wished to advance in the world. For many, their work was ignored while they were alive and celebrated only after their death. In this light, what is the responsibility of the historian-- to dig, to uncover and to elevate the buildings and landscapes that have been relegated to footnotes of history?

Self-taught architecture, like that of Albert Greim, is "a type of architecture that features unique designs made by builders with no formal training."[25] Linked not by style or time period, self-taught architecture is considered as a movement in which the ideology of its creator, often seen as someone on the margins of traditional society, is embodied in the physical creation of a structure through the monumental, often life-long efforts, of that one single person. In a global context today, where buildings are increasingly thought of as scalable, replicable consumer products that are churned out at quick speeds for quick profit, Birdville is unrepeatable, solitary and deviant, not just a shelter for human souls but a site for multi-species communion, radical politics and aesthetic discovery. Today, Birdville stands as a testament to invention, handcraft, personal risk, material exploration and to the growth of a wholly original style that is nonetheless deeply steeped in the traditions and techniques of its time.

Within the footnotes and discarded newspaper clippings that surround Greim's life, there are stories of integrity, grit and an unwillingness to compromise. There are also lessons that we could learn from today: the innovative reuse of found and discarded materials and a commitment to making space in our built environment to be shared by both animals and humans. On any given day, one can witness flocks of tiny English Sparrows chirping happily among the concrete pillars of the Oratory Bethlehem, "House Wonderful," — Birdville.

25
David Patrick Kelly. "Outsider Architecture and Historic Preservation." Athens, Georgia, 2001. https://getd.libs.uga.edu/pdfs/kelly_david_p_200112_mhp.pdf

An installation view of Broadacre 2017, Hector: Damon Rich & Jae Shin with Lucia Thome, Museum of Modern Art, New York. Elsewhere referred to as part of the Fraudacre City project.

Sometimes Vision is the Problem

Founded in a vacated crack
between architecture and
planning, its aim was to rescue
physical urbanism from the
humongous onus of "planning."
—Michael Sorkin

This is our city. Over there
I have my cable car, which goes
across and people can look down
and stuff, so people who come and
visit can see what the city is
like...Today I made a solar-powered garage station in the
wilderness. We live in a country with wilderness everywhere,
animals everywhere. The windmill
makes it really nice...Over here
is the Megabase. You see that
giant cannon right there? That's
where the leader works...
I was hoping to have a city where
everywhere you look, you see
green. So, you have green on
different levels, and maybe have
buildings in the shape of trees
to blend in with the scenery
a little bit.
— *The Fraudacre City Story*

The designers of Fraudacre City,
quoted above, explain endlessly.
Every object, arrangement, and adja-
cency has its reasons and meanings,
earnest and deceptive.

When the museum's education department called, they wanted to create a
"people's studio" to accompany their
institution's forty-fifth exhibition
since 1932 of Frank Lloyd Wright's
architecture. Educational activities
typically occupy marginal spaces of
a museum's facility, cultural pres-
tige, and budget, though they are
also where the institutional message
is most direct. While didacticism
gets finger-wagged in the gallery,
here it remains a proud mission, usually in service of legitimizing the
masterworks and authoring geniuses
on display, as well as the organizational wisdom that selected them for
the honor.

This narrative of masters
obstructs discussions about everyday
environments, place politics, and
spatial conflicts. The underlying
demand of so much pedagogy and discourse remains to "respect the architect" and accompanying ideology of
architecture as control. Fraudacre
City is an unauthorized cover version of Wright and the Taliesin
Fellowship's 1935 Broadacre City
model that attempts to frame questions about how architecture itself
should be controlled. We hope this
demonstration project of reworked
institutional pedagogy helps connect
our own work as endless explainers to
movements for accountable development and democratic environments.

Fraudacre City.

Two Models of Teaching with Architecture

The Fraudacre City Neighborhood Planning Model looks to two pedagogical lineages. The museum has long taught about and with buildings, supplementing exhibitions of modern architecture with hands-on, try-it-yourself activities. Instructive panels illustrate how to judge urban form as good (to be adopted as a model), or bad (to be corrected with architecture). These prescriptive exercises aligned with the legal mechanism to declare blight that supported mid-century environmental modernization programs like Urban Renewal, and therefore also served as professionalized justifications for relations of power that destroyed over 1600 Black neighborhoods across the United States between 1949 and 1973. Putting these objects of moral force into the hands of young people granted them, at least symbolically, the choice to use their powers tyrannically or find other ways of working. Designed as a mobile kit, Fraudacre City takes up this tradition of designing custom hardware to facilitate exchanges that might not happen through conversation alone.

In the Citizenship Education Program, conversations often began with a question about everyday environments like "Where do roads come from?" Empirical and experiential answers could build into structural observations about power, resources, decision-making, and democracy. Developed between the 1950s and 1970s by Septima Clarke and Dorothy Cotton, with the organizational sponsorship of the Highlander Folk School and Southern Christian Leadership Council, these institutions usually operated out of churches and community organizations. Their curricula aimed to provide the civic understanding and skills necessary for putting democracy to use, from reading and writing to voting and banking. Connections between social structure, power, and strategies for change remained central. With adults of all ages as students, educational activities did not begin from abstract principles. They instead began with everyone offering their everyday experiences, then together developing habits of questioning to unravel problems at hand: from roads to relationships, collective action, and strategies for undoing oppression. Tenets of this popular education tradition include the importance of beginning from an examination of people's existing knowledge, continually developing a sense of democratic possibilities, and relying on our abilities to figure things out.

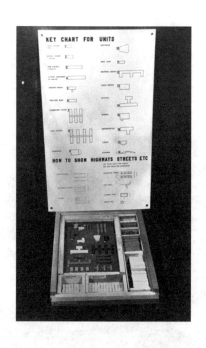

Above: Broadacre City kit.

Facing page, clockwise from top: Free Association word map about the subway, made by Fraudacre City participants; Septima Clark teaching at a Citizenship School on the South Carolina Sea islands; visitors at the original model of Broadacre City.

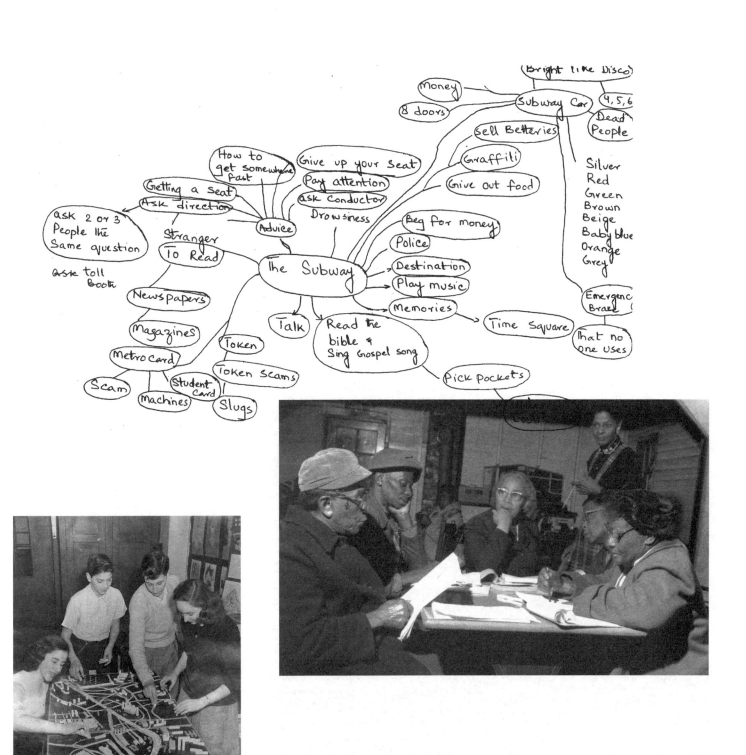

The Subway

(Bright like Disco)

Money

8 doors

Subway Car

4,5,6

Dead People

Sell Betteries

Graffiti

Silver
Red
Green
Brown
Beige
Baby blue
Orange
Grey

How to get somewhere fast

Give up your Seat

Give out food

Getting a seat

Pay attention

ask Conductor

Ask direction

Advice

Drowsiness

Beg for money

ask 2 or 3 People the Same question

Police

Ask toll Booth

Stranger To Read

Destination

Play music

Newspapers

Memories

Time Square

Emergenc Brake

Magazines

Talk

Read the bible & Sing Gospel song

That no One Uses

Metro card

Token

Scam

Token Scams

Student Card

Machines

Slugs

Pick pockets

NO INSTITUTES
NO PETTY OFFICIALISM
NO LANDLORD ——————————— NO TENANT
NO POLITICIANS —— NO ACADEMICIANS
NO TRAFFIC PROBLEM
NO BACK AND FORTH HAUL
NO POLES ——————— NO WIRES IN SIGHT
NO DITCHES ALONGSIDE THE ROADS
NO HEADLIGHTS ——— NO VISIBLE LAMPS
NO POLICEMEN
NO MINOR AXIS ——— NO MAJOR AXIS
NO YARDS FOR RAW MATERIALS
NO SMOKE ——————————— NO HARDRAILS
NO RADIO OR BILLBOARD ADVERTISING
NO SLUM ———————————— NO SCUM

Above: Tenets from Wright's
Broadacre City proposal.

Below: The original model of
Broadacre City.

Truths of Fraudacre City

Schlepper Vision

"The hard-rail, the power-, telephone- and telegraph-pole, signboard, the tin-can, the barbed-wire fence.... Any honest search will give you some faint hint of the hideous waste Broadacre City was designed definitely to repudiate.... The scaffolding still destroying our landscape—poles and wires, sign boards, railroad and lumber yards, etc., etc., do not exist in Broadacres."
— Frank Lloyd Wright, *The New Frontier: Broadacre City*, 1940

Broadacre City's vision rests on a litany of exclusions. A cry of despair against the "hideous waste" that exists, this orgy of negation simultaneously refuses and controls in the name of asserting "A New Freedom for Living in America," painted alongside the no's and other slogans on accompanying plywood display panels.

Another agenda that brought the Broadacre City model into existence was the hope to create a public and commercial attraction for 1935's edition of the National Alliance of Art and Industry's annual Industrial Arts Exhibition at Rockefeller Center. This for-profit event, with fees paid by exhibiting corporate concerns, had lost the confidence of celebrity designers such as Norman Bel Geddes, Henry Dreyfuss, and Raymond Loewy, who boycotted the Rockefeller-backed event because they believed it disrespected the role of designers. Violating solidarity, Wright agreed to participate when Edgar Kaufman Sr, a Pittsburgh department store owner and father of a young Wright fan, showed up at Taliesin, enrolled Junior in the fellowship, and agreed to provide $1000 as long as the model could also be displayed at his store back in Pittsburgh.

In her book *Wright on Exhibit*, Kathryn Smith documents the ongoing antagonisms over Broadacre City's fabrication and display. Arguments go back and forth over travel, money, and square footage. Wright reports to Kaufman that the model's assigned space in the exhibition is "in a back alley between two posts and in behind a couple of automobiles...when we need a space about 45'0" x 45'0" to show the scheme with any forceful effect." Soon after, he threatens "Count us out of the show.... But we will make one of our work some other way.... I am not interested in a motor vehicle and transportation exhibition." In concept and execution, Broadacre City is an act of pushing away, eventually resulting in the final 12-by-12-foot model representing four square miles as "a demonstration of possibilities, a framework for change rather than a fixed plan" (David Smiley, "Broad Acres and Narrow Lots") created by Wright and the Fellows, a group of "apprentices" who pay for this opportunity rather than receive their own piece of Broadacre City.

In Conversation:

Fernanda Canales and Loreta Castro Reguera with Jacqueline Hall

Material Metonyms

For all the heavy rhetoric, the model's materiality is remarkably unheroic, officially recorded by the museum as "painted wood, cardboard, and paper." Its creators basically used the contents of a recycling bin to propose the spatial reorganization of the continent. This great leap between material and meaning, shape and justification, offers a logic of abstraction and storytelling that can be extended and passed along:

> There's a beaver dam and some robotic dinosaurs for the kids to look at. Actually, they are voice-activated so when children ask questions, it will tell them all about themselves… This is an energy resource, this is for the satellite energy, like cosmic energy...If lightning strikes, the electricity will be ejected down this pole, and take the shock and place it into this piece of water...The building is built out of styrofoam and sticks.
> — *The Fraudacre City Story*

Similar to the use of objects in art therapy to manifest thoughts and feelings and facilitate more complex communication, urban planner James Rojas has developed workshops that introduce objects to manifest, describe, and discuss emotions and stories about places. Broadacre City shared this therapeutic function for Wright himself, as a funereal landscape haunted by his own unrealized designs.

However, the therapeutic conciliation most loudly promised by the project—"THE SEARCH FOR DEMOCRATIC FORM AS THE BASIS FOR A TRUE CAPITALISTIC SOCIETY"— instead begs the question, assuming the compatibility of democracy and capitalism while neglecting to study their conflicts. Without holding space for this antagonism, Broadacre City ducks questions of freedom and erects a settler colonial architecture upon a landscape of control. The mechanism of allocating at least one acre per family repeats without reference racialized public land distribution programs like the 1862 Homestead Act that extended the rule of private property and white supremacy across the continent.

Fernanda Canales and Loreta Castro Reguera are architects based in Mexico City. Both their work and research has taken them into communities that typically cannot afford architecture or are informal and, therefore, illegible to conventional architecture practices.

Canales studies the history of housing in Mexico and centers her work in the design of prototypes for low-income housing. She has worked with institutions, such as INFONAVIT, Mexico's workers' housing fund, and SEDATU, the country's territorial development agency. Her current research uses historical precedents to show how people have shared resources in the past. Her work is based on urbanism that is not reliant on individual homes to fulfill all basic needs but, instead, focuses on what is shared between houses — in her words, "a room of one's own, within collective infrastructure."

Castro Reguera, with her practice *Taller Capital*, has conducted in-depth research into Mexico's City's complex relationship with water. Among their wide range of projects, they have worked with SEDATU across Mexico, building high performance public spaces in parts of the country that have an acute lack of both recreational space and water infrastructure. In Mexico City, in collaboration with the National Autonomous University of Mexico, Loreta most recently led the design of *Parque la Quebradora*, a public space designed to both absorb stormwater to prevent flooding and to capture rainwater for reuse.

We spoke about the evolution of their practices and the types of projects they think Mexico needs now. I spoke with them not only because of their focus on housing and water, but also because they find ways to pursue work in challenging contexts, wading into the complicated and ever-changing political landscape in Mexico.

This issue, *Onus*, is devoted to ethics in architecture. But Canales and Castro Reguera both felt that a more important concern was whether architects should even try

Broadfaker City
Fraudacre City
Heartbreaker City
Bellyacher City
Raw Taker City
Dirty Laundry City
Slime City

Fraudacre City illustrations by Hector.

to participate in the design of cities as they actually exist — mostly with few resources and, sometimes, without help from the government. In a world defined by widening inequality and climate change, Canales and Castro Reguera suggest that the specific skill-set of architects could be more useful than ever, if we can be flexible. In today's cities — built among layers of cities that came before — our work may be to read an urban landscape that is full of answers and then use our skills to help edit, rather than author it.

Was there a project or period in your career when you started to feel in control of exercising your personal views, be they social, political or ethical, through architecture?

FC   For me, it started about ten years ago, because I had lost faith in the future of the projects I was designing. When I won competitions, the projects were never executed as designed, and they were built by people who did not care about the project. So, I started changing the scale and details of the projects and working towards a more personal and intimate practice that gave me more control. I decided not to have partners, not to engage in big work with many details that depended on institutions or politicians. I completely changed the way I understood the priorities of a project.

LCR   For me, it was different. The first time that I asked myself how I could offer something to the profession was when I was doing my master's. I thought, "this is a good chance to find out what Mexico City's largest problems are." I decided to focus on water from an urban design and landscape design perspective. I never thought of it as a social service; it was more about how I could read the city through a specific topic. But then, because it's one of those topics that is really public, it became a source for solving social issues. The projects have been fortuitous, in a sense. But, when you have an expertise (or the

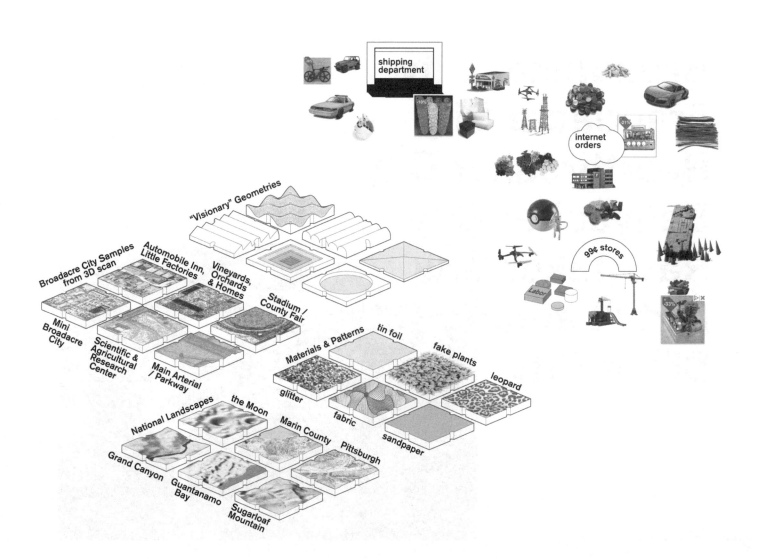

beginning of an expertise) on a certain topic, and then go back to reality, you can start reading sites and providing solutions from that point of view.

Would you say that research allows you to inject your politics and ethics into work for private clients?

FC   Doing research, for me, is creating the time to focus on themes that are usually neglected, that no client or competition asks for and no government or institution pays for. Research is building your toolbox. So, when something comes up, the tools are there. Many projects or competitions arise really fast and results need to be handed in immediately. If you have been working on that theme for years, you are ready to include all the complex situations the project involves, because you had already been doing this, just with no direct application. Sometimes, the opportunity doesn't appear, and it's a challenge to keep doing what you feel is important for the city or for society when you don't have a commission. But, it's the only way to be ready to tackle such vast issues.

What outside work is influencing your thinking and practice now?

LCR   Most are public space and landscape projects, because I'm interested in topography and how topography moves and changes to make space for human beings.

    One of the projects that has deeply impacted the work I do is a square by Peña Ganchegui, a Spanish architect from the mid-20th century. He designed this beautiful open space called *Plaza del Tenis* in San Sebastian, building a topography that results from composing space with granite block modules, similar in size to a brick. By placing these units together, he composes terraces and pavement into a kind of

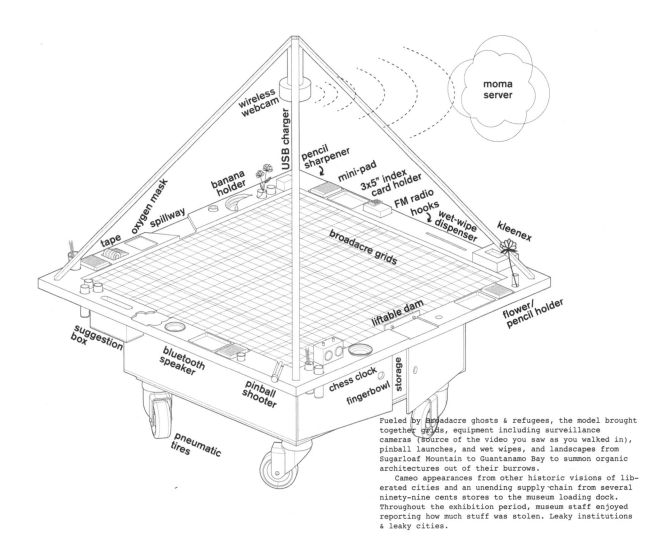

Fueled by Broadacre ghosts & refugees, the model brought together grids, equipment including surveillance cameras (source of the video you saw as you walked in), pinball launches, and wet wipes, and landscapes from Sugarloaf Mountain to Guantanamo Bay to summon organic architectures out of their burrows.

    Cameo appearances from other historic visions of liberated cities and an unending supply chain from several ninety-nine cents stores to the museum loading dock. Throughout the exhibition period, museum staff enjoyed reporting how much stuff was stolen. Leaky institutions & leaky cities.

belvedere. He has another project of the same type, a beautiful square in Vitoria-Gasteiz, where this same granite unit aggregates are used to construct a *Basque Pelota* wall, as well as an open-air amphitheater, a ramp, a stair…

Then, there is a project by Francisco Toledo and Claudina Lopez Morales, CASA, an artist's school, workshop and gallery in a small town in Oaxaca. It's a thoughtful reconfiguration of an old factory. The building acts as a water filter that cleans the adjacent river, through a set of drainage basins and canals. These elements create beautiful common spaces and, at the same time, add needed humidity to the air and provide clean water to the surroundings.

I've also been trying to look into historical precedents, for example, the Hatshepsut Temple in Egypt. The background mountains seem to be sculpted around the construction, unfolding a set of earthen platforms between the visitor and the temple that allow for the landscape to glorify the building.

I'll add another beautiful project here in Mexico, the Baths of Nezahualcoyotl, located to the east of the city. The Baths are one of the most ancient landscape projects of the Valley of Mexico. You can see how the Aztecs were able to transport bathing water from 6 kilometers away. They designed a network of aqueducts and canals to cross several hills. From the top of one of these hills, the viewer can understand the entire irrigation and hydraulic system needed both for worshiping Tlaloc on the mountain top and for the king to bathe overlooking the lake and Pre-Hispanic Tenochtitlan. Just fantastic.

FC   I'm spending most of my time now researching housing projects and designing new prototypes. The research is more about what happens between one house and another house than the design of a house per se. One theme has to do with how people

Take Space / Make Space

Like Wright, we parleyed with our patrons over budget and space. The museum only accommodated a model one-quarter the size of the original. We were kept informed on how different materials were abused and eventually destroyed by the public, and how frequently people were pocketing pieces of the model to take with them. Museum theft has not been excluded from Fraudacre City! Occasionally, situations required staff intervention, like when a kid announced he was building a wall between himself and the Spanish-speaking family across from him. We regularly re-upped the museum with extra supplies, stored in bins within the model. Eventually, staff in the shipping department started sending extra materials that might become looming towers, an exclusive spa for giraffes, or a border wall. They let us drop off as many 99-cent store finds as we wanted.

The most extended conflict with the institution was over the title and how it could manifest the theme of antagonism. Our first suggestion of Fraudacre City and all subsequent suggestions were seen as too negative for the occasion. As someone explained, the museum might mount an exhibition that touched on politics of immigration, but it would be called "People and Borders." Our best attempt at a similarly barbiturate title was the placeholder "Broadacre 2017." When the Broadacre model moved to Kaufman's Pittsburgh department store, Wright feuded with the mayor. The architect unleashed his urbicidal rage and the mayor critiqued his visionary design as driven by social control:

Frank Lloyd Wright:
"Pittsburgh, in common with all cities, becomes more and more a slum as it becomes less and less livable. And no doubt eventually—as new machines and processes are invented—the city will become wholly obsolete—as a factory may become obsolete overnight."

Mayor William Nissley McNair:
"Broadacre City is all right but you could never put Democrats in there. What if they'd want to get drunk or visit somebody's wife? This thing is Utopia. I'll bet they even tell you how many babies to have in each house. I just sent a gang of drunks to the workhouse. Put that bunch in Wright's village and it wouldn't be two weeks before they'd wreck it. This town is built for a lot of social workers."

Frank Lloyd Wright:
"Being Mayor of Pittsburgh, or of any American city, must be a disqualification for seeing anything but bugaboos in Broadacre City. The Mayor knows next to nothing about drunks, babies, or Democracy. As for drunks, a home in Broadacres would be its own saloon if the Broadacre citizen so wished but a more decent one than any the mayor can show in his Pittsburgh."

Scheduled workshops with the Fraudacre model, where groups worked together for 90-minute periods, aimed to inspire similar debates. Starting from points of antagonism, what Myles Horton called "conflict situations," helped identify design's existing and potential connections to identities and political life.

Interior of an affordable housing unit in the State of Mexico
by Fernanda Canales. Photo by Rafael Gamo.

maintain their privacy, a refuge or a place of their own within collective structures and within denser notions of collective living. I'm interested in the blurring between the private and the public and understanding privacy in a shared world. In that sense, I'm not looking as much at housing but at the notion of post-privacy and at the spaces between: what belongs to no one but affects everyone. I'm researching the consequences of the replication of houses in cities: everything the house consumes and the wastes it produces. Since houses represent the most built space in the world, I'm looking at the effects of houses in a plural sense, rather than the specific design of those houses.

What are the ethical questions you believe architects need to address through their work today?

LCR   I've been thinking about the question of how architects should address ethics and our responsibilities in the 21st century. It's a central issue for us, in these times. It has definitely changed from when I was taught or, at least, how I was taught.

In today's world, more than 50 percent of the population lives in cities. However, most of the urban fabric has been informally built, lacking basic infrastructure and services. Architects rarely focus on this, despite the enormous opportunity that it presents. The relevance of our profession is in our ability to address the gaps that unregulated urbanization leaves and to understand how, by filling them, we provide better spaces for the most vulnerable populations, which happens to be the great majority of people in this city. I think we need to reflect upon the close relationship between designing space and mitigating contemporary urban issues. How do we become relevant and useful when faced with the most pressing, glaring problems?

FC I wouldn't even speak about ethics, because, for me, the word has moralistic implications; I would rather not go there and, instead, stick with the realities at hand. When I was studying at the university, the projects we were engaged with were museums and private residences for ideal clients: photographers, artists... There was no connection with the reality that we were facing, not only in Mexico but worldwide. It is said that, in the United States, no more than 2 percent of new houses are designed by architects. The question of ethics and reality is not just about third world countries or poverty; it's that we are not able to understand the economics, the market, the needs, the cities and the links to the people who are paying for the things that are being built. I like a phrase by Giancarlo de Carlo from the 1960s: "architecture is too important to leave in the hands of architects." But I think it's even worse not to put it in the hands of anyone or to leave it in the hands of the market or politicians. 60 years after that statement, we should assert the usefulness of architects, while understanding that it is one of many disciplines that have to work together.

I like that idea that it's not about ethics, because ethics makes it feel like a choice. With this in mind, do you consider yourself an ethical architect? In other words: are you living in the world as it is or are you living in a fantasy of the 1 percent?

FC We are constantly living in a multi-layered world. Not only the one we touch and see every day but the one that is connected and extends beyond national, economic and social boundaries.

You have both worked closely with government officials on your projects. What are the biggest barriers in policy and politics to accomplishing this type of work?

Architecture of Mobocracy

Rather than sell a single formalized vision for the future, Fraudacre City is designed for questioning the forces that shape the places we inhabit. What urban dreams can reflect today's values for living together, and what does this mean for how we design life's basics, including water and food supply, transportation, housing, work, and recreation?

Eight decades after the initial Broadacre publicity campaign, the museum invited visitors to re-envision and update this dream-image of US civilization. Unlike the original model where everything is glued down, here visitors are encouraged to manipulate the landscape to realize their visions or to destroy those of others. Rebooted, this cover vision can now include everything Wright deleted from his city, along with contemporary fantasies, desires, and conditions he never anticipated: self-driving cars, McMansions, Pokémon hunting, bike lanes, data centers, Instagram, and drive-thru coffee shops.

If Citizenship Schools broke down the abstraction of the state so participants could talk about how it worked as if they were its designers, how can design traditions of making images of liberation do similar work around the social production of the physical environment? At a time of pandemic and fury at broken and violent social systems, it may seem crass to write about a visionary city where everything has gone terribly wrong. But let's hold onto the power of negation, and how it might help imagine a world structured so that vision is evaluated by its fine-grained and textured relations to what exists, never dis-embedded and rising up like steam from a utility hatch. Fraudacre City is a challenge to address everything and everybody that is usually left out of Architecture, which is the only way we know to challenge our own good intentions and imagine collective control of the environment.

• • •

Thank you to our generous collaborators Lucia Thome, Jess Van Nostrand, Alethea Rockwell, Sara Torres, and all Fraudacre visionaries.

Fraudacre City.

Early phases of construction at *Parque la Quebradora*.

FC   Even in the US, it's illegal in most cities to build any other typology than single-family dwellings on residential land. That rule stands in Chicago, Los Angeles, Seattle and many more cities. More than 75 percent of residential land is designated exclusively to individual dwellings. So, things need to change in every country, and it is clear that most of the time there will be no government official or client interested in making those changes.

LCR   It's hard to make a government change its mind about the status quo. It takes a lot of effort from the private sector, the community or academia to make them realize something is not functioning as it should.

     I am convinced that citizens from Mexico City have been learning how to apply pressure to the local government, achieving success either by becoming part of the decision-making processes or by organizing think tanks that are able to advocate effectively.

     At our office, we have realized that when a project is the result of a well-identified problem, when it is supported by strong research and evidence and when it is the most intuitive response to a certain issue, the government will easily accept proposals and become very excited about implementing them.

     Then the city becomes an incredible lab to test solutions. If you want to do something different then, of course, you are going to find barriers at the beginning. You must be persistent. As you execute the project, and successfully execute others like it, you build a body of work that might, over time, become the groundwork for public policy. By that time, your work is showing that the existing laws are obsolete. And after that, there are other pressing issues that remain unaddressed, ready to be tackled.

FC   Exactly, laws always come late, and, as Loreta said, they are generally wrong when they are first implemented. For example, stopping the horizontal urban sprawl of single-family dwellings in the outskirts was really important. It sounds really logical. We want to stop urban sprawl; so, let's bring housing back into the city. But you cannot re-densify dwellings or buildings without re-densifying public transport, public space, water and drainage systems. Thus, we are working with the same obsolete infrastructure but now with more people, higher buildings, less public space and no new public transit. That is going to be as bad as the previous model and just as dangerous.

So, the problem is the same in both places; the problem is infrastructure.

FC   Exactly, and a lack of long-term thinking.

LCR   That is the hardest part, I think, for us. You start a project with a systemic, long-term vision, but political cycles are short, three or six years at the most. So, projects must develop super-fast. We architects need to adapt to the pace of reality. This doesn't mean you cannot do excellent work. Understanding reality and pacing yourself accordingly doesn't mean you won't do great projects. It's just that we have to read the world in a different way than how we were taught. In school in Mexico we were deeply influenced by the thought of Le Corbusier, as personified in Mario Pani. He was able to plan and execute important pieces of the city in less than 10 years. But now, cities are different, and we need to understand how to deal with our context as is.

You're both working on public issues in different states across Mexico. How is the current state of political affairs in the country and city impacting your work?

D R A F T

To:-

Dear Sir,

I am writing to confirm the arrangements agreed between
                    Ltd. ("the Company") and APG at our meeting
on   .

1. The Company will grant a Fellowship to
    ("the Artist") to last for a period of one calendar year
    commencing

2. The Company will pay the Fellowship Award of £   in
    instalments as invoiced by the artist - the first
    instalment to be made at the commencement of the Fellowship.

3. The Company will pay to APG at the commencement of the
    Fellowship a commission of 15% on the Fellowship award.

4. The Company has nominated   as a linkman
    who will look after the Artist's needs, making arrangements
    for
    (a) the Artist's brief;
    (b) insurance to cover the Artist's activities;
    (c) technical advice and assistance;
    (d) materials and facilities;
    (e) any necessary travel; and
    (f) any further matters thought desirable.

5. The Artist will work for the period of the Fellowship, and
    after, if necessary, preparing for the Hayward Gallery
    exhibition, within the terms of the brief agreed with APG -
    or any modification thereto arranged with the linkman after
    consultation with APG. It is understood that the artist is
    not committed to devising any work of art, product or idea.

6. It is agreed that all rights in any work of art, product
    or idea devised during the period of the Fellowship shall

Artist Placement Group, *APG Draft Contract*, c. 1970

Artist Placement Group was conceived by artist Barbara Steveni in 1965 and established a year later by Steveni and John Latham along with Barry Flanagan, David Hall, Anna Ridley and Jeffrey Shaw, among others. The organization's goal was to reposition the role of the artist within a wider social context, including government and commerce, and it worked to do so by placing artists at corporate and governmental agencies. Between 1969 and 1989, APG facilitated placements at the British Steel Corporation, British European Airways, Scottish Television, British Rail, Esso Petroleum and the National Coal Board, among others.

The draft contract is a template agreement to be signed by the participating artist and its host organization. It constitutes APG's open brief: artists would be paid a fee by the host with no material output expected. Instead, the artwork was considered the whole process of the placement, which included outreach from APG ahead of the artist's involvement and a report typically written after the fact.

APG believed that artists could have a positive influence on industry, and that the "real world" context was beneficial to artists; their famous maxim reads "Context is half the work."[1] As Steveni and Latham wrote, the placement was more of a collaboration than a residency: "the status of artists within organizations must necessarily be in line with other professional persons, engaged within the organization."[2] She considered APG's work to be "repositioning art in the decision-making processes of society."[3]

[1]
Context is Half the Work website. https://en.contextishalfthework.net/about-apg/artist-placement-group/. Accessed June 23, 2020.

[2]
Frieze website. https://frieze.com/article/context-half-work. Accessed June 23, 2020.

[3]
Barbara Steveni, 'Repositioning Art in the Decision-making Processes of Society', paper given at ELIA, Amsterdam, 1990.

Artist Placement Group, *APG Draft Contract*, c. 1970

LCR   For me, it's been good and bad. On the one hand, a large park that our office
        has been working on, *la Quebradora*, was going really well, or, at least, that
        is what we thought. However, when the new leader of Iztapalapa took over, she
        shut down the largest community projects then underway. One of those was
        la Quebradora. It took several months for construction to re-start, and several
        changes were made to the original design. Some of them were good, but others
        are counter to the original spirit of the project, such as the inclusion of a
        public pool.

        On the other hand, the federal government has a program for implementing
        public infrastructure and public services all around the country. In this context,
        it is evident that when there is political will, things are done super quickly. In
        one example of this, about a year ago, we got asked to design a new public space
        in the city of Nogales, in the state of Sonora. That was less than a year ago, and
        we just finished construction.

        Many things just are not under your control. If you are lucky, you'll
        get a project at the right time and in the right place. Other projects take much
        longer and cost much more effort, especially when they that go against the
        established grain.

        *Was the project in Sonora something you proposed? Or did someone come
        to you?*

LCR   The government reached out to us. They knew about *la Quebradora*. They
        asked us to design a public space adjacent to a dam in a site that, from the aerial
        photos, seemed dry. Once we started research, we realized the area was under

water for more than half of the year. We proposed to re-structure the dam wall, as part of our flood control strategy, and also added several public spaces, both open and covered.

FC   We are always running late to upgrade needed infrastructure, because it's not visible enough. If you're a politician who is looking for projects with very fast media impact, then you're always going to do superficial projects to gain votes. And we are still there; it's not going to change with this administration. We are always starting from scratch. I think that is the history of this city. It's a multi-layer city, built on destroying what has previously been done. The Colonial city was built on top of the indigenous temples. The Neoclassical city destroyed the Baroque buildings, and the Modern city of the 20th century destroyed everything that came before. And now, I think that the 21st century should advance a new understanding of those time-lapses and promote different priorities that don't have to do with the will of a government official or the image of political parties. Urbanism should be about understanding what exists: the place, the history and the resources.

What would you say are Mexico's most urgent housing issues?

LCR   I think, worldwide, mixed-use housing and a new understanding of ownership. Housing can't be about private property anymore. We need to understand sharing economies. Our conception of public and private cannot be the same as it was in the past century. In fact, the dichotomy never really existed. The idea of the nuclear family was an invention of the 1940s. More and more, we want to

The Institutions Must be Designed Before the Buildings

Susanne Schindler

The interior courtyard of a typical *vecindad* in *colonia* San Rafael, Mexico City. Photo by Jacqueline Hall.

I. The Search for a Paradigm

Not so long ago, I was interviewed for a tenure-track position in the urban design program at a school of architecture in the United States. I gave a presentation, and in the interview that followed, I was told that to succeed in teaching urban design, one needed to have a succinct "paradigm." Although unstated, I knew what was implied: morphological and typological frameworks for urban growth that are assumed to generate "good" form. What, exactly, was my take on paradigm, I was asked? I responded that my take on paradigm was a rather different one: namely, that we need to always see formal considerations like type and morphology as intrinsically connected to financial and political aspects. What is the point of "good" design if it benefits only a few at the expense of most? Conversely, what is the point of "good" design if it aims, in and of itself, to solve issues that are beyond its reach, like socio-economic or racial inequality, at which it will invariably fail?

To make my case, I had focused my presentation on a series of urban design proposals from the late 1960s, a contentious moment in the urban history of the United States. As part of the "War on Poverty" and efforts to combat the deep segregation of cities, officials and designers often advanced a new urban design paradigm—generally housing built at smaller scale on infill lots up to the street edge. In parallel, they called for stronger "community" involvement, in an effort to generate the political support needed to move the projects forward, as well as emphasized "implementation" or production, as the measure of success.

Part of my talk focused on Twin Parks, two urban renewal areas in the Bronx, best-known for the architects who designed the buildings there, including James Stewart Polshek and Richard Meier, who with their work had advanced what would become known as the "contextual" urban-design paradigm. However, the "better" designed housing, once implemented, did little to improve the socio-economic conditions which had been the original impetus to develop these projects. This lack of improvement was due, in part, due to the fact the political and financial terms on which these projects were realized had been fundamentally altered between the original idea, which was fundamentally based in community governance, and the projects' implementation. In most cases, these projects, originally conceived as nonprofit ventures, were ultimately realized as for-profit operations.[1] The lesson I tried to draw from these stories is that if designers want their work to have an intended impact, they need to understand their design, a tangible proposition, in relation to intangible aspects of urban life, including the messy, uncomfortable, and contested aspects of money and power. This means expanding the definition of what constitutes "design" to include what is usually summarized under "policy" and sometimes even "finance."

It was clear that my job talk was understood by some committee members as a challenge to the discipline itself. It was as if in simply uttering the word "policy," I was calling into question the relevance of design. In fact, I was arguing quite the opposite: namely that the spatial elements of urban design, such as block dimensions, façade materials, permitted uses and apartment typologies, have extraordinary power to both shape immediate spatial expe-

1
For more on this trajectory, see my article "Model Conflicts," *e-flux Architecture*, July 2018.

live alone. But at the same time, we acknowledge the usefulness of sharing economies. We are questioning how much we want to share and how much privacy we need, which creates a new understanding about ownership and privacy. There are examples of shared housing from all over the world. I'm not talking about the hippie communal living of the 60s. It's *vecindades* in Mexico, *conventillos* in Spain and the *cubiculos* in Cuba. It's about understanding how, historically, people have lived together and apart. It has to do with having the room of one's own, within a collective infrastructure.

LCR   How to design and build housing and infrastructural public spaces in the larger urban fabric, both formal and informal, with scarce resources.

In some ways, issues of climate change, inequality and segregation are global. But Mexico has a strong history of land redistribution and power in indigenous communities in a way that a country like the US does not. Perhaps, there is a more widespread understanding of alternative models of ownership, cooperation and the commons in Mexico. Do you think that is true? If so, could that collective political consciousness influence the way Mexico adapts to climate change and economic inequality?

LCR   Our experience with the parks, *la Quebradora* in Mexico City, *Represo* in Nogales, and an intervention in Tijuana, were all located within informal settlements. Somehow, it's easier to do these sorts of projects. In those communities, people are very conscious

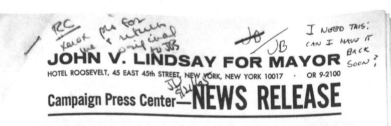

"Remarks to nine questions on urban design and planning." Press release of an address by mayoral candidate John Lindsay to the AIA, annotated by Jonathan Barnett, September 17, 1965.

about the lack of services and the need for better space. They understand the needs of the place. These communities are used to having to ask for the things they need, because, obviously, no one is coming to pave the streets and install lights if they don't demand it. As a result, they are better at understanding ideas that can benefit the whole community. And this is a part of our job as architects: to move out of our comfort zones of legality and our need for everything to happen in a certain way. We were trained as professionals that need a client and a commission: someone to tell us just exactly how many bedrooms they want. It's a shift in mindset, because what we are really dealing with is the lack of services and very low quality of life, spatial and otherwise, in the informal city. We can truly help there if we understand the possibilities of how good architecture can make a difference. It's easier there, because people are conscious of their own individual needs, but, at the same time, they are used to a sense of communal, shared purpose and a high quality of public life. Thus, we may need to become more sensitive about how the city is actually being built and the possibilities that it provides, instead of fighting to twist things based on our own limited perspective.

FC   What we call informality, in Mexico, represents more than 60 to 70 percent of the houses being built. Just because houses are done informally, that is, illegally, doesn't mean that the owners didn't have to pay somebody for their land and the construction of their house. They are not squatting on communal, free properties. They paid for their ownership. That ownership is not recognized legally. Yet, if the largest percentage of houses there are built informally, they cannot be considered irregular. You cannot call the predominant model "marginal." We need to change the laws, the names and the processes.

    In these informal communities, we have examples of what people need and what people can manage and organize on their own. It's not about romanticizing vernacular

Twin Parks Northeast Housing, Richard Meier.

architecture; it's about acknowledging the potential in what they have already accomplished. We associate all of those sharing practices with the internet and new technologies, but the historical examples are even richer than what we have today with new places for co-living, co-working, co-whatever. There are actually deeper understandings of the difficulties, risks and benefits of sharing.

LCR   A sign of success in our culture remains the possibility of building and owning your house. It means that you made it in life. Therefore, people put all their dreams and all their ambitions, everything, into that single event. And that is OK, but it comes from a value system we learned in the last century, based around the idea of private property and western culture. Today, we need to understand that there are other types of values that need to be explored and that also make human life rich, even richer.

rience and communicate to various stakeholders many of the larger, nonspatial issues that are at stake in a proposal. As you might guess, I was not offered the job.

I tell this episode because it reveals how difficult it still seems to be for those who consider themselves designers to acknowledge the entangled nature of their work, even today, when much public dialogue is given over to the task of "breaking down silos" between departments and disciplines, between the academy and the real world. Schools of architecture are grappling with how to conceptualize and address the implication of design in inequality, the question the editors of this issue are framing as "Onus." I say "still" because these debates are remarkably similar to those held at precisely these schools over fifty years ago, the period I spoke about in my talk. How to increase the enrollment of minority students? How to justify the nonprofit, public-benefit status of universities when they serve so few? How to bridge the freedom of research within the academy with aspiring to some impact on the ground?[2] In short, how to connect design to community and implementation?

All this of then is a prelude to a very brief story of the Twin Parks Study, conducted between 1965 and 1967, by five recent graduates of these schools of architecture. The little-known planning process was the basis for the better-known projects designed by Polshek and Meier mentioned before. The story is relevant today because it shows that designers must invariably connect form not only to politics but also to finance, and that occasionally they also have to redefine what needs to be designed if they are to involve the community and make implementation possible. "Policy," or its implied adjectival construction of "socially conscious," is not a dirty word. Rather, it can be a powerful tool to be embraced by designers to advance not only

"good" design, but what is most fundamentally at stake now, just as it was fifty years ago, namely, the conditions for democracy.

II. Machiavelli and the Medici in the Bronx

We hope that you have survived that inferno of conversation without the impression that we are all blinded by Machiavelli. In his day, of course, we would all have dined with the Medicis, and that is the point. Today, the patrons are institutions, and an unfortunate but necessary result of democracy is that architects must learn to deal with institutions politically if their art is to flourish at all—so—we have learned that the institutions must be designed before the buildings.[3]

2
Sharon Sutton has beautifully reconstructed, in a kind of memoir of her time at Columbia, how schools of architecture and planning in the late 1960s launched research institutes and action committees, minority student recruitment efforts and initiatives to bring in public funding, philanthropic support, as well as the business community to address the imbalance between the academy and the worlds often immediately beyond. Some of the efforts at institutional and curricular reform stuck, as design-build programs or community design centers show. Others quickly waned, including proactive student recruitment efforts. Sharon Sutton, *When the Ivory Towers were Black: A Story about Race in America's Cities and Universities*, New York: Fordham University Press, 2017.

3
Letter to "Aldo" from "Giovanni, Jacquelin, Jonathan, Myles, Richard," September 29, 1965. (Yale, Barnett Papers, Group 1733, Box 2, Folder: "Lindsay, John V, Mayoral Campaign Materials relating to urban design, 1966-67.")

The Twin Parks Study first began in early 1965, when five architects in their early thirties joined the mayoral campaign of John Lindsay. Lindsay, a Republican U.S. Congressman, was running on a platform to expand public services, decentralize decision making and create a city more inclusive of its diverse constituents during a time of "urban crisis."[4] Like the prospective mayor, all five architects had significant social privilege. Jonathan Barnett, Giovanni Pasanella, Jacquelin Robertson, and Myles Weintraub had all, like Lindsay, graduated from Yale while Richard Weinstein had studied architecture at the University of Pennsylvania. After graduating, they had worked for well-known New York architectural practices and taught in various schools of architecture.[5] For these five young architects, getting involved in the Lindsay campaign was driven less by political inspiration and more by frustration: a sense that the newly minted architects would never get to build anything in light of citizens' growing opposition to top-down planning. As Robertson put it in a letter to colleagues at the time, he wanted to remedy architects' "shocking impotence" in shaping policy. To do so, he argued, architects would have to engage in "designing the institutions before the buildings."[6] "Gio" Pasanella and "Jacque" Robertson, thus, pitched the idea of setting up "Little City Halls." The goal of these new, localized service points was both to improve and equalize the delivery of municipal services across the city. However, these service points would also alter the structure of planning decisions to facilitate access for local residents by building on the city's existing system of 59 community boards. Appointing professional planners in permanent staff positions would hopefully allow citizens serving on these boards to better understand the often overly technical issues of land-use regulation. By calling on designers

4
For a readable account of Lindsay's campaign and various dimensions of his two administrations, see Joseph P. Viteritti, ed., *Summer in the City: John Lindsay, New York, and the American Dream*, Baltimore: John Hopkins University Press, 2014.

5
Giovanni Pasanella (1931–2011) received his Master of Architecture at Yale in 1958, worked for Edward Larabee Barnes until 1964, when he started teaching at Columbia and established his own practice. The firm is today called PKSB Architecture, known for academic and institutional work. Jacquelin Robertson (born 1933), is a 1961 graduate, also worked for Barnes, then became a founding partner of Cooper, Robertson & Partners. The firm is best known for its take on traditional urban design, as exemplified by the masterplan for Battery Park City. Myles Weintraub (born 1937), is a 1962 graduate. He also worked for Barnes, and he would go on to private and public practice in different partnerships. Jonathan Barnett (born 1937), graduated in 1962 and had worked as an editor at *Architectural Record* since 1964. He is best known for spearheading urban design as an academic discipline at City College of New York and later at the University of Pennsylvania. Richard Weinstein (1932–2018) would become dean at UCLA.

6
Letter by the five architects to the Kaplan Fund, March 24, 1966. (Manuscripts and Archives, Yale University Library. Box 2, Folder: "Lindsay, John V., Mayoral Campaign Materials relating to urban design, 1966-67.")

to focus first on the legal and regulatory framework, rather than jumping to individual objects, Robertson was, thus, articulating a new urban design paradigm; built form was the goal, but new means were needed to get there.

At a moment in which community participation was being called for in governmental programs, responding to citizen pressure, the group's proposal entailed a clear hierarchical distinction be made between experts and citizens. Architects would retain planning authority, while residents contributed local knowledge and suggestions for improvement: "The committee would not be making the plan itself—planning is a highly technical and complex process—but it will participate in making significant decisions at every stage in the planning process."[8] Similarly, and perhaps more significantly, the group was clear that the success of a plan developed in conjunction with the community could only be measured in one way: implementation. As they wrote: "A successful community plan is one that will be carried out. To be carried out, a plan needs the agreement of those who are to implement it and also of those for whom it is drawn."[9] In the proposed test run for a changed planning process, community involvement was seen not as a goal in and of itself but as a means to an end. That end was implementation.

The group had made this understanding of democratic planning processes abundantly clear in a 1965 letter written to Aldo Giurgola. Giurgola was the newly appointed head of the just-created Division of Architecture at Columbia University's School of Architecture, where Pasanella and Robertson had been teaching for over a year.[10] The letter was meant to thank him for a meeting in which they had laid out their reasons for wanting to reshape the city's planning process. The first paragraph, in its reference to Renaissance Italy—cited above—summarized the key motivation. This initiative was driven not by a sense of social responsibility, but by a desire to build. Barnett and his colleagues depicted architecture as an art, but as art in need of patrons. Therefore, in a period in which democracy was the patron, and thus all people—not just families like the Medici—were to be the beneficiaries of art, it was the institutions of democracy that needed to be redesigned in order to give people the tools that would enable them to be clients. However, the five young architects insisted that planning and policy reform could be advanced only through specific projects, for specific places by "testing a developed architectural-planning idea."[11]

In many ways, this approach was not so different from the proposals advanced by advocacy planners at the time. Paul Davidoff, too, argued for new professional roles, albeit for planners. Davidoff believed in the power of a specific proposal for a particular site as a catalyst for the public debate which, to him, constituted the core of democratic processes.[12] In contrast to the five young architects, however, he was adamantly opposed to the idea of any single plan. Instead, Davidoff argued for a new process which

8
Ibid.

9
Ibid.

10
Letter to "Aldo" from "Giovanni, Jacquelin, Jonathan, Myles, Richard," September 29, 1965. (Yale, Barnett Papers, Group 1733, Box 2, Folder: "Lindsay, John V, Mayoral Campaign Materials relating to urban design, 1966-67.")

11
Ibid.

12
Urban historian Mariana Mogilevich clearly distinguishes Davidoff's position from that of the five. She emphasizes the need for planners' to take on an "adversarial role," which she sees as contrasting with the conciliatory, single-client approach embraced by the planners in the Twin Parks Study. See *Designing the Urban: Space and Politics in Lindsay's New York*, PhD Dissertation, 2012, p. 139, forthcoming as a book with the same title with the University of Minnesota Press.

Cameron Rowland, *Encumbrance*, 2020
Mortgage; mahogany handrail: 12 Carlton House
Terrace, stairwell, ground floor to first floor

The property relation of the enslaved included and
exceeded that of chattel and real estate. Plantation mortgages exemplify the ways in which the value of people
who were enslaved, the land they were forced to labor
on, and the houses they were forced to maintain were
mutually constitutive. Richard Pares writes that "[mort-
gages] became commoner and commoner until, by
1800, almost every large plantation debt was a mortgage
debt." Slaves simultaneously functioned as collateral
for the debts of their masters, while laboring intergen-
erationally under the debt of the master. The taxation of
plantation products imported to Britain, as well as the
taxation of interest paid to plantation lenders, provided
revenue for Parliament and income for the monarch.

Mahogany became a valuable British import in the
18th century. It was used for a wide variety of architectural applications and furniture, characterizing Georgian
and Regency styles. The timbers were felled and milled
by slaves in Jamaica, Barbados, and Honduras among
other British colonies. It is one of the few commodities
of the triangular trade that continues to generate value
for those who currently own it.

After taking the throne in 1820, George IV dismantled his residence, Carlton House, and the house of his
parents, Buckingham House, combining elements from
each to create Buckingham Palace. He built Carlton
House Terrace between 1827 and 1832 on the former
site of Carlton House as a series of elite rental properties to generate revenue for the Crown. All addresses
at Carlton House Terrace are still owned by the Crown
Estate, manager of land owned by the Crown since 1760.

12 Carlton House Terrace is leased to the Institute of
Contemporary Arts. The building includes four mahogany doors and one mahogany handrail. These five
mahogany elements were mortgaged by the Institute
of Contemporary Arts to Encumbrance Inc. on January
16th, 2020 for £1000 each. These loans will not be
repaid by the ICA. As security for these outstanding
debts, Encumbrance Inc. will retain a security interest in
these mahogany elements. This interest will constitute
an encumbrance on the future transaction of 12 Carlton
House Terrace. An encumbrance is a right or interest
in real property that does not prohibit its exchange but
diminishes its value. The encumbrance will remain
on 12 Carlton House Terrace as long as the mahogany
elements are part of the building. As reparation, this
encumbrance seeks to limit the property's continued
accumulation of value for the Crown Estate. The Crown
Estate provides 75% of its revenue to the Treasury and
25% directly to the monarch.

Encumbrance, 2020 is an artwork produced on the occasion of Cameron Rowland's solo exhibition at the Institute of Contemporary Arts in London. The work is a mortgage taken out by the Institute of Contemporary Arts in London against four mahogany doors and one mahogany handrail, all original to the museum's building. Rowland's work often takes the form of contractual relations. These projects call attention to and activate the legacy of racial capitalism, with special attention to how it manifests within art institutions.

The caption is an essential and intrinsic part of the work that must accompany it wherever and whenever the work is reproduced, represented or exhibited.

Cameron Rowland, *Encumbrance*, 2020

would encourage the emergence of multiple competing plans, prepared by different stakeholders. Davidoff was motivated by questions of social justice and democratic empowerment, as they played out in urban development. Barnett and his colleagues were likely less concerned with these issues; they wanted to build. This was not cynical or purely self-serving, however. The five young architects took on the Machiavellian work of understanding and changing political processes, as they put it: "designing the institutions before the buildings." They closed their letter to Giurgola succinctly: "The point is that if we must struggle to be politically astute, it is a small price to pay for the chance to build."[13]

The group's "struggle to be politically astute," its investment in writing white papers on institutional redesign, paid off. Lindsay was elected in November of 1965, and, in early 1966, the City gave a go-ahead for a pilot study for the Little City Halls. But while the City may have approved the proposal to "redesign the institutions," it had no public funds to contribute to the Twin Parks Study. The five needed to find financial support elsewhere.[14] They reached out to the J.M. Kaplan Fund, a small, yet influential family foundation with a focus on historic preservation, urban design, and public space. They also reached out to Columbia University, as they needed an institution to administer a possible Kaplan grant. The Twin Parks Study turned out to be a miniscule yet significant contributor to some of the institutional redesign going on at the newly founded Institute of Urban Environment.

III. Institutional Re-design: University, Philanthropy, Community

Our challenge is to revive the spirit and sense of community in this city. We had it once, perhaps we can attain it again. Perhaps we can revitalize our concern for our neighborhoods, for the larger community of the whole city, and beyond that to the larger communities of state, nation, and world.[15]

In the mid-1960s, governmental institutions as well as philanthropic organizations and schools of architecture frantically searched for new ways to define and live up to their social responsibility. In 1965, several East Coast universities reorganized the structure and curricula of their schools of architecture, testing new models of how to relate design, research and action in the field, and they did so in coordination with governmental and philanthropic funding. Creating centers for urban research was part

13
Letter to "Aldo" from "Giovanni, Jacquelin, Jonathan, Myles, Richard," September 29, 1965. (Yale, Barnett Papers, Group 1733, Box 2, Folder: "Lindsay, John V, Mayoral Campaign Materials relating to urban design, 1966–67.")

14
Detailed in Chapter 4, "Neighborhood Planning and Community Participation," pages 84–115, in Jonathan Barnett, *Urban Design as Public Policy: Practical Methods for Improving Cities*, New York: Architectural Record Books, 1974.

15
New York City Housing and Development Administration, T*win Parks Vest Pocket Housing*, p. 8.

"Influencing the Future of New York City." Pamphlet advertising a series of collo-
quiums for senior executives, organized by Columbia University's Institute of Urban
Environment, 1967.

Twin Parks Apartments, SOM.

of this agenda.[16] These urban centers had differing agendas, some tending toward "urban extension" or providing design and planning services to underserved communities. Other organizations focused on "research" to advance knowledge of planning processes. Often, these organizations combined these two approaches. Philanthropic organizations, above all the Ford Foundation, were hugely influential in these efforts. In 1963, for example, Ford and the Rockefeller Brothers Fund had provided the seed money to establish the Pratt Center for Community Improvement. Located within the university's School of Architecture, the Center aimed to work with community organizations from Brooklyn's Bedford-Stuyvesant, one of the city's poorest neighborhoods.[17]

Columbia University had first announced the creation of an "Institute for Urban Environment" in May of 1965. It was the brainchild of Charles Abrams, an esteemed and highly influential researcher and writer on housing and inequality.[18] Columbia was recruiting Abrams as part of the reorganization of its School of Architecture, driven in part by the university's urgent need to address the growing backlash against its expansion into the nearby low-income, minority areas of Harlem and Morningside Heights.[19] Like the Pratt Center, Abrams' Institute for Urban Environment was positioned both to conduct research and take action."[20] In conceiving the Institute, Abrams had counted on funding from the Ford Foundation to establish a university-wide institute to address education, employment, health and other relevant matters in a coordinated and comprehensive manner. By late 1966, the foundation had decided otherwise. Due to a lack of start-up funding, Abrams's Institute was now no longer to operate at the university level but only within the school of architecture.

16
Many were directly inspired by MIT's Joint Center for Urban Studies For a concise history of the emergence and rationale behind urban research at schools of architecture, see Eugénie L. Birch, "Making Urban Research Intellectually Respectable: Martin Meyerson and the Joint Center for Urban Studies of Massachusetts Institute of Technology and Harvard University 1959-1964," *Journal of Planning History* Vol. 10, No. 3 (2011): p. 219–238.

17
George M. Raymond and Ronald Shiffman, "The Pratt Center for Community Improvement: A University Action Program," Pratt Planning Papers, January 1967, n.p. Also: http://www.prattcenter. net/our-mission/our-history, accessed February 14, 2018.

18
Abrams had been one of the lead thinkers in establishing the legal basis of both the public housing and urban renewal in the interwar years. In the post-war years, he gathered further influence as a key advisor on both national and international development. Of his many publications, his 1964 book *Man's Struggle for Shelter* in an Urbanizing World was released in paperback in 1966. That same year he published *The Negro Housing Problem: A Study for Philadelphia*, an influential and nuanced proposal for low-income home ownership, as a solution to fighting racial discrimination in housing. For an overview of Abrams's career, see Scott A. Henderson, *Housing and the Democratic Ideal: The Life and Thought of Charles Abrams*, New York: Columbia University Press, 2000

19
It would be reorganized into three new divisions, Architecture, Technology and Planning. A NYT article characterizes Columbia's reorganization not in terms of its being a trendsetter, but rather as "following the current trend toward the integration of architectural design with city planning and engineering principles" and to expand enrollment. "Columbia Revises Architect School," NYT, May 28, 1965. / A partial synopsis of this history, mentioning the struggle around Morningside Heights, but not the South Campus expansion, can also be found on the GSAPP website, "History of the School," http://old.arch.columbia.edu/ about/history-school, accessed January 23, 2017.

20
The Institute was later described as the "research arm of the school of architecture." "Rules of the School of Architecture," dated April 25, 1969. (Columbia University Central Files, UA#0083 Series I. Office Files, Office of the Provost Records, 1.953–2006, Box 98, Folder: Architecture–General, to June 30, 1969.)

No One Intends to Open an Airport

Julia Walker

This article, created for *Perspecta* 53, has been adapted from Julia Walker's forthcoming book, *Officially Contemporary: State Architecture in Berlin After 1990* (Bloomsbury Publishing).

The Institute had to cover all operating costs through external funding. Thus, it is not surprising that Abrams agreed in mid-1966, shortly after the Institute's official establishment, to administer the comparatively small, $30,000 grant from the J.M. Kaplan Fund for the Twin Parks Study. But hosting the Study was not a purely pragmatic decision. There was a closeness in spirit between the five young architects' emphasis on "designing the institutions" towards the goal of "implementation" and Abrams's own activities. In the fall of 1967, for example, the Institute hosted "Influencing the Future of New York City," a series of colloquia that targeted business "executives" who were to be brought into conversation with "well-known experts."[21] Topics reached from sociological questions ("The Negro in City and Suburbs") to technology-driven design methods ("The Systems Approach to Urban Problems"). But the goal was not just talk. As a brochure advertised, "the total body of knowledge from a variety of fields will not only bring the particular problem into a more constructive highlight, but will hopefully produce relevant proposals worthy of implementation."[22] Its projects were generally sited in nearby Harlem, funded by industry, and involved Columbia faculty and community organizations.[23] The Institute for Urban Environment thus tried to connect the study of race and inequality with a concern for change on the ground, but it was limited in impact from the start by its total reliance on third-party funding.

By June 1966, once both the Kaplan Fund and Columbia confirmed their support, the "Twin Parks area of the Bronx" was selected as the study site.[24] Delimited roughly by the Grand Concourse to the west, Southern Boulevard to the east, Fordham Road to the north and Tremont Street to the south, this part of the central Bronx was developed with five-story apartment buildings in the early twentieth-century with the arrival of mass transit. It was selected, in part, because it included an area designated for urban renewal in 1963, that while championing a new approach to renewal — such as prioritizing rehabilitation and keeping residents in place — had not moved forward, leading to resident turn over, vacancy and disinvestment.[25] The study soon became known as a "vest pocket housing and rehabilitation study," and it was

21
Columbia University, Institute for Urban Environment, brochure announcing the event series "Influencing the Future of New York City," Fall 1967. (Columbia University, Central Files, 1890-1984: Series I: Central Files, 1895-1971, UA#0001, Box 36. Folder 1.1.2917, Charles Abrams, 12/1966–8/1967.)

22
Ibid.

23
For example, there is evidence of a joint venture between Celotec and American Standard investing in a demonstration project in Harlem, as part of the Institute's Urban Action and Experimentation Program, to demonstrate both turnkey and vest pocket approaches to housing. The project involved Max Bond and Wechsler and Schimenti, dated March 15, 1968. What came of this project requires further study. (Columbia University, Central Files, 1890-1984: Series I: Central Files, 1895-1971, UA#0001, Box 36. Folder 1.1.2917, Charles Abrams, 12/1966–8/1967.)

24
Letter to the Kaplan Fund from Columbia University School of Architecture, signature unclear, June 16, 1966. (Yale, Barnett Papers, Group 1733, Box 2, Folder: "Lindsay, John V, Mayoral Campaign Materials relating to urban design, 1966-67.")

25
n.a., no title, NYT, August 16, 1963, p. 26; Alexander Burnham, "City Board Calls for Rehabilitation Of 5 Neighborhoods," NYT, August 15, 1963, p. 1, 23; "Planners approve Renewal in 5 Areas," NYT, December 11, 1963, p. 50.

An architectural ethics relates inextricably to matters of scale, and to the magnitude of a given project's human and environmental impact. Cities, therefore, offer particular object lessons, especially when they become the scene of monumental capital projects intended for the use of the public and the expression of political meaning. This was the case with post-Wall Berlin, whose makers, both public and private, focused on arraying the newly reunified city with eye-catching works of contemporary architecture. By the turn of the millennium, Berlin had become widely known as "the city that let in the architects," as a writer for the London *Times* described it.[1] At sites around the city, new architecture announced Germany's broader ambitions in flashy private-sector commissions, such as Frank Gehry's DZ Bank building and Jean Nouvel's Galeries Lafayette, high-profile cultural projects like Daniel Libeskind's Jewish Museum and David Chipperfield's Neues Museum, and sleek embassies by Rem Koolhaas, Hans Hollein and Christian de Portzamparc. The most famous of these projects, Norman Foster's renovated Reichstag building, anchored a new government district northwest of the Brandenburg Gate, its radiant

1
Rachael Jolley, "The City That Let in the Architects," *The Times*, January 15, 2000, 28.

A view of OMA's Dutch Embassy in Berlin, constructed in 2004.

only one of at least five being pursued under that name by the Lindsay administration at this time. Four were sited, in contrast to Twin Parks, in the city's so-called worst slums, identified as the cores of future Model Cities neighborhoods.[26] But the consultants were to follow a similar task in all cases: to work with local residents to site 800 units of public, low-income housing and 800 units of non-profit sponsored moderate-income housing, either as new construction or in rehabilitated structures.

Documentation of the community engagement process at Twin Parks is lost, but it was likely similar to that in other vest pocket housing study areas, where records document weekly meetings between residents, representatives of local organizations and planning consultants.[27] At Twin Parks, it was clergy of diverse denominations who emerged as the planners' key interlocutors. This is not entirely surprising; whether Catholic, Methodist, Baptist or Jewish, clergy were motivated by the need to preserve their congregations in a period of rapid demographic change. Religious institutions were also some of the few organizations which had existed with some duration in this area. Additionally, they could generally count on political, technical and financial support at a regional level, such as in the case of Catholic parishes from the Archdiocese. In March of 1967, fourteen of these religious organizations created the "Twin Parks Association." At that time, the idea of clergy organizing to promote neighborhood renewal and new housing was not entirely novel. Religious institutions had taken on key roles in urban renewal projects since the 1950s, including on the Upper West Side. Section 221d3, a 1961 federal mortgage subsidy program, gave non-profits preferential terms in accessing financing. However, it was unusual that a single association was to take the lead for two urban renewal areas, rather than only

26
In January 1966, President Lyndon B. Johnson announced a new initiative to tackle these problems, a "demonstration cities program," conceived as a small, but symbolic part of his larger Great Society and War on Poverty initiatives. By mid-1966, as the Model Cities bill was making its way through the US Congress, and the Twin Parks Study was approved, Mayor Lindsay, in anticipation of the forthcoming federal money and eager to demonstrate his philosophical alignment with Johnson's programs, launched what he called a "head start" to the Model Cities program. This took the form of a "vest pocket housing and rehabilitation" program. As its name implied, the focus was on the new construction of small-scale housing on infill sites coupled with the renovation of existing buildings. The administration identified four study sites in the so-called worst areas of the city: Milbank-Frawley Circle at the northeast corner of Central Park in Harlem East New York and Bedford-Stuyvesant in Brooklyn and Mott Haven in the Bronx. These study areas were to be kernels of the future, much larger Model Cities Neighborhoods; Twin Parks constituted the fifth of these vest pocket housing study areas, but it was never conceived as part of the Model Cities program. Model Cities was officially signed into law in November 1966. For more on the five studies, see my article "1966 Can Be The Year of Rebirth for American Cities," San Rocco 14: 66, April 2018, 100–109.

27
The most detailed account of the consultation process in a vest pocket housing study is provided in Walter Thabit, *How East New York Became a Ghetto*, New York: New York University Press, 2003. On the Twin Parks process, there are neither meeting minutes of the various public consultations nor records in public archives on the Twin Parks process. The best summaries are provided by Chapter 4, "Neighborhood Planning and Community Participation," of Jonathan Barnett, *Urban Design as Public Policy: Practical Methods for Improving Cities*, New York: Architectural Record Books, 1974; and Myles Weintraub and Marco Zicarelli, "The Tale of Twin Parks," *Architectural Forum* (June 1973), p. 54–55.

cupola serving as a highly visible beacon that declared its patrons' commitments to contemporaneity in both ethical and aesthetic realms. Flush with investment capital and creative energy, reunified Berlin appeared to many as a realm of boundless possibility, fueled by the euphoria of wide-scale construction. Throughout, a tacit but widespread faith in contemporary architecture's power—to heal a traumatized city, to materialize elusive historical sensibilities and to shape the social life of its users—fueled the building boom within the reunified *Haupstadt*.

At the same time, however, the process of Berlin's "rebuilding" also revealed an increasingly pervasive if rarely voiced doubt that architecture alone could address the accelerating challenges of the twenty-first century. Three decades after reunification, the heroics of the starchitect system (a system that has been challenged in recent years but by no means dismantled) now largely appear powerless to address the most pressing issues of the day, both national and global. The theatrical milieu in which Berlin's gleaming new cityscape was constructed, with renowned architects laboring to manifest symbolic meaning in impressive and novel buildings, seems far removed

from Germany's actual material conditions today, including the capital city's mounting debt, the persistent economic disparities between east and west, the alarming resurgence of far-right extremism, and the increasing fragility of the European Union. These internal problems, of course, relate inextricably to matters of global scale—the ascendance of nationalism and authoritarianism worldwide; the constant threat of cyber insecurity and cyberterrorism; the rapid acceleration of the climate emergency; the newly complex problem of global public health; and the human cost of ongoing conflict and its resulting refugee crisis. Berlin's post-reunification architecture, especially that which was government-sponsored, aimed to convey openness, transparency, and accessibility. But perhaps its designers, both politicians and architects, underestimated the ethical preeminence of questions related to *safety* that the new millennium would pose for public architecture.

In the end, the euphoria was short-lived; by the mid-2000s, many began to declare Berlin's rebuilding a resounding failure.[2] The architectural targets of this widespread sense of disappointment accumulated in the city center,

2
As Simone Hain described it, to use only one example, "The city's grandiose development project is turning into a failure." Hain, "Berlin's Urban Development Discourse: Symbolic Action and the Articulation of Hegemonic Interests," in *The Berlin Reader: A Compendium on Urban Change and Activism*, eds. Matthias Bernt, Britta Grell, and Andrej Holm (Bielefeld: Transcript Verlag, 2014), 60.

sponsoring individual building projects. The emergence of the "Twin Parks Association" thus also attests to the dearth of other institutions able to take on this kind of organizational task and financial risk, reminding us that "community participation" is rarely a matter of independently acting individuals but often a matter of whether there are already existing organizations who have the capacity to assert their interests.

And what came out of this process, in terms of "a developed architectural-planning idea," which the five young architects had argued was necessary to advance a new planning process? In April 1967, the team presented the study to city officials with a proposal that showed that overall coherence and legibility at the urban scale could be achieved through small-scale, infill interventions and the rehabilitation of existing properties. The architects recognized the topography as the opportunity to do so: the escarpment in the west—sometimes dropping off near-vertically toward Webster Avenue—and the expansive flat terrain to the east—the sea of trees in the Bronx Zoo beyond Southern Boulevard. In effect, while not calling it so, the architects proposed two linear cities, much in vogue at this time, but rather than advocating for singular megastructures, their proposal was to be realized incrementally, piece by piece. With their proposal for the Bronx, the five young architects were thus revising the proposal for Harlem they had exhibited a year earlier at the Museum of Modern Art's *The New City: Architecture and Urban Renewal*.[28] For Park Avenue, they had proposed a multi-use megastructure above the elevated rail lines; this would have required a level of planning and investment that was unlikely to happen, something that likely influenced their linear, but incremental vision for the Bronx.

Just like there is little documentation of the debates, considerations or goals articulated as part of the community process, little documentation remains of the actual proposal. An eight-page, black and white brochure with two photographs and two fold-out axonometric plans is all there is. But these fold-out plans are what distinguish the proposal from its vest pocket housing and rehabilitation peers. The designers' intent is clear: to create a sense of density and cohesion within the selected areas. New and existing buildings are barely distinguishable, the former shown merely by slightly thicker lines. The proposals indicate, without further describing or showing in larger-scale drawings, two housing types. The first is the high-rise slab, employed in atypical situations and as an urban marker. The second type is a mid-rise unit, six stories high, utilized for infill situations to create a continuous street front. With rare exception, most existing streets remain, but a few are de-mapped to create larger and, therefore, more easily developed sites. The exuberantly written text compensates for the sparseness of the visual material. Its authors had no problem linking visions for particular parts of the site—to "transform a seven-block stretch facing the Bronx Zoo from an area of gasoline filling stations, automobile repair shops, and parking lots into a first-rate

28
In parallel to the work at Twin Parks, the five architects had, as the "Columbia team," developed a proposal for Harlem with the goal of minimizing resident displacement, for the Museum of Modern Art. *The New City: Architecture and Urban Renewal* was on view from January through March, 1967.

and its most glaring examples were the public and private sites whose design had been zealously controlled by government oversight. Projects directed by official interests, from the oddly incoherent government district to the star-studded, albeit lackluster, ensemble at nearby Potsdamer Platz became symbolic for critics of Berlin's perceived inability to rise to its own historical occasion. In the words of critic Martin Filler, the city amounted to an architectural "lost opportunity."[3] For many, the root of the problem lay with the government itself, whether local, state or federal, and whether acting as sole client or within one of the many "public-private partnerships" forged with private-sector corporations during the capital city's rebuilding. Some committed progressives accused the Bundesrepublik of not going far enough to define a clear and assertive vision for reunified Germany's architectural identity. On the other hand, free-market fanatics blamed government meddling and mismanagement for stifling architectural creativity and dampening the potential of individual projects to enliven key areas of the city. As one journalist described it, the problem was "too much government money, too much

top-down planning, and too great a desire to build a tourist attraction masked as a symbol. So far, the top-down planning model has produced what is at best a tourist trap, at worst an outright failure."[4] The city's luminous examples of adventurous architecture, of which Foster's Reichstag was emblematic, seemed to have been realized in spite of these forces rather than having been auspiciously guided by the government's big plans and heroic aspirations.

Yet the notion of failure itself opens interesting and revealing views beyond the blind spots of contemporary architecture culture. Perhaps, by deflating the iconicity of monumental signature projects, the concept of failure prompts us to look instead to the infrastructure that supports and subtends what is ordinarily identified as architecture for the public. Therefore, in considering the ethical commitments of Berlin's contemporary architecture, we might do well to look past the dazzling dome of the Reichstag to attend as well to the city's airports. After all, the ethics of the contemporary city are made vividly manifest through the liminal zones within its mass transit infrastructure, shaping what the sociologist Manuel Castells has characterized as the

3
Martin Filler, "Berlin: The Lost Opportunity," *The New York Review of Books* 17 (November 1, 2001): 28-31.

4
Dave Copeland, "Poor, Sexy Berlin: The Failure of Urban Planning," *Reason* 36 (December 2004): 56.

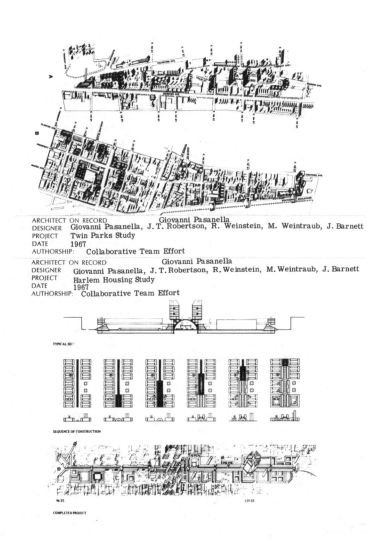

ARCHITECT ON RECORD   Giovanni Pasanella
DESIGNER   Giovanni Pasanella, J. T. Robertson, R. Weinstein, M. Weintraub, J. Barnett
PROJECT   Twin Parks Study
DATE   1967
AUTHORSHIP: Collaborative Team Effort

ARCHITECT ON RECORD   Giovanni Pasanella
DESIGNER   Giovanni Pasanella, J. T. Robertson, R. Weinstein, M. Weintraub, J. Barnett
PROJECT   Harlem Housing Study
DATE   1967
AUTHORSHIP: Collaborative Team Effort

TYPICAL SECTION

SEQUENCE OF CONSTRUCTION

96 ST.   125 ST.

COMPLETED PROJECT

Marketing sheet showing the linear-city approach as projected by the Columbia team for the Bronx (top) and Harlem, Giovanni Pasanella, no date (c. 1969).

"spaces of flows" that regulate the movement of bodies and capital.[5]

• • •

Much like the central railway station that formed a crucial node of the master plan for the government district, as designed by Axel Schultes and Charlotte Frank in 1992, the eventual construction of a new airport was understood to be essential to the success of the *Hauptstadt*. The airport's significance was due in part to the city's historically unique infrastructure. After reunification, the city maintained three functioning airports: Tempelhof, the city's original airfield, and Schönefeld and Tegel, which had respectively served East and West Berlin. In 1991, the federal government, along with the states of Berlin and Brandenburg, formed a limited liability partnership (known as Berlin Brandenburg Flughafen Holding GmbH, or BBF) to fund the construction of a new facility, supplanting the existing three and realizing the "single airport concept" proposed during reunification. However, as with many other projects throughout the city, the momentum of the early 1990s slowed as the decade wore on. By 1996, BBF had resolved to site the new airport on a parcel of land

5
Manuel Castells, "Space of Flows, Space of Places: Materials for a Theory of Urbanism in the Information Age," in *Comparative Planning Cultures*, ed. Bishwapriya Sanyal (New York and London: Routledge, 2005), 45–63. For a discussion of the "transnational capitalist class" and the role of mobility in contemporary architecture culture, see Leslie Sklair, "The Transnational Capitalist Class and Contemporary Architecture in Globalizing Cities," *International Journal of Urban and Regional Research* 29 (September 2005): 485–500. For an example of recent critical scholarship on airport infrastructure, see Max Hirsh, "Design Aesthetics of Transborder Infrastructure in the Pearl River Delta," *Journal of the Society of Architectural Historians* 73 (March 2014): 137–152.

6
"Privatisierung von Hauptstadt-Flughafen gescheitert," *Frankfurter Allgemeine Zeitung*, May 22, 2003, https://www.faz.net/aktuell/wirtschaft/berlin-privatisierung-von-hauptstadt-flughafen-gescheitert-1104085.html.

adjacent to the existing Schönefeld and to incorporate some of its infrastructure. Furthermore, it had farmed the project out to a private investor, retaining the Hochtief consortium to own, construct, and operate the airport. In the first of many setbacks, Hochtief's competition in the bidding process, the rival firm IVG, filed a successful lawsuit alleging that the government review process had been biased. By the end of 1999, the construction contract had been annulled and the project seemed to be back to square one.

In the wake of what was widely viewed as a conspicuous failure of privatization, officials changed tack, deciding in 2003 that the new airport would instead be publicly owned and operated.[6] BBF rebranded itself as FBB (Flughafen Berlin Brandenburg GmbH), with ownership shared by Berlin, Brandenburg and the federal government. Throughout the early 2000s, the project was thwarted by numerous delays and setbacks. In 2004, around 4,000 residents of the neighborhoods around Schönefeld filed suit against the government in objection to the noise pollution that the new airport would cause. The residents eventually lost a protracted court battle with no possibility of appeal, but the legal proceedings slowed

Twins Parks Housing, Giovanni Pasanella.

the project considerably.[7] After a
decade and a half of planning with
little forward motion, ground was
finally broken in 2006 on the future
Willy Brandt Berlin Brandenburg
International Airport (BER), named
after the Nobel-Peace-Prize-winning
former mayor of West Berlin. The
terminal buildings were designed
by Meinhard von Gerkan, whose firm
gmp (Gerkan, Marg & Partners) had
previously completed both the
vast new railway station in the
government district and, some 40
years earlier, Tegel's famously
idiosyncratic hexagonal terminal
building—both widely regarded as
successes. With its futuristic
glass-and-steel facades, polished
marble floors and soaring, mul-
tileveled interiors tastefully
warmed with faux-walnut paneling,
the architecture of the new airport
would speak the global
vernacular of international air
travel at the turn of the new
millennium.

   The design circulated widely
in 2007-2008, as the government
attempted to revive national enthusiasm for this vital symbol of
the capital's growing touristic
popularity. This time, the optimism appeared warranted, at least
in terms of the nation's financial
outlook. While the European economy reeled from the 2008 global

[7]
"Postcard from
Berlin: Can a New
Airport Make this
City Soar?," Der
Spiegel, March 16,
2006, https://
www.spiegel.de/
international/
postcard-from-berlin-
can-a-new-airport-
make-this-city-
soar-a-406321.html.

A vacant terminal at Berlin's Brandenburg Airport.

residential area"—to universal goals that positioned this study as central to a much broader effort. Most strikingly, they articulated a wider understanding of "community," one that connected the neighborhood to the nation and world beyond.[29]

In June 1967, the City's relevant land-use agencies approved the plan. This meant that sites could be acquired, applications for federal funding could be launched, and that architects could be commissioned to move ahead with individual designs. It meant that the pilot project launched by the five young architects to reform the city's planning process had—thanks to a range of institutions under pressure to reconsider their responsibility toward a broader society, including an academic and a philanthropic partner, a Bronx-based neighborhood group and a Midtown-based cultural hub—created the conditions for implementation. Not only this, it created the basis for further institutional inventions: the creation of the Urban Design Group within city government and a professionalized Twin Parks Association as the project sponsor. Some of the outcomes, however, were not those the five architects may have originally aimed for when they argued that "the institutions must be designed before the buildings" two years earlier.

29
All quotes from New York City Housing and Development Administration, Twin Parks Vest Pocket Housing, p. 8.

30
Department of City Planning, Newsletter, October 1967, p.1 (Yale, Jonathan Barnett Papers, Group 1733, Box 3, Folder "Urban Design, first National Conference, Oct 18-21, 1982.)

31
This is how the UDG advertised in a newsletter dedicated to the subject. Department of City Planning, Newsletter, October 1967. (Yale, Jonathan Barnett Papers, Group 1733, Box 3, Folder "Urban Design, first National Conference, Oct 18-21, 1982.)

IV. Groups, Associations, Corporations: New Institutions and Their Afterlives

Imaginative urban design is no longer an idealistic dream. We are now finding practical ways to design the city, based on a creative partnership between government and private enterprise.[30]

The process leading to the Twin Parks Study plan, as well as its approval, led to two simultaneous institutional spin-offs: one at the city level and one at the local level. In April of 1967, just as the Twin Parks Study was wrapping up, and the MoMA exhibition came to a close, the Department of City Planning officially launched the Urban Design Group (UDG). In a department newsletter, which featured a photograph of a model for a Twin Parks building on its cover, the UDG was described as establishing "a new dimension in urban planning."[31] City Planning Commission Chairman, Donald Elliott, defined its relevance through the focus on implementation: the UDG's mission was to develop new ways to incite the private sector, in "partnership" with the public sector, to deliver better design and more public amenities through zoning and other tools. The "community" did not seem to be worth mentioning in this new partnership. The creation of the UDG had immediate consequences for the five architects, with the exception of Giovanni Pasanella, who became the principals of this newly formed entity. Pasanella chose to remain in private practice, likely motivated by the prospect of actually being able to take on commissions to design the new housing— "the chance to build."

At the community level, the Twin Parks Association (TPA) incorporated as an official housing development entity in late September 1967. As stated in its articles of

financial crisis, Germany's GDP proved relatively resilient; in the face of teetering economies in Greece, Spain and Italy, *The Wall Street Journal* wondered, "Is Germany Europe's Safest Bet?"[8] The answer, according to the international corporate development magazine *Site Selection*, was a resounding yes. The country's economic strength was due in no small part to its capital city's grand new airport, as *Site Selection* suggested: "Some have suggested that taking on such a massive project during a global recession was unwise, but in truth not one single German state recorded growth of less than 3.2 percent in the first half of 2011, a rather startling and remarkable feat." It was thus clear, the magazine concluded, that the new mega-airport would have a long-term positive economic effect, not only in the capital but throughout the country, making it the "safest investment spot" in the eurozone.[9] On track to open in March 2012, the airport's future finally looked rosy, while its contributions to national security—from an economic perspective, that is—seemed assured.

Yet once again, the optimism proved unfounded, as costs, delays and scandals mounted. Beginning in 2012, it became clear that major

8
Thorold Barker, "Is Germany Europe's Safest Bet?," *The Wall Street Journal*, video, June 5, 2012, https://www.wsj.com/video/is-germany-europe-safest-bet/93BD887D-9B28-411D-A533-9A79AA9A29A2.html.

9
Adam Jones-Kelley, "Is Germany Europe's Safest Bet?," *Site Selection*, November 1, 2011, 868.

Drawings of Tempelhof Airport by architect Ernst Sagebiel.

incorporation, its purposes were "to promote and improve living conditions ... and to sponsor and promote the construction and rehabilitation of housing in that area for persons of low and moderate income, including families displaced from urban renewal areas or as a result of governmental action, for whom no adequate housing exists."[32] Its mode of operation was to be resolutely nonprofit: "No earnings of the Association or any such corporation shall inure to the benefit of, nor shall any of the assets thereof be distributed to, any individual or any private firm, corporation or other association; provided, however that compensation may be paid or services rendered and interest on money borrowed."[33] As announced in the press, the TPA sought to launch this community-based development process with a 160-unit apartment building.[34]

Implementation, however, was not so easy. By 1968, the urgency of urban problems coupled with the culture wars and opposition against the war in Vietnam, which was consuming ever-growing parts of the federal budget, had made new forms of development like Twin Parks more difficult. Federal funding was being redesigned. In August 1968, the Housing and Urban Development Act introduced a new series of programs. Most importantly, the Section 236 mortgage subsidy replaced Section 221d3, emphasizing production—with greater quantity and efficiency—by now giving for-profit developers preferable conditions over non-profit sponsors. This had immediate consequences for the Twin Parks Association. By late 1968, the TPA found that securing federal funds proved to be more difficult than expected. Moreover, the political future under newly elected President Richard Nixon seemed uncertain. In the name of implementation, the TPA decided to hand off its development rights for all sites not already co-sponsored by other entities to the newly formed New York State

Urban Development Corporation (UDC). This public-interest authority—itself an institutional innovation—had unprecedented development rights. More importantly, it was able to raise private capital for new housing by issuing bonds that would surely move the projects forward.[35] While the TPA would remain the "community sponsor" in this arrangement, by agreeing to work with the UDC, it had given up any semblance of community control. The TPA consoled itself by pointing to the fact that all involved agreed on the importance of "good" design.[36] Indeed, the UDC, together with the TPA and the UDG, selected Richard Meier, James Stewart Polshek, Prentice, Chan, Ohlhausen and, yes, Giovanni Pasanella as architects for the building projects. The design was widely recognized in the nation-

32
"Articles of Association," in Twin Parks Study (1967), Canadian Center for Architecture, Giovanni Pasanella Papers, Subseries AP154.S1.1967.PR01.SS1.001.

33
Ibid.

34
This was the site that would later become part of Richard Meier's Twin Parks Northeast. n.a., "Housing Project Planned in Bronx," NYT, September 28, 1967.

35
There is substantial recent scholarship on the UDC. To cite just two: for a recent article explaining its origin of the UDC's funding mechanism, see Eric Peterson, "The Urban Development Corporation's 'Imaginative Use of Credit': Creating Capital for Affordable Housing,"

Journal of Urban History, September 2018, https://doi.org/10.1177/0096144218796466 and a book focused on the UDC's director, Edward Logue: Lizabeth Cohen, *Saving America's Cities: Ed Logue and the Struggle to Renew Urban America in the Suburban Age*, New York: Farrar, Straus and Giroux, 2019.

36
As Mario Zicarelli, a Catholic pastor and head of the TPA would later write, "The decision was made an easier one with the knowledge that the TPA's last and most important demand had been met: the architects to be selected would be of outstanding ability." Myles Weintraub and Marco Zicarelli, "The Tale of Twin Parks," *Architectural Forum* (June 1973): p. 54–55.

problems with the building's fire protection and alarm system, constructed by the European technology company Imtech, would demand many years and millions of euros to repair. This would be only one of numerous structural and technical flaws to hamper the airport's progress in the coming years. Meanwhile, charges of corruption surfaced in the press, including the bribery of an airport construction official by an Imtech manager in 2012.[10] Perhaps most embarrassingly, an official 2013 study revealed that the airport, as it had been conceived, would already be operating at the limit of its capacity when it opened, necessitating a total redesign well after construction was underway.[11] When the architect von Gerkan objected, his contract was unceremoniously terminated.[12] Later that year, the opening of the airport was postponed indefinitely, prompting *Schadenfreude*-laden quips about "German efficiency" from the international press.[13] In a particularly hard blow, the director of the Willy Brandt Foundation publicly stated that he regretted giving permission to attach Brandt's name to such a disastrous project.[14] The following year, Berlin's mayor Klaus Wowereit resigned, in part due to his role in the mismanagement of the airport.

10
In August 2016, the BER manager was found guilty of accepting 150,000 euros in bribes at a 2012 gas station rendezvous with the Imtech contact. See Thorsten Metzner, "Ehemaliger BER-Manager gibt Erhalt von Schmiergeld zu," *Der Tagesspiegel*, August 23, 2016, https://www.tagesspiegel.de/berlin/korruption-am-berliner-flughafen-ehemaliger-ber-manager-gibt-erhalt-von-schmiergeld-zu/14443604.html.

11
The impetus for the redesign came partly from the desire to accommodate the A380-Airbus, with its capacity of up to 800 passengers. See Jobst Fiedler and Alexander Wendler, "Berlin Brandenburg Airport," in Genia Koste and Fiedler, eds., *Large Infrastructure Projects in Germany: Between Ambition and Realities* (London: Palgrave Macmillan, 2018), 115. Behind the scenes, the aircraft would eventually pose yet another problem for the airport, as it was announced in 2019 that production of the plane would cease in 2021.

12
Von Gerkan later published a book on his experience with the project, declaring the airport a "self-made catastrophe." See Meinhard von Gerkan, *Black Box BER: Vom Flughafen Berlin Brandenburg und anderen Großbaustellen* (Munich: Bastei-Lübbe-Verlag, 2013).

13
See, for example, Nicola Clark, "Airport Delays Undermine Image of German Efficiency," *The New York Times*, September 4, 2012, B3, and Derek Scally, "New Airport Proves Not to Be Best Example of German Efficiency," *The Irish Times*, January 12, 2013, https://www.irishtimes.com/news/new-airport-proves-not-to-be-best-example-of-german-efficiency-1.957296.

14
Interview with Wolfram Hoppenstedt, "Verliert der Airport seinen Namen 'Willy Brandt'?," *Das Bild*, January 15, 2013, https://www.bild.de/regional/berlin/flughafen-berlin-brandenburg/verliert-der-airport-seinen-namen-willy-brandt--28103598.bild.html.

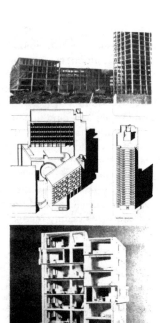

UDC in TWIN PARKS

In September 1970, construction began on the first of 1554 units of new housing in the Twin Parks section of the Bronx, between Crotona and Bronx Parks. An additional 729 units are scheduled to start construction this summer. In close cooperation with the City and the Twin Parks Association, the community sponsor behind Twin Parks renewal, UDC is building this housing for low and moderate-income families in four different project areas (see map).

Long-standing Need for New Housing

The need for more housing is well-known to the residents of Twin Parks. Many of the old buildings are badly deteriorated. And many homes have been demolished over the years for public projects.

Not Only New Housing

The new development—to prevent overburdening existing community facilities—will include three day-care centers, a special childhood center, more than 27,000 square feet of commercial space, community meeting rooms, and off-street parking, a new intermediate school (I.S. 137), and a Youth Services Center.

A Statewide Program

In addition to Twin Parks, plans are underway for UDC housing, commercial, and industrial developments in the West Bronx, Brooklyn, Manhattan and Queens, and in 24 other cities and towns across the State. Construction is getting started this year on nearly 7,500 housing units, in 12 different cities.

(upper left) Twin Parks Northeast (Richard Meier & Associates, architects)—two sites under construction and one to start construction this summer generally bounded by Garden and E. 183rd Sts., Crotona Ave., and Southern Blvd. for 523 units, a day-care center, shops, and vest pocket park on 3.4 acres at $18.3 million development cost.

(middle left) Twin Parks Southeast (James Stewart Polshek, architect)—two sites on E. 180 St. between Southern Boulevard and Mapes Avenue for 408 units, a day-care center, and shops on 5.3 acres at $16.4 million development cost.

Applications for UDC housing are not yet being accepted. Extensive public announcements will be made to show how and when to file such applications. The first Twin Parks tenants should be moving into their apartments by the Fall of 1972.

(lower left) Twin Parks Southwest (Giovanni Pasanella, architect)—sectional model showing typical apartments on three sites between Webster and Valentine Aves., north of Tremont Ave. and south of E. 181st St., for 536 units, a day-care center, and shops on 4 acres at $20.9 million development cost.

(upper right) Twin Parks Northwest (Prentice and Chan, Ohlhausen, architects)—two sites. This shows site bounded by Marion and Webster Aves., north of E. 184th St. The other site is between Webster and Tiebout Aves. north of E. 180th St. Total: 334 units and a center for preschool children on 2.6 acres at $12.4 million development cost.

"UDC in Twin Parks." Pamphlet explaining the Urban Development Corporation's involvement in the vest pocket housing project, no date (c. 1971).

By 2018, yet more money had been spent but the airport seemed no closer to completion. The BBC reported that the so-called "ghost airport" "looks exactly like every other major modern airport in Europe, except for one big problem: more than seven years after it was originally supposed to open, it still stands empty."[15] Despite the fact that no movement of people or planes was transpiring through this Brobdingnagian space of flows, the structure was nonetheless filled with ghostly motions and gestures. At a nearby airport hotel, a small staff reported to work in an empty building, regularly mopping floors, airing linens and checking taps for the nonexistent clientele. At one point, a glitch in the computer system made it impossible to turn off the lights in the terminal for a stretch of several months, skyrocketing energy costs and making the airport appear eerily occupied from a distance. In a tunnel below the terminal, Deutsche Bahn conductors piloted passenger-less trains once every weekday at precisely 10:26 a.m. to the airport's new, vacant railway station in order to keep air moving through the tunnels and prevent the tracks from rusting. Empty luggage carousels rotated spectrally to prevent their belts from atrophying. Expensive monitors parasitically displaying information for flights at Schönefeld eventually burned out; all 750 were eventually replaced, at a cost of 500,000 euros. Tourists — some of them German citizens keen to see exactly how their taxes were being spent at the now-infamous money pit — arrived in double-decker buses to survey the construction site from an observation platform, gazing over a windswept landscape of dormant runways, desolate parking lots and empty terminals. Along Unter den Linden, souvenir shops sold postcards blazoned with the facetious phrase "No one intends to open an airport," an ironic appropriation of Walter Ulbricht's notorious dissimulation in June 1961 — "No one intends to build a wall" — only weeks before the first coils of barbed wire were laid. A pair of locals designed and sold a board game called "*UnberechenB€R*," the objective of which was to waste the most taxpayer euros possible.[16] The sardonic slogan on the front of the box read, "Building an airport — it's not child's play!"

If the Reichstag circulated internationally as the signature image of Germany's post-reunification optimism, the new airport became the face of its humbling dénouement. By 2016, a decade after

15
Emily Schultheis, "Whatever Happened to Berlin's Deserted 'Ghost' Airport?," BBC Worklife, November 5, 2018, https://www.bbc.com/worklife/article/20181030-what-happened-to-berlins-ghost-airport.

16
Ava Johnson, "Airport Delay Byproduct," *Exberliner*, November 21, 2017, https://www.exberliner.com/whats-on/insider-tips/airport-delay-byproduct/.

Twin Parks Housing, James Stewart Polshek.

ground was broken, the only way for the public to experience the airport was from a 105-foot-tall "InfoTower," housing an observation deck and a gift shop ingenuously selling a variety of souvenirs embellished with the airport logo. As Claire Colomb has noted, this last gasp of reunification euphoria was part of a larger trend: "While the 'spectacularization' of the built environment faded away with the completion of Berlin's largest urban development projects, it did not disappear."[17] The skeletal, decommissioned quality of the airport construction site uncannily echoed the skyline of cranes that defined the city's euphoric rebuilding, yet the ceaselessness of construction on the site now read as farce. The apparent indolence still felt foreign to a city recovering from the whiplash of rapid post-*Wende* change, and the failure of contemporary architecture seemed endemic. "Germany's long-awaited Berlin airport falls short of expectations—such as opening," declared the *Los Angeles Times* satirically in May 2019.[18] In November of that year, officials announced, with minimal pomp, that the airport would open on October 31, 2020, at a final cost of 7.3 billion euros—an astronomical sum nearly four times the original

17
Claire Colomb, "Staging Urbanism: Construction Site Tourism and the City as Exhibition," in *Staging the New Berlin: Place Marketing and the Politics of Urban Reinvention Post-1989* (Abingdon: Routledge, 2012), 216.

18
Erik Kirschbaum, "Germany's Long-Awaited Berlin airport Falls Short of Expectations—Such as Opening," *The Los Angeles Times*, May 20, 2019, https://www.latimes.com/world/la-fg-germany-berlin-empty-airport-20190520-story.html.

19
Over the past decade, the government has spent millions of euros each month simply to maintain the building. Steven Perlberg, "Berlin's 'Ghost' Airport Might Finally Open—Billions over Budget and Eight Years Late," *Fortune*, January 26, 2020, https://fortune.com/2020/01/26/berlin-brandenburg-airport-open/.

20
Arthur Sullivan, "Berlin's New Airport: A Potted History," *Deutsche Welle*, December 12, 2019, https://www.dw.com/en/berlins-new-airport-a-potted-history/a-41813465.

estimate.[19] Journalists wondered cynically whether the announcement truly marked "the beginning of the end, or merely the end of the beginning."[20] At the time of this writing, the date of the grand opening remains in place—while over the course of only a few months, the future of air travel itself has been thrown into turmoil by a global pandemic whose final human and economic toll will likely remain unknown for years to come.

• • •

In 2008, about three miles due south of the Brandenburg Gate and 10 miles northwest of the new international airport, planes were grounded at Tempelhof Airport in premature anticipation of BER's opening, prompting a contentious discussion of the old airfield's future. As one of Germany's oldest airports, with infrastructure dating to 1923, it was also firmly embedded in both the urban fabric and the history of the city. Constructed at the southern edge of Kreuzberg, Tempelhof was one of Europe's largest pre-World War II airports, built in the very earliest days of civilian air travel. The site, a wide-open green plain on the Teltow Plateau unfolding south of the city, had originally

al and international architectural press at the time. And yet the housing, while made affordable by local, state and federal subsidies, would be developed, built, owned and managed by for-profit entities—not the TPA. So, while the community's physical plan had been implemented (the same measure of success defined by Robertson in 1965), it was on an entirely different financial model than had had been envisioned earlier with an entirely different new set of stakeholders: private investors.

The further fate of the Twin Parks Association is also indicative of this broader shift from a belief in gradual, non-profit based approach for housing to for-profit driven models that prioritized production. The TPA's loss of the control over the development and management of the new housing, thereby, become a mere facilitator for-profit development, foreshadowing what "community development" means today. Since the mid-1970s, across the United States, such Community Development Corporations (CDCs) have become the main developers of low-income housing. The locally based organizations, whose mission is promoting the economic and social wellbeing of their neighborhoods, have not been able to pursue these goals without a partnership with the private sector. Given current funding programs, the private sector is central both for financing—in the form of corporate investment through the low-income housing tax credit (LIHTC)—and as a partner in actual construction and management. To achieve and maintain permanent non-profit status is as difficult to accomplish today as it was fifty years ago. To balance between an original mission of advocating for local interests and the pressure to fund itself through development fees is not an easy task.[37] The TPA itself dissolved, without trace, in the mid-1970s; in 1981, some of its portfolio was transferred to a newly formed CDC, the Belmont Arthur Avenue

Local Development Corporation (BAALDC), which continues to operate on the community-capital model.

The fate of the Urban Design Group, too, reflects the shift toward public-private partnerships, which has eclipsed both non-profit development models and a public-sector lead in planning. The UDG was renamed and re-constituted multiple times over the decades, but its central function remains—as the opening quote to this section shows—to wrest some measure of public benefit from the private sector. As Jonathan Barnett pointed out in 1974, looking back at his work for the UDG: "The game of real estate goes on and some method needs to be found to direct and improve it."[38] Today, over forty years later, the role of urban design within the Department of City Planning largely consists of rezoning the city's low-income areas with that aim.

And what about those academic institutions founded amidst the mid-1960s sense of urgency that something must be done? The fate of Abrams' Institute for Urban Environment demonstrates how difficult it is to conceive of ways to connect research, design speculation and

37
For an excellent, albeit uncritical, history of the emergence, evolution and reasons for the endurance of community development corporations in the US as a main vehicle for producing below-market rate housing in partnership with the private sector, see David J. Erickson, *The Housing Policy Revolution: Networks and Neighborhoods*, Washington, DC: The Urban Institute Press, 2009.

38
Barnett, *Urban Design as Public Policy*, p. 16.

served as military drilling and parade grounds for the Berlin garrison. Its proximity to the city center made it useful to the National Socialists when they took power, while its dramatic alignment with Karl Friedrich Schinkel's neo-Gothic Prussian National Monument for the Liberation Wars atop the Kreuzberg appealed symbolically to Nazi hubris. Albert Speer's steroidal north-south axis for the city would have been anchored at its southern terminus by the expanded airport, intended to serve as the international gateway to the *Welthauptstadt Germania*.

Between 1935 and 1936, a massive terminal building was constructed from a design by the architect Ernst Sagebiel, fresh off his successful completion of the Ministry of Aviation along Wilhelmstrasse. Consistent with the "Luftwaffe modern" style Sagebiel developed for Hermann Göring's headquarters, the airport was characterized by a disciplined grouping of architectural volumes, in this case a series of curved, slab-like segments that responded to the adjacent circles of a ceremonial entry plaza and the Tempelhof Field.[21] From the plaza, a sightline would be opened northward through Speer's gargantuan (and never-built) triumphal arch, visually connecting the airport to other symbolic structures testifying to the Third Reich's world conquest. The facades were treated with Sagebiel's characteristic streamlined classicism, and the terminal interiors were simplified and modern, typical of Nazi architecture in its techno-triumphalist mode. Like the Ministry of Aviation, the airport building has remained standing into the present — both strangely intact traces of Nazism whose ongoing use is evidence of the complex intertwining of classicism and modernism in the architecture of the twentieth century.[22] Despite its unsavory political pedigree, Tempelhof's architecture remained well-regarded enough for Norman Foster, a longtime flight enthusiast and amateur pilot, to describe it, in 2015, as "one of the really great buildings of the modern age;" indeed, for Foster, it is "the mother of all airports."[23] To be sure, Tempelhof had accrued positive political valence in the interim owing to its central role in the Berlin Airlift of 1948-49, when Allied planes dropped millions of tons of food and supplies to citizens blockaded in West Berlin after the Soviet Union closed land routes into the city.

Upon the government's announcement in 2008 that all future air

21
Elke Dittrich, *Ernst Sagebiel: Leben und Werk* (1892-1970) (Berlin: Lukas Verlag, 2005), 14. In the late 1920s, Sagebiel worked in the office of Erich Mendelsohn before joining the NSDAP in the early 1930s. The modernist tendencies that are apparent in his later work are frequently attributed to the influence of his former employer.

22
This intertwining of tendencies is what Jeffrey Herf famously and controversially characterized as "reactionary modernism" in Herf, *Reactionary Modernism: Technology, Culture and Politics in Weimar and the Third Reich* (Cambridge: Cambridge University Press, 1984).

23
Alexandra Lange, "Seven Leading Architects Defend the World's Most Hated Buildings," *The New York Times Magazine*, June 5, 2015, https://nyti.ms/219RZJ9. Nicolai Ouroussoff has identified Tempelhof as a precedent for Foster's terminal building at Beijing International Airport. See Ouroussoff, "In Changing Face of Beijing, a Look at the New China," *The New York Times*, July 13, 2008, A1.

action on the ground in a university setting. In 1972, only six years after it had started to operate, James Stewart Polshek, the newly appointed dean of Columbia's School of Architecture, closed the Institute. This was part of a reorganization in which Polshek moved urban design to architecture, distinct and separate from the questions of policy he assigned to planning.[39] The legacies of this division are still with us today, not only at Columbia. Yet, Abrams's Institute was not the last of the school's attempt to somehow set up a "research arm" while also trying to answer to the demands that the school address socio-economic questions by drawing on philanthropic support. In September 2019, for example, Columbia announced the creation of the IDC Foundation Professor of Housing Design. The endowed position has goals, if not methods, remarkably similar to those Abrams articulated for his Institute: "The funds ... will encourage the development of new housing models urgently needed to address shifts in demographics, household composition, challenges of climate resilience, affordability, and the widening inequality gap."[40] Developing new housing models to address these challenges will only have a chance at success if these models consider design in its mutual entanglements with financial and political conditions.

V. Two Questions

The Twin Parks Study was never about form for its own sake.[41] But it was also never just about political change, even in the initiators' views. What the story of the Twin Parks Study makes clear is that form, politics and finance are inextricably intertwined. It tells us that designers may have to be "politically astute" and recognize the need to "design the institutions before the buildings," sometimes taking on roles beyond the making of form, even if their ultimate goal is just that. However, with its trajectory from original intentions to institutional afterlives, the Twin Parks Study prompts me to question two assumptions which shape how we often conceive of architects' social responsibility today.

First: do the key criteria for evaluating plans result from community participation, whether or not they were implemented? "Implementation," understood as building, is what the five young architects stipulated at the time, and in the case of Twin Parks Study, indeed, the plan was largely realized. By 1974, most sites that had been designated for development were acquired and developed. This did not take place in the non-profit way the sponsors had originally envisioned but as low-income housing owned

39
In an email exchange between the author and Polshek in February 2018, he wrote: "I do not remember any specific action but it is possible that I simply transferred urban design to the architectural division so that the planning school could focus on policy not on anything related directly to bricks and mortar." Ironically, Polshek did so just the moment in which he added "Planning" to the school's name. Other schools of architecture, too, came to distance themselves from an involvement with planning, the social sciences and on-the-ground action. Princeton's Research Center for Urban and Environmental Planning, to which Chester Rapkin moved from Columbia in 1973, was closed in 1980. Concurrently, Princeton, in contrast to Columbia, dropped the name "Urban" from its name.

40
Columbia GSAAP, "Columbia GSAPP Receives Historic Donation to Advance the Study of Housing Design," September 10, 2019, https://www.arch.columbia.edu/news/idc-foundation-professor, accessed January 19, 2020.

41
A recent example of a scholar's emphasis on Twin Parks as built form, see Brent D. Ryan, *The Largest Art: A Measured Manifesto for a Plural Urbanism*, Cambridge, Mass: MIT Press 2017.

traffic would be channeled through the new main airport, thousands of Berlin residents protested, gathering signatures for a referendum to keep Tempelhof open and functioning. For many Berliners, especially those in the city's western districts, Tempelhof's central location made it both practical and historically significant. Yet the initiative was bootless, and the final commercial flight departed from the runway on October 30, 2008, as hundreds gathered for a candlelight vigil below. Though the site would no longer function as an airport, both federal and local governments put forth ambitious plans for its reuse. The range of proposals included a Berlin Airlift museum, a commercial space for startups, sports facilities and parks. In August 2009, city officials announced that the sprawling meadowland to the south of the terminal would be transformed into a public park and dedicated 60 million euros to its conversion.[24] At the same time, the city of Berlin became the sole owner of the park, purchasing remaining shares from the federal government at a cost of 35 million euros. At over 300 hectares, significantly larger than the city's beloved Tiergarten, the park proved enormously popular, attracting bicyclists, picnickers

24
A. J. Goldmann, "Repurposing Tempelhof," *The Wall Street Journal*, August 25, 2011, https://www.wsj.com/articles/SB1000142405 27023038231045763915727 09176418.

An aerial view of Berlin's shuttered Tempelhof Airport, as seen in 2016.

and managed by for-profit developers, made possible by local, state and federal funding. Affordability restrictions have expired in recent years; the projects have been sold and re-financed at enormous public expense. At the same time, the original impetus for the Twin Parks Study — to reform the city's local planning process in order to equip citizens appointed to local community boards with professional guidance — has remained unrealized.[42] Implementing this kind of institutional redesign may have had a far greater impact on addressing the inequities of urban life than building a certain number of housing units. How might we reconsider what implementation means, and how might we take into consideration a new measure of time when doing so?

Second: given the trajectory and afterlives of the Twin Parks Study, might we need to challenge the notion of "community" itself? Rather than invoking "community" as an unquestionably positive goal, might we rather need to ask, more precisely, as to who constitutes "the community," and, thereby, who has the right to speak for whom? Why do we use a malleable, imprecise term in the singular, rather than use notions in the plural — citizens, residents, owners or investors — to describe the multiplicity of interests in any one community at any given time? Defining the stakeholders and boundaries — of who is in and who is out — is key to defining the conditions for democracy. As designers, we need to better understand and articulate what is at stake and for whom in a democracy divided along lines of race, class, gender and political ideology. We need to ask, again and again: on whose terms? That, to me, is a powerful paradigm for urban design and a reason to situate design as inextricably connected to money and power.

42
For a critique and history of the limited power of community board system, see Paul Angotti, New York for Sale: Community Planning Confronts Global Real Estate, Cambridge, Mass: MIT Press, 2008. For a more recent take on the lack of power in community organizations in New York City and the increasingly conflicted role of planners therein, see Samuel Stein, *Capital City: Gentrification and the Real Estate State*, London/New York: Verso 2019.

and plant enthusiasts eager to
work in the community gardens lining its eastern edge. The undis-
turbed green space even became a
significant habitat for rare and
endangered bird species. In the
meantime, the airport's hangars
were used to host trade expositions
and auto shows. Though the passen-
ger hall remained empty, tenants,
including the Berlin police force
and a male strip club and revue
called "*La Vie en Rose*," rented
office space within the terminal,
supervised sternly from the Platz
der Luftbrücke by the sculptor and
Luftwaffe pilot Wilhelm Lemke's
bronze eagle's head.

In 2011, the city proposed to
sell a portion of the former airport's land to private developers
for the construction of several
new commercial areas, a zone of
office buildings and 4,700 homes.
A citizens' initiative called "100%
Tempelhofer Feld" fought back,
with its supporters protesting the
private acquisition of this public
land and arguing that increasing privatization in the capital
had been responsible for many of
its failures. As part of the new
plan, the prospect of a major new
public library—a pet project of
Wowereit's prior to his resignation—did little to assuage the
general attitude of skepticism.

The emergency shelter for refugees at the shuttered
Tempelhof airport, as seen in 2017.

Though the Berlin Senate alleged that the new construction would be "affordable housing," the numbers told a different story—and when confronted, politicians and developers hedged. As one writer reflected, "This government hasn't built a single social apartment for 10 years—are they going to start right when park-side real estate opens up?"[25] After months of heated debate, 64.3% of voters elected in 2014 to maintain the public park at Tempelhof, prompting a journalist for *The Guardian* to marvel, "The people decided they didn't trust big business not to mess up the park they loved. It's a state of affairs that would be almost unimaginable in Frankfurt or Munich, let alone London or New York."[26] Unfolding alongside the privatization debacle at BER, the success of Tempelhof's defenders over private interests seemed to indicate a still-vital public sphere in the rapidly gentrifying city.

Yet the following year, the very character of Berlin's "public" was called into question, and the fragility of the consensus surrounding the park was thrown into high relief. In September 2015, as Germany struggled to address an influx of refugees from Syria, Iraq, Afghanistan and elsewhere, the federal government announced

25
John Riceburg, "Everyone is Lying about Tempelhofer Field," *Exberliner*, May 12, 2014, https://www.exberliner.com/features/opinion/everyone-is-lying-to-you-about-tempelhofer-feld/.

26
Ciarán Fahey, "How Berliners Refused to Give Tempelhof Airport over to Investors," *The Guardian*, March 5, 2015, https://www.theguardian.com/cities/2015/mar/05/how-berliners-refused-to-give-tem

27
Raziye Akkoc, "Refugee Crisis: Europe's Borders Unraveling as Austria and Slovakia Impose Frontier Controls," *The Telegraph*, September 14, 2015, https://www.telegraph.co.uk/news/worldnews/europe/eu/11863246/Refugee-crisis-EU-ministers-Germany-border-control-Austria-army-live.html.

28
In June 2019, the United Nations High Commissioner for Refugees (UNHCR) reported that, at the end of 2018, there were 1.06 million refugees in Germany. Most of these individuals—nearly one million—arrived over the course of 2015 as part of what Merkel termed Germany's "*Wilkommenskultur.*" Merkel's administration tightened Germany's borders significantly in 2018.

that it would open a center at Tempelhof to provide temporary housing for up to 1,200 of the displaced in two of the airport's hangars.[27] Over the next months, those numbers only grew as a result of Chancellor Angela Merkel's polarizing "open door" policy.[28] By the end of 2015, nearly 2,500 refugees took up temporary residence in cubicles arrayed beneath the 52-foot-high ceilings of the hangars. Sentimental media accounts quickly associated the refugee center at Tempelhof with the humanitarian feats of the Berlin Airlift. Instead of the supplies delivered by the airlift's "candy bombers," the refugees were provided with shelter and safe haven, but the narrative of international altruism seemed poignantly parallel. Rather than the city that let in the architects, Berlin had now become capital of the country that saved the refugees.

Of course, the reality was far more difficult, revealing Germany's unresolved relationship with its own past and with the very idea of "foreignness." Merkel's policies, and the new migrant populations of cities across Germany, laid bare the nation's deep political schisms and brought the simmering racial and ethnic tensions in its cities to a boiling point. At Tempelhof, officials attempted to accommodate the new population while also respecting the protective legislation forbidding changes to the building—a direct result of the 2014 victory against privatization intended to stave off the development of the site. Little in the way of architectural intervention could be managed beyond the sterile row of cubicles, each housing up to twelve people, huddled inside the cavernous space. Some residents enlivened their limited allotments by scribbling brightly colored drawings on the wall panels, but an official ban against graffiti was put in place after offensive marks appeared in some areas.[29] Privacy was virtually nonexistent, despite the blankets and sheets that refugees hung from their bunk beds to create tent-like enclaves. Even the smallest noises echoed from the glass-and-steel walls of the enormous cavernous hangar.[30] Amidst crowding, poor living conditions and harsh treatment from guards, as well as the relentless boredom of waiting, a mass brawl broke out in November 2015. Photographs of Berlin police struggling to subdue unruly refugees appeared in the right-wing press, presented as evidence of mass migration's dangers, while journalists on the left strained to downplay the scuffle's

violence. However, what was missing from most journalistic accounts of the conflict was the central role that the architectural inadequacy of the meager shelter at Tempelhof had played. The flimsy, serial, makeshift architectural quality of the center made it just one more of the "waiting rooms" that form what the political philosophers Sandro Mezzadra and Brett Neilson have termed the "temporal borders" of the larger mobility regimes in which global migration takes place.[31] As one refugee from Baghdad stated, "We were hurting in Iraq, but now we're hurting maybe even more. We were afraid of rockets. But we were living in a stable house comfortably. Here, there's no stability; the only benefit is safety."[32]

By 2017, the refugee population at Tempelhof had largely been dispersed. Frustrated by the slowness of the asylum process, some returned to their native countries; others were relocated to "Tempohomes," somewhat more commodious temporary housing arranged around the periphery of the park. These forms, which are the very opposite of the stylish contemporary architecture for which Berlin is now famous, are no less a manifestation of architectural contemporaneity—with safety as the

29
Toby Parsloe, "Appropriating Buildings to House Refugees: Berlin Tempelhof," *Forced Migration Review* 55 (June 2017): 36.

30
A former journalist from Afghanistan stated in the *Washington Post* that the acoustics of the space alone had contributed to significant mental strain: "Imagine in one hangar, there are more than 500 people…They say one word, and it makes more than 500 echoes because the ceilings and walls are made of iron." Quoted in Luisa Beck, Rick Noack, and Joyce Lee, "Inside an Enormous Abandoned Airport in Berlin That's Coming Back to Life," Washington Post, March 17, 2018, https://www.washingtonpost.com/world/inside-an-enormous-abandoned-airport-in-berlin-thats-coming-back-to-life/2018/03/16/65ca90a6-2642-11e8-b79d-f3d931db7f68_story.html.

31
Sandro Mezzadra and Brett Neilson, *Border as Method, or, the Multiplication of Labor* (Durham, N.C. and London: Duke University Press, 2013).

32
Quoted in Sonia Narang, "Pregnant Inside Tempelhof, Germany's Largest Refugee Camp," *Refugees Deeply*, August 16, 2016, https://www.newsdeeply.com/refugees/articles/2016/08/17/pregnant-inside-tempelhof-germanys-largest-refugee-camp.

In the Shadow of Information

Michael Young

insufficient ethical goal of their design.

In recent years, individual politicians with hardline anti-immigration policies and organizations like the far-right party *Alternative für Deutschland* (AfD) have received a groundswell of support, especially from economically disadvantaged former East German regions. Today, Germany continues to wrestle with the newly overt discrepancy between the official doctrine of openness affirmed during the process of reunification and the factious reality of politics on the ground. Therefore, the central role of architecture itself in either inciting or assuaging these conflicts, as well as addressing the problems I described above, must become better understood. In 2013, *Der Spiegel* conducted an interview with three high-profile architects: von Gerkan, Pierre de Meuron and Christoph Ingenhoven, whose projects in Germany have come to represent notorious failures of public architecture. The interviewer began the discussion with the adversarial assertion that "Architecture's reputation in this country is worse than ever."[33] This striking statement might serve as a judgment that resonates beyond Germany and the specific examples of contemporary architecture I have invoked here. Despite the profession's recent obsession with risk management, we seem—at a global scale—to be caught continually unawares by disaster, whether natural or human-made. In interrogating the foundations of a practice forever reconsidering its ethical purchase, we must continue to train attention on problems both structural and infrastructural, viewing the forms of contemporary architecture as useful evidence of whose safety we prioritize, and at what cost it is achieved.

33
Susanne Beyer and Ulrike Knöfel, "The Men Behind Germany's Building Debacles," *Der Spiegel*, June 14, 2013, https://www.spiegel.de/international/germany/de-meuron-von-gerkan-and-ingenhoven-on-german-construction-headaches-a-905472.html. As well as von Gerkan's Berlin airport, the projects in question were Ingenhoven's Stuttgart railway station (known as Stuttgart 21) and Herzog & de Meuron's Elbphilharmonie in Hamburg.

The surfaces of our environments are scanned, stored, monitored, cross-referenced and monetized. This is done by governments, militaries, corporations and you. It is done by satellite imaging, LIDAR scans, Google Street View, Bluetooth beacons and what was formerly known as photography. Knowledge of this monitoring produces an unavoidable dystopian anxiety, the fear of constant surveillance and the disappointment in knowing that everywhere will soon be transformed into information. Yet all technologies of mediation produce residual effects. In the case of our digitally mediated environments, this excess is the very real space lost between and behind the discrete instances of scanned points. This loss manifests as shadows—gaps where scans skip and stutter, struggling toward fidelity. These shadows also open zones for occupation; they are inherently political.

There is a concept that relates to these hidden zones, emerging initially in the late fifteenth century as a graphic abstraction in architectural representation. This chapter argues that the shadows that hide behind and between the scanned imaging of the environment can be understood as a transformation of the concept known as *poché*. The way in which architecture understands these gaps as alternative possibilities for inhabitation is a pressing issue, given that reality is increasingly mediated through the digital image.

Image as Information

Our cameras are not cameras anymore. Data scanners, photon collectors, discrete energy arrangers: these are more apt names. Not everyone has noticed. Though we still treat the images that our digital cameras reproduce as if they are photographs, our digital cameras do not index light as a chemical interaction with film emulsion. Instead, they capture, translate and store arrays of energy intensity as information.[1] As John May articulates, "In our lives, imaging is a form of photon detection. Unlike photographs, in which scenic light is made visible during chemical exposure, all imaging today is a process of detecting energy emitted by an environment and chopping it into discrete, measurable electrical charges called signals, which are stored, calculated, managed, and manipulated through various statistical methods."[2]

Display screens are performance spaces where captured information is transformed into luminous pixels, pulses of energy that human eyes evaluate as images. These images are typically engaged through the conventions of previous visual arts, such as painting and photography, which offer important avenues for understanding such loaded concepts as realism and abstraction. Yet these aesthetic categories take on different aspects when mediated through technologies of reproduction, where concerns are less interpretive questions of representational resemblance than the disinterested record of scanned points. How these differences manifest discursively is a key question. Let us begin with *resolution*.

Resolution is the product of a technological, economic and aesthetic negotiation. The discretization of the environment into bits of information begins with the

1
John May, "Everything Is Already an Image," *Log* 40 (Spring/Summer 2017): 12.

2
John May, *Signal, Image, Architecture* (New York: Columbia Books on Architecture and the City, 2019), 45.

technology of capture and carries on into storage, display and transmission. As higher resolutions take longer to process, requiring faster and more expensive computational power, image information is compressed in order to be manipulated, transmitted and consumed. There is a constant struggle in the appearance of digital images between the fidelity of the resolution and the econometrics of attention and distribution. Resolution is a valuation made through digital information, an exchange between competing priorities.

If our eyes perceive the pixels of the discrete array, we call the image "low-res"; if they don't, we call it "high-res." These terms may feel quantitative and objective; after all, we key specific numbers for PPI (pixels per inch) in Photoshop. But the difference between what is "high" and "low" is ultimately subjective, a differentiation made based on human perception. Gaps between points of scanned data are often discussed with a sense of mourning, a nostalgia for a lost analog richness of reality. This sentiment reflects an aesthetic judgment of realism in its guise as mimetic resemblance, comparing the sense of vision to the representational artifice. However, a digital image does not operate within the realm of representation, it is a mediation, and thus the aesthetic questions are different. Representations are constructed through cultural conventions and require knowledge regarding the manners through which specific disciplines regulate interpretation. Mediations attempt to record everything without an imposed bias. The gaps, noise, errors that occur in "the attempt to record everything" are terms used to describe aspects presented by mediations that lie outside familiar sensation, affects that have not yet been culturally valued. These are aesthetic responses and when coupled with techniques of manipulation and modes of

performance-display particular to the mediation, become key features for working with these technologies. Yet, as important as these aspects are, they elide a crucial fact: digital images are also information captured by machines for machines.

Trevor Paglen reminds us, "The image doesn't need to be turned into human-readable form in order for a machine to do something with it."[3] In this context, resolution is little concerned with the human eye, yet the quantity and density of data contained in an image will determine how it will be analyzed, filtered, and combined with other data sets. For a machine exchanging information with another machine, gaps are a given as digital information is and always has been discrete. This discretization structures how it is processed in relation to other information and then acted on by very real forces in the world. In their study of how scanning, computation and visualization are expanding into political, ecological, legal and cultural realities, Eyal and Ines Weizman write, "The exclusion of people from representation is thus complemented by their gradual exclusion from the increasingly automated process of viewing and also . . . from the algorithmic process of data interpretation."[4] Digital images are used today to determine the reality of everything from human rights violations to the quantified extent of glacier retreat to

3
Trevor Paglen, "Invisible Images (Your Pictures Are Looking at You)," *New Inquiry*, December 8, 2016, https://thenewinquiry.com/invisible-images-your-pictures-are-looking-at-you.

4
Eyal and Ines Weizman, *Before and After* (Moscow: Strelka, 2013), 38.

Detail of Room portrait, by Veronica Skeppe, Cecilia Lundbäck and Ulrika Karlsson 2019, from Interiors Matter: A Live Interior.

This study of the domestic interiors combines the measured LIDAR point scan with coordinated photos at each pulse. The shadows appear as white areas behind objects. The overlapped shadow gaps of three scanning passes can be seen behind the flower vase. The reflective material of the lamp stand is missing altogether, unable to be registered by the sensors.

potential military targets. Furthermore, as they are evaluated by machines using criteria foreign to humans, every digital image also redistributes the background of reality. In this, the gaps between points are real, only this reality means very different things depending on who, or what, is engaging the mediation.

Blind Pockets

Information carried through electromagnetic radiation generally cares very little for the built environment it passes through. Only a small specific range of energy is reflected off surfaces and detected by human vision. It is this range that digital cameras simulate. The question of "seeing" the world through digital mediation in a manner similar to vision takes on a different implication when expanded to technologies that uses images to build three-dimensional models. The information captured, stored and processed through lidar and photogrammetry is not only trying hard to *see* as many qualities of environmental surfaces as possible, it is also trying to give them spatial depth, it is trying to *touch*.[5]

The representation of depth is a fundamental question for all visual media, especially for drawing, painting, photography and digital images, which all occur on a flat plane. Lidar and photogrammetry appear to have resolved it through automation. Depth is computed as part of image capture itself.

The image no longer signifies depth through representation but instead measures space as an inherent component of its computation. Our environment, our objects and ourselves are being collected as three-dimensional digital bodies. These scanned approximations of the environment determine what is stored, cross-referenced and

distributed, which aspects are "real" for the valuations of digital exchanges and how that in turn alters our occupation of the world. A loss of information or a lowering of resolution literally changes the shape of reality.

The scanning of the environment is also its surveillance. Liam Young has made a series of films that explore the narrative possibilities of a world known through LIDAR scans. *Where the City Can't See* (2016), codirected by Tim Maughan, looks at the potential for inhabitation in relation to the scanning technology of our urban environments: "Set in a futuristic Detroit that has become heavily surveilled, . . . it tells the story of teenagers organizing illegal parties while hiding themselves — and even whole buildings — by wearing clothes made from 'deflection fabrics.' These materials, the patterns of which are designed to deflect and diffuse the LIDAR's laser scans, make them invisible to the eyes of automated vehicles."[6] These zones hidden from the scan become spaces for occupation. Young and Maughan suggest that these spaces open possibilities for human activities that require freedom from surveillance. Architecture can create these gaps through a kind of camouflage that intervenes and "deflects" the capture of surface location as energetic information. Or, to put this another way, the decoration of surfaces alters the information that is collected in a digital scan, all objects in the environment can potentially intervene in its energetic capture.

5
Lucia Allais, "Rendering: On Experience and Experiments", *Design Technics: Archaeologies of Architectural Practice*, Zeynep Celik Alexander and John May ed. (Minneapolis, MN: University of Minnesota Press, 2019), 60.

6
Tim Maughan, "No One's Driving," in *Machine Landscapes: Architectures of the Post-Anthropocene*, ed. Liam Young (Oxford: John Wiley & Sons, 2019), 96.

Equivalent Interiors

Curtis Roth

Such blind zones can also be described as shadows, *sciographias*, invisible to data collection, dark pockets looming on the other side of the scan.[7] Shadows are an occlusion of light, and there is a long history in architectural representation that entwines optics, perspective projection, and shadow drawing.[8] In its attempts to record surfaces, scanning technology does not differentiate between the articulated layers of decoration (*mosaïque*); transitory objects such as people, cars, furniture and vegetation (*entourage*); or the solidity of architectural mass (*poché*).[9] These are all smushed together into a thin glitchy body of surface topology floating in three-dimensional space absent of thickness and solidity. The differences between lidar and photogrammetry will be discussed later. For now, it is important to note that both have linear relations between the capturing source and the first surface struck, occluding all that exists behind that instance of reflected energy. The intersected line of sight, or ray of light, connects art and mathematics through projection as formulated by painters, surveyors, and stonecutters in order to represent visual depth on a two-dimensional plane. Architectural representation was born of this exchange between the metric computation and visual image of the environment, and it is the history of this entanglement that allows architecture to engage these questions in significant ways.

These relations to projection, optics, and photography, tends to classify lidar and photogrammetry within ocular and visual media. But this is only part of how they operate. What is imaged in a three-dimensional scan is an interference between matter and energy. Scanning passes over things evenly, distractedly, objectively; it is as tactile as it is visual, its mediation is a point not a line, and the gaps consist of what is skipped as much as what hides behind.

Poché emerged through the representational technologies of the Northern Italian Renaissance and was codified in the pedagogy of the French Academies and the École des Beaux-Arts during the eighteenth and nineteenth centuries.[10] According to the most common architectural understanding, *poché* is the representational convention of using graphic hatch or colored fill to denote cut material in plan and section drawings. But this definition of the term is complicated by other associations, such as "pocket," "hidden" and "swollen."[11] *Poché* presents contradictory issues simultaneously. First, it renders figure-ground relations, where spatial voids become aesthetically sensible and conceptually legible. Second, in the abstraction of notation, it conceals all information regarding material, construction, assembly and building systems. When a drawing is rendered with *poché*, it is concerned not with

7
Sciographia is derived from *scio-*, "shadow" and *graphy-*, writing or inscription.

8
Thomas Kaufmann, "The Perspective of Shadows: The History of the Theory of Shadow Projection," *Journal of the Warburg and Courtland Institutes* 38 (1975): 258–87.

9
"A good plan sustained a depth and transparency achieved through the dessin techniques of entourage, *poché*, and *mosaïque*—graphic codes that made the plan legible to an architectural audience." Hyungmin Pai, *The Portfolio and the Diagram* (Cambridge, MA: MIT Press, 2002), 52.

10
Michael Young, "Paradigms in the Poché," *Proceedings of the ACSA Annual Meeting* (Washington, DC: Association of Collegiate Schools of Architecture, 2019), 190–95.

11
Wiktionary, s.v. "poché," accessed June 1, 2020, https://www.en.wiktionary.org/wiki/poché.

This article is published in collaboration with *Third Rail*. It first appeared in *Third Rail* issue 13, 2019.

According to Richard Upjohn's keynote lecture at the American Institute of Architects' First general Convention in 1867, "Our merchandise is our brain, we sell our ideas." By "our," Upjohn circumscribed an emerging body of mostly middle-class design professionals, distinct from the mostly lower-class master builders of previous centuries. By "selling our ideas," Upjohn suggested that in order to make this distinction visible within the competitive economies of construction, the minds of architects needed to be disentangled from the bodies of builders. But if the century of architectural professionalization, following Upjohn's declaration, consisted of drawing increasingly sophisticated borders between *authorship* (creative intellection) and *construction* (anonymous physical labor), we might also remember that the concept of Upjohn's architect as a sovereign author is only possible by erasing alternative forms of creativity that have yet to be named.

Take for example: "*...or equivalent*," that peculiar postscript appearing at the tail-end of an architect's specifications, intended to emphasize the notion that unwieldy matter submits to the ideas that attempt to organize it. The writ of "*...or equivalent*" obligates a worker to preserve an idea's coherence, as it travels through the unpredictable networks of production: substituting 5/8" sheetrock for its 3/4" equivalent or replacing Benjamin Moore's *Whisper White* with *Frothy Surf*. Yet, while anyone might be excused for mistaking two oily off-whites, any assertion of the equivalence between *this* and *that* becomes a creative proposition, one in which the decisive and authorial brainwork of *design* leaks into the anonymous physical labor of *construction*.

That being said, for all that "*...or equivalent*" would seem to undermine Upjohn's aging model of authorship, its obligation to substitute this for that is only successfully fulfilled when the worker's creative substitution remains invisible. In other words, "*...or equivalent*" places an onus on laborers to creatively erase the evidence of their authorship to better preserve an architect's intellectual merchandise.

This is all to suggest that, perhaps, by re-staging the problem of equivalence, we might also begin to imagine another model of authorship altogether. One that transcends Upjohn's distinction between minds and bodies. Building upon the premise that the construction of the architectural imagination has always been the construction of boundaries between themselves and others, we point toward

Photo taken using the Snoopy Highway Mapper LIDAR System, 2019.

In this study, the LIDAR sensor is mounted to the roof of a car travelling down a street. This is an aerial top view of a captured moment, where the directionality of the laser pulses is clearly noticeable in the data shadows, occluded by cars and other street objects.

another creativity that is more difficult to discern within the competitive economies of construction.

• • •

In a small gated development, located three kilometers outside the Special Economic Zone of the Chinese megacity Shenzhen, over one-hundred painters gather every year for a competition, producing one-hundred copies of paintings, such as Ilya Repin's 1883 portrait of Russian art critic Vladimir Stasov. This is Dafen Village, the turpentine-soaked capital of copied art. Established during the post-socialist economic reforms of China in the early 1990s, Dafen is responsible for over 60% of the earth's total volume of reproduced paintings.[1] Paradoxically, the marginalized and mostly migratory painters participating in this annual competition are competing for liberation from the US$43,000,000 copying economy itself.

If Walter Benjamin's "The Work of Art in the Age of Mechanical Reproduction" claimed, "…that which withers under modernity is the *aura* of the work of art," then Dafen is nothing less than a paragon for the mass remanufacturing of modernity's lost auras. Dafen's

economy is partially premised on the painter's ability to reinvest oversaturated images like Van Gogh's *Self-Portrait* or da Vinci's *Mona Lisa* with the financial premiums associated with hand-crafted auras.[2] Additionally, Dafen's industry runs on a state-sanctioned narrative that the perfect resurrection of such auras might even elevate the brute labor of copying into an "original" artistic act in itself. Call it Dafen's dream: original authorship born out of the perfect copy while supplying Dafen's economy with a steady stream of low-cost painting labor. A competitor's ability to convincingly resurrect Repin's aura is judged by the local propaganda department, and the top ten painters are awarded state sponsorship as *original artists*. More importantly, these artists are afforded the right to legally register as citizens of Dafen.[3]

This aspiration turns upon two competing accounts of painting's value: a culturally profitable form of artistic expression and a financially profitable organization of surplus labor. The worker's proficiency in resurrecting auras, adjudicated through competitions like the Dafen Copying Competition, attempts to disentangle artistic expression from economic factors and, ultimately, humans from nonhumans.

1
Damien Gayle, "The World's Biggest Art Factory." *The Daily Mail*, July 23rd, 2013.

2
Walter Benjamin, *The Work of Art in the Age of Mechanical Reproduction*. (New York, Penguin Adult, 2008).

3
Winnie Wong, *Van Gogh on Demand*. (Chicago, University of Chicago Press, 2014).

conveying how to build the design but instead with imaging architecture in a way that exists as representation, for an audience that will evaluate the spaces through imaginary projection. *Poché* exchanges construction labor for intellectual labor, material assembly for spatial conceptualization. It is economic; one reality withdraws to allow another to become sensible.

Services of Surveillance

The pockets of space that exist between the interior and the exterior; the basements, attics, back stairs, passages, plenums, shafts and cavities are not empty, they are filled with services, both human and nonhuman. These residual spaces are purposefully hidden to keep them from disrupting the cohesive visual image of the environment. As Mark Wigley explicates:

> No building form is as complex as the systems that service it or the activities it services. Architecture is an act of simplification or of veiling complexity. It is dedicated to the skin more than it can ever acknowledge. Perhaps nothing can be as thin as architecture, the art of suspending perforated surfaces within a myriad of flows to paradoxically represent seamless solidity.[12]

Energetic pulses captured on cellphones relay through floors and walls, in route from phone to satellite to server to database. These wireless networks determine much of what currently defines the background of our daily interactions.[13] We have come to depend on and expect connectivity at the same time that we increasingly feel the need to escape this constant surveillance. Broadband connectivity

is legally an infrastructural public utility.[14] Like water and electricity, it is expected to be continuously available, thus backgrounded and blackboxed; its operations withdrawn from human attention.[15] We notice it only when it provides faulty service. Wireless media not only provide access to information; they produce information by monitoring user interactions. In this exchange, both sides prefer its operations to be invisible. The consumer wants digital information at the highest fidelity possible, in real time, and constantly accessible everywhere. The provider of these services wants the consumer to use them habitually as a normal everyday interaction with the world. This integration into the background of the environment is important, for it is the unconscious behaviors of daily life that are the most easily monetized. This agreement is also the foundation of contemporary surveillance.

The temptation is to locate surveillance entirely in the technology of internet, but what turns these networks into apparatuses of control is not just computational

12
Mark Wigley, *Buckminster Fuller Inc. Architecture in the Age of Radio* (Zurich, CH: Lars Muller, 2015), 77.

13
Mark Wigley, *Buckminster Fuller Inc. Architecture in the Age of Radio* (Zurich, CH: Lars Muller, 2015).

14
Cecilia Kang, "Court Backs Rules Treating Internet as Utility, Not Luxury," *New York Times*, June 15, 2016, https://www.nytimes.com/2016/06/15/technology/net-neutrality-fcc-appeals-court-ruling.html.

15
This combination of "blackboxing" and "withdrawal" owes a significant debt to Bruno Latour and Graham Harman and will be explored in greater detail in other writing.

The Wall of Jack's Studio, as specified by: Curtis Roth,
painted by: Jack and erased by: Bella, Stuttgart/Dafen, 2016/2017.

algorithms; it is the way they have been naturalized as part of the environment. Which brings us to architecture. What is withdrawn in the *poché* is not removed from knowledge. It is simply removed from attention, yet nonetheless continuously produces the environment as a distraction for consumption. We know that our walls and floors are full of pipes, insulation, structure, wires, ducts, membranes, and fasteners running all over the place and connecting "somewhere" to an "outside." The internet is an extra-planetary piece of infrastructure hidden outside the atmosphere, beneath the crust of the earth, below our city's streets, and within our building's shafts. Hiding "the internet" in the pockets of the *poché* allows us to behave as if our environments are material, solid, real enclosures, and information is an ephemeral cloud-like flow of data.

Surveillance means to "keep watch", it is an idea based in sight. Jeremey Bentham's panopticon, with its single, all-seeing watchtower at its center has played a paradigmatic role within the cultural discourse of ocular centric surveillance at least since Michel Foucault noted its architecture of control and discipline.[16] Within this model, inhabitants of the periphery behave as if watched, even if there is no one watching inside the tower. Extending the panoptic model into the internet seems to make sense as all users become increasingly subject to constant surveillance by a handful of powerful private companies. But aspects of this paradigm do not seem accurate in describing internet monitoring. For instance, we all know we are being watched, we just typically ignore it. Furthermore, we are not really being "watched", we are being recorded and exchanged, scanned and statistically filtered. This should still instill anxiety, if not more so given that all interactions on the internet are searchable and stored forever regardless of their importance, but it is exactly

this constant tracing of meaningless data noise that seems to undermine the ocular-centric control of vision. Petra Gehring has challenged the extension of the pan-opticon into internet surveillance. "It may well be that the presence of mass-media pictorial rhetoric is overes-timated. Other techniques penetrate deeper, techniques that include knowledge of automatic registration and the permanent possibility of processing the traces that I leave."[17] Gehring continues on monitoring technologies, "…in their core they are post-panoptic. They rely on registration that is performed out of sight and on data acquisition procedures that run unawares—and which thus as a rule do not merely result in behavioral discipline, but rather lead to a fundamental subjective disquiet."[18]

Poché offers a potential paradigm for the type of monitoring that operates in contemporary society—one more apt, perhaps, than the panopticon. Our actions are no longer watched from an analogical, geometrical or dia-grammatic center but instead from a zone hidden within and behind the screens and surfaces of our environmental background. Monitoring occurs below the threshold of

16
Giorgio Agamben, "What Is a Paradigm?" in *The Signature of All Things* (New York: Zone Books, 2009).

17
Petra Gehring, "The Inverted Eye. Panopticon and Panopticism, Revisited", *Foucault Studies*, No. 23, August 2017, 60.

18
Petra Gehring, "The Inverted Eye. Panopticon and Panopticism, Revisited", *Foucault Studies*, No. 23, August 2017, 62.

The Wall of Polly's Studio, as specified by: Curtis Roth,
painted by: Polly and erased by: Jing, Stuttgart/Dafen, 2016/2017.

attention not at a focal center. "Image" is simply a visual metaphor for the sound, light, heat, movement, time, attention, and currency exchanges that service our desires and monitor our behavior. What hides in the *poché* is the hum and hiss of the infrastructure, recording, mixing, and filtering reality.

Capture and Process

Though the historical development of LIDAR and photogrammetry are closely related, there are some important differences to emphasize regarding how each captures and processes environmental surface data to build spatial models. LIDAR works by measuring distances in the environment, photogrammetry calculates depth through images. What is hidden, then, depends on how the environment is sensed, stored, and processed.

LIDAR (light detection and ranging) uses lasers to scan the environment. An electromagnetic pulse is sent out and bounces back to the imaging source, and a measurement of the time it takes for the signal to return allows distance to be calculated.[19] This is considered an active sensor, as it emits energy. Every point is an individual measurement in *x-y-z* coordinate space, independent of ambient environmental lighting, color, texture, and pattern. The type of material (concrete, tree foliage), its reflectivity (glazing, wet) and the distance from the scan source all affect the return of the signal and can produce noise, irregularities and other errors in the scan.

Photogrammetry, on the other hand, measures depth by comparing two photos. Photogrammetry has been in use as long as we have had photography for surveying, most often in engineering and military contexts.[20] The transformation that has occurred, thanks to computational

technologies, is that huge sets of "photos" can be rapidly processed to produce spatial models. The identification of surface edges and detail depends on pixel comparison, which relies on the resolution and intensity of energy captured in the initial photographs.[21]

A ground-based lidar scan can be created from a single sensor origin, however this will have large areas of occlusion. In order to get a more complete dimensional model of the space measured, scans from multiple origins are necessary. Photogrammetry, by contrast, requires more than one scanning position to produce any spatial information. The calculation is done through differences between two images of a single object, that is through motion.[22] The movement of scanning is wedded into the computation of spatial depth.

19
Todd Neff, "Lidar History Timeline," online supplement to *The Laser That's Changing the World: The Amazing Stories behind Lidar, from 3D Mapping to Self-Driving Cars* (Amherst, NY: Prometheus Books, 2018), https://toddneff.com/books/lidarhistory/extras/lidarhistory-timeline.

20
Helen Wickstead, "Drawing on Photographs: Aerial Photogrammetry and Virtual Mapping 1865 to 1900" from *Royal Anthropological Institute Conference*, British Museum 28th, May 2014.

21
Methods of pixel comparison are fundamental for machine vision, CNNs, GANs and image search algorithms; i.e. facial recognition, atmospheric pollution emissions, traffic patterns, etc.

22
Matthew Magnani and Matthew Douglass, "Photogrammetry and Stereophotogrammetry," *The SAS Encyclopedia of Archaeological Sciences*, ed. Sandra L. Lopez Varela (New York: John Wiley & Sons, 2019).

In 2004, in an effort to rebrand Dafen as a Bohemian tourist attraction, the village was rezoned, from a migrant worker's settlement into a residential community.[4] The select minority of original-artist citizens were afforded a collection of human rights, such as housing and political representation that differentiated these *artists* from the scores of undocumented *laborers* anonymously "frankensteining" the lamp-lit auras lining hotel lobbies across the earth. Today, this aspirational dream separates artists from their undocumented counterparts, dividing the city itself. This kind of ambition relocates the fraction of original artists to highly-visible, ground-floor studios along popular tourist avenues. This move segregated scores of undocumented laborers into the unregulated recesses of corporately-owned image factories in which painters collectively sleep, live and labor.

My work *Equivalent Interiors* attempts to render the segregation of Dafen's aura economy visible through the deployment of architecture's own instrument for managing the authority of authorship over labor: in other words, the write of "*…or equivalent.*"

The project began by soliciting ten images from ten Dafen copying corporations. Each corporation was contracted

4
Ibid.

5
Robin Evans, "Translations from Drawing to Building," *AA Files* no. 12, (London, Architecture Association School of Architecture, 1986), 6.

to reproduce a single historical example from the marginal 19th-century painters' subject, Pliny's mythic origin of drawing. Each commission was accompanied by an architectural specification, dictating the precise conditions for each image's reproduction. Where Pliny's myth portrayed the origin of drawing in Kora of Sicyon's tracing of her lover's shadow across the wall of an architectural interior, each attached specification obliged a painter to produce the equivalent or to depict the historical painting itself on the factory wall against which they toiled.[5] Upon the completion of these original ten equivalent images, the canvases were mailed to one of the original painter's local competitors who were supplied with a second specification. The second painters were obliged to erase all but the studio wall of the original painting's producer.

On its surface, the collection of images represents an attempt to render the urban erasure of Dafen's labor visible in the frame of the image itself. However, the successful execution of each image was also compromised by the state-sponsored onus on originality under which each painter labors. In other words, each of the ten paintings raises a strange question: whose agency *caused* these spaces to appear? Within each image, three

Edges in scanned models are jumps between points representing different surface planes. Edge in this context is thus not the geometric intersection traditionally represented and controlled through the graphic drawing of a line. Edges in three-dimensional scans often look funny; they smudge and fray, sometimes drifting into the shadowy void behind. Multiple scans increase the model's definition and tighten its corners. When a model is lowered in resolution in order to be manipulated or transmitted, one of the first places distortions appear is at the edges and corners.

The number of points determines the level of detail. Lower resolution scans or increased distance from the object produces less accurate mapping of the surfaces. For photogrammetry, color and brightness of reflected surface energy can produce data capture confusion also resulting in loss of surface detail. Resolution in capture extends into the performance of the model as a point cloud. From a distance, these models can have a somewhat disturbingly high degree of realism. As one zooms in, the point cloud disintegrates: points spread, gaps open and eventually the surface dissolves entirely. In this, the difference between realism and abstraction is but a matter of degree, or literally a matter of zoom.

The shadows of occluded information are reduced by having multiple scans, but there will always be pockets the scanner cannot access. Gaps in LIDAR scans are caused by occluded lines of sight and resolution, which are a function of the number of scanning passes. Gaps in photogrammetry, on the other hand, are dependent on the electromagnetic range that is captured by the sensing technology, in simpler terms, the color and resolution of the initial digital images. What is missing and how those gaps are accounted for is different for each technology. In

both cases, however, the most "successful" models work to complete the surfaces as they are seen from certain privileged views, which are different depending on the industry for which the model is intended. "View" should not be equated with vision; it is as likely to be an aerial drone or a satellite image as it is to be the height of a human eye. In the efforts to fill the gaps, an interesting side effect is produced: the scan turns images into objects.

Image-Objects

All digital models are double. They consist of an interior surface model floating inside an exterior surface model. Though this is true of all digital modeling, it is rarely commented on, perhaps because most digital models are developed as a single surface that is then offset, making one surface the result of the other. This offset does not produce "thickness," however, and all digital models that develop both their interior volume and exterior mass are objects inside of objects, connected by funnels called "apertures." A modeled building's interior volume is independent of its exterior mass and is made sensible as a figured void, appearing as a solid object. In his book *Baroque Topologies*, Andrew Saunders writes,

Although not technically able to see through external surfaces to the underlying hidden layers of composite structure, 3D scanned point clouds produce a novel effect of transparency on the thin membrane surface of enclosure due to the spacing of points. This enables a unique topological vantage point to view the spatial envelope of the interior from the "outside" as well as from the "inside" simultaneously. It is as if the entire internal poché of the churches has been completely

irreconcilable accounts of authorship seem to coexist.

First, in those instances in which a viewer believes that the specification was diligently executed by the original painter, then the author of the painting's content seems caught in roughly equal measure between the authority of my specification — as an instrument *causing* the institutionally erased recesses of Dafen to appear in the image's frame — and the original architect, whose own specifications resulted in the construction of the wall depicted by the representation. Whether the painting's observer locates the authorial act in the specification of the painting or that of the original wall, either account relies on the manifestation of Upjohn's model in which the creative work of the mind organizes the anonymous physical labors of fabrication.

Yet, in most instances, the paintings themselves would likely fail to convince the observer that my own specification was ever executed at all. In other words, a viewer might suspect that the idealized studio interiors depicted in the paintings are less acts of documentation than they are aspirational renderings of the fictive artist-personas, manufactured by the state itself. Rather than an authorial act caught between myself and the wall's original

architect, this reading would locate the painting's authorship somewhere between the imagination of the contracted painter herself and the imagination of state bureaucrats fabricating Dafen's dream through zoning codes, residency permits and tourism advertisements.

However, for all that this second account would replace the minds-versus-bodies duality with an imagination diffused across a vast array of anonymous factory painters and unnamed civil servants, this account itself is undermined by second painter's act of erasure. She is asked by the specification to creatively decide which elements of a painted image constitute a wall and which elements constitute erasable content. Here, like a construction laborer creatively executing the "...*or equivalent*" postscript of a construction document, the second painter operates within the inherently ambiguous nature of a wall to draw distinctions between planar surfaces, perpendicular porticos or the chamfered edges of crown molding profiles. Each distinction between the wall and everything else, or what's erased and what remains, is turned into a speculative redefinition of a wall itself.

Which is all to say that each of the ten images highlight the ambiguity of

the architectural specification to further complicate the apparent binary between authorial thought and manual labor. In doing so, the images also suggest that the professional conventions, through which the discipline constructs authority over certain forms of the imagination, rely on the distinctions made between the mental work of architects and the physical work of laborers. To imagine forms of architectural work that resist historical distinctions between brains and bodies is not just to reimagine the conventions of authorship but to redesign the instruments through which architects construct themselves.

Andrew Saunders, LIDAR scan of San Lorenzo, Tornio, 2019.

The point-cloud model seen here is the product of multiple scans from different origins. It is a good example of the diaphanous veil-like appearance of point-cloud models, the volumetric objectification of interiors, and the strange effect of being able to see through surfaces that are closer to the viewpoint.

The Wall of Vera's Studio, as specified by: Curtis Roth,
painted by: Vera and erased by: Kevin, Stuttgart/Dafen, 2016/2017.

removed to reveal only a thin spatial residue of the
interior shell volume, a view never before imagined.
To view the inside from the outside and the inside
turned out paints a completely new understanding of
the total working of the interior volume as a whole.
The interior becomes a manifold body providing an
unprecedented representation of the complete spatial
capacity of Baroque interior.[23]

The digital model, as captured by three-dimensional
scans and imaged as a point cloud, reveals this "volume
as object" aspect. As Saunders points out, the technology
of capturing these surfaces, as points mapping surfaces
rather than lines representing edges, is not only a more
accurate model but is also a novel mode of representation
and visualization. Point-cloud models render the interior
volume as a coherent whole, a "figured void" (a phrase
that comes very close to ideas—such as "detached lining," "spatial nest," "space within a space" and "things
in things"—developed by Robert Venturi in his efforts to
describe qualities of *poché*[24]). In a way, all three-dimen-
sionally scanned environments are interior volumes, even
the exterior spaces of streets, parks, and public squares.
The scan is a discrete-point registration of a bounding
volume of the surfaces surrounding the sensor-camera.
This capturing origin is *within* the space; it records all that
surrounds it and manifests the information as a model
of discrete points. When the model is then displayed—and
especially when it is viewed from locations that humans do
not typically inhabit—the gaps created by resolution and
occlusion are revealed. In other words, to "see" the
missing spatial information requires a disembodied eye,
or more accurately, the acknowledgment that the model
is a thin liminal layer of something not quite an image,

an object or a volume. The *poché* lies within, behind, and
between the non-dimensional surface of points.

Our environments are assumed to be continuous. This
quality is part of how we define reality: there are no holes,
no gaps. Energetic scans of the environment attempt to
collect this continuity. But because electronic storage
and transmission requires signals, the environment must
be cut into discrete bits of energetic information that can
be processed.[25] This discretization produces gaps, frays,
and tears in the mediated surface. As Hito Steyerl points
out, these models are never fully two-dimensional or
three-dimensional:

> 3D technologies don't only render the parts that are
> actually captured as locational measurements by a
> lidar scanner, but also the parts that are missing from
> 2D images: the shadowed, covered or cut parts of
> the image. The missing data are assigned a volume or
> a body. The shadows and blind spots are not off frame,
> masked or cut off as they might be in a 2D shot,
> but treated as equal parts of the information.
> What emerges is not the image of a body, but the body
> of an image that itself presents information on a thin
> surface or differentiation, shaped by different natural,
> technological or political forces.[26]

23
Andrew Saunders, *Baroque
Topologies* (Modena:
Palombieditori, 2018).

24
Robert Venturi, *Complexity and
Contradiction in Architecture* (New
York: Museum of Modern Art,
1966), 71–86.

25
Friedrich Kittler, *Optical Media:
The Berlin Lectures* (1999;
Cambridge: Polity Press, 2010), 26

26
Hito Steyerl, *Duty Free Art*
(London: Verso, 2017), 197.

The Wall of Chao's Studio, as specified by: Curtis Roth,
painted by: Chao and erased by: Erwin, Stuttgart/Dafen, 2016/2017.

There is a mistaken belief that to resolve the "glitches" and errors in the scanning of the environment, all that is required is a more advanced, higher-resolution, faster-processing technology. This line of thinking misses the point, for all technologies of mediation substitute abstractions for reality. It is the tensions and frictions that give each medium its aesthetic characteristic. In the case of the three-dimensional scan these are; the point cloud as energetic interference, the edge as fray of resolution, and the data shadow as *poché*.

The Electromagnetic Threshold

In the history of urban representation, poché is most often associated with the "Nuova Pianta di Roma" by Giovanni Battista Nolli (1748). Commonly known as the "Nolli map," this engraving abstracts the city into figure and ground; roads and squares, as well as the quasi-public space of civic-religious interiors are left blank, while the mass of the rest of the built fabric is hatched black. The Nolli map makes legible the infrastructure of movement, the economics of private ownership, and the shared zones of public exchange. It is still popular because as a representation it allows people to analyze, interpret, and act on the city though a mode of abstraction. It is also a highly problematic representation that reduces urbanism to a private-public, figure-ground dichotomy.

The differentiation of figure from ground, solid building from empty space, becomes irrelevant when edges no longer constitute linear bounding contours but instead the falloff at energetic thresholds. The point-cloud model highlights this variability. It is no longer a hard edge, no longer a figure on a ground, determined by drawing a line, but instead a diaphanous fray of marks in a matrix. Edges

scatter, scumble, and jump between surfaces. Since all objects have an equal opportunity to interfere with the electromagnetic spectrum, the traditional hierarchies between object, architecture, and landscape flatten into a background environment of reflection and interference. The city is modeled as a ground of variable energy intensities with gaps, rips and tears from lossy resolution and surface occlusion.

The desire to map the physical world with energetic pulses appeals to governments, militaries, mining industries, archeologists, agriculture conglomerates, advertising agencies, traffic planners, ecologists and architects. Each of these industries, corporations, bureaucracies, and disciplines wants this digital double not only because it "looks like" the world but also because an environment modeled as information can be combined, compared, filtered and augmented to allow it to be understood, controlled, exploited, and manipulated in ever new ways. The expansion of electromagnetic scanning into the infrared and thermal has, since World War II, been part of the development of photogrammetry, used to create images that can be analyzed in ways foreign to human perception. This has been applied to everything from the extraction of "landscape features" for ballistic targeting to ecological studies that cross-reference heat maps with moisture models.[27] Furthermore, the environment, modeled as information, can be combined and cross-referenced with other sets of information. Data is meaningless in its raw

27
John May, "Sensing: Preliminary Notes on the Emergence of Statistical-Mechanical Geographic Vision," *Perspecta* 40 (2008).

The Wall of Jiang's Studio, as specified by: Curtis Roth,
painted by: Jiang and erased by: Mei, Stuttgart/Dafen, 2016/2017.

These images are point clouds generated through a photogrammetry scan of Giovanni
Battista Piranesi's altar in Santa Maria del Priorato. The model is seen from above and
rotating towards the rear of the church. The pink "fill" on the right set highlights the
poché of missing information. Some areas are inside the sculpture; some are outside the
image collection. For instance, the face of St. Basil is seen through the top of his head in
the lowest image. All images by author, 2019.

The Wall of Ting's Studio, as specified by: Curtis Roth,
painted by: Ting and erased by: Gustav, Stuttgart/Dafen, 2016/2017.

state but gains value when combined with other data to become interpretable as a statistically legible pattern of behaviors.

For industries with an interest in rendering the environment as an augmented three-dimensional model, the gaps, errors, and tensions between energetic scans and the physical world become problematic. For instance, as the movement of commodities are mapped for the purposes of storage logistics, on-demand delivery, and location-information accrual, the zones of absent information appear as lost capital or the mismanagement of services. Furthermore, a misregistered depth or fraying edges present significant problems for all applications using machine vision, such as; self-driving cars, facial-recognition software and drone-missile targeting; technologies that exceed but also extend "capital services."

The digitally scanned environment is not a simple doubling, however. Technologies of mediation store, transmit, and process information.[28] Mediations are models of reality. The question is not which one is closer to the "real", but how these models alter human and nonhuman engagement with the world. As Shannon Mattern reminds us, "We inhabit a data space defined by various levels of intersecting protocols that direct our connections, facilitate or close off access, and thus subtly shape the geographies — both informational and physical — we are then able to explore."[29] For the discipline of architecture seeking to occupy the city in alternative modes, knowledge of how the environment is scanned is indeed essential, but it is not enough to simply locate and identify the errors or gaps in these scans.

The Aesthetics of the Unregistered

Poché has always been residual. It now includes the unregistered zones produced through interferences in the electromagnetic spectrum. This is an extension and mutation of the traditional concept of *poché*. As residual, information shadows are an entanglement of the material with the energetic, an aesthetic redistribution that shifts away from the sharp distinction between figure and ground into the scumbled lacunae located behind, between and within the image-objects of clustered points.

Scanning mediates this background, both in terms of how machines capture and store the environment, and how our lives are ever more defined by the data trails we excrete and inhabit. In this, resolution is a cultural-economic negotiation between information and visualization, a political zone that entangles humans and nonhumans in the computational mediation of the environment.

Framing transformations in technologies of mediation within the disciplinary history of architectural representation is crucial for the development of discourse. Every new technology is initially posited as being more faithful, more accurate, more "real" than the previous. Tracing the relationships between concepts and aesthetics challenges the assumption that each new technology is a revolution in the representation of reality. It is important to remember that no mediation has a privileged access to the real. Each produces its own aesthetic and conceptual traits, which

28
See Kittler, *Optical Media*.

29
Shannon Mattern, "Ether and Ore: An Archeology of Urban Intelligences," in *Ways of Knowing Cities*, ed. Laura Kurgan and Dare Brawley (New York: Columbia Books on Architecture and the City, 2019), 125.

The Wall of Mabel's Studio, as specified by: Curtis Roth,
painted by: Mabel and erased by: Zhu, Stuttgart/Dafen, 2016/2017.

come to define its qualities. The digitally surveilled world
runs parallel to the material world, but also intersects
and is entangled with it as well. If we assume authenticity
is something to be found only in one or the other, we let
an imbalance of political power be given over to technology, economy, ecology, or the institutional entities that
enforce, police and monetize how reality appears. For
architecture, the complexity of these issues will require
a transformation and expansion its disciplinary concepts
to engage, occupy, and subvert these mediations.

The Wall of Gene's Studio, as specified by: Curtis Roth,
painted by: Gene and erased by: Norman, Stuttgart/Dafen, 2016/2017.

The Wall of Huang's Studio, as specified by: Curtis Roth,
painted by: Huang and erased by: Bao, Stuttgart/Dafen, 2016/2017.

The Wall of Giacomo's Studio, as specified by: Curtis Roth,
painted by: Giacomo and erased by: Alan, Stuttgart/Dafen, 2016/2017.

Frontiers
of Design

Ronald Rael
and
Virginia San
Fratello

On July 28, 2019, our office gathered a team of collaborators, friends and community members along the 18-foot-high steel wall that divides the cities of El Paso and Juárez. Over the course of a few hours, we installed three pink teeter-totters that bobbed between a desolate stretch of Sunland Park, New Mexico[1] and the Mexican *colonia* of Anapra, on the outskirts of Ciudad Juarez.[2] That afternoon, at our humble gathering along the border, mothers, children, artists, designers and curators from both sides of the divide congregated and shared a moment of *convivencia*. This word, *convivir*, doesn't have a direct translation in English. "Co-exist" or "fellowship" might come close; however, one translation seems too scientific, while the other sounds too religious. In this context, the closest translation would probably be simply "hanging out and having fun."

Unexpectedly, this event was shared by millions across social media. Many called it an important moment of release from the tensions fueled by continued media coverage of family separation at the border, as well as the never-ending quest by the Trump administration to acquire funds for more wall construction. For us, the work also demonstrated that there is another borderland that exists outside the *white gaze*. It's something that we do not often hear or see about

[1]
Sunland Park is a city in southern New Mexico, immediately east of El Paso, on the borders of Texas and the Mexican state of Chihuahua.

[2]
The teeter-totters are pink, a color used to pay respect to the hundreds of women and girls killed since 1993 in Ciudad Juárez.

when communicating the realities of the borderlands; these
territories are not simply a barren desert landscape comprised of "bad *hombres*" but, rather, an ecologically rich and
socially diverse set of communities filled with intelligent
and caring families, who live with their children in communities where they laugh, play and take pictures with their
cell phones despite the hardships of poverty, xenophobia and
the oppression reflected in the construction of walls.

Our architecture workshop has worked on projects near
the United States—Mexico border since 2001, but our ancestors have lived along the Rio Grande watershed for millennia.
This region extends from where the Rio Grande currently ends,
in El Paso, TX and Juárez, Chihuahua, to where it begins: the
San Luis Valley in southern Colorado, which was the northern-
most borderland prior to 1848, known as the Mexican territory
of *Santa Fe de Nuevo Méjico*. As designers, we recognized that
our own work, in our own land, did not have to contort our own
understanding of the borderlands in response to the vantage
point of the white gaze. Instead, we could demonstrate who
borderland people are, not who others *think* they are.

Working outside the lens of the white gaze has been
an increasing focus of our borderland work. Seen together, it
questions the limited range of processes, materials, agendas and technologies that architecture institutions uniformly
agree upon as relevant. This emphasis is particularly true
for those institutes that reflect a Euro-centric, modernist

At left and right, photos of the Teeter Totter Wall show three bright pink seesaws slotted into gaps of the steel border fence between the United States and Mexico. It was a day filled with joy, excitement, and togetherness.

perspective that has traditionally dominated architectural discourse, as well as the more recent "-isms" that have pervaded recent the recent history of discourse in our profession, including deconstructionism, post-modernism and parametricism.

That moment of *convivencia* demonstrated that play and design can too be a form of activism, as illustrated by our *Teeter-Totter Wall*. Using a similar approach, earlier during that summer of 2019, we concluded a project called *Mud Frontiers*.

In 2010, on the 40th anniversary of the *Smithsonian Magazine*, the publication announced the "40 Things You Need to Know About the Next 40 Years." Number one proclaimed: "Sophisticated Buildings will be made of Mud" — a bold, if not controversial prognostication at a time when digital fabrication and computer-aided design was seen as the *avant-garde* in architecture. Even before the Smithsonian put their prediction in print, we already believed in the power of mud having grown up in the same adobe house that we currently live in today, as did Rael's mother, her mother, and her mother before her.

Mud Frontiers was a two-part research project to better understand the capacities and potentials of the traditional pottery and the earthen construction traditions that have guided our ancestors for centuries. Over the course of our investigations, we journeyed from the contemporary borderlands along the Rio Grande watershed in El

The Maker's Mark

Kyle Dugdale

Paso to the ancient borderlands and the headwaters of the Rio Grande in southern Colorado's San Luis Valley. During this trip, we explored technologies and traditions that challenge the standard tropes of robotic fabrication most commonly found in architectural research.

Each phase of *Mud Frontiers* consisted of on-site research and a set of built explorations that posed new possibilities for architecture, using the most traditional of materials: clay, water and wheat straw. Within our profession today, these materials would be categorized under the unfortunate term, "alternative," connoting a sense of otherness. Instead, we use these materials to push the boundaries of sustainable and ecological construction in a project that explores traditional clay craft in the context of both architecture and pottery. The end goal of this endeavor was to demonstrate that low-cost and low-labor construction should not be relegated to an "alternative choice" but as an intuitive choice that is simultaneously accessible, economical and safe.

The first phase of the project analyzed the earthen architecture and clay pottery of the *Mogollon* culture (200 C.E.- 1450). These artifacts define the archeological history of the *Jornada Mogollon*, the region where the borderland cities of El Paso and Juárez are currently situated. Excavated pit houses and above-ground adobe structures characterize *Mogollon* architecture. By 400 C.E., this region witnessed the development of a distinctive, indigenous coil-and-scrape pottery technique, known as El Paso Brownware.

Fig. 1. Zaha Hadid Architects, One Thousand Museum,
Miami, June 2016. Photo by Field Condition.

Taos Pueblo is an ancient pueblo belonging to a Taos-
speaking (Tiwa) Native American tribe of Puebloan people.
It lies about 1 mile (1.6 km) north of the modern city
of Taos, New Mexico, USA. The pueblos are considered to
be one of the oldest continuously inhabited communities
in the United States. This has been designated a UNESCO
World Heritage Site. Photograph by John Fyfe, 1992.

This is a story of four things: a vinyl banner, a stained-glass window, a ceramic tile and a glowing screen bearing the promise of architecture. Two of these things belong to the fifteenth century; the others are ours. They contradict one another in curious ways; but when juxtaposed, they also speak of the limits and responsibilities of the architectural project as such.[1]

ONE

On a recent visit to Miami I found myself driving along the Atlantic shoreline of South Florida, past the site of Zaha Hadid's One Thousand Museum condominium tower. The project was, at that moment, still very much under construction. Cranes stood poised to supervise the rising structure. The precast shell of its concrete exoskeleton, recently shipped from Dubai, stood exposed in a posture of temporary anatomical embarrassment, set against the voids of the unenclosed floor slabs beyond. Painted hoardings lined the boundary of the building site, drawing the public's attention to the identity of the building's designer. But the architect herself was absent.

Instead, workers had hung a banner from the tower's unfinished Biscayne Boulevard façade: a four-story portrait, presented as a tribute to the life of a great architect.[2] Reproduced in black and white on vinyl, tied back to the building's structure, its taut surface rippling in a stiffening Atlantic breeze, the architect's image looked out eastward through the tracery of the surrounding scaffolding, a face substituting for the façade. Below the portrait, in smooth modern letterforms, was printed a brief text:

ZAHA HADID
1950–2016

Above, also in capital letters, stood a more explicit claim:

HER LEGACY
LIVES ON

I found myself unexpectedly troubled by this encounter. Why? Perhaps I was simply unaccustomed to seeing the image of the architect hung from the façade of the contemporary city at such a super-human scale. More familiar is the image of man as the measure of all things, architecture included; here, instead, was the image of a woman scaled to the measure of the architecture. Or maybe I was rendered uncomfortable by the easy juxtaposition of commemoration with

1
This essay builds on an earlier essay in a previous issue of this journal: "They Too Were Silent," *Perspecta* 48, Amnesia (2015): 108–17. I am grateful to the editors and to Philip Bess for comments on earlier versions of this text.

2
The image appears to be the 2007 portrait by celebrity photographer Steve Double, widely circulated online, and here printed in reverse.

163

Our research in this region unearthed and re-examined these traditions using 21st-century technological capabilities, coupled with local skills and emerging craft practices. Local clays were gathered from various sites throughout the Juárez and El Paso communities. Using customized, accessible software and additive manufacturing robotics, we produced over 170 ceramic vessels and a 3D-printed adobe structure to connect the forefront of digital manufacturing with the traditional coiled pottery techniques, as well as the subterranean, adobe architecture of the area.

In the project's second phase, we explored the earthen architecture and clay pottery traditions of ancestral Pueblo cultures (700 C.E.-Present) and both the indigenous and colonized cultures of northern New Mexico and southern Colorado (1598 C.E.-Present). We examined how collectively these regional-defining architectures tell a story of an evolving and merging set of craft traditions, all centered around earthen materials. Here, our explorations were inspired by numerous techniques. In one investigation, we studied the puddled mud building traditions found in the Pueblos of Northern New Mexico, most notably Taos Pueblo, which was constructed largely of hand-molded mud to create a multi-story dwelling, which also incorporated adobe bricks, a technology imported from Spain. Other analyses studied the pottery traditions of the Taos and Picuris Pueblos, who used harvested, wild micaceous clay dug from the Sangre de Christo and San Juan Mountains.

marketing. Immediately adjacent, Chad Oppenheimer's Ten Museum Park — a self-described exploration "of the hedonistic possibilities of architecture in a futuristic tropical playground of urban sophistication" — offers space on its façade for three-story backlit advertisements, celebrating the narratives, rituals and spirits of modern consumer culture: Lacoste, Equinox Fitness, Havana Club, Maker's Mark, their translucent images glowing with appeal.[3] Or perhaps I am guilty of a self-righteous distaste for the commodification of architecture and the architect — a commodification conveniently contained within that term *starchitect*. Perhaps I simply remain, in this regard, retrograde, preferring that the architect's legacy be materialized in the architecture itself, rather than represented through the medium of advertising.

And yet — should we not, in fact, celebrate the life of the architect? — not least, the life of an architect as brilliant as Zaha Hadid? Should we not honor the memory of a woman with an acclaimed capacity for pioneering new models for the discipline, overturning the prejudices of history, serving as idol for new generations of emerging voices, building a legacy that lives on?

3
Ten Museum Park," Oppenheim Architecture, accessed January 23, 2019, http://oppenoffice.com/project/957/.

4
1000 Biscayne Tower and The Regalia Group, "About: Zaha Hadid (1950–2016)," One Thousand Museum, accessed January 14, 2019, https://1000museum.com/about/.

Certainly, the publicity for One Thousand Museum is explicit about its ambitions; the visitor to the project's marketing website will find the architect's name, here too reproduced in capital letters, providing the headline for a notably personal tribute:[4]

ZAHA HADID (1950–2016)

On March 31, 2016, the world unexpectedly lost one of its brightest stars. A revolutionary who redefined architecture for her generation, Dame Zaha Hadid left behind a body of work that is and will remain an inspiration to those within her field, as well as countless others well beyond it… We are deeply committed to ensuring that the single residential skyscraper she designed in the western hemisphere during her lifetime will live up to every expectation she had for it.

Zaha Hadid, the architect, is here identified as one of the world's "brightest stars" — a designation not unfamiliar to the contemporary reader. The tone of this assertion is, after all, in keeping with the spirit of its time and place, perhaps even with the proverbial will of the epoch: in this instance the will of early

In order to gather samples for our research, we worked with an industry partner, 3D Potter, co-designing and deploying customized but low-cost and portable robots into the environments where we worked. The robots were engineered to be carried into a site where local soils could be harvested, tested and used immediately to make large-scale 3D printed structures, experiments that we conceptualized under four themes: *Hearth*, *Beacon*, *Lookout* and *Kiln*.

Hearth explores how thin mud wall construction can be reinforced using local, rot-resistant juniper wood. The wood holds the walls together, but it also extends beyond the walls of the structure on the outside, while remaining flush on the inside. This dynamic of construction references the cultural differences between the architectural traditions of Pueblo and indigenous *Méjicano* buildings. The interior contains a 3D-printed adobe bench (also known as *tarima* in the local dialect), surrounding a *fogón* (fireplace), which burns the aromatic juniper.

Beacon tests how the texture and undulation of 3D-printed mud coils can produce the thinnest possible structural enclosures. These coils are then illuminated at night, contrasting the difference between the concave and convex curves that create the mud walls.

Lookout is an exploration in structure, a 3D-printed staircase made entirely of adobe. A dense network of undulating mud coils is laid out to create a structure strong enough

twenty-first-century modernity — which differs, we presume, from that of the previous century. The will of twentieth-century Modernism, in contrast, was tied by official accounts to a well-publicized commitment not to individual celebrity but to architectural anonymity, understood as a characteristic that could be read into architecture at its most vital moments throughout history. Gothic architecture, in particular, was the frequent object of such descriptions: Ludwig Mies van der Rohe may be imagined to have spoken for many when he argued, in 1924, that "medieval cathedrals are significant to us as creations of a whole epoch rather than as works of individual architects. Who asks for the name of these builders? Of what significance are the fortuitous personalities of their creators? …We are concerned today with questions of a general nature. The individual is losing significance; his destiny is no longer what interests us."[5]

It will not escape the reader's attention that this lapidary statement reaches us through the pages of Philip Johnson's monograph on Mies's life work, its frontispiece a portrait of the great architect himself. The commitment to architectural anonymity has, in practice, rarely been as absolute as Mies's statement might suggest. That said — is this not the appropriate moment at which to set aside at last any surviving pieties regarding the superiority of architectural anonymity, along with remaining stereotypes of the Gothic? Is it not curiously fitting that the world's largest portrait of Zaha Hadid should be found in the city of Miami, attached to a block of super-luxury high rise apartments at the city's "most prestigious new residential address?"[6] Miami is not committed to anonymity either; on the contrary, it has a reputation as "a city obsessed with image," where "branding and popularity are everything."[7] The city itself accumulates labels: "the epitome of modern man . . . a tropical urban lifestyle where all is streamline, bright, and sunny"; "the Rome of the Caribbean . . . the best city of its age"; simultaneously the "city of the future" and a "city of today."[8] How does One Thousand Museum fit into this context? According to its general contractor, "People here appreciate greatness…. A long time ago, 25 years ago, you would never see a building like this in Miami, and now all the great architects from around the world want to have their mark on Miami."[9] *A long time ago, 25 years ago.*

Hadid's architecture has itself occasionally been described as a form of modern Gothic. This is no doubt a

5
Ludwig Mies van der Rohe, "Architecture and the Times" (translating his 1924 "*Baukunst und Zeitwille*"), in Philip C. Johnson, *Mies van der Rohe* (New York: Museum of Modern Art, 1947), 186. For a discussion of the implications of this passage (which includes Mies's famous assertion that "architecture is the will of the epoch translated into space"), see David Watkin, *Morality and Architecture: The Development of a Theme in Architectural History and Theory from the Gothic Revival to the Modern Movement* (Oxford: Clarendon Press, 1977), 37; for a partial biography of imagined Gothic anonymity as an influence on modernity more generally, see the chapters entitled "Brave New World" and "The Historic Mission." Note especially J. M. Richards, "The Condition of Architecture and the Principle of Anonymity," in *Circle: International Survey of Constructive Art*, ed. J. L. Martin, Ben Nicholson, and Naum Gabo (London: Faber and Faber, 1937), 184–86, discussed at Watkin, *Morality and Architecture*, 49.

.6
1000 Biscayne Tower and The Regalia Group, "One Thousand Museum: Residences by Zaha Hadid Architects," One Thousand Museum, accessed January 4, 2019, https://1000museum.com.

7
Juan J. Alayo, "Fair Weather Fans," *Clog: Miami* (2013): 103.

8
For these and other epithets see the contributions to *Clog: Miami* (2013); here Rose Bonner, "The Treason of Miami," 25, Andrés Duany, "Miami," 29, and Cathy Leff, "The Magic City: Past, Future, Present," 95.

9
Brad Melzer, president of Plaza Construction, quoted in Travis Cohen, "Zaha Hadid's 1000 Museum Lights Up the Downtown Skyline," Miami New Times, February 14, 2018, accessed January 25, 2019, http://www.miaminewtimes.com/arts/zaha-hadids-1000-museum-lights-up-the-downtown-skyline-10085308.

The portable robot performs early tests. Photo by the authors.

misrepresentation. But the tower of One Thousand Museum might at first glance fit the description quite well, its skeletal structure looking wistfully back across the Atlantic toward the geographic origins of an earlier Gothic. In adopting the vocabulary of a "modern Gothic," the emphasis is typically placed, after all, on a perceived synthesis of structural clarity and ornamental effect, and if structural clarity has not always been the hallmark of Hadid's architecture, the demands of the condominium-tower typology have in this instance evidently permitted a certain focusing of attention.[10] Less frequently does the speaker cite any affinity with the figure of the anonymous Gothic architect — a figure that is today, doubtless for good reason, less familiar than it once was. Anonymity is not the primary characteristic of Zaha Hadid Architects. Certainly the portrait hung on Biscayne Boulevard does little to support this association.

TWO

On the far side of the Atlantic, its conception separated by veritable chasms of space, time and architecture — by four thousand miles, by five hundred years and by a comprehensive reversal of attitudes toward the architect himself, or herself — another representation gazes back. In a small town in the west of England, set beneath the rounded profiles of the ancient Malvern Hills, themselves softened by the action of a prehistoric sea, stands the Priory of Great Malvern, founded in the eleventh century, built in the language of Norman architecture, and subsequently enlarged in the vocabulary of the Perpendicular Gothic. Despite this later extension, it is not a structure of extraordinary dimensions. However, it contains what is arguably among the finest surviving stained glass of the fifteenth century, declared truly magnificent by no less a critic than the Gothic revivalist A. W. N. Pugin.[11] Its glowing images can be appreciated only from within the building's interior, being intended to instruct the devout believer rather than to seduce the passing consumer; and it cedes, on the exterior, to the architectural order of its Gothic framework. Yet inside, the painted glazing comes alive with embodied narratives articulated in deeply saturated colors. From the tracery of a window belonging to the south clerestory of the nave, there emerges a familiar figure.[12] This is the master builder, the ἀρχι-τέκτων or architect, holding the compass that serves as symbol of the discipline

10
Kurt Dannwolf, Principal at ODP, Architect of Record for One Thousand Museum, states that "the ideology of the way in which it is built is to expose the columns, rather than hide them behind a wall." "One Thousand Museum," O'Donnell Dannwolf and Partners Architects, September 16, 2016, accessed January 4, 2019, http://odparchitects.com/news/2016/9/16/onethousand-museum.

11
A. W. N. Pugin to William Osmond, October 27, 1833, in The Collected Letters of A. W. N. Pugin, ed. Margaret Belcher, vol. 1, 1830–1842 (Oxford: Oxford University Press, 2001), 18.

12
The glass was subsequently moved, in the mid-nineteenth century, to a window in what is now St Anne's Chapel. See James Nott, Malvern Priory Church: Descriptive Accounts of its Ancient Stained Glass, Old Tombs, Tesselated Pavements, and Other Antiquities (Malvern: John Thompson, 1894), 48–49, reproducing, with some errors, the text of J. T. Fowler, "Notes on Some Painted Glass in the Priory Church, Great Malvern," Associated Architectural Societies' Reports and Papers 17, no. 1 (1883): 115–120, and Gordon McNeil Rushforth, Medieval Christian Imagery as Illustrated by the Painted Windows of Great Malvern Priory Church, Worcestershire, together with a Description and Explanation of All the Ancient Glass in the Church (Oxford: Clarendon Press, 1936), 16–17.

to be walked upon. This method also demonstrates how wide, airy walls can create interior enclosures that represent new possibilities for insulation, especially in the harsh climate of the San Luis Valley, which can drop below -20° F in the winter.

Kiln iterates several of the techniques we studied, including undulating or interlocking mud deposition to create structural and insulative walls. Kiln is also used to enclose an area that draws in oxygen and keeps in heat to fire locally sourced clay with burning juniper wood. The products of the kiln, fired micaceous clay derived from the traditions of Taos and Picuris Pueblos, are hybrids of technology and technique. Each 3D-printed ceramic vessel holds areas in which the carbon has not been burned out, leaving a deep black color, evoking Taos Pueblo traditions. Each vessel also features micaceous slip on its surface, that when the carbon burns out completely reveals itself as brilliant gold.

As a body of work, The Teeter-Totter Wall and Mud Frontiers explore sustainability, accessibility and open-source technology through the lens of local tradition. Yet, the work is also a form of activism, standing as physical manifestations of the belief that design is an integral component of the activist agenda.

While developing these projects, we were incensed by the news that chronicled how nearly 2,000 children had been separated from their families at the U.S. border. In

Fig. 2. Unknown artist, Creation Window, Priory Church, Great Malvern,
ca. 1485. Photo by Groenling, 2014.

response, we created an open-source, downloadable sign that
anyone could use to protest these horrific acts. The work
was adapted from an image, originally created in the late
1980s. The image was designed by the Navajo graphic artist
John Hood, a Vietnam War veteran from New Mexico, who worked
for the California Department of Transportation. Hood was
tasked with creating a sign in response to the sharp rise in
immigrant traffic deaths. People who immigrated from Mexico
without documents were not able to cross through ports of
entry. Instead, they were being dropped off on the side
of the highway by *coyotes*, leaving them with no choice but
to run across the dangerous roads.

The image Hood developed was meant to elicit empathy,
as well as the immediate recognition of a potential traffic
hazard. A little girl's flowing pigtails are illustrated to
evoke the motion of running. She is accompanied by a father
whose profile was modeled on Cesar Chavez, an intentional
move by the designer.

This iconic sign was a subversive work of design activism. Hood believed that drivers would be more cautious if a
little girl was the face of the campaign, as he felt they "are
dear to the heart, especially for fathers." Hood also likened
the immigrants' plight to those endured by the Navajo tribe,
such as the 1864 Long Walk of the Navajo and the conditions
of present-day reservations in northeastern New Mexico.

and as guarantor of its authority both in measurement and in drawing — in judgement and in creation, in assessing the world as it is and in imagining the world as it could be.

It is an exquisitely crafted window, to be sure; but in other ways, it is not calculated to astonish. The name of its maker is unknown. It is, by any standard, a rather small representation, just a few inches in height. Yet the implications of this window are massive. Setting aside the disputed anonymity of the Gothic, it is in itself unremarkable that a work of architecture should contain within its iconography the image of an architect. But what is significant is the identity of this particular architect.[13] For this figure is not anonymous. This architect is God.

To be precise, the figure of God is here presented in the context of an account of the first day of creation — described in the sonorous words of the first sentence of the book of Genesis, reproduced in fragmentary Latin immediately below. *In principio creavit Deus caelum et terram*: "In the beginning God created the heaven and the earth."[14] This architect is none other than the architect of the universe. One is tempted to suggest that this is, quite literally, the original *starchitect*, shown at the very

moment of the creation of the heavenly bodies.[15]

What are the implications, for architecture, of this image? — of this identification of God and architect? It is of course possible for the modern reader to speculate on the question without suspending a presumed disbelief in the very existence of a creator of heaven and earth. The architectural reader, in particular, is well equipped to imagine that which cannot be seen.

At the very least it might be said that the conception of God as architect implies a certain affiliation between creator and creation. We speak, today, of architecture as a domain of *intellectual property*, and thus we objectify what is often a rather personal association, which might find a more appropriate analogy in the relationship between parent and child. The architectural creation *belongs* in a peculiarly personal way to its architect, even after the moment of project delivery. One Thousand Museum *belongs* to Zaha Hadid.[16] Even after the project is handed over to the vicissitudes of the marketplace, it still bears the architect's name. As we are inclined to declare, the architect's legacy lives on in the architecture. Thus, it is presumed to be the architect who has the fullest understanding

13
See Nott, *Malvern Priory Church*, 50–51, and L. A. Hamand, *A Little Guide to Malvern Priory Church* (St. Albans: Campfield Press, 1933), 17, with further reference to Anthony Charles Deane, *A Short Account of Great Malvern Priory Church* (London: G. Bell, 1914), 82. For the listing in the *Corpus Vitrearum Medii Aevi*, see the entry for Malvern Priory, St Anne's Chapel, south window, main light, window III, panel 3a.

14
See Rushforth, *Medieval Christian Imagery*, 149–52.

15
For an account of this architect, see Christine Smith, ed., *Before and After the End of Time: Architecture and the Year 1000* (New York: George Braziller, 2000). "The bibliography on the image of God as architect . . . is large" (75).

16
For a very similar statement applied by Louis Kahn to Frank Lloyd Wright's Johnson Wax Research Tower, see Louis Kahn, Paul Weiss, and Vincent Scully, "On the Responsibility of the Architect," *Perspecta* 2 (1953): 47.

John Hood's original iconic sign (left) and it's reinterpretation by the authors (right).

of the project's intent. Indeed, her vision may endure, in text or image, even if posterity does violence to her design intent. And the architecture may, in due course, be restored to the glories of the architect's original plan. These ideas are architectural, yes; but they are also theological — or, at least, they can readily be translated into their theological analogues. The creator claims a legitimate authority over the creation, over the creature.[17]

By the same token, when the creatures in question are human beings, traditionally distinguished from the rest of creation by a peculiar capacity for moral responsibility, the obligations do not extend only in one direction. The conception of God as architect implies a certain reciprocal obligation on the part of the creature toward its creator. To be responsible, after all, is to be answerable — to owe a response. And a response presupposes a prior address. So a responsibility, by definition, is a responsibility *to* someone. The very word *responsibility* is derived from the Latin *spondere*, which is, in turn, tied back to the Greek σπένδειν, used to describe the act of *making an offering* — a drink offering, to be precise, poured out to the gods. It might, therefore, be argued that

17
Architects curious about the texture of theological discourse on this subject may enjoy Robert Jenson's brief "Creator and Creature," *International Journal of Systematic Theology* 4, no. 2 (July 2002): 216–21, with reference (218) to the architecturally intriguing eighth-century formulation of John of Damascus, "God is his own space."

any responsibility worthy of its name is, first of all, a responsibility to the divine.

Be that as it may, we creatures of modernity are no longer inclined to recognize that responsibility or to credit that creator. The image of God as architect is no longer current. In its place, we have other images, other portraits — among them, that portrait on Biscayne Boulevard. We may well be hesitant to speak of the architect as God — after all, our discipline is still recovering from a reputation for wanting to play God. But it is certainly the case that in the absence of a divine creator, whose intent may be understood to shape all things, and from whom all subsequent authorities and obligations may be derived, the human creator accrues to herself a certain freedom — and, along with it, certain new and rather awesome responsibilities.

For the architect is the figure in whose image we see the capacity to shape the world — to imagine its possibilities, maybe even to right its wrongs: to rebuild its ruins, to restore its damaged fabric so as to correspond to the conception of a more just, a more equal, a more sustainable world. Architecture here assumes a redemptive role. And where might we turn for our conception of redemption? In the absence of divine

When building upon the genius of this work to protest family separation for our own sign, we made one simple design move. We turned the family to face each other. As the last of Hood's original signs were being removed from the southern California county where they were first placed, we saw an unexpected outcome. Our open-source, downloadable sign found itself returning to the highway in the form of a massive billboard, seen by hundreds of thousands of motorists. Our sign had been mounted by the *For Freedoms* campaign, a set of programs, exhibitions and public art installations, led by the artists Hank Willis Thomas and Eric Gottesman. The campaign's main intent was to deepen public discussions on civic issues and core values in order to advocate for equality, dialogue and civic participation.[3] This act became a catalyst. To us, it demonstrated the power that architects have to reconsider the topics, landscapes and "clients" with which we choose to invest our time and energy, even if such an approach does not necessarily fit within the dogmas of the discipline. This form of power can be transformative and demonstrates that our relevance as a profession can emerge from materials that are often not considered, forms and landscapes that are unfamiliar to the majority, and the voices of the least represented—the participants in the built environment that the profession hears from the least.

3
https://forfreedoms.org/about/

revelation, must we not create it for ourselves?

In fact, have we not come to think of religion itself in architectural terms — as something that may bear the name of an individual, but is ultimately fabricated over time by societies and cultures? The modern view of religion is that of an essentially human construct. And if religion is best understood as a construct, in the manner of a work of architecture, can it not also be judged according to architectural criteria? Notions of truth are replaced with other, more circumspect principles: commodity, firmness, delight, or any number of less poetic substitutes — sustainability, criticality, intellectual sophistication, or sheer viability as a return on investment. Indeed, is not the very notion of God understood as a product of human design, as a figure of our own invention? And in this regard, do we humans not effectively position ourselves as God's creators, best understood in the image of the architect? We have neatly reversed the meaning of that window at Great Malvern; we have become the architects, not only of our world, but of God himself.[18]

For the discipline of architecture, this is no light responsibility — quite the contrary. For the onus now lies on the architect to do what was previously intimated: to shape the world, to right its wrongs, to restore its damaged fabric so as to correspond to the conception of a more just, a more equal, a more sustainable world. That burden lies heavier on the discipline today, perhaps, than ever before. Its weight can be measured in the groaning curricula of schools of architecture that seek to redirect future architects' attentions, as they feel they must, away from narrowly aesthetic, tectonic or formal speculations toward the weightier problems of our time.

Just at the moment when that weight lies more heavily than ever before, it has become harder to reach consensus on an appropriate response. If architecture must by necessity impose onto the world — quite literally — a vision of a better future, we architects have with good reason grown increasingly reticent about the premises of that project: the validity of imposing on others our own, private conceptions of what constitutes a firm, commodious and delightful future. Zaha Hadid was not, herself, known for dispensing sweeping theoretical screeds, and the more ambitious arguments of Patrik Schumacher, sole remaining partner of Zaha Hadid Architects, have not met with universal acclaim. Generally speaking, ours is no longer an age of consensus or of promises to create the new building

18
For more on this see my "Faith in Architecture," in "Ethics in Architecture: Festschrift for Karsten Harries," ed. Eduard Führ, special issue, *Wolkenkuckucksheim | Cloud-Cuckoo-Land | Воздушный замок: International Journal of Architectural Theory* 22, no. 36 (2017): 71–82.

of the future, "which will rise one day toward heaven from the hands of a million workers as the crystal symbol of a new faith."[19] Who am I, after all, to tell you how to live? There is an expectation, yes, that the architect lead the way in shaping the good life, in building the *città felice*; but in the absence of shared narratives, it has become increasingly difficult to prescribe the nature of that life and the boundaries of that place.

So, in practice, the market rules. Consumer culture steps in. One Thousand Museum "creates a six-star lifestyle within an exceptionally elegant private residential tower. Over 30,000 square feet of beautifully designed venues for swimming, sunning, socializing, fitness, and pampering cater to fewer than 100 residences, offering the luxury of abundant space."[20] And the architectural project takes upon itself an increasingly transactional quality.

THREE

A few steps away from that window in Great Malvern Priory can be found a small fifteenth-century encaustic tile, one of many in the church, set into a massive Norman pillar near the west end of the nave. It is, by all accounts, of local manufacture, burned in a kiln on the monks' property, two hundred yards east.

19
Walter Gropius, "From the First Proclamation of the Weimar Bauhaus," in *Bauhaus 1919–1928*, ed. Herbert Bayer, Walter Gropius, and Ise Gropius (New York: The Museum of Modern Art, 1938), 18, with one word of the translation substituted to preserve the strength of the original German. For a discussion of this text and its implications see Dugdale, "Faith in Architecture," 73.

20
1000 Biscayne Tower and The Regalia Group, "Building: Overview," One Thousand Museum, accessed January 14, 2019, https://1000museum.com/building/.

Fig. 3. Unknown artist, Executor's Tile, Priory Church, Great Malvern, ca. 1450. Photograph Bob Embleton, 2010.

Commonly known as the "Executor's Tile," it is famous, today, for its inscription, imprinted onto its surface by means of fixed wooden type — a method that allowed for the fabrication and distribution of multiple copies.[21] The text is worn by the intervening years, but it remains legible. And it proves to be a remarkable exhortation: nothing less than an appeal to posterity, voiced by the very fabric of the architecture. Transposing the original Middle English letters, the following lines of verse may be read:[22]

Thenke.mon.yi.liffe
mai.not.eù.endure.
yat.yow.dost.yi.self
of.yat.yow.art.sure.
but.yat.yow.kepist
un.to.yi.sectur.cure.
an.eù.hit.availe.ye.
hit.is.but.aventure

Think, man, thy life
may not ever endure;
that thou dost thyself
of that thou art sure;
but that thou keepest
unto thy executor's cure,
and ever it availe thee,
it is but aventure.

Although the letterforms may be hard to make out, the message is clear. You, the reader, are urged to *think*. And this form of thinking is not mere intellectual thought, but rather something closer to the exercise of historical and existential honesty. You are urged by the architecture of the past to recognize the ephemerality of your present and to acknowledge your powerlessness over the future. Yes, you may believe in the future; you may even aspire to shape the future for the better. And while you live, you may exert a degree of control over your work. But then? Will your executor carry out your plans according to your wishes? Will your legacy live on? The outcome is unknown: *it is but aventure*.

Conspicuously located near the entrance to the church, this tile has been interpreted as an encouragement to liberality on the part of the reader toward the immediate needs of the institution and its building.[23] But we architects might read its message differently. Yes, it articulates a general diffidence as to man's capacity to shape the future with any certainty. But architecture is not only a prophetic art, but also an enterprise that depends heavily upon the care of its various executors, who accept the architect's design, build it out into a material

21
For this early form of printing, compared with contemporary developments on paper in Germany and the Netherlands, see Jane Marshall, *Three Tours of England's Wonderful Abbeys* (London: Chancery Books, 1961), 206.

22
For more on this tile, along with the transcription and transposition (using the letter *y* for the Middle English *þ* or *thorn*) quoted here, see the chapter entitled "The Tesselated Pavements of Malvern," in Nott, *Malvern Priory Church*, 71–103, especially 82–83, reproducing a description drawn from Albert Way, "On Pavements of Figured Tiles, Particularly Those at Great Malvern," *Gentleman's Magazine* (May 1844): 492–96. See also H. Card, *A Dissertation on the Antiquities of the Priory of Great Malvern, in Worcestershire* (London: J. G. and F. Rivington, 1834), 34. The reader may compare the rendition by Robert Chambers, "Spirit of Old Inscriptions," in *Essays Moral and Economic* (Edinburgh, 1847), 201. The author comments, at 199, on the well-established tradition of writing on architecture: "It was a custom of our ancestors in the middle ages, and particularly in the fifteenth and sixteenth centuries, to label every house and public building with inscriptions. . . . Thus, while modern structures are generally dumb even as to the date of their erection, old ones are often found to be curiously eloquent and readable."

23
See for instance Deane, *Great Malvern Priory Church*, 44–46.

Fiona Connor, *#4*, 2019 — ongoing

Fiona Connor's #4 is an artwork that consists of an annual window cleaning in a residential apartment in Long Island City, Queens. The work was produced on the occasion of Connor's 2019 exhibition at SculptureCenter, an art space in the same neighborhood. The piece is presented to the passers-by through a modest plaque on the building. The Long Island City neighborhood is a rapidly developing area home to many new high-rise buildings, a symbol of New York City's accelerated rate of luxury development. The apartment tended by Connor's work is in an older three-story vernacular building, a remnant of a disappearing era.

#4 takes place both physically on the exterior of the apartment and legally, as it is inscribed in the lease for the unit, which now features this service clause in perpetuity. As an artwork, the piece remains invisible to viewers beyond the parties directly involved: tenants of the apartment, the landlord, the artist and the museum. The work is a hyper-local intervention in a single lease. Yet, given its context, it highlights the proximity of art and high-end residential properties and forefronts the maintenance labor that surrounds artistic production.

Fiona Connor, #4, 2019—ongoing

reality, and then maintain and inhabit it over the course of subsequent generations. So this text can also be interpreted as an assertion of the limits of the architectural project. Architecture is such that its products are not created *ex nihilo*, or brought into existence by *fiat*, but rather made with a great deal of labour and collaboration. Indeed, it would once have been said that it is the mark of God the architect to *create*; the mark of the human architect is to *make*.[24] And that making is itself constrained. As an architect, you may exert a degree of control over your sketches, renderings, graphic materials, plans and specifications, however limited by budget, code, program or schedule. But then? Will your executors carry out your plans according to your wishes?

And this is not even to begin to consider the uncertainties of history, politics, reputation, litigation, economic decline, climate change, material failure or so-called acts of God. No assurance can be given. Your executors can modify your plans without prior notice. *It is but aventure.*

What are the effects of this condition? One could list a full range of possible outcomes. At one end lies a certain cynicism, a cold, clear-eyed pragmatism that surrenders all too easily to the guaranteed rewards of the short-term transactional exchange. At the other end stands an overheated proprietary attitude that must protect at all costs the maker's mark, the individual architect's carefully crafted identity. The effects of both extremes are all too visible in the contemporary disciplinary landscape. Indeed, the furthest extremes meet again on the dark side, in a paroxysm of marketing brilliance that has left its own distinctive mark on the Florida coastline and, more broadly, on the torn fabric of the twenty-first century city.

To the believer in the creator God — God the architect — this condition of *aventure* provokes little in the way of existential anxiety. Quite the contrary. The work of the individual architect takes place within a larger narrative of creation, redemption and eventual restoration; and the name that warrants exaltation is the name of God — the compassionate, the merciful, the God of past, present and future. To the incredulity of a faithless modernity, the believer insists that true freedom is found in submission to this God, and that this submission grants to the architectural project a freedom of its own — and with it, a freedom to commit to the great project of justice, equality and sustainability, without

24
See Smith, *The End of Time*, 28–75, and especially 67: "The Christian distinction between creating and making also set God's activity apart from that of the human artisan who shapes things out of preexisting matter. The absolutely unique character of God's creativity is an unchanging tenet of medieval theology, reiterated from St. Augustine in the fifth century—"the creature cannot create" (*De Trinitate* 3:9)—to St. Thomas Aquinas in the thirteenth."

Fig. 4. One Thousand Museum marketing website.
Screen capture: https://1000museum.com, January 16, 2019.

assuming the full burden of a redemptive obligation.

The analysis of this claim lies beyond the scope of this essay. But to modern readers in their presumed unbelief, this particular consolation is not so readily available.

FOUR

On the second day of my visit to Miami, I passed along Biscayne Boulevard once again. Unsurprisingly, little had changed on the site of One Thousand Museum, and although the general contractor had no doubt made an incremental advance toward the distant goal of final completion, that progress was invisible to the casual observer. But a detail caught my eye. The architect's portrait had apparently torn loose during the night, and the four-story vinyl banner now flapped listlessly in the wind, exposing to the public its blank rear face.

It was hurricane season in the Atlantic Basin. The coast of Florida had recently been pounded by 130-mile-per-hour winds, and the rising architecture of One Thousand Museum had survived the storm intact. Yet, just days later, the architect's portrait had fallen victim to a lesser hazard — as if in silent concession to the warning on that tile embedded into the structure of Great Malvern Priory.

In itself, this is, of course, hardly significant. The banner was, at best, a temporary tribute, as it was to be taken down soon after to allow work on the façade to proceed unencumbered. More significant for the future is the legacy of Hadid's architecture itself, a legacy that may live on. And indeed, the developers of the project remain conscious of that ambition. As of the time of this writing, the visitor to the marketing website for One Thousand Museum is met with a quotation, reproduced on the glowing screen in capital letters:[25]

"I BELIEVE IN THE IDEA OF THE FUTURE"
— ZAHA HADID

Deeper into the structure of the website, the interested reader will find the more explicit statement quoted earlier: the executors of Hadid's plans "are deeply committed to ensuring that the single residential skyscraper she designed in the western hemisphere during her lifetime will live up to every expectation she had for it."[26] Deeper still, there exists a rather longer and more circumspect disclaimer, written in the boilerplate language of

25
1000 Biscayne Tower and The Regalia Group, "One Thousand Museum: Residences by Zaha Hadid Architects," One Thousand Museum, accessed January 4, 2019, https://1000museum.com.

26
1000 Biscayne Tower and The Regalia Group, "About: Zaha Hadid (1950–2016)," One Thousand Museum, accessed January 14, 2019, https://1000museum.com/about/.

aventure, and evidently pieced together from varying sources, with the occasional modification specific to this particular work of architecture:[27]

> *The building is* currently under construction but not yet completed. Any images of a competed building are artists' renderings incorporating the proposed building into the existing skyline. As depicted in the developers brochures or on the developers website, sketches, renderings, graphics, plans, specifications, services, amenities, terms, conditions and statements contained in this brochure are proposed only, and the Developer reserves the right to modify, revise or withdraw any or all of same in its sole discretion and without prior notice.

And there is more:

> Use and operation of the helipad are conditioned upon obtaining FAA and other governmental approvals. No assurance can be given about whether the approvals can be obtained, and/or if so, the timing of same.
>
> Although described in the present tense, all amenities and services described herein are proposed only and are subject to change during the development of One Thousand Museum. Actual improvements may vary and views may not be available from all condominium units. Future development can limit or eliminate views from a particular condominium unit.
>
> All dimensions are approximate, and all floor plans and development plans are subject to change…. All references to square footage (or square meters) are approximate and the actual configuration may vary…. You should not rely upon any listed figures….
>
> The sketches, renderings, graphic materials, plans, specifications, terms, conditions and statements contained in this brochure are proposed only, and the Developer reserves the right to modify, revise or withdraw any or all of same in its sole discretion and without prior notice…. The developer expressly reserves the right to make modifications, revisions, and changes it deems desirable in its sole and absolute discretion…. The photographs contained in this brochure may be stock photography or have been taken off-site and are used to depict the spirit of the

27
1000 Biscayne Tower and The Regalia Group, "Disclaimer," One Thousand Museum, accessed January 16, 2019, https://1000museum.com/disclaimer/.

Violation City

Ann Lui and Craig Reschke

lifestyles to be achieved rather than any that may exist or that may be proposed….

The condominium units are being sold for personal use and enjoyment and 1000 Biscayne Tower, LLC is not making, nor does it condone, any representations about future profit…. Prospective purchasers of condominium units should not base their buying decision on an expectation of profit.

Prospective purchasers may, if they read these materials too carefully, note a certain inconsistency between the language of confidence — of the architect who believes "in the idea of the future" and the developers who "are deeply committed to ensuring" that her project "will live up to every expectation she had for it" — and the admonitions of the lawyers, who must note that, while "the condominium units are being sold for personal use and enjoyment," the associated images are merely used "to depict the spirit of the lifestyles to be achieved rather than any that may exist or that may be proposed." What, in the end, can interested parties expect from this project? Is it true that this architecture can create for them a specified lifestyle, six-star or otherwise? Will ever it availe

them, financially or existentially? As it turns out, "1000 Biscayne Tower, LLC is not making, nor does it condone, any representations about future profit."

This story is, of course, far from over — whether for the purchasers or for the developers. On the far side of the Atlantic, the future is similarly uncertain. As of the time of this writing, the public battle over Zaha Hadid's legacy is ongoing, and her executors have taken the matter to Britain's High Court "in order to defend her great name and legacy."[28] The maker's mark is contested. Indeed, we read that there have been efforts to disassociate the architect's name from her continuing practice. Those efforts may or may not prove successful; it is not yet clear whether the personality of the creator will give way to anonymity. But that outcome is no longer the architect's responsibility.

What remains the responsibility of every architect is the articulation of a response to the challenge embedded into the surface of that encaustic tile in Great Malvern. After all, if we are hesitant to identify with the attitudes and artefacts of the makers of the fifteenth century, we may also, with good reason, be reluctant to place our faith in those surrogates that bear the distinctive mark of the twenty-first.

28
Rana Hadid, quoted in Jonathan Hilburg, "Patrik Schumacher Sues to Become Sole Executor of Zaha Hadid's Estate," *The Architect's Newspaper*, November 14, 2018, accessed January 7, 2019, https://archpaper.com/2018/11/patrik-schumacher-sues-sole-executor-zaha-hadid-estate/. See also Katharine Keane, "Details of Patrik Schumacher ZHA Executorship Suit Revealed in Legal Documents," *Architect: The Journal of the American Institute of Architects*, January 4, 2019, accessed January 7, 2019, https://www.architect-magazine.com/practice/details-of-patrik-schumacher-zha-executorship-suit-revealed-in-legal-documents and Jonathan Hilburg, "Patrik Schumacher Claims He was Forced to Drop Zaha Hadid's Name from ZHA," *The Architect's Newspaper*, January 4, 2019, accessed January 23, 2019, https://archpaper.com/2019/01/patrik-schumacher-claims-forced-drop-zaha-hadids-name/.

Cities, like dreams, are made of desires and fears, even if the thread of their discourse is secret, their rules are absurd, their perspectives deceitful...
— Marco Polo to the Kublai Khan, *Invisible Cities* (Italo Calvino, 1974)

All of Chicago's buildings are illegal. Since 2006 in Chicago, the city's Department of Buildings inspectors have issued over 1,126,569 building violations at the time of writing.[1] These citations, used by the city to regulate and enforce the building code, are pervasive — exceeding in number even the total number of individual buildings in the city overall.[2] Violations are issued in every neighborhood, in every census tract. These violations are used to describe a myriad of building types: from garages to churches to tall towers, including structures of seemingly all ages and styles. Inspectors issue violations to document their evaluation of buildings' non-compliance with city ordinances, which range from trivial infractions, such as piled-up refuse in a side yard (Violation Code #138056), to major structural damage in foundations (Code #069014) or exterior walls (Code #61014). In the eyes of building inspectors, all of Chicago's buildings are in a process of continuous *slow emergence into violation* — from the splintering of a window sill after rain to the slow movement of a foundation over decades, slipping out of alignment. In 2019, the "conservation bureau" of the Department of Buildings, responsible for existing buildings, undertook 22,273 individual complaint-triggered inspections. City-wide, the majority of these inspections resulted in building violations.[3] In some neighborhoods, as little as 2% of buildings were inspected without finding fault.[4]

What if, when walking the streets of Chicago, one only saw the violations, the errors, and the flaws? If the totality

of the brick wall was obscured in favor of its slowly growing cracks? What if you never saw the person in the window but only the window's uneven frame? What if every city block was not composed of the totality of these conditions but, instead, only the broken porch members, the unaccounted-for smoke, and the crumbling masonry? What opportunities would we see? What stories would we miss?

Violation City revisits Italo Calvino's 1972 novel *Invisible Cities* through the lens of Chicago's building violations.[5] In *Invisible Cities*, the explorer Marco Polo visits with a weary Kublai Khan. Marco Polo tells tales of fifty-five seemingly magical cities from his travels: a city of a

1
All data sourced from the City of Chicago's public open data portal, including building violations since 2006, publicly accessible and updated daily. This data includes all violations, not only those administrated by the Department of Administrative Hearings. For this text, we looked specifically at violations issued by the "conservation bureau" of existing buildings, not violations of permits in new construction. City of Chicago, "Building Violations," Chicago Data Portal, accessed May 25, 2020, https://data.cityofchicago.org/Buildings/Building-Violations/22u3-xenr.

2
The Department of Buildings' "Building Footprints" data counts 820,606 unique buildings in the city of Chicago. "Building Footprints (Current)," Chicago Data Portal, accessed May 25, 2020, https://data.cityofchicago.org/Buildings/Building-Footprints-current-/hz9b-7nh8.

3
We compared 311 complaints for building violations from 2019 with inspections in 2019 and 2020, which produced building violations through address matching. Over 60% of inspections resulted in subsequent violations. However, this does not include the buildings which already had building violations assessed in previous years that would have increased that percentage. An assessment of the full city-wide data is outside the scope of this text.

4
This statistic is from sociologist Robin Bartram's analysis of a "typical" neighborhood in her text: Robin Bartram, "The Cost of Code Violations: How Building Codes Shape Residential Sales Prices and Rents," Housing Policy Debate 29, no. 6 (November 2, 2019): 934.

5
Italo Calvino, Invisible Cities (New York: Harcourt Brace Jovanovich, 1972).

thousand deep wells — a city without thresholds — a city on stilts — a city of eternal markets — a city comprised only of water pipes — a city which throws out all its possessions and begins anew every day — a city with water instead of roads, or with soil instead of air. Through these stories, Marco Polo outlines to Kublai Khan a heuristic technique for understanding cities. Marco Polo teaches us that city is not one monolithic thing; instead, it is a "desert of labile and interchangeable data," a collection of "signs to be deciphered," a place that is constantly constructed and re-constructed by seemingly irreconcilable subjectivities and systems.[6] *Violation City* appropriates this technique to render visible the simultaneous impact and banality of building violations and the institutions which produce them.

In four drawings, *Violation City* zooms into one city block, using an act of fictional subtraction to highlight the twenty most frequently issued building violations since 2006. A single block is drawn through the eyes of Chicago's building inspectors, isolating a form of observational assessment which in conjunction with the city's building code construct and produce the state of "violation" — of buildings in the wrong. Each house collages together a group of misdeeds or failed maintenance that together describe an unspoken form of collective risk. Welcome to Violation City.

6
Ibid., 22.

HOUSE
OF EGRESS

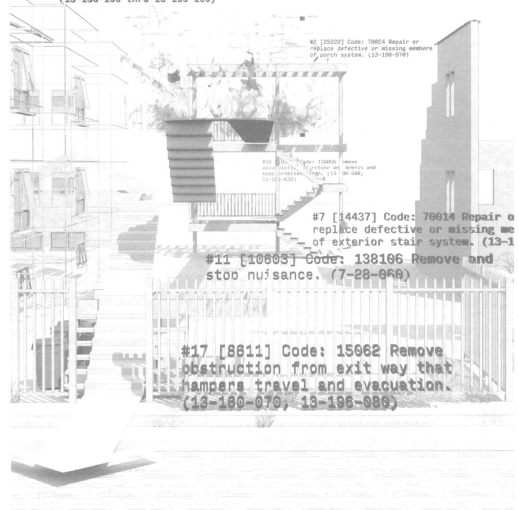

#8 [13436] Code: 197019 Install and
maintain approved smoke detectors.
(13-196-100 thru 13-196-160)

#2 [25220] Code: 70024 Repair or
replace defective or missing members
of porch system. (13-196-570)

#10 [____] Code: 138056 remove
accumulati_ of refuse and debris and
keep premises clean. (13-_96-580,
13-196-630)

#7 [14437] Code: 70014 Repair o_
replace defective or missing me_
of exterior stair system. (13-1_

#11 [10603] Code: 138106 Remove and
stop nuisance. (7-28-060)

#17 [8611] Code: 15062 Remove
obstruction from exit way that
hampers travel and evacuation.
(13-160-070, 13-196-080)

House of Egress

**This house carries the memories of the Great Chicago
Fire; it is a house of smoke and warnings; it is defined by
the constant need for multiple ways out; it is tangled
by obstacles and obstructions; its bones reverberate with
the harmonic rhythm of the well-placed alarms.**

— **Repair or replace defective or missing members
of porch system. (13-196-570)**

— **Repair or replace defective or missing members
of exterior stair system. (13-196-570)**

— **Install and maintain approved smoke detectors.
(13-196-100 thru 13-196-160)**

— **Remove accumulation of refuse and debris and keep
premises clean. (13-196-580, 13-196-630)**

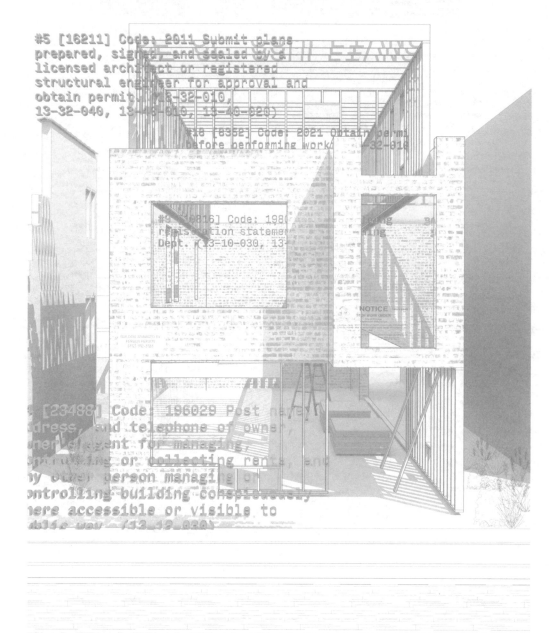

House of Compliance

This is a house of regulations and a house of rule-break-ers; it is formed by marks on paper, notarized forms and ProjectDox 9.1.8.5; its enclosure is built around the ongoing arguments of administrative courts, city legal counsel and zoning attorneys; its archives are both infinite and always missing.

— Post name, address, and telephone of owner, owner's agent for managing, controlling or collecting rents, and any other person managing or controlling building conspicuously where accessible or visible to public way. (13-12-030)

— File building registration statement with Building Dept. (13-10-030, 13-10-040)

— Submit plans prepared, signed, and sealed by a licensed architect or registered structural engineer for approval and obtain permit. (13-32-010, 13-32-040, 13-40-010, 13-40-020)

— Obtain permit before performing work. (13-32-010)

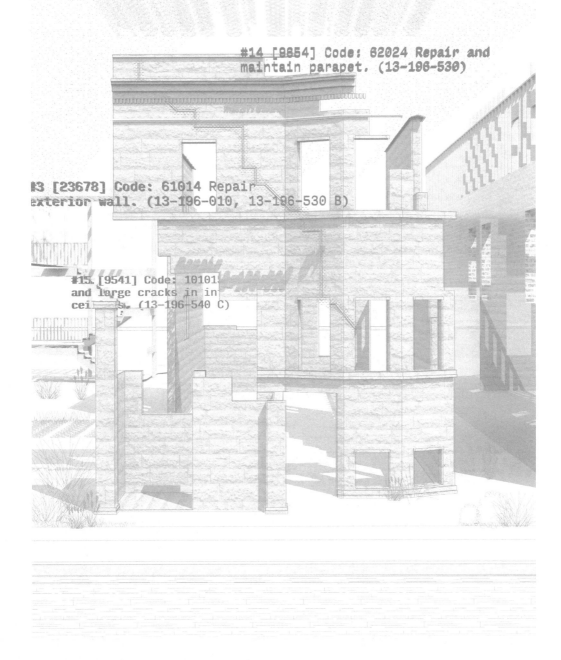

#14 [9854] Code: 62024 Repair and maintain parapet. (13-196-530)

#3 [23678] Code: 61014 Repair exterior wall. (13-196-010, 13-196-530 B)

#15 [9541] Code: 10101 and large cracks in in cei s. (13-196-540 C)

House of Enclosure

This is the house of exteriors (it has no interior). It is made of all the stories that can be captured in a single wall—the refuse left by the framers between the wall studs, the history of the Chicago brick, the weeping of the weep holes in the masonry wall. It is the leak and the crack and the joint left untuckpointed.

— Repair exterior wall. (13-196-010, 13-196-530 B)

— Repair and maintain parapet. (13-196-530)

— Repair holes and large cracks in interior walls or ceilings. (13-196-540 C)

#20 [7820] Code: 63014 Repair or rebuild chimney. (13-196-530, 13-196-59

#8 [15919] Code: 104015 Replace broken, missing or defective window panes. (13-196-550 A)

#19 [7862] Code: 65034 Replace defective window sills. (13-196-550)

#16 [9508] Code: 73014 Repair or replace defective door. (13-196-550 D, E)

House of Openings

This is the house of ways in and out; inside, one can always hear the doors slamming shut, the windows creaking open, the hail on the skylight. It is the opening which lets in the breeze, the friend, the stranger and the unintentional gust of cold air.

— Replace broken, missing or defective window panes. (13-196-550 A)

— Repair or replace defective door. (13-196-550 D, E)

— Replace defective window sills. (13-196-550)

— Repair or rebuild chimney. (13-196-530, 13-196-590)

What is the role of architects in this ongoing push-and-pull between regulation and compliance — an endless war against crumbling parapets and missing smoke detectors — with the city's residents caught in the middle? Building violations work is unglamorous for architects: ungainly in execution, requiring bureaucratic paperwork, rarely producing magazine-worthy photography and poorly paid. However, the fifth most issued building violation since 2006, with over 16,211 occurrences, is the requirement to *"Submit plans prepared, signed, and sealed by a licensed architect or registered structural engineer for approval and obtain permit. (13-32-010, 13-32-040, 13-40-010, 13-40-020)."* Building issues, which require an architect's seal to resolve, often comprise the most serious infractions with risk to public health and safety, ranging from illegally converted basement and attic units to structural failure. Yet, despite this pervasive need for design services across Chicago, registered architects and design firms capable of absolving building violations are located in exactly the areas where this specific building violation is least common, like a bizarre inverted image.^(Fig. 1) The stakes are significant: left unaddressed, building violations can sometimes lead to receivership, forfeiture, and demolition by Chicago — upstream of the city's well-known issues of vacant lots.[7]

 Despite the ubiquity of building violations in Chicago, their impact on communities is uneven. Far from being monolithic in their judgments, the prosecutorial actions by

7

For a call to action in response to the impact of building violations, see: Ann Lui, "Toward an Office of the Public Architect," *Log* 48 (2020): 39-52.

Fig. 1. Map of Chicago showing location of architects and open building violations requiring an architect's stamp. Architects located as Registered Design Firms [IDFPR] as large points and State of Illinois registered architects self-provided addresses. Courtesy of Future Firm.

the Department of Buildings both index and reproduce the city's complexities. Chicago's regulation of new construction and existing buildings acts to maintain public health, accessibility and sound building practices. It enforces provisions hammered out through generations of lobbying, professional expertise, and activism in the city on issues, including fire safety, accessibility, and energy performance. However, while regulations protect welfare, the non-objective and sometimes discretionary systems of building code regulation and compliance continue to reproduce existing inequalities. Building violations include notes from the inspectors, which, in their minutiae capture the many interpretations for how a single violation might be adjudicated. Amongst the violations issued under the code for "Repair Window Sills," inspectors includes notes such as "not seal[ed] properly," "rotted," "air seepage," "gaskets worn." In the book *Objectivity*, on the construction of the same idea, historians of science Lorraine Daston and Peter Galison describe the emergence of "trained judgment" in the early 20th century which supplanted mechanically-produced images to produce objectivity.[8] This epistemic change to prioritize of "judgment-inflected vision" to evaluate what is true — in fields from psychoanalysis to geography to astronomy — coincides with Chicago's establishment of the building code in 1875, which deployed a legion of building inspectors as the human interface of the legal code. When (and with whom) does a crack become a crack?

Studies by sociologist Robin Bartram have found that building inspectors have created a culture of subjective violations assessments. Inspectors, often themselves from working class backgrounds, "go easy" on individual homeowners while "going after" perceived nefarious landlords by more aggressively issuing violations.[9] Yet, despite the intentions of the inspectors to prosecute those they consider more culpable or with deeper pockets, the ripple effects of these efforts can propagate in unexpected ways. While resolving building violations through repair or construction has no positive impact on raising home sale prices, the cost of resolving violations is often displaced directly onto tenants — systematically reproducing housing insecurity for already low-income homeowners and tenants.[10] Complaints triggering inspections to the city's 311 hotline or to its webpage mostly come from tenants; those tenants then find themselves paying these for the expenses through next year's rent, such as the porch repair they themselves reported as a hazardous risk.

Further, discretionary approaches may also reveal an unconscious bias: building violations are more frequently issued in the city's African-American and Latinx communities.(Fig. 2) Current building violation "hot spots" in Chicago align with south and west side neighborhoods, carrying the multi-generation burden of redlining, a practice which disproportionately deprived African-American communities of inherited wealth through the mechanisms of property ownership, home equity and affordable housing.[11] Beyond discretionary actions of building inspectors, these historic

8
Lorraine Daston and Peter Galison, *Objectivity* (New York; Cambridge, Mass.: Zone Books ; Distributed by the MIT Press, 2007).

9
Robin Bartram, "Going Easy and Going After: Building Inspections and the Selective Allocation of Code Violations," *City & Community* 18, no. 2 (2019): 594–617.

10
Ibid., Bartram, "The Cost of Code Violations," *Housing Policy Debate*.

11
Beryl Satter, Family Properties: How the Struggle Over Race and Real Estate Transformed Chicago and Urban America, (New York, N.Y.: Picador, 2010).

and ongoing forms of discriminatory lending policies have prevented owners from undertaking needed maintenance and repair, ultimately producing and compounding maintenance issues.[12] Other studies in planning reveal that building code regulations hamper economic growth in cities, especially in underserved neighborhoods.[13] The burden of increasingly complex and costly compliance requirements outstrips economic growth, stymying single-family home construction and commercial remodeling, whereas a "business friendly" approach to compliance might, nonetheless, continue to protect public health and safety.[14]

Architects' obligation to uphold and adhere to the building code — taught in professional practice, evaluated in licensure examinations and maintained by professional organizations — is often described within the framework of new construction. Yet, what about the ongoing project of maintenance and the difficult acts of care which comprise the ongoing work of maintaining a city's collective building stock? How do we reframe violations from acts of criminality, enforced by fines and court actions, to a collective responsibility for the city's residents at large, as well a potential avenue for design expertise? Is there a way

Fig. 2. Open (unresolved) building violations by census tract since 2006. Census tracts with majority black populations outlined in grey and with majority hispanic/latino populations (over 50%) outlined in dashed grey, based on 2010 American Community Survey data. Courtesy of Future Firm.

12
Keeanga-Yamahtta Taylor, *Race for Profit: How Banks and the Real Estate Industry Undermined Black Homeownership* (Chapel Hill: The University of North Carolina Press, 2019).

13
Raymond J. Burby et al., "Building Code Enforcement Burdens and Central City Decline," *Journal of the American Planning Association* 66, no. 2 (June 30, 2000): 143–61.

14
Ibid., Raymond J. Burby et al., and Mayer, Christopher J., and C. Tsuriel Somerville. "Regulatory Implementation: Examining Barriers From Regulatory Processes," *Cityscape* 8 (1): 209–232. 2000.

Soil, Walls, and their Funambulists

Sumayya Vally

to make architectural design services—which currently require a voluminous drawing set to absolve even simple violations—nimbler and more streamlined and, therefore, more financially accessible? In the absence of architects, the work of resolving building violations and performing building maintenance falls solely to contractors and tradesmen. Work known as "cash jobs," construction work occurring without permits as a transaction between a homeowner and a tradesman, can leave low-income homeowners vulnerable to further exploitation. How can we both address the conditions flagged by building violations, which both produce and reproduce the city's inequitable histories—while also keeping a critical eye on the biases within the Department of Buildings and the Building Code itself?

In *Invisible Cities*, the final city that Marco Polo recounts to Kublai Khan is the city of Berenice, named for the bearer of victory. Berenice is the "unjust city, which crowns triglyphs, abaci, metopes with the gears of its meat-grinding machines," filled with "perfumed pools [...] where the unjust of Berenice recline and weave their intrigues."[15] But lurking just below the surface, there is also "the hidden Berenice, the city of the just, handling makeshift materials in the shadowy rooms behind the shop and beneath the stairs," where the just folk, "always cautious to evade the spying sycophants and the mass arrests, recognize one another by their way of speaking." In fictional Berenice, in Chicago and in any city, both the seeds of justice and injustice produce and reproduce each other through buildings—sometimes visibly, often not. "Berenice is a temporal succession of different cities," Marco Polo continues, "alternately just and unjust. But what I wanted to warn you about is something else: all the future Berenices are already present in this instant, wrapped one within the other, confined, crammed, and inextricable." This dialectical condition describes the landscape of building violations: alternately protecting and prosecuting, serving and undermining, constantly being issued and resolved at a scale dozens of times more prolific and at a velocity unknown to any architecture firm's individual production. *Violation City* counters the risk of reading the city through the lens of the building inspector—as a series of unscrupulous and anonymous misdeeds—by rendering visible the systemic conditions that produce Chicago's "illegal" buildings, presenting opportunities and untold stories that might rebuild, just hidden below the surface, a more just version of the violation city.

Using multiple visual thinking...eclectic maps help us to recognize the physical change in contemporary action. They spring from a belief that many of the complex tensions uniting space and society, inhabitants and places, only take on form and "weight" within a vital flux.
— Stefano Boeri, *Eclectic Atlases*

The soil and earth of a place make up an archive of its past, present and future. Soil and earth are the physical and material condensation upon which the histories of its movements, visions, rituals and politics of place are physically sedimented. The soil and earth of a place — its soul — constitutes something generative: a call to action.

Johannesburg was born out of a meteor strike (which landed at what is now known as the Vredefort crater site in South Africa) billions of years ago that brought gold close to the surface of the earth. Before the discovery of gold, it was conceived through the concept of *uitvalgrond*. Loosely translated from Afrikaans into English, *uitvalgrond* is the concept of left-over, discarded or surplus land.[1] In 1886, at the founding of Johannesburg, the city was mostly based around where the property lines of three large farms met. Yet, at the center of the city, there was a triangular piece of surplus ground, the *uitvalgrond*. Today, after centuries of growth and continuous sprawl, this idea of interstitial, shifting land, as well as the apertures, crevices and ambiguities that house unsanctioned and unregulated people, remains central to the physical and psychological condition of Johannesburg. Our work as an architecture studio explores this spatial tension within the city, as well as the oscillating membranes that shift and conflate geographies, making visible this tension between vast human needs and scarce resources.

In the Post-Apartheid and Post-Gold Rush eras, some of this *uitvalgrond* has recently taken on new functions. For example, in Johannesburg, the presence of *zama-zamas* (a colloquial term for illegal miners, translating to "*try your luck!*" in Zulu) has sparked entirely new urban practices and underground economies — a loaf of bread may be R20 above ground and R400 underground.

Through one lens, the mine dumps, where the *zama-zamas* work, hold remnants of clandestine religious, economic and recreational practices, such as illegal mining, ritual slaughter, informal trade, housing, sandboarding and church gatherings. Through another lens, they are places that reveal and announce historical artefacts: the bones of enslaved bodies, porcelain plates and fragments of the first structures of the city.

In Johannesburg, people interested in accessing worlds like that of the *zama-zamas*, including the informal spaces,

1
Uitvalgrond: Original piece of triangular ground at the center of eight farms claimed for mining diggings, in 1886 Johannesburg. *Uitvalgrond* translates to "surplus ground" in Afrikaans, given by the ZAR as a word to describe land left over between farm portions, whose perimeters were defined by the distance a Boer farmer could ride in the day from his or her farmstead. Beyond simple surplus land, the Afrikaans etymology is based on something falling out or falling away, something unable to fit into a premeditated scheme but also a waste product.

economies and people in the *uitvalgrond*, must be shape-shifters. For those who cross the boundaries of accents, mother-tongue, body language, class and culture, practices must ebb and morph as we traverse physical space. In Johannesburg, ways of being are represented through languages and the walls that include some while excluding others. Different parts of the city — though they may be adjacent to each other, sometimes even within each other — have different codes of understanding. The city is there, if you know how to see it. Though innate to many, to some, these languages are trade-speak, which is conscious and learned, used to access underworlds and their infrastructures.

Within this context, those who are able to circumvent these divides are able to define themselves and to discover the city in a way that is much more expansive than the normative citizen's daily interactions. The word *funambulist* means "tight-rope walker." It originated in 1793, coined from the Latin *funis*, "a rope, a line, a chord" and *ambulare*, "to walk." The *funambulist* steadily and dexterously walks along a length of wire or cable, often elevated high above ground level, sometimes with extreme danger lurking below. In Johannesburg, metaphorical *funambulists* exist on many dividing lines in the city. Many Johannesburgers live in the city without ever confronting or moving across stark, spatial dividing lines. Often, these discrepancies are associated with a different race or income background from their own. However, there are several characters who manage to circumvent them. Tracing along lines on the plan, the *funambulist* rejects the delineation of the border or buffer, the division between two sides.

Migration has always been, and is still, almost synonymous with Johannesburg. Ethnically- specific,

economically-defined enclaves, through which migrants enter, endure and find livelihoods in the city, form part of highly-coded and systematic networks of trade. Codes and rites for different cultural enclaves exclude those who aren't in the know. As a result, adept Johannesburg street-traders often learn and navigate within and around these systems. As a result, they are able to gain access to economies that they would otherwise be excluded from, according to culture and language.[2] If we think of the divisions within the city, whether they be physical, psychological, economic, social or cultural, how can architects begin to engage with the *funambulists* who balance precariously over both sides of these walls? Furthermore, like the *zama-zamas* or the street traders, how can architects become *funambulists* themselves? The spatial, policy and planning professions are largely seen and practiced through top-down, empirical and regulated methods, even though the decisions they make often affect inhabitants of the *uitvalgrond* in ways that these professionals cannot imagine, conceive of or engage with.

• • •

In the most literal sense, a wall is usually denoted by a line on a plan. It is a necessary and primordial element, and its omni- and ever- presence in our environment has rendered it almost subconscious, easy to be overlooked. The English word "wall" is derived from the Latin, "*vallus*," meaning "a stake" or "post," usually seen on the outer edge of a

2
S. De Villiers & T. Govender,
(eds.) *Rogue Economies* Vol 1
GSA UJ (Johannesburg, 2017), 38.

CONVENTION ON THE USE OF SPACE

Acknowledging that this legal document is a continuous collective process subject to yearly review,

The adherers to this Convention,

Considering that space insofar as it is a scarce resource in relation to the common good, should be addressed according to use-value principles;

Considering that the use of space for financial accumulation based on its exchange-value cannot interfere with the use-value of space;

Considering that housing, as granted by the UN High Commissioner for Human Rights under the "Right to Adequate Housing" (2009), entails protection from forced eviction irrespective of title;

Recognizing that varying forms of occupation are reactions to the social-economic circumstances that produce inequality, vacancy, gentrification, and displacement, and limit access to affordable space, and therefore, should not be criminalized;

Considering that a community's right to use, and a grass-roots management of space should be acknowledged, in accordance with the "World Charter for the Right to the City" (2004);

Considering that the real estate sector and the "Commercial Vacancy Industry" stimulate speculation on the value increase of property with the prospect of financial securitization, effectively sustaining rightlessness and reproducing the social-economic circumstances that lead to inequality, vacancy, gentrification, displacement, and limiting access to affordable space;

Considering that detailed knowledge of public and private real estate development, including plans, urban impact assessments, and transparency in contract awarding, should be publicly accessible to provide for accountability and effective tools for arbitration, allowing for local communities to utilize their right to challenge, agree to the following:

1

Casco, *Convention on the Use of Space*, 2015

The *Convention on the Use of Space* was drafted between March and May 2015 in the Netherlands, as a response to the housing crisis in Utrecht. It was developed during a series of workshops led by artist Adelita Husni-Bey and supported by Casco, a non-profit art center in the city. Contributors included lawyers, squatters, undocumented people, advocates for the undocumented, academics, activists and the general public.

The founding claims of the convention assert that space should be managed according to use-value principles. It states that occupation of physical property should be protected, and housing as a commodity should be dissolved. The text is a para-legal document, meaning that it borrows legal language and outlines a set of standards agreed to by its signers, but the claims it makes are not legal. In this sense, it is also an example of "movement-perspective legislation," a term used by criminologist and activist Deanna Dadusc to describe legal frameworks that are deliberated and written in public.[1]

Although not legally binding, the document is legitimized by its signatories, including organizations, associations, collectives, houses, trade unions, groups, individuals and municipalities. In signing, the signatories agree to abide by the Convention and can be guarantors for articles and their values. The growing community of signatories puts political pressure on existing institutions to recognize the legality of the convention's claims. Furthermore, the intention is that the text could be cited in court as a supporting document to defend spaces threatened with eviction or by groups wishing to make a claim to a space.

The Convention on the Use of Space has been exhibited in gallery settings and used as an activist tool, either pasted on a wall or read aloud. Currently, it circulates as a pdf, and is hosted on a website where users can sign the convention.

1

FAQ, What is movement-perspective legislation, Convention on the Use of Space, https://www.useofspaceconvention.org/qa/, accessed June 23, 2020.

Casco, *Convention on the Use of Space*, 2015

Aerial view of a mine site in Johannesburg.

fortification. Palisades like these are mentioned by Homer in the 8th century B.C.E., later by the Greek historian Polybius (c 200-118 B.C.E.) and the Chinese historian Sima Qian (145-86 B.C.E), among others. Although the exact origin of the first walls is unknown, they may have been used to fortify man against nature — against tides and currents, elements and predatory species. But the history of the wall is not just protective but often painful and brutal. The wall separates here and there, this and that, us and them. Its beginnings are rooted in exclusionary ideologies, even down to its very instinctive and early origins — in our distinctions between culture and nature, inside and outside and between hierarchically-regimented city spaces.

And so, the wall, the most primordial of architectural forms, is always a political ideology in physical form. Lambert argues that the line is a legal diagram, instantaneously denoting a dichotomic political arrangement.[3] As soon as the pen marks the paper in a stroke, a wall is represented. In his work *Forensic Architecture*, the architect Eyal Weizman (2017) suggests that architecture is "political plastic," describing the elastic way in which abstract forces — political, economic and military — are condensed into material form. In Johannesburg, largely because of our apartheid legacy, our spaces are divided manifold with "walls" of varying thicknesses, sizes and gradients with varying degrees of perceptibility and visibilities. As Lindsay Bremner (1998) writes in *Blank: Architecture, Apartheid and After*, "Pockets of privilege and ghettos of shame, business men clutching briefcases and taxi-industry hit-men bearing

3
L. Lambert, *The Law Turned into Walls*. Volume 4 (2013).

Anticolonial Remedies: From Colonization to Globalization

Samia Henni

AK-47's exist side by side in this extraordinary conflation of space, time, powers and cultures." There are walls that act as thresholds between races, ethnicities, belief systems, economic brackets and ideologies.

Indeed, beyond physical walls, other forms of "walls," such as *soft* walls, are less tangible, experienced only through the legacies of economic, class, ethnic and language divisions. For example, since the turn of the 20th century, several discourses have emerged on "inconvenient" women of color in the city.[4] These women were present in patriarchal roles or spaces in the city. Beer brewers in the 1910s and 1920s of Johannesburg, forced to adjust their families and work for an income, are one example of this. The contemporary equivalent may be caregivers, maids, washerwomen and nannies. In this way, the trope of the *uitvalgrond* applies. However, in this context, the trope does not just apply to land but to people. People operate in the margins, as an unseen surplus; their existence is unwritten in the formal definitions of worlds that are constructed to exclude them.

By understanding the various conditions and various types of walls in Johannesburg and, in turn, understanding the ways in which these walls are subverted and circumnavigated, we may start to produce new ways and languages for understanding architecture. In doing so, we may find alternatives to normative architectural discourses. It is my hope that, as spatial practitioners, we will start to engage in a more critical and nuanced dialogue with our city. By recognizing architecture in the rituals and practices of the city and its people, we can find clues for making and understanding our city differently.

• • •

One way to see the development of new languages and new conversations for architecture is to start to understand the other forces that affect, subvert and form architecture. For this, it is illustrative to look to history. In the 1990s, under the direction of Archbishop Desmond Tutu and a number of other notable political and cultural leaders, South Africa embarked on a self-reflective program under the general banner of the "Rainbow Nation."[5] The name represents a summary of the kind of nation-building language that was necessary in the early stages of South Africa's liberation narrative to loosen the grip of racist regimes. Although the Truth and Reconciliation Commission was an important

4
M. Matsipa, "Urban Mythologies," in O. Barstow and B. Law-Viljoen (eds.), *Fire Walker: William Kentridge, Gerhard Marx* (Johannesburg: Fourthwall Books, 2011), 61.

5
Rainbow nation is a term coined by Archbishop Desmond Tutu to describe Post-Apartheid South Africa, after South Africa's first fully democratic election in 1994.

The phrase was elaborated upon by President Nelson Mandela in his first month of office, when he proclaimed: "Each of us is as intimately attached to the soil of this beautiful country as are the famous jacaranda trees of Pretoria and the mimosa trees of the bushveld — a rainbow nation at peace with itself and the world."

The term was intended to encapsulate the unity of multi-culturalism and the coming-together of people of many different nations in a country once identified with the strict division of white and black.

Colonialization has different forms of existence. It exists through the physical invasion and occupation of lands and people. It exists through both military operations and civil measures. It exists through the material and psychological subjugation and exploitation of human and natural resources. It exists through man-made environmental transformations and ecological interventions. It exists through technological threats and digital strategies of businesses and surveillance. It exists through the uncritical imposition of specific language, literature and knowledge. It exists through global mechanisms of accumulation by dispossession and profound socio-economic and gender inequities. It exists through the implicit or explicit alienation and maintenance of power, domination and war. It exists through forced traditional, religious and cultural erasures. It exists at the very heart of destructed, projected and built environments. It exists through the labor force of construction, material extractions and industries. These processes are often violent and traumatic.[1] So how are we to examine the ethical responsibilities that arise from these manipulations of space?

Modern histories, theories and practices of architecture and urbanism are intimately interrelated to processes of colonialization and globalization, as well as to the principles of what Frantz Fanon (1925–1961), psychiatrist, political philosopher and activist, had called "absolute evil." Territories and people around the world have been constantly and continuously permeated and marked by violent activities

part of the country's transition to freedom and democracy, an attempt to collectively heal and move beyond our country's traumas, many believe that it was insufficient in affecting any real reversal of past atrocities. Both "Rainbow-ism" and the TRC may be seen as very necessary attempts to create a veneer of peace to move beyond the chaos of the early 90's, avoiding unrest, civil war and the destruction of our nation. These attempts were necessary and arguably fulfilled the important task of avoiding strife and projecting a national ethos of tolerance at the time. Yet, it was not enough to merely rephrase or expand the discursive field to include more dialectical considerations (for example, adding "privacy" to balance the rhetoric of "transparency" and/or "economic freedom" to "human rights"). It is, instead, necessary to engage in the production of entirely new languages with which to express possibilities that transcend the limitations of the current political imagination.

As we have seen, architecture takes on and solidifies the ethos of its city-makers, for both politicians and inhabitants. Apartheid city-planning is a clear example of this, where the legal systems and the ethos of the ruling party was (and still is, in most instances) concretized, a scene played out upon the city's fabric. Even at the smallest scale, represented in the protective bars on public entrances and the spikes on planters and benches in Johannesburg, we know that architecture represents ways of seeing.

With this in mind, how can architecture contribute to the development of a new language? Architects, planners and those engaged in city-making need to become practitioners who can draw the real architecture of our society in terms of what exists in the unplanned and the *uitvalgrond*. For that, we must draw on radically new methods. To do

Aerial view of a John Masowe church congregation on a former mine site in Johannesburg.

of war, occupation, exploitation, dispossession, destruction and construction. In fact, since the 15th century, European architects, both for civil and military purposes, have been actively participating in constructing empires and framing their representations. These designers were commissioned to imagine and realize various infrastructures, public complexes and private settlements across the multiple lands of the empires of which they represented, including the British, Dutch, French, German, Italian, Ottoman, Portuguese, Russian and Spanish empires. The vastness and diversity of colonial spaces around the world—including the United States of America—that resulted from these conditions have been instrumental in colonizing territories, exploiting and transporting resources and representing an uneven distribution of power. To this end, the making of spaces in the colonizer world cannot be differentiated from the making of spaces in the colonized world. The production of architecture between these two spaces is closely interconnected, and these rapports must be studied and understood together: both along and against the grain.[2] The study of these legacies is an onus.

What Fanon theorized as "absolute evil" is a manifesto of a colonial world order and of a constructed system of values. Being con-

1
Samia Henni, "Colonial Ramifications" e-Flux Architecture, History/Theory, gta Institute, ETH Zurich (October 31, 2018). https://www.e-flux.com/architecture/history-theory/225180/colonial-ramifications/.

2
Ann Laura Stoler, *Along the Archival Grain: Epistemic Anxieties and Colonial Common Sense* (Princeton: Princeton University Press, 2009).

this, architects must engage in action, and not just the lip service of peace, tolerance, freedom, transparency and rights. Any intervention must not simply be a rebranding exercise. Rather, we must meaningfully transform the structures of society.

In this era of Post-Rainbowism, as we are starting to engage with the redress of past inequalities, ruptures are beginning to interrupt this veneer of peace and tolerance (through movements like #FeesMustFall, for example), we need more meaningful tools to understand and move beyond the architectures of our past society (both in our built environment and in the architectures of our societies).

In this context, the Italian architect and urbanist Stefano Boeri's work on new vocabularies for contemporary spatial conditions that are useful for reflecting on our own situation.[6] Using these tools, alternative ways of seeing space and spatial conditions, beyond the conventionally architectural and orthogonal narratives, will emerge.

In his essay, *Eclectic Atlases*, Boeri mentions four different types of gazes: the detective, the sampling, the oblique and the mobile gaze.[7] These gazes de-emphasize "empirical," mathematical forms of understanding space as effective and significant to understanding and developing new design languages. A top-down, autocratic perception does not reveal the realities and qualities of our city, particularly its *uitvalgrond*. The realities of Johannesburg necessitate multiple gazes, multiple ways of understanding that cannot be deduced from the plan alone. Much of the city is comprised of subversive and informal activities occurring beyond the limits of formal planning and design. As such, we need new and different ways to understand them. Text and narrative may be one such gaze. Photographic studies, radio-active readings, sound, etc. may all be other points of entry into understanding our city.

Architecture is as much concerned with communication and story-telling as it is with shelter. Architects create and imagine new places and bring them into being, altering and shaping our realities. The relationship between our experiences, our mental images and our physical existences are never settled; all of these continuously form, inform and undo each other. There is no truly objective way of seeing. For spatial practitioners, rather than describe Johannesburg conditions through empirical planning technologies alone, we need to supplement our inventory of design language to include new ways of seeing. What can be recorded and described, in ways we are not accustomed to, can offer entirely an entirely new understanding of architecture.

6
S. Boeri, *USE: Uncertain States of Europe* (Milano: Skira, 2003), 424.

7
Ibid.

Frantz Fanon. *The Wretched of the Earth*.
New York: Grove Press, New York (1963).

cerned with the analysis and critique of the psychology and psycho-
pathology of colonialism, dispossession, oppression and violence,
Fanon attempted to dismantle colonial protocols and doctrines, which
he himself experienced in colonized Martinique, France and colonized
Algeria. Thus, he crafted the ethical quintessence of decolonialization
theory as a commitment to human dignity, accountability and responsibility.[3] In his book *The Wretched of the Earth*, Fanon argued: "The
colonial world is a Manichaean world. It is not enough for the settler to
delimit physically, that is to say with the help of the army and the police
force, the place of the native. As if to show the totalitarian character
of colonial exploitation the settler paints the native as a sort of quintessence of evil."[4] Architecture is no exception. On the one hand,
European colonizers erected a variety of civil and military and religious
buildings "to delimit physically" and impose their own norms and
forms; and on the other hand, they depicted local populations, the
so-called "Indigenous," "Native," "First Nations," "Brown," "Black,"
Muslim,"... and their respective habitat as "absolute evil." This

[3]
Fanon's most influential books include: *Peau noire, manqué blans* (*Black Skin, White Masks*, 1952), *L'An V de la révolution algérienne* (*A Dying Colonialism*, 1959), and *Les Damnés de la Terre* (*The Wretched of the Earth*, 1961). Some of his writings were published postmortem, such as *Toward the African Revolution* (1964) and *Alienation and Freedom* (2015), edited by Jean Khalfa and Robert J.C. Young.

[4]
Frantz Fanon. *The Wretched of the Earth*. New York: Grove Press: 2004 [1961], 41. On the mechanism of this Manichean world, see *Black Skin, White Masks* (New York: Grove Press, 1967 [1952]).

tendency continues to this day. A number of architects who build in "the other" countries, as well as architectural theorists and historians who write about "the other" architecture, tend to obey this violent mechanism and constructed system of values.

For Fanon, violence is both a human (political) and a medical (scientific) notion. He identified at least three categories of violence: offensive colonial violence, defensive anti-colonial violence and violence in the international context, opening up possibilities for constructive reconsiderations of world orders, spaces and assumptions. His ambition was to scrutinize the "them-or-us" or "the other-or-the self" dichotomy of both the colonial world and the Cold War—including the threat of nuclear war—and to map the complex nuances that the colonizer might have, consciously, unconsciously, censored, distorted, or obliterated. His pathology (political and scientific) of colonial ideologies and anticolonial struggles incites an intersectional approach of architectural practices and theories that considers race, class, religion, gender, resources, climate and violence. This ethic of decolonial reason helps us reflect on the ongoing cartographies of so-called "globalization" that often echo the colonial world order of possession and dispossession, including the production and transportation of cement, glass and other material constructions, as well as the exportation and circulation of forms that do not respond to specific environmental and socio-economic conditions. Moreover, part of architectural vocabulary, such as formal/informal settlements, modern/traditional architecture, private/public spaces and other well-known categories, belong to this Manichaean world order.

The presence and dominance of the colonizer resulted in forcibly destroying existing spaces, buildings, traditions and languages, thereby imposing certain forms of being, living and governing. Whether it was called the "civilizing mission" in the context of colonization, or "development" and "investment" in today's context of globalization, these measures wear a mask that expresses imperial ideology in regard to a particular colonial/global order. Ethical responsibilities or anticolonial remedies, emerging from the manipulation of physical and psychological spaces, must consider and operate in relation to these aspects of dispossession. These actions must be transformative. They set out to intervene on the order/disorder of the world and acknowledging that the primary encounter between the colonizer and the colonized people and their spaces was marked by violence. Fanon contended: "Violence in its practice is totalizing and national. As a result, it harbors in its depths the elimination of regionalism and tribalism."[5] Architectural examples of this violence can be found, for example, in Australia, Canada and the Americas. These are places in which a harsh extermination of native people occurred, along with the destruction of their habitat and the imposition of imported forms and construction materials from England, France, The Netherlands and other European countries.

The legacy between colonization and globalization was scrutinized in Frederick Cooper's book: *Colonialism in Question: Theory, Knowledge, History*. The US historian raised fundamental questions about the notions of globalization and modernity, which are relevant to the social sciences and the humanities, including architecture, along with its histories, theories and practices. Cooper refuses to locate the colonial world between 1492 and the 1970s, arguing that "the globalization story claims as new what is not new at all, confuses 'long-distance' with 'global,' fails to complement discussion of connections across space with analysis of their limitations, and distorts the history of empires and colonization in order to fit it into a story with a predetermined end."[6] This enduring story is interconnected with Fanon's analysis of the colonial world and its intrinsic physical and psychological violence. Although empires have a gigantic place in history, and their changing maps cover a huge portion of the world, they are barely discussed and studied in architecture schools and departments. But if the spatial manifestations of empires do not become an integral part of architectural education, then architecture students (and ultimately architects) will possibly ignore these histories and fail to

dismantle the ways in which powerful corporations and states —
potential clients — act and operate. Analyzing and understanding the
spatial witness to imperialism and colonialism is to study and consider (to cite a few examples among many others) the consequences
of the demarcation of random borders such as those in the United
States and African countries, and the provenance and transportation
of coal, oil, gas, water and building materials, which are of vital importance to the existence and life of cities around the world.[7]

     The stories of globalization are the extension of Western
European colonial history. Fanon's insistence on the Manichean nature
of the colonial world and the Cold War was an anticolonial determina-
tion that identified and defined the cartographies of dispossession and
alienation, rejecting the fabricated narrative of modernization. An effort
to understand architecture, along with its histories and theories, as
part of the dynamics of world order/disorder and not simply as passive

[6]
Frederick Cooper. *Colonialism in Question: Theory, Knowledge, History*. Berkley:
University of California Press, 2015, 10.

[7]
On specific case studies, see, for example, Jiat-Hwee Chang. *A Genealogy of Tropical
Architecture: Colonial Networks, Nature and Technoscience*. London: Routledge, 2016;
Samia Henni. *Architecture of Counterrevolution: the French Army in Northern Algeria*.
Zurich: gta Verlag, 2017; Anthony Douglas King. *Spaces of Global Cultures: Architecture
Urbanism Identity*. London: Routledge, 2004, and *Colonial Urban Development:
Culture, Social Power, and Environment*. London: Routledge, 1976; Itohan Osayimwese.
*Colonialism and Modern Architecture in Germany: Culture, Politics, and the Built
Environment*. Piitsburgh Pa: University of Pittsburgh Press, 2017; Peter Scriver, *Colonial
Modernities: Building, Dwelling and Architecture in British India and Ceylon*. London:
Routledge, 2007; and Gwendolyn Wright, *The Politics of Design in French Colonial
Urbanism*. Chicago: University of Chicago Press, 1991.

Grounded Bodies, Flying Plasma: The Origins of Hemogeography

Ivan L. Munuera

spectators and suppliers of spaces, is fundamental. Such attention should neither evade the inherent violence of exploitations — human, animal, material, territorial, atmospheric, underground and environmental — nor fetishize them. Architecture is no exception. Architecture operates on a planetary scale and it depends on accumulated capital. The historical proximity of colonialism and other forms of dispossession and violence, such as slavery, suggest that it should inform architects, architectural historians and theorists. Unlike other disciplines and professions, architecture imposes the built environment upon the physical landscapes of the colonized and exploited territories. They are exiting carriers of particular socio-cultural and politico-economic histories and signifiers. They are open-air archives. Both liberated and colonized lands contain the physical presence of these "ruins of the present."

Anticolonial remedies do not cure the colonial disease of architecture. They invite educators, designers, scholars and students to commit, or they keep committing to forms of pedagogy and practice — designing, building, writing, exhibiting, lecturing... — that are realistic, inclusive, egalitarian, nondiscriminatory, intersectional, sustainable and responsible. They encourage historical, environmental, social and spatial justice. They promote proactive approaches and methodologies that respond to current political landscapes and engage with the unbalanced distribution of wealth. They address subjects, places, and

1. Blood Pride

On April 20, 1990, tens of thousands of demonstrators—50,000 by police estimations, 80,000 according to the rally organizers—crossed the Brooklyn Bridge in New York City from Cadman Plaza to Manhattan's City Hall in what came to be known as the "Haitian AIDS March." They were protesting against a Federal health policy on blood donations that stigmatized certain communities, with Haiti being at the very center of the polemic. In February of that year, the Food and Drug Administration (FDA) prohibited all Haitians in the United States from donating blood under the suspicion of their being infected by HIV/AIDS.[1] Dr. Jean Claude Compas, chairman of the Haitian Coalition on AIDS and one of the organizers of the march, remarked on the restriction: "This policy is on the basis that Haitian blood is dirty, that it is all infected with the HIV virus."[2]

The demonstrators met in the morning and then crossed over the bridge from Brooklyn, tying up traffic and ultimately shutting down Wall Street and several businesses in Lower Manhattan. One of the banners stated "Proud of Our Blood." If the Haitian population had been reduced to their blood by the medical and political institutions, as well as the media that echoed the FDA recommendations, their response was to generate an aneurysm, a stroke in one of the central arteries of the city, the Brooklyn Bridge, collapsing the flow of daily life to demand urgent attention and, thereby, reclaiming their place in the body of the city. The urbanism of New York enacted and shaped the controversies and debates surrounding HIV/AIDS from the beginning of the epidemic, generating a battleground for identity, activism and politics with architecture and blood at the center of the debate.

The notion of Haitians and their blood as the original agents of HIV/AIDS ran parallel to the outbreak of the epidemic. Since being first diagnosed in 1981 as a "gay cancer"[3] or GRID (Gay-Related Immune Deficiency), Haitians were rapidly targeted as a focus of contagion when the then-unknown disease escalated into public consciousness as affecting four risk groups[4] known as the 4Hs: homosexuals, heroin addicts, hemophiliacs and Haitians, following a list provided by the Centers for Disease Control and Prevention (CDC) on March 4, 1983.[5] Haiti was the only nation labeled as a risk group, an idea spurred by the data supplied by the CDC the previous year.[6]

1
This policy also included Sub-Saharan people as well. Recommendations for the Prevention of HIV Transmission by Blood and Blood Products. FDA Memorandum. February 5, 1990.

2
Donatella Lorch, "FDA Policy To Limit Blood is Protested," *The New York Times*, April 21, 1990. P. 27.

3
Lawrence K. Altman, "Rare Cancer Seen in 41 Homosexuals," *The New York Times*, July 3, 1981.

4
During the first years of the HIV/AIDS epidemic, the words "group" and "community" were often mixed, referring to the same part of the population affected by HIV/AIDS. Nowadays, the Center for Disease Control and Prevention (CDC) has defined group—as in "control group" or "test group"—as a segment of the population affected by specific conditions, a definition that does not link the individuals in a greater context outside of the study. These individuals share common characteristics, but they do not necessarily share common values. The word "community," however, suggests a link in a much broader sense, relating to locality, state and region, even when the individuals are taken out of the context of a study. These individuals share common values in a given geographical area. In this sense, the words "group" and "community" are used in this paper following the CDC recommendations but also with a historical sense. Territorial connotations, national definitions and other

5
"Current Trends Prevention of Acquired Immune Deficiency Syndrome (AIDS): Report of Inter-Agency Recommendations," *Morbidity and Mortality Weekly Report*, vol. 32, no. 09 (March 4, 1983): 101-3.

6
"Opportunistic Infections and Kaposi's Sarcoma Among Haitians in the United States," *MMWR*, vol. 31, no. 26 (July 9, 1982): 353-54, 360-61.

spaces both as sites of becoming and transforming and as moments for belonging and intervening. They reject an illusory neutrality and embrace a situated positionality. If one follows the claims made by those who believe that we live in a Postcolonial world, then one needs to ask the following question: if the forms of production and consumption, capital and commodity exchange systems and technologies of accumulation and communication have changed enormously, why didn't the forms of dispossession follow suit? The creation, formation and production of built environments epitomize these forms of possession and dispossession, participating implicitly or explicitly, in the theory of "the absolute evil." To practice, historicize or theorize architecture is to take into account the processes of colonization and globalization and to be aware of the ethical consequences of circumventing such implications and of the "danger that ahistorical history encourages an apolitical politics."[8]

8
Ibid., 25.

GRID was renamed AIDS (Acquired Immune Deficiency Syndrome) during the summer of 1982[7] and was described as a syndrome "at least moderately predictive of a defect in cell mediated immunity, occurring in a person with no known case for diminished resistance to that disease"[8] and "a rare and rapidly fatal form of cancer,"[9] manifested by Kaposi's sarcoma and/or PCP (Pneumocystis Carinii Pneumonia). To understand the weight of the epidemic, it is important to keep in mind that before 1981, cases of Kaposi's sarcoma—an uncommon form of cancerous purple skin tumors and one of the most visible AIDS related illnesses in the epidemic's early years—were so infrequent that it struck just two Americans out of every three million. The NYU Cancer Registry archives show only three cases of Kaposi's sarcoma for the entirety of the 1970s.[10] In July of 1981, there were at least 41 cases, a number that increased every day.

In the early 1980s, the general assumption was that the source of the disease was American gay men who had returned from "sex holidays" in the Caribbean,[11] specifically Haiti, resulting in what Paul Farmer labeled a "geography of blame."[12] This powerful narrative continued over the decades, even

7
Both names, GRID and AID or AIDS were commonly used during these years: Lawrence K. Altman, "New Homosexuals Disorder Worries Health Officials," *The New York Times*, May 11, 1982.

8
Idem.

9
Lawrence K. Altman, "Rare Cancer Seen in 41 Homosexuals", *Op. Cit.*

10
Lillian & Clarence de la Chapelle Medical Archives. NYU Cancer Registry

11
Richard A. McKay, *Patient Zero and the Making of the AIDS Epidemic* (Chicago and London: The University of Chicago Press, 2017), p. 55.

12
Paul Farmer, *AIDS and Accusation: Haiti and the Geography of Blame* (Berkeley, Los Angeles, London: University of California Press, 1992).

13
David France, *How to Survive a Plague* (New York: Alfred A. Knopf, 2016), 37.

when available medical evidence suggested otherwise. The name GRID, as well as the common "gay plague" and "gay cancer," strengthened the idea of a specifically gay disease related to a certain environment-specific villain, a theory that was adopted by doctors like Yehudi M. Felman of New York City's Bureau of Venereal Disease Control, who declared that the disease's cause "could be the bugs out of the pipes in the bathhouses"[13] or poppers (amyl nitrite), a recreational inhalant popular among gay, bisexual men, transwomen and transmen, used to enhance experiences on the dance floor and in sexual intercourse, generating a public perception that there is an inherent connection between queer sexuality and HIV/AIDS. This powerful narrative continued over the decades, even when available medical evidence suggested otherwise.

This geography of blame generated a diasporic map in which a plasmaregime emerged—that is to say, a governing authority based on the liquidity of material and immaterial assets from economies to geographies and a mechanism of control, surveillance and redistribution based on the agency of fluids, the retrovirus' main way of transmission. HIV/AIDS was enacted by a myriad of uncontainable spatial

A Haitian Patriot [sic], "The US Blood Drain in
Haiti," *Clone*, April 1973, New York.

U.J.A. tax evaders invade Commons

5

By Mary Beth Yakoubian

The tax-exempt status of the United Israel
Appeal and the United Jewish Appeal, which
have channeled over $2.5 billion in U.S.
funds to Israel since 1948, is the target
of a suit filed in Federal District Court
in Washington, D.C., on Oct. 25, 1972.

This same U.J.A. is using valuable student-
peddler space on Commons to collect contributions from unwitting Hunter students.

There are only ten booths available for
either individual students or student groups
for the sale of merchandise or publicizing
club activities. During the day, eight
booths are available to Day Session students
and two to S.G.S., while at night eight are
for S.G.S. and two for Day Session. This
means that this space, from which many students earn their food money, is at a premium.
Which makes it even more ironic that it
should be used by a group of Zionist stu-

dents to exploit their fellow religionists
for the benefit of a foreign country, a
racist imperialist one at that.

The law suit mentioned above asks the
Internal Revenue Service and U.S. Treasury
to end the tax-exempt status of the U.J.A.
and U.I.A. because:
-- the two agencies "are not organized or
operated for charitable and educational
purposes but substantially for political
and ideological ones," contrary to IRS
regulations;
-- they do not retain control over the
funds they collect, as required by the IRS;
-- funds given to the agencies contribute
to racial discrimination contrary to the
Civil Rights Act of 1963;
-- The United Jewish Appeal, the United
Israel Appeal, the Jewish Agency in Jerusa-
lem and the World Zionist Organization all
are agencies of the state of Israel, and
gifts to them represent contributions to a
foreign government, in violation of IRS
regulations.

SCENE MACABRE EN HAITI   by a Haitian Patriot

THE US BLOOD DRAIN IN HAITI

For the past two years Hemo-Caribbean, a
white firm led by Austrian Bio-chemist Werner
Thell; has been "dealing" in blood bought from
poor Haitian people, particularly children.
The African is given three dollars and a coca-
cola in return for his blood. This is his alternative to hunger pains, lack of clothes,
and a place to sleep at night.
     Hemo-Caribbean blood center accumulates
20,000 pints every two weeks. The white para-
sitic firm has already stolen blood from over
three-million Haitians during the last two
years, and are still doing capacity business.
     Once the blood reaches the U.S., according
to Thell, it's broken down into several medical
products and shipped off to various states including Illinois, Indiana and California.
     Because of the severe criticism that pro-
gressive Haitians voiced about the Black blood
drain, President Jean Claude Duvvalier recently
issued a decree which supposedly outlawed the
Hemo-Caribbean contract. However, any decree

issued by Duvalier and his puppet administration is meaningless. The corrupt Haitian government, and its white controllers have only
one primary interest--Money!
     Like many of the natural resources drained
from the Caribbean as well as Africa and Asia,
this drainage of the Blackman's blood by U.S.
exploiters is seen as the most blatant example
of Genocide.
     The struggle will go on in Haiti. The at-
tempt in January by Haitian guerillas is only a
fraction of the real fight against neo-colonial
ism and the Jean-Claude Duvalier fascist regime.

Free all Political Prisoners
 in the Haitian cellars

Free the people from Duvalier, the
 U.S., and NATO exploiters

Vive La Revolution Haitienne

David Bartel, "Haiti" Queen's Quarterly: The
Magazine for Gay Guys Who Have No Hangups.
October 1973, Vol. 5, Issue 5.

HAITI
ISLAND OF LAZY LOVERS

by David Bartel

IF you've been racking up too many ciphers on your sexual scoreboard lately and are puzzled about how you can quickly reverse this dismaying trend, *QQ* has the ideal solution to your problem. Pack your bag with some summer-light clothing and take the next Pan-Am flight to Haiti.

From the moment you deplane in Port-au-Prince until you regretfully head back home, you can flirt and fuck, be screwed and sucked by the horniest young humpyhungs in the Caribbean . . . and the laziest. Fast john-cruisers and numbers guys take notice: the fuckalazy, suckalazy Haitian hustler (they're mostly all hustlers here . . . they're just too poor to do it for free) likes to take his time. It figures: given his subtropical climate, his native resistance to speed in anything, plus the fact that it takes time for him to wheel his huge sexual catapult into place and fire the first depth charge, he's not one to race the clock . . . he's in no hurry for the 'catapullout'. Lay a few bucks on him and he's yours for hour-r-rs . . . even all night.

'Gangbusters', as well as those devotees of the 'slow-poke' group encounter, should find this of singular interest. *Because* of him and *through* him you will learn where the wildest orgies are likely to be taking place back in the hills . . . or up the mountainside . . . 'back of the moon'.

He will know because all day his ears will have been 'antennaed' to the telegraphic drumbeat of the voodoo *hougan* (priest). The African drum came along with the slaves to Haiti in the late eighteenth century and it is as much a part of Haitian life now, as then. As a visitor you may not be conscious of its variations in pitch, rhythm and pattern. Only the Haitian knows what the subtle differences mean.

VOODOO PROTOCOL

The sex orgies that inevitably follow the voodoo ceremony are not planned. They're spontaneous, being irresistible postludes to the religious ritual—a further letting-off-of-steam in response to a primitive religious enthusiasm (much as the Japanese over-respond to the erotic stimulation of their famed religious Festival of the Phallus). The voodoo ceremony always takes place at night—when it's cool—in secret places. It is nothing like those staged affairs that the downtown Port-au-Prince hotels put on for a gaggle of giggly tourists. It is a hair-raising, freaked-out orgy that occurs nowhere else in the world except, perhaps, in Dahomey where so much that is Haitian has its primal roots.

We should like to emphasize that these post-voodoo orgies are not specifically gay. *(Continued on page 39)*

constituencies that together comprised a transnational geography
that formulated the concept of a
hemogeography: a distribution power
structure based on the meaning and
circulation of blood, a radical
rearrangement of the bodily,
spatial, material, technological,
political, legal, economic and
symbolic global order.

2. Hemo-Caribbean: $3 and a Coca-Cola

The contemporary classification of
Haitians and Haiti as a focus of
disease started in the early 1970s
with the constitution of Hemo-
Caribbean. From May 1971 to November
1972, Hemo-Caribbean, a large
plasmapheresis[14] center, operated in
Port-au-Prince, Haiti while being
managed in Miami. It was a transnational and multifaceted company
founded by Joseph B. Gorinstein, a
Florida businessman, and Luckner
Cambronne, a Haitian politician
under François "Papa Doc" Duvalier
and his son Jean-Claude "Baby Doc"
Duvalier's dictatorships.[15] This
business, along with others, such
as the one that exported corpses to
American medical schools, earned
Cambronne the nickname "Vampire of
the Caribbean."

Hemo-Caribbean was founded as
a real estate development business
connected with Northeast Airlines,
which operated in the United
States, Canada and the Caribbean,
until it was acquired by and merged
into Delta Airlines in August
1972.[16] The involvement of Cambronne
does not appear in any legal documents; but different classified
reports from the United States
embassy in Port-au-Prince to the US
Department of State declared that
Cambronne was "the contract's chief
negotiator"[17] until 1972—the year
when Cambronne left Haiti to live
in political exile in Miami until
his death in 2006. He was in charge
of the Haitian operations.[18]

In January 1972, Hemo-Caribbean
was exporting up to 6,000 liters
of plasma to the United States
each month. Hemo-Caribbean could
accommodate 350 donors per day at
its two-story center on Rue des
Remparts in Port-au-Prince and
was building a second facility to
increase capacity to 850 donors
per day. The process was described
as "plasma farming."[19] Donors, most
of them children, laid down in a
series of gurneys in the same room,
attended by Hemo-Caribbean staff,
while their blood was extracted
through hypodermic needles. They
were paid between three and five
dollars each (the plasma sold
in Miami for thirty-five dollars)
and "a coca-cola."[20] They donated

14
Plasmapheresis is
a process that
consists in the
removal, treatment
and return of blood
plasma throughout the
circulatory system.

15
Hemo Caribbean,
Inc. filed as a
Domestic for Profit
Corporation in the
State of Florida,
active between
August 11, 1970, and
1976, as recorded in
documents filed with
Florida Department
of State with the
address: Suite 1405,
150 SE 2nd Avenue
Miami, Florida 33131.
In article VI of
this file, it was
stated that it had
the "privilege of
having its office and
branch offices at
other places within
or without the State
of Florida." Doc.
No. 368180. P. 5.
Florida Department of
State, Division of
Corporations.

16
Idem.

17
"Other Factors
Influencing Prospects
for Resolution of
Dispute Between GOH
and Dupont Caribbean
INC." Original
Classification:
Limited Official Use.
1974 August 20. ID:
1974PORTA01620_b.
Department of State,
Secretary of State.

18
"Hemo-Caribbean
Operation Still
Suspended." Original
Classification:
Limited Official Use.
1973 March 28. ID:
1973PORTA00472_b.
Department of State,
Secretary of State.

19
Richard Severo,
"Impoverished
Haitians Sell Plasma
for Use in the U.S,"
The New York Times,
January 28, 1972.

20
A Haitian Patriot
[sic], "The US Blood
Drain in Haiti,"
Clone, April 1973,
New York. P. 5.
Lesbian Herstory
Archives, New York
Public Library.

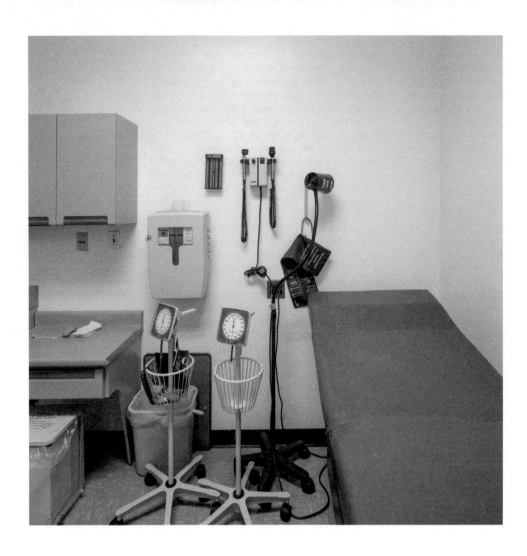

West, Bellevue
Hospital.
Photograph by
Ivan L. Munuera
& Miguel de
Guzman, 2019.

plasma at least once a week, even though the CDC recommended adult donors wait at least eight weeks between donations.

The facilities at Rue des Remparts, located in Portail Saint Joseph in the La Saline area—a neighborhood famous for its hospitals near the maritime port—were less than a 45-minute drive to the François Duvalier International Airport through the principal highway of Port-au-Prince, the RN-1.[21] Rue des Remparts was one of the only routes of transportation for semi-rural, regional and urban markets at the center of the old colonial settlement. It was also a route used by rural migrants. At the roadside of Rue des Remparts, a parking area was habilitated, making terminals that were, in fact, streets just used for truck parking.[22] This was a commercial transit course that was highlighted constantly in the maps commissioned by Duvalier's regime, making it one of the essential routes of Port-au-Prince.[23] The frozen plasma was exported on Air Haiti—Cambronne's air company which had the monopoly on transportation—to Miami, where it was sold to four American enterprises: Armour Pharmaceutical (now CSL Behring, Chicago), Cutter Laboratories (Berkeley, California), Dade Reagents (Deerfield, Illinois

21
The airport was renamed Port-au-Prince International Airport in 1986 and Toussaint Louverture International Airport in 2003.

22
Plan de Development de port-au-Prince et de sa Region Metropolitane, Tome 2, Janvier 1977. P. 97. Source: *CIAT-Comité Interministériel d'Aménagement du Territoire,* Port-au-Prince, Haiti.

23
Map of Port-au-Prince by Capital Air Services, ltd. December 1976. Source: ISPAN-*Institute de Sauvegarde du Patrimoine National,* Port-au-Prince, Haiti.

24
Douglas Starr, *Blood: An Epic History of Medicine and Commerce* (New York: Perennial, 2002).

and Glasgow, Delaware) and Dow Chemical (Midland, Michigan), as well to clients in Germany and Sweden.

During the 1970s, it was discovered that Hemo-Caribbean never practiced safety measures among its donors, scanned for diseases, nor did they collect data about the plasma itself or the sale of it. In addition, the international organizations responsible for the control of plasma commerce, like the CDC or the World Health Organization, also neglected to monitor the supply.[24] Different diseases spread because of Hemo-Caribbean, including malaria, syphilis and hepatitis. These outbreaks were possible because a form of transnational piracy was enacted, one that had its roots in the colonial map; transnational companies and pharmaceutical firms made their business without regulations or oversight.

In the 1980s, the conception of Haiti as a focus of disease proliferated, mixing prejudice, discrimination and stigmatization. It was based on the construction of an ill colonial body in which news about bizarre voodoo practices were published alongside medical records, hiding the United States's and the international organizations' implication in Hemo-Caribbean, thereby constructing the

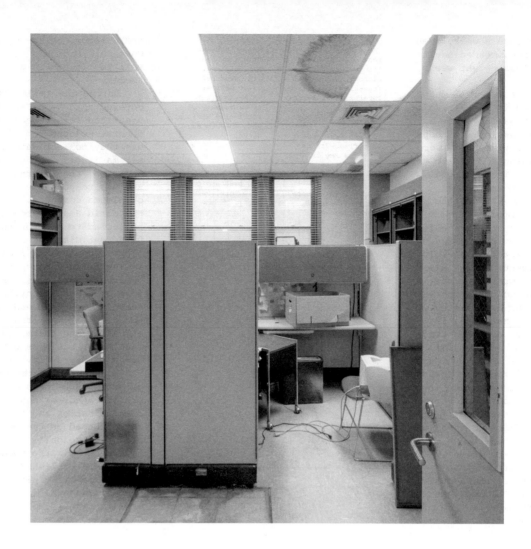

West, Bellevue
Hospital.
Photograph by
Ivan L. Munuera
& Miguel de
Guzman, 2019.

West, Bellevue
Hospital.
Photograph by
Ivan L. Munuera
& Miguel de
Guzman, 2019.

powerful narrative of Haiti as a focus of contagion. In the October 1983 edition of Annals of Internal Medicine, physicians affiliated with the Massachusetts Institute of Technology related the details of a brief visit to Haiti and wrote "it seems reasonable to consider voodoo practices a cause of the [AIDS] syndrome."[25] This body was rapidly sexualized through the developed argument about Haiti as a spot for gay sexual tourism, embedded in Western fantasies about black sexuality.[26] As Mirko D. Greek explained, "speculations abounded on the germ-bred misery, on the filthy water, on the intestinal and skin parasites, on the alcoholism of the Haitians, on their use of marijuana and all sorts of other privations and deprivations."[27] The concept of an ill colonial body with multiple locations was manifested in the blood trade of Hemo-Caribbean, the laboratories of Port-au-Prince, the flow of plasma through Air Haiti and the failure of organizations, such as the CDC and the World Health Organization, to adequately regulate blood commerce.

If Haitian plasma flew freely during this time, their human hosts- the Haitian bodies- did not benefit from the same regime of circulation. As Laurent Dubois recounted, by the early 1980s,

25
Richard Beach and Laura Peter, "Nutrition and the Acquired Immune Deficiency Syndrome", *Annals of Internal Medicine* (99:565-566, 1983).

26
Paul Farmer, *AIDS and Accusation*, Op. Cit. pp. 146-147.

27
Mirko D. Greek, History of AIDS: Emergence and Origin of a Modern Pandemic (Princeton, NJ: Princeton University Press, 1990), p. 35.

28
Laurent Dubois, Haiti: *The Aftershocks of History* (New York: Picador, 2012), p. 354.

Haitians themselves had become Haiti's most significant export. The three decades of Duvalier rule were a time of massive exodus; A tally of Haitians in New York City was approximately 150,000 in 1976, and that figure would climb to at least 400,000 by the end of the 1990s. Although a precise count is difficult to come by, it is estimated that up to a million Haitians—about 15 percent of the country's population—fled during the thirty years of Duvalier's rule. This diaspora was later dubbed the "Tenth Department," an international supplement to the nine official districts within Haiti itself.[28]

Through Hemo-Caribbean, a transnational biopolitical economy was instated. wherein medical technologies articulated a definition of bodies and nations through different architectures: laboratories, medical facilities, airlines and, ultimately, blood, plasma and bodies. Haitians were reduced to plasma, reassuring the urban constitution of a microbiological operation, where the exchange of plasma could flow freely among different countries. However, the human hosts were banned from this kind of mobility. This was a fluid sociopolitical urbanism, where legislations and the constitution of borders were embodied in its own citizens. The urbanism that was described through Hemo-Caribbean stated a movement of interscalarity in which the relationships between the local situations and histories of Haitians were intermingled within the context a wider world view: a contradictory space characterized by contestation, internal differentiation and continuous border crossings.[29]

3. Biohazard Architecture

As Jacques Pépin explained, Haitians were described during the HIV/AIDS crisis by some New York doctors as black people who could not speak English or could only do so with a "peculiar accent." They were also often referred to as "illegal migrants, asylum seekers and not-yet American citizens."[30] Access for Haitians to the American healthcare system was particularly difficult, since they could not obtain legal immigration status in the late 1970s and early 80s. In 1980, US Congress passed a law that permitted Central Americans to obtain legal immigration status, although Haitians were left out. That same year, the "Mariel boatlift," in which 125,000 Cubans and 40,000 to 80,000 Haitians tried to immigrate to the United States, caused President Jimmy Carter to reevaluate US-Haitian policies. A new class of immigrant—the "Cuban/Haitian entrant (status pending)"—was created, allowing Haitians who had entered before October 10, 1980 to apply for asylum.[31] Any Haitian entering after that date faced incarceration and deportation.

During the HIV/AIDS crisis, hospitals became the laboratories of the urban operations of the new plasmaregime, linking different geographies with the microbiological debates of the virus itself and the configuration of borders, bans and mobility operations. As late as 1990, the Gay Men's Health Crisis could barely find fifty doctors in private practice willing to put their names on a referral list for those with HIV/AIDS in New York.[32] As David Oshinsky recounted: "Stories appeared of funeral directors refusing to embalm the bodies of AIDS victims and EMS workers ignoring calls in gay neighborhoods. A number of state dental associations recommended that non-routine procedures for AIDS patients (…) be postponed. And a poll of 350 New York City dentists showed '100 percent' of them opposed to treating someone with the disease."[33]

Meanwhile, different hospitals improvised spatial solutions to confine HIV/AIDS carriers. Dr. Saul

29
On interscalirity: Albena Yaneva, "Scaling Up and Down: Extraction Trials in Architectural Design", *Social Studies of Science* (Vol. 35, Issue 6, 2005).

30
Jacques Pépin, *The Origin of Aids* (Cambridge: Cambridge University Press, 2011).

31
Jena Gaines and Stuart Anderson eds., *Haitian Immigration* (Broomal, Pa.: Mason Crest, 2003).

32
The Gay Men's Health Crisis is a New York city non-profit organization that provides support for HIV/AIDS patients. The organization was founded in January 1982 when the disease was still referred to as GRID.

33
David Oshinsky, *Bellevue: Three Centuries of Medicine and Mayhem at America's Most Storied Hospital* (New York: Doubleday).

Farber, the head of internal medicine at NYU Medical Center, said that after the first cases of AIDS were detected among his patients "[it was] just the beginning of a disaster, but why does NYU have to be the Titanic?"[34] Farber adopted an anti-AIDS policy, ruling that those patients could not be admitted to shared rooms—even though it was known at that time that HIV/AIDS carriers posed no risk to roommates—and consequently that they had to be held in the ER when the limited number of isolation rooms filled up. Farber considered the containment policy necessary, because applications for residencies at NYU from top medical schools had lagged. The effect was to build different entrances and doors for the med applicants and for the patients. The latter architecture would be organized through corridors full of beds in which the patients would be confined, keeping them on temporary gurneys lining the first-floor hallways, hidden from other patients, visitors and especially prospective applicants from med schools.

This hidden biohazard architecture instituted an asymmetrical regime, wherein the doctors and medical staff were aware of the situation (the confinement spaces, the habilitation of corridors

34
David Oshinsky,
Bellevue. Op. Cit.
p. 290.

and ER for HIV/AIDS patients), while the other patients and even the ones affected by the epidemic were never informed of the reasons behind the arrangement. It was an example of bio-chemical zoning, dividing the space into different areas in which the circulation through certain parts were permitted and others prohibited based on the perception of the epidemic. If the zoning scheme was described under the same ideology used to plan neighborhoods in which proximity is used as the desired urban configuration based on property and residence, HIV/AIDS showed the dark side of this zoning process. It was a segregationist and ideological kind of zoning, based not on the possible contagion but on the economy and academic agreements with med school applicants. This arrangement proposed a protocol based on the narratives associated with HIV/AIDS patients being seen as non-desirable subjects on the margins of society. This system was certainly not based on the available data on the epidemic and the usual protocols of biohazard in which the relationship between the given scientific information on the outbreak and the spatial configurations and medical measures used to combat it are both transparent and central. The architectural layout

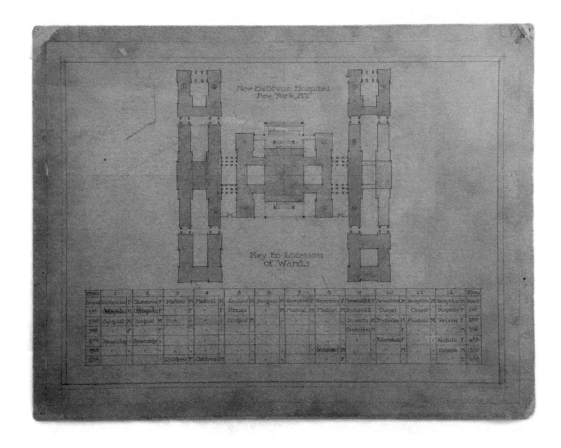

West, Bellevue Hospital. Floorplan by
McKim Mead & White.

West, Bellevue
Hospital.
Photograph by
Ivan L. Munuera
& Miguel de
Guzman, 2019.

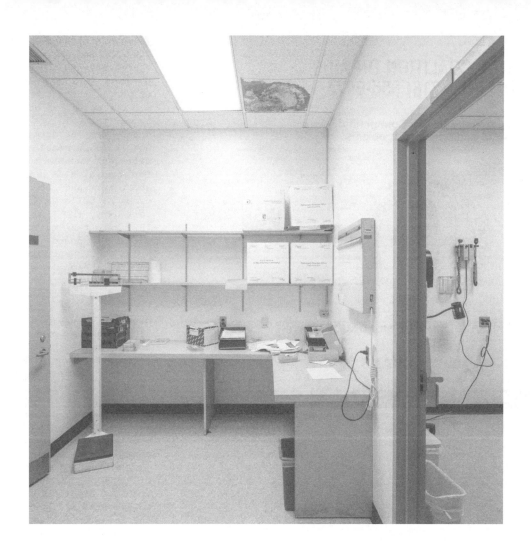

West, Bellevue
Hospital.
Photograph by
Ivan L. Munuera
& Miguel de
Guzman, 2019.

HAITIAN COALITION ON AIDS
HOTLINE: (718) 855-0972

Serving the Haitian Community:
AIDS and/or related problems

LANMÒ AVÈTI PA TOUYE KOKOBE
SIDA
PA BA W 2 CHANS

50 Court Street, Suite 605, Bklyn, NY 11201
A Project of the Haitian Centers Council, Inc.

"The Haitian Coalition on AIDS is partially funded by
the New York City Department of Health."

Graphics: Kiudi Lemone
Printing: KAPAB

"Haitian Coalition On AIDS" poster.

conveyed the stigma attached to HIV/AIDS and formed ideological hierarchies with the prescription of movement in space and the control of people through and within space.

The evolution of the epidemic showed that, in the mid-1980s, a cure was far from being found, so hospitals increased the design of different architectural solutions for special AIDS units to provide short-term and intensive primary care. At Bellevue Hospital in New York City, the AIDS unit began in 1987 as a ten-bed operation that quickly expanded to a whole wing known as 17 West, named after its location: Area 17 in the West Wing at 426 First Avenue. The unit was singled out on account of sanitation (the huge volume of vomit and diarrhea of the patients) and HIV/AIDS patients' protection (their extreme vulnerability to hospital germs). Bellevue, the oldest public hospital in the United States, accepted all of the patients that came to its doors, even if they held irregular citizenships, making it one of the central hubs for Haitian HIV/AIDS carriers and the other 4Hs.

Dr. Fred Valentine, in charge of the HIV/AIDS unit, explained that the architecture of Area 17 was central in the response to the epidemic. It was located on

Toxic Geographies

Meredith TenHoor

the fifth floor of the new wing in order to hide it from other patients and assure the anonymity of visitors. Testing facilities, waiting rooms, information points, offices and laboratories were located there, making the space an autonomous entity within the hospital that could respond rapidly to the new protocols and measures that were implemented almost daily during the height of the epidemic.[35]

The hierarchies in the medical organization also changed. As one nurse said at that time, HIV/AIDS was "a nurse's disease" rather than "a doctor's disease," not only because nurses spent more time with patients, but also because their skills were better than anything "a doctor [could] prescribe" at a time when anti-retrovirals were unknown.[36] It was an architecture of caring rather than healing, creating another confinement space: the nurse bubble. Nurses even contested some of the ideologies prescribed by the doctors with irony, like Saul Farber's declaration comparing HIV/AIDS crisis with the Titanic by hanging a block letter sign taped above the nurse's station at 17 West: "THE ONLY THING BETWEEN THIS PLACE AND THE TITANIC—THEY HAD A BAND!"[37] In 1987, when the possibility of refusing HIV/AIDS patients based on moral issues was discussed

35
Dr. Fred Valentine interviewed by the author. November, 2018.

36
David Oshinsky, Op. Cit. p. 292.

37
Idem. p. 295.

38
"When Doctors Refuse to Treat AIDS," *The New York Times* (August 3, 1987).

39
See: Bennedict R. O'G.Anderson, "Long Distance Nationalism. World Capitalism and the Rise of Identity Politics," The Wertheim Lecture 1992 (Amsterdam: Centre for Asian Studies, 1992).

among the medical community, the American Nurses Association declared that nurses "are not backing away from caring for AIDS patients. They have from the beginning and they will to the end."[38] HIV/AIDS also changed the protocols in hospitals and other medical facilities, like dental care clinics, introducing the mandatory usage of protective gear, such as disposable gloves, needles and masks. This was an infection control measure that was not indispensable until this moment.

Through a series of operations, HIV/AIDS created an urbanism that reflected and performed the political, legal, economic, colonial, symbolic and administrative regulations and ideologies. This kind of urbanism manifested a kind of "long-distance nationalism," where the agents of diaspora stories explore the sense of belonging outside their nation-states through their access to other media and representations.[39] HIV/AIDS was enacted (and still is) in a series of spatial configurations: from plasmapheresis centers to laboratories, from bio design to state borders, from airlines to international organizations, from bathhouses to hospitals. HIV/AIDS influenced the formation of an architectural organization based on a system

In these months of quarantine, we've become intimately and perhaps overly familiar with the insides of our homes. Similarly, the insides of our bodies have become charged as battlegrounds against COVID-19. Both of these interiors, however, have already been under attack for many years in a kind of slow and largely invisible assault from toxic composites used in common building materials. The "slow violence" of these materials' assaults on our bodies compounds the unequal violence of the virus, putting all of us who make, work and live in, and deal with waste from buildings produced after 1970, at risk.[1] What does it mean to understand and take this risk seriously from within the field of architecture?

Most of us are familiar with the neurotoxic and carcinogenic legacies of older, regulated, toxic building materials, such as lead and asbestos, and know that these forms of environmental risk are unevenly distributed through processes of environmental racism and environmental inequality.[2] We may also know about dangers from newer materials if they have been heavily mediatized; many try to avoid the endocrine system-disrupting compound BPA found in can liners and rigid plastic water bottles. Or perhaps we may have learned about the carcinogenic perfluorinated compounds

1
The term "slow violence" is Rob Nixon's; see *Slow Violence and the Environmentalism of the Poor* (Cambridge Mass.: Harvard University Press, 2013).

2
For more on the history of these concepts see Laura Pulido, "A Critical Review of the Methodology of Environmental Racism Research*," *Antipode* 28, no. 2 (1996): 142–59; Andrew Szasz and Michael Meuser, "Environmental Inequalities: Literature Review and Proposals for New Directions in Research and Theory:," *Current Sociology*, June 30, 2016

of production, distribution and consumption of different agents: plasma, bodies, materials, media, narratives and spaces. This was possible through a series of operations: from the confinement of the disease into specific groups (the 4Hs) to the simplification of these groups and its possible belongings (male homosexuals, Haitians, and so on)—a coordinated operation enacted by the media, medical organizations and government representatives. This was a confinement operation, a zoning that was rapidly contested by a series of activists, like the Haitian Coalition on AIDS and ACT-UP, showing that HIV/AIDS was not a disease located and confined in certain groups or communities but an epidemic that was enacted through a techno-social recomposition based on a multiscale operation.

The disease created a biohazard architecture, a microbiological, embodied urbanism based on the relationships between the virus, the treatments, the human hosts and the spaces that they created. This was framed by the postcolonial decisions and agreements of different governments before and after the rise of HIV/AIDS. The epidemic gave forth an architecture that considers the agency, history, politics and economic circumstances of the period, as well as the construction of the identity of its inhabitants. HIV/AIDS is an architecture of biohazard, wherein the politics and narratives of its subjects and spaces come hand-in-hand, depicting a hemogeography. HIV/AIDS was and still is an architectural construction, the invention of a trans-national boundary, a way to give continuity to the territorializations and discriminatory subject-specializations of the post-colonial world in the urban age. These same operations of segregation and confinement formulate new ways of spatialization—and also of resistance.

or "forever chemicals," used in Teflon manufacture from popular journalism, or from Todd Haynes' 2019 film *Dark Waters*.[3] But few architects, unless they do a deep dive into the literature on green building, realize the extent to which the everyday materials, that comprise the buildings they design, shape our biological lives.[4] To see the consequences of the materials used in our work, we would need to be able to map the biological, ecological and social impacts of these chemicals at the multiple sites in which they are created, used and circulated, and we would have to rethink our current understanding of the connections between architecture, the environment and embodied life.[5] Along with my colleague Laura Diamond and our student-researchers at Pratt Institute, I have been doing research on the geographies and architectures of toxic materials, tracing their impacts on workers and the environment at sites of extraction, manufacture, distribution and installation. We hope to expose the necropolitics — we have found Achille Mbembe's term to describe the ways that power over death is part of modern liberal society is the best way to describe this — of contemporary building.[6]

Toxic chemicals infiltrate buildings at various points and impact our bodies in different ways. One of the most common toxins we encounter is the carcinogen and lung irritant formaldehyde, volatile organic compound (VOC). Daily, but especially after we renovate, repair or redecorate, our bodies absorb formaldehyde that soaks the particleboard in our furniture, binds layers of most plywood, or coats or infuses walls via paints, wallpaper and foam insulation. While it dissipates over time, becoming less dangerous in the years after a product has been installed, the picture is more grim inside the bodies of manufacturers and contractors producing and installing materials that contain it, or architects who receive constant high levels of exposure during their frequent site visits.[7] Other VOCs — some carcinogenic, others damaging to our nervous and endocrine systems, kidneys or livers, such as benzene, toluene and acetylaldehyde, — evaporate from newly installed paints, flooring and plastic fixtures, making us dizzy, nauseated and more susceptible to headaches and infections.

Semi-volatile organic compounds (SVOCs) — found in piping, windows and cladding panels, as well as furniture — are a class of chemicals

3

Nathaniel Rich, "The Lawyer Who Became DuPont's Worst Nightmare," *The New York Times*, January 6, 2016, sec. Magazine, https://www.nytimes.com/2016/01/10/magazine/the-lawyer-who-became-duponts-worst-nightmare.html.

4

While I can't begin to introduce the bibliography in the space available here, environmental historians have a growing literature on these chemicals. One of the most useful theoretical frameworks is presented here: Soraya Boudia et al., "Residues: Rethinking Chemical Environments," *Engaging Science, Technology, and Society* 4, no. 0 (June 28, 2018): 165–78, https://doi.org/10.17351/ests2018.245.

5

This text draws from a research project on the recent history of toxic building materials that I've been conducting with architect and historian Laura Diamond, with research assistance from Jada Cannon, Sebastian Lopez Wilson, Owen Spangler and Ida Hansen. I am very grateful to biochemist Joan Ruderman for sharing research and insights on this with me.

6

See Achille Mbembe and Libby Meintjes,"Necropolitics," *Public Culture* 15, no. 1 (March 25, 2003): 11–40 and Achille Mbembe, *Necropolitics* (Durham; London: Duke University Press, 2019). For an analysis of the application of this term to environmental destruction see Thom Davies, "Toxic Space and Time: Slow Violence, Necropolitics, and Petrochemical Pollution," *Annals of the American Association of Geographers* 108, no. 6 (November 2, 2018): 1537–53, https://doi.org/10.1080/24694452.2018.1470924.

7

Healthy Building Network and Hansen, Jean, "Toxic Chemicals in Building Materials: An Overview for Health Care Organizations" (Healthy Building Network, May 2008), https://s3.amazonaws.com/healthy-materials-lab/resources/toxic-chemicals-in-building-materials.pdf; "Formaldehyde in Your Home: What You Need to Know," Agency for Toxic Substances and Disease Registry, February 10, 2016, https://www.atsdr.cdc.gov/formaldehyde/home/index.html.

Fig. 1. Still from a film depicting the futures of toxic materials in Cancer
Alley after petrochemical companies are forced to relocate residents.
Renderings by Abhishek Thakkar.

that also accumulate in our bodies, though they enter the air a bit less readily than VOCs. Halogenated flame retardants, which were in most upholstered furniture until recently when California stopped requiring them, and phthalates, a class of chemicals commonly used to make vinyl pliable, are some of the most threatening SVOCs to our health.[8] Phthalates are also found in carpets, food containers and often in cosmetics. SVOCs like phthalates disrupt endocrine systems in the bodies of both manufacturers and users of products that contain them. This can lead to early puberty for children, or to problems with metabolic function, including obesity and other illnesses.[9]

These chemicals leave themselves in unexpected places. They are not just in our bodies; they also infuse animal bodies and our landscapes. Coatings on roofs slough off in storms, polluting the soil and the water supply.[10]

8
Z. Liu and J. C. Little, "5 - Semivolatile Organic Compounds (SVOCs): Phthalates and Flame Retardants," in *Toxicity of Building Materials*, ed. F. Pacheco-Torgal, S. Jalali, and A. Fucic, Woodhead Publishing Series in Civil and Structural Engineering (Woodhead Publishing, 2012), 122–37, https://doi.org/10.1533/9780857096357.122.

9
The threats of phthalates are explained further in Leonardo Trasande, *Sicker, Fatter, Poorer: The Urgent Threat of Hormone- Disrupting Chemicals on Our Health and Future ... and What We Can Do about It* (Boston: Houghton Mifflin Harcourt, 2019). See also "Toxicological Profile for Vinyl Chloride" (U.S. Department of Health and Human Services Agency for Toxic Substances and Disease Registry Division of Toxicology and Environmental Medicine/Applied Toxicology Branch, 2004), https://www.atsdr.cdc.gov/toxprofiles/tp20.pdf; "Toxicant-Associated Steatohepatitis In Vinyl Chloride Workers," *Hepatology* 51, no. 2 (February 2010): 474–81, https://doi.org/10.1002/hep.23321.

10
Nancy Winters and Graunke, Kyle, "Roofing Materials Assessment: Investigation of Toxic Chemicals in Roof Runoff" (Olympia, Washington: Washington State Department of Ecology, February 2014), https://fortress.wa.gov/ecy/publications/documents/1403003.pdf.

Durable perfluorinated coatings in cladding systems (again, the "forever chemicals" of *Dark Waters*) make these materials waterproof, but this very durability is what makes these chemicals virtually impossible to destroy or remove from our ecosystems. Materials that appear to be ecologically beneficial from some perspectives — think about the thick foam layers that make a SIP panel energy-efficient, the "fun" vinyl used to create a temporary inflatable dwelling, or many of the resins used to make renewable mass timber structurally sound — often contain these chemicals. Yet we have still not proven their long-term safety for human occupation, let alone for the people who manufacture these products.

Bought and sold *en masse*, toxic chemicals are put in products whose ingredient lists are industry secrets. While toxins can be sensed in our bodies, or measured with expensive test kits, they are mostly invisible, and in the U.S., largely unquantified and unregulated. Although toxic building materials are found in the bodies of nearly everyone living in the contemporary US, this invisibility allows us to displace their impact onto racialized and gendered bodies, and therefore to minimize it. This process of creating invisibility is the subject of Todd Haynes' other film about toxins, *Safe* (1998) about a woman who suffers from an untraceable and not-medically-verifiable-but-still-debilitating form of "sick building syndrome." Because the impacts of materials on her body can't be quantified, her concerns are dismissed as hysteria, and the links between her

Carolyn Lazard, *Accessibility in the Arts:
A Promise and a Practice*, 2019

Carolyn Lazard, *Accessibility in the Arts: A Promise and a Practice*, 2019
Commissioned by Recess; edited by Kemi Adeyemi; designed by Rosen Tomov & Riley Hooker.

Carolyn Lazard's *Accessibility in the Arts* is an accessibility guide for small-scale arts nonprofits. It exists as an online guide, an open-source pdf and an audio recording. Paper copies were distributed at the 2019 Common Field convening, and the text is now available for free to stream or download from several websites.

    Across four sections, the guide identifies the ways in which disabled people are excluded from cultural spaces and offers possible solutions. It outlines accommodations, i.e. actions an institution can take to make their space more accessible, suggestions on how to list access information and guidelines for budgeting. The text considers the unique capacity of small-scale art organizations to meet the needs of disabled communities, in particular the advantage of increased flexibility.

    In its approach, *Accessibility in the Arts* moves away from historical and juridical definitions of accessibility, such as ADA, and towards principles of disability justice. As the guide reads: "Within this framework, disability is defined as an economic, cultural, and/or social exclusion based on a physical, psychological, sensory, or cognitive difference." The solutions outlined in the guide range from changes to the physical space, to guidelines about how to handle content or even support visitors with auxiliary services such as childcare or harm reduction measures.

Carolyn Lazard, *Accessibility in the Arts:
A Promise and a Practice*, 2019

body's reaction to chemicals and the psychological suffering she endures are constantly collapsed. What we see in the film is a simultaneous dismissal and naturalization of the risk that is everywhere in the Anthropocene (actually, I prefer a term that is between Donna Haraway's Cthulhucene, which denotes the unpredictable impacts of our environmental decisions, and Jason W. Moore's Capitolocene, which rightly understands the role capitalism has played in environmental degradation) where the impact of environmental damage is widespread, unpredictable, and unmanageable, and the canaries in the coalmine who sense it first are constantly dismissed.[11] It's hard not to see the parallels between this discourse and the one we have experienced during the COVID-19 pandemic; the proven but still variable impacts of everyday toxins mirror the unknowable impacts of the coronavirus in our bodies as well as the gross racial and economic disparities in its impact. Blame for the disease, in parallel to blame for being visibly impacted by toxins, is unfairly displaced onto vulnerable, stressed and taxed bodies.[12] Toxins are equalizing, in that we are all impacted by them, but also sensed unequally.

[11]
See Donna J. Haraway, *Staying with the Trouble: Making Kin in the Chthulucene*, (Durham: Duke University Press Books, 2016); Elmar Altvater et al., *Anthropocene or Capitalocene? Nature, History, and the Crisis of Capitalism*, ed. Jason Moore, (New York: PM Press, 2016).

[12]
For more on our epistemological position in relationship to coronavirus see Daston, Lorraine, "Ground-Zero Empiricism," *In the Moment: Posts from the Pandemic from Critical Inquiry* (blog), April 10, 2020, https://critinq.wordpress.com/2020/04/10/ground-zero-empiricism/.

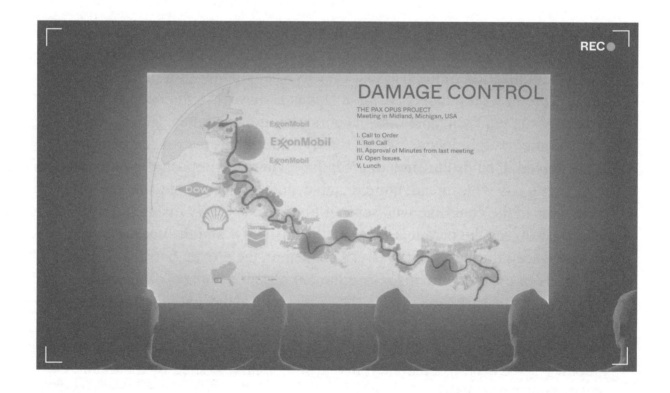

Fig. 2. Still from a film depicting the futures of toxic materials in Cancer
Alley after petrochemical companies are forced to relocate residents.
Renderings by Abhishek Thakkar.

To end these inequalities and the damage they create in our bodies and landscapes, architects must not only learn more about what lurks in our homes but call for new curricula that takes material risk and impact more seriously. Now more than ever, architectural education must include teaching on the unequal vulnerability of our bodies and biomes, and on how architects can design for these vulnerabilities, rather than erase or minimize them. Architectural historians have been laying a strong groundwork for this pedagogical shift; soon-to-be published dissertation research by Laura Diamond, Meagan Eardley, Erin Putalik, Desirée Valadares, Jessica Varner and others explores the recent history of measuring toxins and quantifying risk in landscapes and bodies. And major works on the history of architectural specification by Katie Lloyd Thomas and Michael Osman document the architectural production of industrial materials and materialisms, showing how specification has performed a kind of pseudo-regulatory function of these materials.[13]

13
Michael Osman, *Modernism's Visible Hand: Architecture and Regulation in America*, Buell Center Books in the History and Theory of American Architecture (Minneapolis: University of Minnesota Press, 2018); Katie Lloyd Thomas, "Specifications: Writing Materials in Architecture and Philosophy," *Arq: Architectural Research Quarterly* 8, no. 3–4 (December 2004): 277–83, https://doi.org/10.1017/S1359135504000296; Katie Lloyd Thomas, Tilo Amhoff, and Nick Beech, *Industries of Architecture* (Routledge, 2015). Note that the questions Osman and Thomas pose about material differ significantly from how "materialism" has been understood in architectural conversations around object-oriented ontology.

1. Exterior Cladding & Siding

Arsenic, Creosote, Phthalates/PVSs, SVOCs
Semi-volatile organic compounds (SVOCs) are a class of chemicals that become partially airborne at room temperatures, at which point they enter our bodies through the air we breathe or sometimes through skin contact or ingestion. They can impact our organs, metabolisms and endocrine systems.

2. Insulation

Halogenated flame retardants, Formaldehyde, VOCs
Halogenated flame retardants release harmful dioxins when heated, posing health threats to installers, at the end of a building's life cycle, or in the event of a fire.

3. Furniture

PFCs, Formaldehyde, Phthalates/PVCs, VOCs
Volatile Organic Compounds (VOCs) emitted by furniture and other domestic items are ten times higher concentrated indoors,[1] and pose health risks to humans and animals.

4. Paints

Cadmium, BPA, VOCs
Paints containing cadmium pigments are especially toxic carcinogens, and pose health risks to installers.

5. Finish Flooring/Decking
6. Subflooring/Sheathing

Arsenic, Creosote
PFCs, Formaldehyde, Phthalates/PVCs, VOCs
Formaldehyde is a volatile organic compound (VOC) that is a known carcinogen and lung irritant.
Perfluorinated chemicals (PFCs) damage ecosystems at the site of manufacture, and at high levels can disrupt our endocrine systems and cause cancer.

7. Windows

Lead, Hexavalent Chromium, Phthalates/PVCs
Phthalates are endocrine disrupters used to make vinyl flexible; we encounter them in houses through dust and off-gassing and they reach our bodies at higher concentrations at the site of manufacture.

[1]
US EPA, OAR. "Volatile Organic Compounds" Impact on Indoor Air quality." Overviews and Factsheets. US EPA, August 18, 2014.

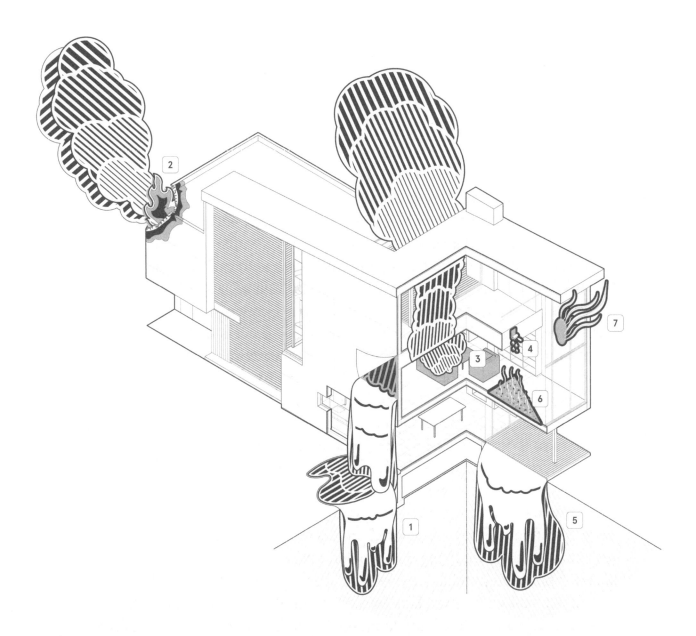

Fig. 3. A standard post-1970 house. Drawing by Owen Spangler.

Architects, too, have played increasingly active roles in creating and sharing knowledge about building materials by making specification a medium for activism. Much of this work has been undertaken by large firms and in-house planners at large technology companies, such as Google, who realized it was in their economic self-interest to mitigate the threats to worker productivity posed by indoor air pollutants, and to specify safer materials. (Indeed, the fumes from sitting in a sunny office with a standard-issue vinyl window shade can slacken our powers of concentration.) Professional organizations are beginning to take action; a recent report issued by the AIA synthesizes and makes available some of the data gathered by firms who have researched this issue.[14] Academic material labs, particularly at the New School, have been established to research risks and alternatives to toxic materials. And crucial databases, like the Pharos database created and maintained by the Healthy Building Network, collect and attempt to quantify risk as a service to designers and builders alike. The growing field of lifecycle and supply-chain analysis also offers some hope. The Grace Farms-sponsored project to end supply chain slavery is researching and publicizing this problem; participants hope to use architects' social capital and purchasing power to shame manufacturers and distributors who abuse their workers into changing their ways. In all of these incontrovertibly important knowledge-gathering initiatives, however, architects have taken the onus of regulation on themselves. But architects are not and will never become biochemists. As our team of research assistants have found, researching the material provenance of even common products is difficult when they are closely-guarded and unregulated industrial secrets. And what is challenging in an academic context is nearly impossible for a small firm to add to billable hours.

Beyond specification, and within a more established set of disciplinary conventions, architects can make the toxic both visible and intolerable through representational work. Through renderings, drawings, maps and plans for future projects, we can depict why a healthy house is desirable and how poisons created in seemingly far-off factories penetrate our bodies. As my student research collaborator Owen Spangler shows in his drawing of toxins that are commonly found inside homes, the house is everywhere compromised. Toxins seemingly contained within walls leak into exterior landscape and the interior of the house[Fig. 3]. Other work can examine the scales of the landscape or city: Lindy Roy's project *Cancer Alley* (2001), and Richard Misrach and Kate Orff's book *Petrochemical America* mapped the relationships between sites of production and environmental consequences of industrial pollution in Southern Louisiana.[15]

14
Frances Yang and Sara Tepfer, "Prescription for Healthier Building Materials: A Design and Implementation Protocol" (Washington, D.C.: AIA/ARUP, Spring 2018).

15
For more on Lindy Roy's *Cancer Alley* project see Kristine Synnes, *Roy: Architecture of Risk*, vol. 11, Michigan Architecture Papers (Ann Arbor: University of Michigan, College of Architecture & Urban Planning, 2004); See also Kate Orff and Richard Misrach, *Petrochemical America*, 1st ed. (New York: Aperture Foundation, 2012).

Heating the Bauhaus

Daniel A. Barber

This article is published in collaboration with the Kleinman Center for Energy Policy at the University of Pennsylvania. An earlier version appeared as a KCEP paper, and can be found online at https://kleinmanenergy.upenn.edu/paper/heating-bauhaus.

Drawing from these projects and that of the activist Rev. Dr. William Barber, Pratt Institute B.Arch. student Abhishek Thakkar imagined that a future court case forced the owners of petrochemical factories along the Mississippi River to remediate the ruined landscape of Cancer Alley and relocate residents living on polluted land, building new houses and towns. Thakkar produced a series of renderings of this new world as a set of film stills, depicting the chemical companies' continued attempts to find a use for their toxic output, and the residents' attempts to resist chemical colonization.(Fig. 1-2). Future work depicting the geographies of pollution can make the extent of the uneven geographic distribution of damage even clearer.

In spite of the enormous value of all of this documentary and critical work within our field, it would be best if toxic products were not made at all. If hazardous materials were never extracted, transformed, added to building parts, and dumped into landscapes, we would not be faced with the racialized, gendered and globally unequal consequences of environmental racism. If biocides were never added to products, landscapes impacted by them would never need to be remediated. If our buildings were not made of toxic materials, we might all have a better chance at surviving pandemics such as the current one. Though we can impact the lives of building workers through careful specification, architects cannot perform the regulatory role that our federal government has largely abdicated.[16] Our best

What is architecture after carbon? It's not just a question of "How do we build?" or even "How do we take care of the buildings we love?" Rather, the question should be: How do we attend to what is clearly an atrophied discipline, one to which so many are nonetheless devoted? How do we render creative once again, though on different carbon terms, the process of spatio-energetic adaptation? How can we rebuild the discipline, using its complex historical relationship with energy as a guide?

Hydrocarbon fuels, economic growth and the built environment have co-created each other over the last century. They exist in a suspension of feedback over-productivity, with buildings acting as both medium and mediator. Architecture, which always exists in a cultural relationship with the larger built environment, has been a mechanism of fuel intensification, both through willful acts and process of adaptation. All of the familiar debates of modern architecture—habitat and "the man on the street," the Grays and the Whites, the proliferation of computational neo-modernisms (to name just a few)—occurred during a historically brief period of hydrocarbon-fuel expansion, which is now coming to an end, albeit far too slowly. The "post-war flowering

1
Philip Johnson, "Preface" in *Built in USA: Post-war Architecture* (New York: Museum of Modern Art, 1952): 7; J. R. McNeil and Peter Engelke, *The Great Acceleration: An Environmental History of the Anthropocene since 1945* (Cambridge, MA: Belknap Press, 2016).

2
Stephanie LeMenager, *Living Oil: Petroleum Culture in the American Century* (New York: Oxford University Press, 2013); Sheena Wilson, Adam Carlson and Imre Szeman, editors. *Petrocultures: Oil, Energy, and Culture* (Montreal: McGill-Queen's University Press, 2017).

3
Dominic Boyer and Imre Szeman, *Energy Humanities: An Anthology* (Baltimore: Johns Hopkins University Press, 2017).

of modern architecture," to use Philip Johnson's memorable phrase, correlates precisely with the Great Acceleration, the spike of the Anthropocene.[1]

Cultural relations to fuel sources are foundational both to the patterns and contours of social life and also to understanding how to adjust these patterns, as new contingencies emerge in relation to energy systems. *Architecture* sits in the center of this dynamic relationship, as both a cultural reflection of existing energy systems and as a material force for a possible transition to other energetics. With substantive roots in the energy transitions of the nineteenth century, twentieth century culture is decidedly a carbon culture, and is so in part due to buildings, systems, infrastructures and habits of modernity.[2] Architecture, again, is a *medium*, a means of conveying and expressing energy: it is both a screen on which to *watch* energetic change and a material from which to *produce it*.

Many scholars have argued that to be modern is to depend on the capacities and abilities generated by hydrocarbon fuel.[3] Given this tight connection, it is striking that so little attention has been paid to the intersecting histories of architecture and energy sources.

hope to act against our toxic risk is to agitate for better regulation. We can do this best by aligning ourselves with frontline communities and with longstanding advocates for environmental justice, by seeing that our risk is shared. Yet architectural work within existing disciplinary channels is also not uncoupled from regulation. Regulation has, in crucial ways, drawn from the work of architects and architecture to come into being, as I and others have long argued. Thus architectural work — in ways I have briefly sketched here and also in ways I have not yet imagined — can gather steam for, render desirable, and even give the form to a better-regulated material supply. Our onus is to find ways within politics and within our discipline to push for this transformation of material processes and products. Only then can we find a way to a world where our interlinked biomes and bodies can flourish free of toxins.

16
The state of California and Sweden both have somewhat comprehensive material safety regulations, but federal US regulation of building parts has never truly existed, and it has been significantly dismantled in the Trump administration, especially in light of the recent decision to re-permit the use of carcinogenic asbestos. See Oliver Milman, "Russian Mining Firm Puts Trump's Face on Its Asbestos Products," *The Guardian*, July 11, 2018, sec. US news, https://www.theguardian.com/us-news/2018/jul/11/asbestos-trump-face-seal-uralasbest-russia.

Carbon was essential to the development of modern architecture on both cultural and technological terms.[4] Histories of the environment more generally have, until recently, been in the background of architectural discussions. In the context of energy sources, this gap in the scholarship is even more pronounced.[5]

Through investigating a prominent building in the history of architecture, the Bauhaus Dessau, I hope to clarify and begin to unravel the mutual dependencies of architectural innovation and fuel transition. While the building has been extensively written about, documented and criticized, little mention has been made of the heating system, or of the importance of innovations in heating technology and coal availability to the formal, technological and programmatic ambitions of the building. Heating and cooling systems of buildings are often subject to renovation and transformation, usually with little evidence of these changes in the interiors spaces or on the surface. Documents of the last ninety-plus years of the Bauhaus Dessau's fuel dynamics help to frame concerns that are re-emerging in relation to the history of architecture more generally, and specifically relative to the material impact of buildings on

the living conditions of the uncertain present.

The Bauhaus Dessau was an early example of coal-powered modernism: its façade, volume and height were determined, in part, by (under) estimations of available coal for heating fuel, coupled with a pervasive sense of design as an expression of aesthetics rather than of performance. Increasingly today, architecture sees itself as a climate-mediating system: a means of both mitigating carbon emissions and also encouraging a culture of low-carbon living. Design plays a role in the technological intensification of fuel efficiency; design is also crucial to fostering a culture of low-carbon living and encouraging new discussion about policy, lifestyles and urban transformation. The history of the Bauhaus Dessau provides a concise case study on these terms, and helps frame architecture and its history as a contingent aspect of socio-energetic relations.

• • •

The history of the heating system of the Bauhaus Dessau suggests a number of interesting inflections to familiar narratives of architectural history. As an initial, large-scale reframing, it provides

4
Daniel A. Barber, *A House in the Sun: Modern Architecture and Solar Energy in the Cold War* (New York: Oxford University Press, 2016.)

5
Exceptions include Giovanna Borasi and Marko Zardini, *Sorry, Out of Gas: Architecture's Response to the 1973 Oil Crisis* (Montreal: Canadian Centre for Architecture, 2007); Carola Hein, "Oil Spaces: The Global Petroleumscape in the Rotterdam/The Hague Area" in *Journal of Urban History* vol. 44, no. 5 (2018): 887-929; Thomas Leslie, Saranya Panchaseelan, et. al., "Deep Space, Thin Walls: Environmental and Material Precursors to the Postwar Skyscraper" in *The Journal of the Society of Architectural Historians* vol. 77, no. 1 (March 2018): 77-96.

Fig. 1. The workshop wing of the Bauhaus
Dessau, from across the street. Photograph
by the author.

Fig. 2. Close up of the curtain wall as seen
from the connecting bridge. Photograph by the
author.

evidence that many of the formal and programmatic innovations associated with German modernism were reliant on the changing conditions of energy policy and fuel provision. Put simply: the Bauhaus Dessau, as did many buildings before and after it, relied on coal.

The Bauhaus Dessau was designed by Walter Gropius and completed in December 1926. The building was home to the experimental school, the Bauhaus, which Gropius led only until 1928. The building's organization, while innovative, was quite simple. It consisted of four major components: the three levels of open workshop spaces, the dormitory block, a third volume to the north that housed an unrelated school, and the connecting bridge, which included the oft-photographed director's office.

The programmatic and design components of the Bauhaus Dessau required a novel and aggressive heating system. *Open-ness* was an explicit desire of the social and pedagogical program of the school: physically open workshops would allow "master" and "student" to interact, and they would provide a new model for design engagement with industry. Numerous design collaborations emerged as a result of this pedagogical and professional method. The workshop of Marcel

6
Kathleen James-Chakraborty, ed. *Bauhaus Culture: from Weimar to the Cold War* (Minneapolis, MN: University of Minnesota Press, 2006).

7
Paul Overy, *Light, Air, and Openness: Modern Architecture between the Wars* (New York: Thames and Hudson, 2008).

8
Reyner Banham, *A Concrete Atlantis: U.S. Industrial Building and European Modern Architecture* (Cambridge, MA: MIT Press, 1986).

9
Anke Fissabre and Bernhard Niethammer. "The Invention of the Glazed Curtain Wall in 1903 — the Steiff Toy Factory" in *Proceedings of the Third International Congress on Construction History* (May 2009): n.p.

Breuer, for example, worked closely with the furniture manufacturer Thonet to mass produce bent aluminum chairs; other collaborations led to innovations in textile design, typeface and photography.[6] All relied on the open space as an arena for relatively egalitarian interactions.[7]

The building was designed with one of the first curtain walls: a thin, uninsulated single pane of glass in iron spandrels that surrounded three sides of the building.[fig. 1-2] The curtain wall enclosed a remarkably open interior—modeled, as many have noted, on American factories, including those for the Ford motor company, then aiming to maximize daylighting on the interior;[8] the Steiff toy factory in Geingen, Germany, completed in 1903, was an important precedent.[9] Perimeter radiators, situated against this thin wall, were, in cold weather, pumped with enough coal-generated steam to keep the interior of this thin shell relatively comfortable. While effective in producing a sense of openness and a space for engagement, this design and construction approach exhibited remarkably poor thermal conditions. Indeed, due to the poor insulation of the curtain wall, the large amount of heat generated to warm this open space was also effectively drawn out of the interior and into the lower atmosphere.

Evidence of the building's thermal strain includes awkward placement of radiators. In addition to the perimeter radiators in the workshop, one is hung on the wall in the central stairway.[fig. 3] Concern over thermal conditions is also evident in the operability of window openings for summer ventilation. The wall of the auditorium provides a clear example of these innovations: radiators lined the wall, and the windows were opened or closed with a wheel.[fig. 4-5]

The school's pedagogical innovations depended on the open, difficult-to-heat workshop space, at least symbolically. It was the core of the project, the image and the activator of the school's novel program. It was a space for socio-political negotiation and contestation. Spatial conditions were integral to the method of education, suggestive of a connection between the school and factory and conditions, and part of a program of social and industrial relations that were imagined within the building itself. Adaptation to a new kind of spatio-sociability was encouraged, sparked and facilitated: a new way of life was modeled in the form itself. Coal was essential

to these prospects for social transformation.

The Bauhaus Dessau's heating system is a complex historical object. It was installed and then changed and reinstalled and reconfigured almost a dozen documented times. It has always been *in process*, an indication of the fluid state of architecture as an energy interface. The Bauhaus Dessau's energy demands were significant and relied on increased access to heating energy from coal. In the context of emergent energy policy in the consolidated German state, using coal as heating fuel was a welcome gesture towards intensifying productivity and economic growth. Development, in all its senses (national, suburban, colonial and post-colonial), has also always been at least in part about energy intensification: the extraction and exploitation of resources.

The Bauhaus Dessau represents a significant moment in this history of intensification. Peter Behrens, of course, designing for the Allgemeine Elektricitäts-Gesellschaft (AEG, often referred to as the German General Electric) in the previous decade, represents another. Numerous other examples could also be invoked during the heroic Inter-War period, the Post-War economic and architectural

boom, amidst the strains of Post-Modernism and up to the eclecticism of the present, albeit complicated by shifts from coal to petroleum. The Bauhaus Dessau is just one example. The causal diagram holds: innovations in building design are often also evidence of how new kinds of energy have been taken advantage of for novel social effects. The building is a medium to process fuels and render them social, cultural and political. Historically, this processing has also been intensification—Mies' Seagrams Building is one other potent example of fuel profligacy that followed these transitions and traditions; Eero Saarinen's thin curtain wall for the IBM complex in frigid Rochester, Minnesota and Louis Kahn's Exeter Library in Vermont offer additional data points. Until very recently, that is, the adoption of fuel sources also meant a marked increase in fuel use and, thus, the building became as a cultural medium for energy intensification. Renewable energy has begun (but just barely) to redraw this causal diagram of energy and architectural innovation.

...

Over the past ninety-four years, the Bauhaus Dessau's heating plant underwent a number of significant renovations.[10] The heating plant was located just to the left of the main entry, where the workshop building intersected with the connecting bridge and under the auditorium. When the building opened in 1926, it had a low-pressure steam system, consisting of five pulverized coal (P.C.) boilers that used coal dust as fuel. The coal was stored next to the workshop building and under the connecting bridge. At the time, this was an innovative approach; P.C. boilers have since become commonplace, especially in large-scale power generation, in which the conditions of feeding the boiler have been mechanized.[11] Pulverized coal has significant health risks for those exposed to it directly. In the case of the Bauhaus Dessau, a single boilerman was initially employed to manage and maintain the system.

By the end of 1927, alterations were already being made, including a more precise control system and an early iteration of a watering system to help reduce free particulates. Two of the five boilers were replaced in 1931, because the insulation conditions were so poor that they had cracked due to over-firing. During the brief period that the school was in operation, students were often expected to assist in transporting the coal piled near the dormitory into the boiler room.[12] The Bauhaus Dessau was shut down by the Nazi's in October of 1932 (aspects of the school continued in Berlin for another year).

The building was damaged during World War II, but it was haphazardly repaired by 1946. Only two of the P.C. boilers still worked; pulverized coal and coal dust were now harder to come by, as they were being used in larger scale power plants rather than in small, building-scale systems. The boilers were converted to raw coal, so that they could use numerous available variations of coal briquettes or high-temperature coke. These systems were considerably less efficient and significantly more toxic. A ramp was installed between the coal storage bunkers (still under the bridge) and the boiler room, breaking through exterior and partition walls to provide more convenient access. By the early 1960s, coal was also stored outside in exposed piles next to the coal bunker, so that there would be enough fuel on hand for colder periods.

By this time, however, the boilers were outdated and inefficient. A sixth boiler was added around 1967; there were now two full-time boiler operators, keeping all of them firing in the winter from 4 A.M. to 8 P.M. and for 24 hours

10
Oliver Blomeier, et. al., *Rekord: die Spur der Kohlen* (Dessau: Herausberger, 1993).

11
Sonia Yeh and Edward S. Rubin, "A centurial history of technological change and learning curves for pulverized coal-fired utility boilers" in *Energy* vol. 32 (2007): 1996-2005.

12
Eric C. Cimino, "Student Life at the Bauhaus, 1919-1933," MA Thesis, University of Massachusetts Boston, 2003.

Fig. 3. The staircase and view onto the bridge
leading to the north wing. Note the radiator
hung on the wall in the landing. Photograph by
the author.

Maria Eichhorn, *Building as unowned property*, 2017, conversion of a building's
legal status, lot at Stavropoulou 15, documenta 14, Athens

Maria Eichhorn's artwork *Building as unowned property* sets out to purchase a vacant building in Athens and convert the real estate to a piece of legally unowned property. The work, as exhibited at *documenta 14*, appears in the form of documents that result from research and legal/bureaucratic activities that went into achieving this goal. The process of establishing the building's legal status as unowned is still ongoing.

Conceptually, the unowned building ceases to participate in the commodification of space, which Eichhorn argues forms the basis of "disaster capitalism." Practically, the building stands at odds with the consistent speculative purchasing of abandoned buildings in Athens — buildings left behind by tenants or landlords unable to pay their debts due to the economic crisis in Greece. Although the unowned property is still physically extant, it cannot directly benefit people who profit from rentals, mortgages or gentrification. Eventually the building will house the Rose Valland Institute, another work by Eichhorn in the form of an independent interdisciplinary project that "researches and documents the expropriation of property formerly owned by Europe's Jewish population and the ongoing impact of those confiscations."[1]

The success of *Building as Unowned Property* will constitute a legal precedent. As the artist writes, "The work is an attempt to use the law, as a proper language, to produce, or rather to reproduce, something that doesn't exist."[2]

[1]
Rose Valland Institute website. http://www.rosevallandinstitut.org/about.html. Accessed June 23, 2020.

[2]
Maria Eichhorn in Polly Staple, "1000 Words: Maria Eichhorn", Artforum International Vol. 55, No. 8, 180-183.

Maria Eichhorn, *Building as unowned property*, 2017, conversion of a building's legal status, lot at Stavropoulou 15, documenta 14, Athens

Fig. 4-5. Window opening mechanisms, in
the auditorium and in the workshop wing.
Photographs by the author.

during frost conditions. The building could not be left unheated in the winter, even for a short period, for fear of negative impacts on furnishings, electrical wires and other interior systems.

In 1970, records indicate that the boilermen were not able to keep enough coal on hand, due to a combination of supply inconsistencies and rising demand by virtue of the boilers' inefficiency. In 1972, the six boilers were repaired and updated; a third boilerman was hired, and a larger space behind the dormitory wing was used to store the fuel, which was then mostly brown coal. Smoke from the boilers was also an issue, discoloring the walls on the interior and exterior of the building. And yet, the increased capacity still proved inadequate. In March 1973, the six furnaces were replaced by five new boilers, which were both more efficient and had a higher capacity; this led to increased demand and increased use of coal as the more efficient system sought to maintain a higher temperature on the interior.

The Bauhaus Dessau building underwent another renovation in 1976 in preparation for its 50th anniversary celebrations in 1977. The main concern, relative to the heating system, was to obviate the need for the unsightly hill of coal

next to the building. An initial plan to build an underground storage area was dismissed as too costly. Instead, largely out of concerns for the discoloration resulting from the furnace exhaust, it was decided to switch to a gas-fired system. A system was purchased, but it was never installed, as there was no means to provide an adequate supply of gas.

Attempts were then made to connect the building to the district heating system of Dessau. Due to technical concerns and the fact that the city of Dessau had consistently distanced itself from the school and its building during the Communist years, the district heating plan fell apart in 1977. The inefficient, polluting, coal burning system remained. The 1976 renovation also led to the replacement of many windows, especially in the dormitory and the north wing. Many operable windows were now sealed to marginally increase insulation. However, these windows were still of single-paned glass instead of more insulative double-paned, glass panels.

On New Year's Eve of 1978, a sudden temperature drop froze parts of the heating system. During the holidays, the system was run at a minimum, which proved inadequate to the plummeting temperatures.

A number of pipes and radiators cracked, and again the heating system was subjected to an overhaul. A warm water system was set up to supply the radiators in the workshop building, while the bridge and dormitory wing were still heated by steam from the boilers. By the end of the year, the entire system was converted to warm water that heated the radiators.

A few years later, attempts were made again to connect the building to a district heating system. Pipes had been laid on site in 1976. Yet in 1982, negotiations to make the connection stalled again, due to changes in the city's management. Up until the dissolution of East Germany in the early 1990s, the building relied on the pile of coal in the back, feeding an inefficient and inadequate system. Finally, in 1998, the building was connected to a district heating system. The boilers, and the coal pile, were removed; the space that contained the boilers is now the coat room and bathrooms for visitors to the building.[fig. 6-7]

The story of the Bauhaus Dessau building, amidst all of its specificity, is normal enough. When issues emerged relative to the means of heating interior space, the solution tended to be: "more fuel." The details of the

Fig. 6. The control system for the district steam heating system now in the former site of the heating plant, which is also the coat room with lockers for visitors to store bags and coats. Photograph by author.

pedagogical program and the value of the building to architectural history obviously suggest that it requires some special treatment, but the general diagram persists: before concerns about carbon emissions became acute, the solution to heating problems was to increase throughput. In other words, rather than renovate, insulate, upgrade the system or reconsider forms of habitation, the solution was just to increase energy availability—again, due to the need to maintain the aesthetic integrity of the building. Generally speaking, hydrocarbon fuels in various forms have been kept cheap by subsidy and other national government scale interventions. Aside from a brief moment in the 1970s, the most economically viable solution to heating deficiency has been to simply turn up the radiator and feed in more coal. This default setting has led to an atrophied technological trajectory, relative to the relationship of buildings to hydrocarbon fuels and, thereby, to carbon. This dynamic calls into question the viability of buildings (and of architecture in general), as we look towards a future of increased climatic instability. We lack a historical and conceptual foundation for understanding architecture's energetics and

its social relationship to fuels. Thus, we strain to collectively transform it.

In 1996, the Bauhaus Dessau was included on the UNESCO World Heritage List; this was a process that involved restoring the building to its original condition, while also respecting the need for substantive mechanical upgrades.[13] In 2011, Brenne Architekten, a Berlin-based firm that focuses on the fuel retrofit of modernist buildings, was hired to renovate the building according to changing thermal standards and increased concern over carbon emissions, yet without compromising the heritage value of the structure.

An important decision was made as part of this most recent renovation process, the significance of which cannot be overemphasized: the workshop wing was functionally abandoned during seasonal extremes of heat or cold. Due to the poor insulative conditions of the single-paned windows and the scale and position of the radiators that could not be altered, it was determined that no ongoing public activities could persist in the workshops. In short, the architects could not retrofit the space so that it could be consistently maintained above 16 degrees Celsius (60 degrees Fahrenheit) without either

13
Margret Kentgens-Craig, "Art and Politics: no 'new unity'" in *The Dessau Bauhaus Building 1926-1999* (Basel: Birkhauser, 1998): 66-85.

Architects Draw the Anthropocene

Lili Carr, Feifei Zhou, and Anna Tsing

Fig. 7. A close up of the district steam heating system as it enters the building in the coatroom. Photograph by author.

transforming the building from its heritage state or significantly exceeding carbon emissions targets.[(fig. 8)]

Following this decision, the offices and remaining student activities were moved to the north wing. When the TU Anhalt relocated its faculty of architecture to Dessau in 2001, new buildings were constructed next to the Bauhaus Dessau, with classrooms, design studios and computer facilities. The Bauhaus library was also expanded and relocated. The original building's workshop area still contains the gift shop on the first floor and a café on the ground floor; the latter is better insulated because it sits partially below grade. The upper floors are occasionally open for tours.

A number of other renovations increased the fuel efficiency of the dormitory wing, the bridge and the north wing. Photovoltaic panels were installed on the roof of the north wing; black-out curtains, insulative curtains and new windows were implemented where possible. The most significant change was to the window profiles of the north and dormitory wings. On the dormitory wing, a number of windows had been replaced in 1976 with un-openable, sealed panels. These were removed and replaced with windows that

Humans did not produce the Anthropocene by themselves. Instead, the Anthropocene is a patchwork of "feral" ecologies, encouraged by landscape altering human infrastructure projects — dams, drilling rigs and industrial parks — which then develop and spread beyond human control. *Feral Atlas* brings together 75 reports by scientists, humanists, artists, researchers and architects who witness and study how these ecologies change the conditions under which humans interact both with each other and non-human others, whether biological, technological or ephemeral. These infrastructural effects, *Feral Atlas* argues, *are* the Anthropocene.

Insistently attuned to more-than-human histories, *Feral Atlas* does more than catalogue sites of imperial and industrial ruin. Feral Atlas stretches conventional notions of maps and mapping, drawing on the relational potential of the digital to offer new ways of analyzing and apprehending the Anthropocene. In insisting that heterogenous ways of knowing and telling are essential for its study, each report in *Feral Atlas* is presented in a manner related to the author's training, whether through painting, poem, essay, field reportage, documentary film or music. In insisting that spatial analysis is required in following the fragile and complex dynamics of feral effects, observations and analyses are told across different spatial scales, angles and modes of representation, depending on the issue being mapped. The scaly side of a salmon is a terrain for a salmon louse, but

Fig. 8. Insulating curtains covering the
windows in the gift shop, on the first floor
of the workshop wing. Photograph by author.

it does not scale up into a global map. A map of stratospheric winds
is a useful way to consider the travels of a coffee rust spore, but it cannot depict the travels of a cane toad. Held in relation with each other,
these materials reveal worlds full of connection and overlap, as well
as worlds full of difference and multiplicity. Unlike 15th century carto-
graphic maps or GIS mapping systems, *Feral Atlas*' maps do not
come together neatly.

One of the key categories in *Feral Atlas* is "Anthropocene
Detonator," by which we refer to that set of historical conjunctures that
changes landscape-making projects in a radical way. The atlas has
chosen four Detonators—Invasion, Empire, Capital, and Acceleration—
to show how infrastructure making programs have changed historically,
and into the present, through these "detonations." We explain each
through a landscape, which shows world making as brought into being
through a landscape-transforming program. Each incorporates multiple representational techniques to bring multi-scalar, cross-temporal
events into conversation across a canvas.

As we continue to seek new ways of seeing and doing in the
Anthropocene, architects must play a crucial role. Architects are
trained in the practice of drawing as a method of observation and projection, yet often overlook crucial aspects of the ecologies in which
they practice. Just as *Feral Atlas* stretches conventional notions of
mapping, we encourage architects to use their skill at drawing to em-

could be opened for ventilation in the summer. According to the Brenne Architekten's subsequent monitoring, due to this combination of factors the dormitory wing saw a 72% reduction in fuel demand.

While considering the history of this century of changes to the heating system, it is important to keep in mind that Dessau is in the former territory of East Germany. In keeping with a familiar narrative of an East/West industrial imbalance, the building was not seriously attended to until the mid-1970s. In the context of the Great Acceleration, the use of coal and petroleum increased around the world, specifically in mid-size industrial buildings across Europe and the U.S. and in many decolonizing spaces of the Global South. This accelerated usage coincided with the deregulation of the energy industry. Buildings were organized to pump through coal and other fuels and were often then neglected, neither upgraded nor maintained. The solution, if needed, to any heating deficit was, again, just to feed more coal into the boiler. The Bauhaus Dessau is an icon of Modernism in this important sense as well — hungry for hydrocarbon fuels, and eager to participate in the system of growth and expansion that has led to our contemporary polluted and overdeveloped world.

German energy policy was unfocused during the period of the Bauhaus Dessau's design, construction and the short period when the building was used for the school (1928 to 1932). There was little incentive to reduce smoke or waste. While there were substantive efforts across the German industrial economy to render coal furnaces more efficient, this was not done systematically. During the Cold War, buildings like the Bauhaus Dessau were viewed in the East as evidence of Western cultural excess, at least until 1976, which further isolated the building from related technological and policy improvements.

By contrast, in more recent years, both the engineering and policy communities in Germany have, by and large, supported the prospect of an energy transition away from hydrocarbon fuels.[14] The German *energiewende* is celebrated as a model for a broader, global energy transition, and the specific goal of moving buildings off of coal is, in general, praised.[15] The Bauhaus Dessau represents a high-profile example of extensive retrofit activities occurring much more broadly with the support of government policies; building heritage and the management of energy systems is taught in prominent schools and encouraged through

14
Carol Hager, "Germany's Green Energy Revolution: Challenging the Theory and Practice of Institutional Change" in *German Politics and Society*, vol.33, no. 3 (Autumn 2015): 1–27.

15
Christine Sturm, "Inside the Energiewende: Policy and Complexity in the German Utility Industry" in *Issues in Science and Technology* vol. 33, no. 2 (Winter 2017): 41–47.

brace "arts of noticing". *In situ* observation and heterogeneous modes of analysis offer ways of becoming attentive to lively, messy more-than-human activities. Practices that bring together knowledge, materials and people in collaboration across disciplines can attempt to build dialogue across many forms of difference. Polyphonic methods of description and storytelling can aid in translation, helping cultivate recognition and response to the environmental challenges of our times.

internships and other professional development mechanisms.

The *energiewende* has been, until quite recently, mostly about integrating new forms of power generation and providing incentives for reduced consumption rather than encouraging dramatic social transformations. Increasingly, through both policy and cultural initiatives, issues around consumption, habits and social behaviors more generally have also come to the fore. Germany's excellence in this realm has from exploring a wide range of energy potentials: from solar and wind to methane and geothermal. At the same time, the recent resurgence of the country's right-wing political parties have pointed to the uneven-ness of the costs and benefits of the approach. Schematically, the hinterlands have become energy production sites that feed the densely populated cities. Buildings have played an important material and symbolic role, at least, schematically, since Sauerbruch and Hutton Architects' GSW Headquarters in Berlin—a competition winning project that aimed to reduce energy use through façade treatments and the thoughtful organization of mechanical systems.[16] Germany has arguably become the center for architectural and engineering innovation relative to the design and construction of low-carbon buildings. However, in many cases, such innovations have not played well in the global architectural discourse: in biennials and high-profile awards, praise for the design relevance of high-performance buildings is an exception rather than a rule. And most such examples exhibit a reliance, still, on technological transitions rather than social transformations.

• • •

Energetics, as a concept, is relatively new. It describes a social relationship to fuel: how human habits, patterns and practices develop in relationship to material resources.[17] Architecture, again, is here a medium and a media, a cultural expression of possible energetic conditions. The field of architecture has been attempting to be sustainable for at least seventy years, and intensively, unevenly, for the last thirty. It is not easy. Design is overwhelmed by capitalist development, to paraphrase Tafuri. Forces of capital and regulation resist possible evolution towards a more climatically engaged framework for architectural practice. That is obvious enough. The less obvious question would be: What are the new opportunities available for design and innovative energetics? How can

16
Louisa Hutton, Matthias Sauerbruch, et. al, editors, *GSW Headquarters Berlin: Sauerbruch Hutton Architects* (Zürich: Lars Müller Publishers, 2000).

17
Kiel Moe and Rini Srinivasan, *The Hierarchy of Energy in Architecture: Emergy Analysis* (New York: Routledge, 2015); Cara New Daggett, *The Birth of Energy: Hydrocarbon Fuels, Thermodynamics, and the Politics of Work* (Durham, NC: Duke University Press, 2019).

Capital presents an idealized, "God's eye" view of a commodified and monoculture world. Yet, notice where the grid collapses: the scarred landscape after the forest fire, the crumbling buildings meant to be replaced by new investments, the striking algal bloom as a result of industrial dumping and the traffic jams and street protests that break the order of the urban system.

architecture and spatial formations be deployed to help turn heads towards questions of comfort, climate and ways of living in a post-carbon world? How can architectural specialties begin to rearticulate themselves towards retrofit, maintenance and care? Rather than a so-called "energy transition," the future of the field depends on its capacity for *transformation*, a whole-cloth reconsideration of the role of architecture and other cultural practices in adjusting desires to accommodate a changed atmosphere.

In considering this new role for architecture, one quickly discovers another potent reason to resist the framework of "energy transition:" the historical record clarifies that "transition" has usually meant "addition" or an equally problematic "substitution." Every transitioned-to fuel (wood, hydro, hydrocarbon, nuclear and even renewables) has benn an addition of more fuels into the energy mix. One only need think of the hybrid SUV; it is still a gas guzzling engine, only now with an electrical assist. Renewables are added on top of hydrocarbon fuels for marginal increases in efficiency. A *transformation*, by contrast, indicates changing the way we live in the world and particularly in

buildings: changing habits and desires, pursuing different aspirations and finding opportunities, anywhere and everywhere, to be less carbon-intensive. This is the creative opportunity for architecture, more than both the computational parametrics of designed novelty or the efficiencies of high performance. Architecture can help society imagine a life without carbon, and then build it.

Most prominent modern buildings perform horribly on the terms of energetics. It is ridiculous, on some level, to even consider the fuel efficiency of a pre-World War II building according to contemporary standards. Prominent Modernist structures, such as the Bauhaus Dessau, were built with little regard for energy conservation, since policy makers and architects of that era saw fuel use as a positive contribution to economic activity. Buildings that required a lot of fuel were, until quite recently, welcome. And today, many are still being built. Architecture and building culture have developed an industrial infrastructure rooted in fuel profligacy, to such a degree that most performance metrics continue to aim for the least consumption of fuel, rather than carbon-neutrality or carbon-sink construction.

The Bauhaus Dessau is exemplary for the planimetric arrangement of its energy collapse; it is not atypical. Other icons in the historical canon are similarly environmentally misapprehended, from the sealed, conditioned interiors of mid-century skyscrapers to any number of museums, cultural centers, archives and urban developments. Energy has not been a concern for architects in the way it has suddenly become the issue: towers, malls and suburbs demand intensive energy throughput, even when using efficient fuel sources. Too many modern buildings and projects stand as monuments to the apparent inevitably of growth. They are stranded assets, isolated objects in the urban landscape—object lessons in how *not* to live and build.

• • •

A final point of interest, in the case of the Bauhaus Dessau and more generally: If the workshop space was so thermally inadequate, what were the conditions of its occupation during the short period in which the school was active? In the winter, it must have been quite cold. The current thermal conditions do not meet standards for occupation.

Comfort is a central issue to re-imagining social relationships

to fuels. Was the workshop wing comfortable for its users in the 1920s and 30s? Presumably, students and masters during the Weimar Era wore a lot of sweaters and coats in the winter and shirtsleeves in the summer. Comfort standards have increased dramatically over the last century. Air-conditioning has been, to no small extent, people-conditioning: as a society, we anticipate, even expect, specific thermal conditions in spaces of work and leisure, as well as in our homes. These expectations are hydrocarbon-fuel dependent, artifacts of a culture soaked in petroleum. These expectations are also the medium for an epochal social transformation, elicited by reduced carbon emissions; we (collectively, as local groups and unevenly, as a species) have to be willing to be less comfortable.

It is difficult to articulate the extent of the climate emergency and to understand the obstacles to its penetration into architecture culture. Every day, an attentive reader can find new reports indicating updated data and new knowledge about the urgency of the climate crisis, and the intensity of its effects. Yet, this year (2019) is on track to see the highest amount of carbon emissions *ever*. Things are not getting better; they are getting worse. Social patterns are not transforming to reduce carbon output. It is, of course, a systemic problem—the basic premise of economic growth, the basic structure of Late Capitalism, continues to rely on hydrocarbon fuel as the driver of security and social well-being.

One is desperate, all the same, to find discursive opportunities that might encourage architects to collectively reassess familiar patterns and expectations. In architecture and elsewhere, as both professionals, citizens and desiring beings, our *aspirations* are subject to transformation. New expectations of the future can open up unexpected pathways that disrupt the patterns of the present. It is likely that in this familiar space of novel affect—within the aspirations of architectural discourse and practice—one could outline a different set of experiences and expectations. Considering these novel aspirations, architects can help design the carbon-free future, beyond metrics and sustainability. The Bauhaus Dessau becomes an index for these desires and their possible realization, not only for the last century but also for the next.

Author's Note
The narrative of the Bauhaus' heating system was drawn from material in the city archives of Dessau, thanks to the archivist Monika Markgraf for her assistance. The material from Brenne Architekten was based on in-person interviews and unpublished presentation material provided by the firm and summarized with permission; thanks to both Winfried Brenne and Fabian Brenne for their time, hospitality and interest. I am grateful to Urlike Beck who assisted me at the archive, in the interview and in translating relevant material. Thanks also to Kiel Moe for reading a draft and sharpening the language around fuel and energetics, to Kathleen James Chakrabarty for helping me clarify the details and experience of German modernism, to Mark Alan Hughes and his colleagues at the Kleinman Center for Energy Policy for research support and to Jürgen Renn and Department 1 at the Max Planck Institute for the History Science in Berlin for hosting me during my Alexander von Humboldt Fellowship, which also supported the research. Any and all errors remain, of course, my own.

Scale should serve as a tool to think with, rather than restricting the resolution of our imagination. Here, factory lines, supermarket shelves, shipping container stacks and nuclear power plants are aligned in almost identical sizes. Euclidean scale has no significance in a world of simplification and replication.

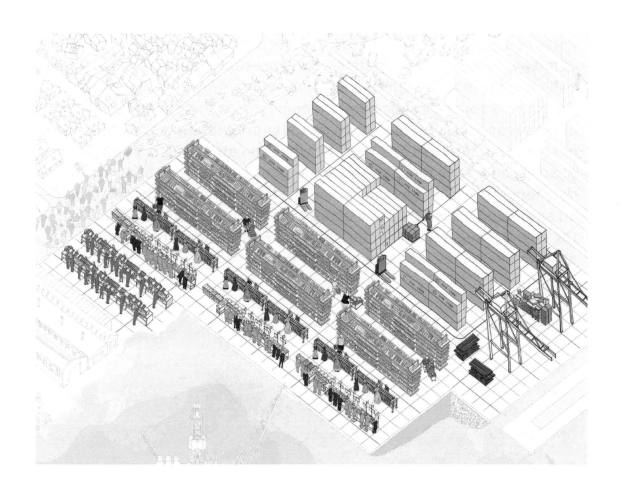

Parts of stories in *Feral Atlas* are told through the hands and eyes of indigenous and native artists who express certain acts of violence and struggle in their own way. Filipino artists Amy Lien and Enzo Camacho's collage in *Acceleration* comes from their work on the figure of Manananggal, a mythological monster originating in the Philippines; one half is in the form of a woman, while the other half is in the form of an organ-eating monster. Manananggal's bifurcated body is only tenuously joined by the invisible robe-like tongue, hidden behind an entangled mass of marine plastic. As her head levitates above the colonial sugarcane plantation in the Philippines, she haunts a strangely modified landscape once familiar to her.

Australian Aboriginal artist Nancy McDinny's painting in *Invasion* describes a striking scene of colonial encounter and resistance; her great grandfather faces the first wave of mining prospectors, seeking to exploit her ancestral lands. The tension and violence are vividly illustrated through her striking composition and compellingly bright colors.

Empire presents the Anthropocene through the landscape of plantations. This particular section charts the entangled planting relationships between peasant farms and imported colonial crops in Southeast Asia, showing the particular vegetation and vivid colors of the area's indigenous landscape.

Mature teak plantation

Young teak

Cassava

Mature Sugarcane

Young Sugarcane

Rice

Tea

Opium

Another section within *Empire* juxtaposes a cruise ship with a hybrid island that combines the features of the southern United States and the Greater Caribbean, which also serves as the destination of a slave ship. The same land that once went through a unique and violent history of political ecology has now transformed into destinations for ecotourism, itself a form of exploitation and commodification of human and nonhuman resources.

Afterword

The very idea of responsibility relates to a burden: the notion of being accountable for something within one's control. With this as our topic, how could we not come away with some kind of certainty? In the first pages, we frame the topic of *onus* through a prism of questions, shining light on different facets of ethics, obligation and responsibility during the multiple phases of the design process. Seen together, these inquiries seemed to offer, at least, a few clear parameters — a sound basis for answers.

But uniform answers are difficult to come by, since they are, by nature, non-existent. Numerous factors lie beyond our professional control. There are ideals to strive for, visions to achieve, but the design invariably differs from its realization. The tension between the perfect model and its physical manifestation is at the heart of architecture. As architects delve more deeply into the task of assuming responsibility, questions linger, compound and multiply. They remain unresolved not for lack of consideration, but because uncertainty is part of the story.

As the voices here acknowledge, a large part of assuming responsibility in architecture is not just creating one defined narrative about what architects must do and what is right. Rather, we are responsible for asking better, more nuanced questions, which we can use to discover new moments of possibility within the established narrative of the built environment and our role in it.

The scholars, artists and practitioners of this volume begin to probe at this narrative, to re-frame the limits of what architecture might be concerned with and to give architects meaning and power outside traditional dialogues. Essays, such as Susanne Schindler's, analyze community building in the design process through the lens of history, underscoring that change is not linear but messy. The effects of activism sometimes only emerge generations later in ways we cannot anticipate. Other contributions are rooted in contemporary struggle, drawing from all scales and geographies, to tell us that if we fail or refuse to question, the world will not stop building. Rather, building will continue but without intention. In this regard, Meredith TenHoor traces the toxic impacts of building materials on human health at the scale of one home, while Anna Tsing works on a macroscopic, global scale to show these same effects on diverse ecological systems.

In these early months of 2020, the COVID-19 pandemic and the protests against systemic racism across American cities make evident that there is essential ethical work for architects to do and key questions for us to ask of ourselves and of others. Although the authors included here have started to consider our effects as a profession, they represent only a small fraction of the issues and voices that demand further visibility and discussion.

By its nature, design is the practice of examining multiple constraints and applying ingenuity and inventiveness to create better outcomes. We must take responsibility to craft the questions we want to answer and the stories we want to tell, as architects, workers and humans. Opting out is a tempting but false choice. Whether architects are involved or not, there will always be buildings, neighborhoods, streets and cities. We must not hide behind established norms and contracts that dictate an architect's role. Rather than being seen as stifling, these considerations can provide opportunities to build in a more meaningful, equitable, aesthetic and sustainable way. It's a heavy, complex burden. Yet, if we can carry it together, we begin to see the cracks of lightness, revealing the openings that make real progress happen.

Contributors

Daniel A. Barber is an Associate Professor and Chair of the PhD Program in Architecture in the Stuart Weitzman School of Design at the University of Pennsylvania. He is co-founder of the *Current* platform for environmental and architectural histories, and co-editor of the Accumulation series on *e-flux architecture*. His latest book is *Modern Architecture and Climate: Design before Air Conditioning* (Princeton University Press, 2020).

Fernanda Canales (b. Mexico City, 1974) holds a PhD in Architecture (ETSAM, Madrid), and has been distinguished with several international awards, such as the Emerging Voices Award from The Architectural League of New York. Author of *Private Spaces; Shared Structures* (Actar, 2020), *Vivienda Colectiva en México: El derecho a la arquitectura* (Gustavo Gili, 2017) and *Architecture in Mexico 1900-2010: The Construction of Modernity* (Arquine, 2013), she has been visiting faculty member at Yale School of Architecture and invited speaker at the Architectural Association School in London, Edinburgh School of Architecture and Landscape Architecture, and Columbia University Graduate School of Architecture in New York.

Loreta Castro Reguera (b. Mexico City, 1979) studied Architecture at the Universidad Nacional Autónoma de México (FA UNAM). She holds a Master in Architecture from Mendrisio Academy of Architecture, and a Master in Urban Design with Distinction from the Harvard GSD. She has been awarded prizes for her work such as a Fulbright scholarship, the CEMEX Marcelo Zambrano scholarship, and the Druker Traveling Fellowship. In both 2017 and 2018, she received the LafargeHolcim Gold Award for her work as design director and technical coordinator of the UNAM project *Hydropuncture* in Mexico City, which became *Parque la Quebradora*. She co-founded Taller Capital in 2010, which she leads with José Pablo Ambrosi. They have received several national prizes: the installation of the 2015 Eco Pavilion and a silver medal at the 2017 Architecture Biennale. She is a Professor in the School of Architecture at UNAM. Since 2018, she has been part of the National Creators System of Mexico.

Nicholas de Monchaux is Professor and Head of Architecture at MIT, and a partner in the architecture practice modem. He is the author of Spacesuit: Fashioning Apollo (MIT Press, 2011) and Local Code: 3,659 Proposals about Data, Design, and the Nature of Cities (Princeton Architectural Press, 2016). His work has been exhibited at the Venice Architecture Biennale, the Lisbon Architecture Triennial, The Storefront for Art and Architecture, SFMOMA, and the Chicago MCA. He is a Fellow of the American Academy in Rome.

Kyle Dugdale is an architect and historian. He teaches history, theory, and design at Yale School of Architecture and at Columbia Graduate School of Architecture, Planning and Preservation. He holds a BA from Corpus Christi College, Oxford, an MArch from Harvard's Graduate School of Design, and a PhD from Yale. His work has been published in journals including *Perspecta*, *Clog*, the *Journal of Architectural Education*, and *Utopian Studies*; his first book, *Babel's Present*, was published in 2016. He maintains an interest in architecture's claims to metaphysical significance, with a particular curiosity for architecture as a recurring figure in biblical narratives.

Justin Duerr is a self-taught artist, musician, and art historian. His artwork has been featured in gallery and museum exhibits across the United States, and he has toured as a musician throughout most of the continental US. His research efforts can be seen in the documentary film, *Resurrect Dead: The Mystery of the Toynbee Tiles*, which won the award for Best Director at the 2011 Sundance Film Festival and has had a wide release in art-house theaters and on online streaming platforms. His first book, *The Temple of Silence: Forgotten Works and Worlds of Herbert Crowley*, was published in 2018 by Beehive Books. Justin is currently researching and writing a multi-volume work centered on the life and achievements of artist, bookshop owner and landscape architect Mary Mowbray-Clarke.

Feral Atlas is a collective work of more than a hundred scientists, humanists and artists, united in examining the non-designed effects of human infrastructures. Feral Atlas is curated and edited by anthropologist Anna Tsing, visual anthropologist Jennifer Deger, environmental anthropologist Alder Keleman Saxena and architect Feifei Zhou. The project is being developed in collaboration with architect Lili Carr (directing maps) and an international network of makers, including an array of designers, artists, editors and coders. Feral Atlas is developed in association with AURA (Aarhus University Research on the Anthropocene) and James Cook University, Australia. It will be available, open-access, from Stanford University Press digital publications at www.feralatlas.org in October or November 2020.

Jacqueline Hall has worked in architecture and landscape architecture, most recently as a designer at Reed Hilderbrand. She holds a dual Master in Architecture and Environmental Management from Yale where her research focused on environmental justice in water management in Mexico City from a design and political ecology perspective. She completed her BA at New York University's Gallatin School of Individualized Study.

Elisa Iturbe is a critic at the Yale School of Architecture (YSoA), where she also coordinates the dual-degree program between YSoA and the Yale School of the Environment. In addition, she is an Adjunct Assistant Professor at The Cooper Union, where she teaches studio, formal analysis, and a course titled The City as Carbon Form, which explores the spatial expression of our dominant energy paradigm in both urban and architectural form. Her writings have been published in *Log*, *Dearq*, *Pulp*, and *The New York Review of Architecture*. Most recently she guest edited *Log* 47, titled *Overcoming Carbon Form*. She has also co-written a book with Peter Eisenman titled *Lateness*, forthcoming. She is co-founder of the firm Outside Development.

Maroš Krivý is Associate Professor and Director of Urban Studies at the Faculty of Architecture, Estonian Academy of Arts. He was previously a Research Associate in the Department of Geography, University of Cambridge, where he worked on the ERC-funded project entitled "Rethinking Urban Nature". His work, situated at the intersections of urban geography and architectural history, has been published in journals such as *Architectural Histories*, *The Journal of Architecture*, *JSAH*, *Planning Theory*, *Footprint* and *Avery Review*. Maroš also contributed to a number of edited collections, including *Neoliberalism on the Ground* (University of Pittsburgh Press, 2020), *The Botanical City* (Jovis, 2020) and *Second World Postmodernisms* (Bloomsbury, 2019), and is a member of the EAHN's Architecture and Environment interest group. This research was supported by an ERC Advanced Grant entitled "Rethinking Urban Nature."

Samia Henni is an Assistant Professor of History and Theory of Architecture and Urbanism at Cornell University, Ithaca, New York. Her work focuses on the intersection of the histories and theories of manmade environments with colonial practices, forced displacement, resources extraction and exploitation, and military measures from the European colonization of the Americas to the present, with a particular attention to urban, rural and desert environments in North Africa. She is the author of the multi-award-winning *Architecture of Counterrevolution: The French Army in Northern Algeria* (2017, EN; 2019, FR), the editor of *gta papers 2: War Zones* (2018), and the curator of *Discreet Violence: Architecture and the French War in Algeria* (2017–19). Henni taught at Princeton University, ETH Zurich, and Geneva University of Art and Design. She received her Ph.D. in the history and theory of architecture (with distinction, ETH Medal) from ETH Zurich. She has published, exhibited, and lectured widely.

Ann Lui is a registered architect and founding principal of Future Firm, a Chicago-based architecture and design research practice. She is also Assistant Professor of Practice at Taubman College of Architecture and Urban Planning at the University of Michigan. Ann's work focuses on spaces of collectivity in cities. She was co-curator of the U.S. Pavilion at the Venice Architecture Biennale 2018 titled *Dimensions of Citizenship*. She co-edited, with Gediminas Urbonas and Lucas Freeman, *Public Space? Lost and Found* (MIT/SA+P Press, 2015) on aesthetic and spatial practices in the civic realm.

Jala Makhzoumi studied architecture in Iraq, received her Master in Environmental Design from Yale University and her PhD in Landscape Architecture from Sheffield University. Her design expertise includes energy efficient landscape planning, sustainable urban greening, landscape heritage conservation and postwar recovery. Publications include *Ecological Landscape Design and Planning: the Mediterranean context*, co-author Pungetti (Spon, 1999) and *The Right to Landscape, contesting landscape and human rights*, co-editors Egoz and Pungetti (Ashgate, 2012). Jala is co-founder and president of the Lebanese Landscape Association, recipient of European Council Landscape Architecture Schools "lifetime achievements award" in 2019 and the Tamayouz Award for Women in Architecture and Construction in 2013 and was profiled by the Aga Khan in 2014.

Ivan L. Munuera is a scholar, critic, and curator working at the intersection of culture, technology, politics, and bodily practices in the modern period and on the global stage. Since 2015 he has been developing his dissertation at Princeton University on the architecture of HIV/AIDS. His research has been generously sponsored by Princeton Institute for International and Regional Studies and the Canadian Centre for Architecture. He has presented his work at the Association for Art History, Cornell AAP, Columbia GSAPP, the Architectural Association in London, Cooper Union, University of Virginia, Princeton University, Sussex University, Het Nieuwe Instituut, and Manchester University. His work has been published in *Log*, *Thresholds*, and *The Architect's Newspaper*, among others.

Rael San Fratello has attempted to rethink the art and practice of designing and constructing buildings by crossing the disciplinary borders between architecture and art for eighteen years. Their work spans two geographic borders, from the historical boundary that defined the U.S.-Mexico Border prior to the Treaty of Guadalupe Hidalgo in 1848 to the contemporary border today. The work is both defined by, and bleeds over, these territorial demarcations, in order to connect, and expose the violence of disconnection. Their desires for an ecological practice come from their indigenous and traditional knowledge base and are rooted in the belief that architecture and art have a social responsibility first and foremost, and with that is aligned beauty. Their projects connect activism, traditional earth building practices, social art practice, and technology, aligning themselves with a concept described by the Nahuatl term *rasquache*, which extols the condition of the underdog having more capacity for inventiveness and ingenuity.

Craig Reschke, AIA is a registered architect and founding principal of Future Firm. He is also Teaching Assistant Professor in the Department of Landscape Architecture at the University of Illinois at Urbana-Champaign. Before founding Future Firm, Craig was a project architect at SOM and RODE Architects, where he led the design of buildings at many scales in the U.S. and abroad. His research explores "fast matter" and public space in rural landscapes. This work was awarded Harvard GSD's Penny White Prize and was recently published in *Codify: Parametric and Computational Design in Landscape Architecture* (Routledge, 2018).

Damon Rich PP AICP is a designer, urban planner, and partner at HECTOR. He previously served as planning director and chief urban designer for the City of Newark and is the founder of the Center for Urban Pedagogy (CUP), an internationally recognized nonprofit organization that uses art and design to increase meaningful civic engagement. His work has been recognized by the MacArthur Fellowship, American Planning Association National Planning Award, the Cooper Hewitt National Design Award, the Loeb Fellowship in Advanced Environmental Studies at the Harvard University Graduate School of Design, the MacDowell Colony, and the United States Pavilion at the

11th International Architecture Exhibition in Venice. Curtis Roth is an Assistant Professor at the Knowlton School of Architecture at The Ohio State University. He studied at the Massachusetts Institute of Technology, and was previously a resident fellow at the Akademie Schloss Solitude in Stuttgart, a partner of OfficeUS, and a Howard E. Lefevre Emerging Practitioner Fellow. His research consists of images, objects and software that examine new subjectivities within networks of computation and labor. His work has been published in *e-flux*, *Thresholds*, and *Volume*, and has been exhibited at the ZKM Karlsruhe, the Venice Biennale, and elsewhere.

Susanne Schindler is an architect and historian focused on reconceptualizing the intersection of policy, finance, and design in housing in a comparative urban perspective. In her current book project, provisionally titled *On Whose Terms? Architecture, Housing, and Democracy in the Age of Model Cities*, she analyses how largely discredited urban renewal programs of the late 1960s in fact shaped the assumptions that still guide design and development practices in the United States today. Schindler co-directs the MAS program in the history and theory of architecture at ETH Zurich and is currently a visiting lecturer at MIT's School of Architecture and Planning. From 2013 to 2016, she was lead researcher and co-curator of the research project *House Housing: An Untimely History of Architecture and Real Estate* at Columbia University, and co-author of the related book *The Art of Inequality*.

M. Surry Schlabs is a critic at the Yale School of Architecture, where he is the Director of Undergraduate Studies in Architecture. His ongoing research engages a range of aesthetic, political, and pedagogical practices, characterized by their distinctly public character and decidedly architectural and urban contexts. He received both his MArch and PhD degrees from Yale, where his dissertation explored the aesthetic theory of Pragmatist philosopher and educator John Dewey, and its evolution relative to the emergence of American modernism during the middle decades of the 20th century. A longtime resident of the New Haven area, Surry lives with his family in Hamden, CT.

Lola Sheppard is a Registered Architect and founding Partner at Lateral Office and founding editor of the journal *Bracket*. She is Professor at the School of Architecture, University of Waterloo where she also serves as the Graduate Officer. She has taught at the University of Toronto, Ohio State University, and California College of the Arts. She is committed to architecture's new relationship to social and ecological possibilities, not just solutions. Sheppard is the recipient of the 2012 RAIC Young Architect Award and the 2003-04 Howard Lefevre Fellowship from Ohio State University.

Jae Shin is a designer and partner at HECTOR. She recently served as an Enterprise Rose Architectural Fellow at the New York City Housing Authority (NYCHA), where she facilitated efforts to define and implement design principles for preserving and rehabilitating New York City's public housing. She holds degrees in painting from Rhode Island School of Design and architecture from Princeton University. Her projects have received support from the MacDowell Colony and the National Endowment for the Arts, and she has led design studios at New Jersey Institute of Technology and the Harvard Graduate School of Design.

Meredith TenHoor is an architectural and urban historian whose research examines how architecture, infrastructure, urbanism and landscape design participate in the distribution of resources. She does both scholarly work in architectural and urban history, and public history projects about environmental and urban transformation. Publications include the forthcoming *Architectures of the Market: Food, Infrastructure and the Management of Life in 20th Century France*, as well as *Black Lives Matter* (2015), *Governing by Design: Architecture, Economy, and Politics in the Twentieth Century* (2012), and *Street Value: Shopping, Planning and Politics at Fulton Mall* (2010). Meredith is Associate Professor in the School of Architecture at Pratt Institute, the editor and a founding board member of *Aggregate*. She has a Ph.D. in Architecture from Princeton University and a B.A. in Art-Semiotics from Brown University.

Sumayya Vally (b. 1990, South Africa) carries obsession for Johannesburg and her work around narrative, identity and memory in the city have admitted her into a host of conceptual and investigatory projects, including a position as assistant curator and film producer for La Biennale di Venezia 2014 (South African Pavilion). Sumayya has recently been selected as a finalist for the Civitella Ranieri Foundation architecture residency prize (2019) and was a finalist for the Rolex Mentorship and Protege award in the 2018/2019 cycle to be mentored by Sir David Adjaye. Sumayya founded the design-research studio Counterspace, where she practices, and she currently teaches at the Graduate School of Architecture, as Unit Leader of Unit 12, which focuses on finding design expression for issues of identity and contested territory. She is presently based between Johannesburg and London as the lead architect for the 2020/20 Plus 1 Serpentine Pavilion.

Julia Walker is Assistant Professor and Director of Undergraduate Studies in the Art History department at Binghamton University, where she specializes in modern and contemporary architecture and theory. Her first book, *Berlin Contemporary: Architecture and Politics After 1990* (Bloomsbury Visual Arts, 2020), examines the architecture and urban planning of reunified Berlin and reveals how its iconic new government structures embody the unsettled contradictions that animate global contemporary architecture culture as a whole. Her second book, tentatively titled *Why They Left: Women After Architecture*, recovers the histories of women who studied and practiced as architects before leaving or being pressured out of the field. In addition to recuperating stories of individual architects, this project is intended to expand architecture's intellectual scope, connecting it to fields as diverse as religion, science, politics, and music. She has also published articles on Daniel Libeskind, Zaha Hadid, and Rem Koolhaas, and others.

Mason White is a founding Partner at Lateral Office and founding editor of the journal *Bracket*. He is Professor at the Daniels Faculty of Architecture, Landscape, & Design at the University of Toronto. He has taught at Harvard University, Cornell University, Ohio State University, and UC Berkeley. He is convinced that there are new roles for architecture out there that we do not know because we are not looking, really looking. White is the recipient of the 2012-13 Howard Friedman Visiting Professorship in the Practice of Architecture at UC Berkeley College of Environmental Design and the 2008-09 Arthur Wheelwright Fellowship from Harvard Graduate School of Design.

Michael Young is an architect and educator practicing in New York City where he is a founding partner of the architectural design studio Young & Ayata. Young & Ayata have received a Progressive Architecture award, the Design Vanguard Award from Architectural Record, and the Young Architects Prize from the Architectural League of New York. In 2015 they received a first-place prize for their design for the new Bauhaus Museum in Dessau, Germany. Michael is currently an Assistant Professor at the Cooper Union. He was previously the Louis I. Kahn Visiting Assistant Professor at Yale University and has taught studios and seminars at Princeton, SCI-Arc, and Columbia. His published essays have appeared in *Log*, *The Cornell Journal*, *Thresholds*, *AD*, and the book titled *The Estranged Object*. He is the 2019-20 Rome Prize Fellow at the American Academy in Rome.

Caroline Acheatel holds a Master of Architecture and a Master of Environmental Management from Yale University, where her research centered on the social, ecological, and political dimensions of climate change in Mexico City. She also holds a Bachelor of Arts in Architecture from the University of Pennsylvania. While at Yale, she pursued her interest in teaching through Teaching Fellow appointments in the history and theory of global architecture and urbanism, with Professor Elihu Rubin and Professor Keller Easterling. As a practicing urban designer in Chicago, she studies how an area's ecological context can guide the design process towards more equitable spatial outcomes.

Paul J Lorenz graduated from Yale University with a Master of Architecture degree. He also holds a Master of Fine Arts degree from the University of Wisconsin. His sculpture and installation work has focused primarily on digital fabrication and parametric design, and has been exhibited in galleries in Chicago, Beijing, and Lausanne, London, and Athens. His work at the Yale School of Architecture has been regularly selected for publication in *Retrospecta*, the annual journal of student work, and has been nominated for the RIBA President's Silver Medal. Paul has also been awarded the James Gamble Rogers Fellowship for exceptional design work and the AIA Henry Adams Certificate for the second-highest academic ranking. Paul is currently a practicing architect in Philadelphia.

Alexander Stagge graduated from Yale University with a Master of Architecture degree. He also holds a Bachelor of Science in Architecture degree from the Ohio State University from which he graduated magna cum laude with honors in Architecture. He earned Knowlton School of Architecture's Honors Research Distinction for his research interrogating representation methods within architecture. His design work at the Yale School of Architecture was regularly selected for publication in Retrospecta. His writings for Kyle Dugdales' seminar, Babel, were also featured in the publication. He is currently working at an architecture firm as a designer in New York.

Paul Rasmussen came to the field of architecture through both his theoretical training in art history and his years of practical experience in construction management. He holds a Master of Architecture degree from the Yale School of Architecture. While at Yale, Paul was appointed to numerous Teaching Fellowships and Assistantships in both design studios and theory seminars, and his work was consistently featured in the school's annual publication, *Retrospecta*. Today, Paul works as a designer in Brooklyn, and focuses on how to create affordable, dignified, and equitable housing solutions for New York City's most populous borough.

Rosa McElheny is an artist and graphic designer based in New York. McElheny's work derives from research and everyday life, and for now includes subjects such as: listening, reading, getting dressed, the voice, the archive, the smart phone, institutional critique, independent publishing, social movements of the late 1960s, art movements of the early 1960s, jokes, puns, money, temperature, traffic, New York City, and more generally the circulation of things through space and time. McElheny holds an MFA from Yale Universityand teaches interactive design.

Nilas Andersen is an independent graphic designer, researcher, and editor, who produces objects, images, texts, and exhibitions in collaboration with other designers, artists, and institutions. His work examines the circuits information take in its production and dissemination – from communication infrastructure, to protocols, and interfaces – often by complicating these systems and rerouting attention to their seams and vulnerabilities. He holds an MFA from Yale School of Art and lives in Copenhagen.

Duerr
p. 76: Photo courtesy of Francois Valocchi via Wikimedia Commons.
p. 77: Photo from Library of Congress, Prints and Photographs Division (Historic American Buildings Survey Collection).
p. 78: Photo from Library of Congress, Prints and Photographs Division (Historic American Buildings Survey Collection).

Rich and Shin
Fig. 5. Image courtesy of Victor D'Amico papers in the Museum of Modern Art Archives.
Fig. 6. Image courtesy of the Avery Research Center for African American History & Culture. College of Charleston, South Carolina.
All other images courtesy of the authors.

Canales and Castro Reguera
All images courtesy of the authors and Rafael Gamo.

Walker
p. 124: Photo courtesy of the architect.
p. 129: Images courtesy of TU Architekturmuseum

Young
p. 140: Interiors Matter: A Live Interior, is funded by The Swedish Research Council and hosted by KTH School of Architecture and the Built Environment in collaboration with Konstfack University of Arts, Crafts and Design. The research is carried out by Ulrika Karlsson, Cecilia Lundbäck, Veronica Skeppe, Daniel Norell and Einar Rodhe. Image by Ulrika Karlsson, Cecilia Lundbäck, Veronica Skeppevp.
p.143: Photo Courtesy of LiDARUSA.

Rael San Fratello
p. 162: Photo by John Fyfe, via Wikimedia Commons.

Munuera
p. 205: Lesbian Herstory Archives, New York Public Library.
p. 206: Lesbian, Gay Bisexual and Transgender Periodical collection, New York Public Library.
p. 215: McKim Mead & White architectural records and drawings, 1879-1958, Avery Architectural & Fine Arts Library, Columbia University.
p. 218 Credit: New York City Department of Health/US National Library of Medicine.

McElheny & Andersen
p. 117: Courtesy the artist and Essex Street/ Maxwell Graham, New York.
p. 225: Courtesy the artist and Essex Street/ Maxwell Graham, New York.
p. 243: Courtesy Maria Eichhorn. © VG Bild-Kunst/Artists Rights Society, Bonn 2017, photo: Mathias Völzke.

Perspecta 53 is indebted to the countless individuals who provided us with their support, time, and guidance as we worked to create this volume. We would like to thank all of our professors at Yale University, especially Keller Easterling for her time, generosity, and belief in us as we tested and iterated experimental modes of working and publishing. We would also like to thank Dean Deborah Berke for her consistent encouragement and support during all phases of the project. Thanks to Richard DeFlumeri and Kate Rozen for their constant help, and especially to A.J. Artemel for his multiple years of kindness and patience with us.

This issue would not have been possible without the financial support of the Perspecta Fund, which includes a gift in honor of Tom Beeby from the Robert H. Driehaus Foundation. It was also made possible through the financial generosity of Marc F. Appleton, '72 M.Arch, Hans Baldouf, '81 BA, '88 M.Arch, Austin Church III, '60 BA Family Fund, Fred Koetter and Susie Kim, Cesar Pelli, '08 DFHA, Robert A.M. Stern, '65 M.Arch, Jeremy Scott Wood, '64 BA, '70 M.Arch and F. Anthony Zunino, '70 M.Arch. In addition to this financial support, we are also grateful for the years of feedback, criticism, and support from the Perspecta Board, composed of Dean Deborah Berke, Barry Bergdoll, Sheila Levrant de Bretteville, Keller Easterling, Gavin Macrae-Gibson, Alan Plattus, Harold Roth, and Robert A.M. Stern.

Previous Perspecta editors Teo Quintana, Samantha Jaff, Dante Furioso, and Shayari De Silva deserve our immense thanks for taking time out of their days over the course of multiple years to guide us through the editorial process.

We would also like to call attention to the work of Ross Lipton, who diligently, quickly, and precisely copy-edited and proofread all of the texts in this volume at a moment's notice. Alexander Velaise, Juan Pablo Ponce de Leon, and Gregory Cartelli all contributed their time, contacts, and ideas to help garner contributions, and we are truly grateful. Thanks to Laurel Lorenz for her time, support, and exceptional hosting capabilities. We are also appreciative of our co-publishers, Cameron Gainer at Third Rail, Lindsey Austin Samahon at the University of Pennsylvania, and others. Special thanks to artists Maria Eichhorn, Carolyn Lazard and Cameron Rowland, and to Maxwell Graham for their images and insight.

Finally, we were lucky to be joined in this endeavor by the expansive talents of Nilas Andersen and Rosa McElheny. They are two designers who consistently revealed new possibilities and ideas for this journal, and worked closely with us to re-imagine its format not only during the final design phase, but rather, ever since we began to solicit contributions. We could not have done it without you both.

Perspecta 53: Onus
The Yale Architectural Journal

    Editors
Caroline Acheatel
Paul J Lorenz
Paul Rasmussen
Alexander Stagge

    Design
Nilas Andersen
Rosa McElheny

    Copy editor
Ross Lipton

    Printing
NPN Drukkers, the Netherlands

    Perspecta Board
Deborah Berke
Barry Bergdoll
Sheila Levrant de Bretteville
Keller Easterling
Gavin Macrae-Gibson
Alan Plattus
Harold Roth
Robert A.M. Stern

    Director of Communications
AJ Artemel

Perspecta, The Yale Architectural Journal is published in the United States of America by Yale School of Architecture and distributed by the MIT Press

Massachusetts Institute of Technology
Cambridge, Massachusetts 02142
http://mitpress.mit.edu

© 2020 Yale

ISBN: 978-0-262-53942-5
ISSN: 0079-0958

THE
LONG
WALK
BACK

BY DOUGIE BLAXLAND

Published by Playdead Press 2019

© Dougie Blaxland 2019

Dougie Blaxland has asserted his rights under the
Copyright, Design and Patents Act, 1988, to be
identified as the author of this work.

A CIP catalogue record for this book is available from
the British Library.

ISBN 978-1-910067-77-2

Playdead Press
www.playdeadpress.com

The Long Walk Back was first performed at The Chipping Norton Theatre on Tuesday 2nd April 2019.

CAST (in alphabetical order):

THE OTHER MAN	**Scott Bayliss**
CHRIS LEWIS	**Martin Edwards**

CREATIVE

Director	**Shane Morgan**
Movement Director	**Moira Hunt**
Designed by	**RoughHouse Theatre**
Original Music by	**Owen Morgan**

The company would like to thank:

Rondo Theatre Bath, Hampset Cricket Club, Matthew Engel, Prior Park College Bath, The Professional Cricketer's Association, Christopher Norwood Greaves, Colin Blumenau.

Please note: This is an early rehearsal copy of the script and was subject to change during the rehearsal period. There may be differences between this version and the performance.

DOUGIE BLAXLAND | Writer

Award winning writer Dougie Blaxland is also Director of South West based Live Wire Theatre. His writing credits include *That Moment, Never Any Fruit, Chauntecleer and Pertelotte, Hands Up For Jonny Wilkinson's Right Boot* and *When The Eye Has Gone*. He has also written stage adaptations of *Wuthering Heights* and *Jane Eyre*.

SCOTT BAYLISS | The Other Man

Scott was a member of the Bristol Old Vic's Made In Bristol Programme (2014/2015) and trained at Identity School of Acting.

Stage credits include: *SPILL* for Propolis Theatre at The Edinburgh Fringe Festival, *Wild Men* for Hotel Echo Theatre and *You Know What You Are* for Doppelganger Productions.

MARTIN EDWARDS | Chris Lewis

Martin was a journalist for more than a decade before training professionally as an actor at ALRA. Since then he has performed at various venues including Soho Theatre, Theatre503, Greenwich Theatre and The Old Red Lion. As a playwright, he is currently developing a play with The White Bear theatre in London for performance next year. His play *The Glory Road* was shortlisted for The Alfred Fagon Award in 2013.

MOIRA HUNT | Movement Director

Credits include: *Glitz Dies!* (Performance Space, Sydney as Director in Residence), *The Sneeze* (Director, Victoria and Albert Museum, London), *The House of Bernarda Alba* (Movement Director for Theatre Royal Bath), *Henry Walker and the Wheel of Death* (Movement Director, Rondo Theatre,

Bath), *Hands Up For Jonny Wilkinson's Right Boot* (Movement Director and Director, National Tour) and *When The Eye Has Gone* (Movement Director, National Tour). Moira is Director of RoughHouse Theatre.

SHANE MORGAN | Director

Shane's credits include: *The Two Character Play* (Red Rope Theatre), *When The Eye Has Gone* (National Tour), *Hands Up For Jonny Wilkinson's Right Boot* (National Tour), *The Tenant of Wildfell Hall* (Butterfly Psyche Theatre), *Venus and Adonis* (Theatre Royal Bath, Engage), *The Sneeze* (Victoria and Albert Museum, London). He has also adapted for the stage Daniel Wallace's novel *Mr. Sebastian and the Negro Magician* and Nick Hornby's *NippleJesus*. He is an Associate Director of the Rondo Theatre Bath and Director of RoughHouse Theatre.

OWEN MORGAN | Original Music

Owen is a musician, producer and DJ from Sydney, Australia. His previous projects include *3.3*, *Nazuri*, and *Trictum Sound*. This is his first work for the stage.

ABOUT ROUGHHOUSE THEATRE

RoughHouse Theatre was formed in Sydney and after successful collaborations and residencies, including Sydney Fringe, Old Fitzroy Theatre, Cat and Fiddle and the Performance Space, moved to the UK in 2005. Since then, RoughHouse collaborations have included the Victoria and Albert Museum London, Ben Crystal, Theatre Royal Bath, Tobacco Factory Theatres Bristol, Rondo Theatre Bath, writers Nick Hornby and Daniel Wallace, the Rugby Football Union and the Professional Cricketer's Association.

www.roughhousetheatre.com

For Suzie

The Long Walk Back

(*The Chris Lewis Story*)

By Dougie Blaxland

THE SET

Centre stage is an area exactly 10 feet in length and 6 feet wide. It is a prison cell and comprises an open toilet, a bed and a suitcase. The rest of the stage is variously a bar/pub, Gatwick Airport Customs area, the Courtroom in Croydon and various rooms/areas in and around a prison setting.

PROLOGUE

Lewis and The Other Man are standing downstage centre, looking out to the audience with a suitcase between them.

OTHER MAN: Have we got everything?

LEWIS: I think so.

OTHER MAN: Good – in which case –

LEWIS: (*speaking directly to the audience*) I know why I've come – the reason I'm here –

OTHER MAN: (*mimicking the man at the bar from Scene 3*) 'You ever need anything – know what I'm saying Chris – just let me know.'

LEWIS: And that's why I'm here – that's how it works.

SCENE 1

May 2009 – Dovegate Prison Uttoxeter. Before the lights come up there is the sound of a cell door being unlocked and then locked again. The Lights come up to reveal Lewis in his prison cell. He sits on the bed.

LEWIS: (*looking around his cell and speaking to himself*) 'Welcome to Dovegate' – Jesus – – I mean – look at it – just look – ten by six – can't be more than that – and the toilet – my head will be right next to the toilet – when I'm on the bed – I'll be lying with my head by the toilet – (*He stops himself mid flow as a counter thought/feeling comes to him*) Hey – come on – come on – stop this – you hear me – stop it – do something – find something to do – put

9

something on the walls – a bit of colour – cheer it up a bit – posters – photos – make it more like – like – well – more than this – more than 10 by 6. (*He stops himself again as the negative side of his thinking takes over*) 10 by 6 – shit – I mean – Christ – how do you…. (*he struggles to overcome the negative thinking*) – don't dwell on it – best not dwell on it – best not – no – stop – stop it – you hear me Chris – stop it – just stop it – (*he is unable to stop the negative thoughts from coming through and he is in visible anguish*) – but – Jesus! – 10 foot – that's all – 10 foot – 3 and a bit yards – I mean – 6 of these cells laid end to end – 7 in fact – 7 of them – 7 laid end to end would barely make the length of a cricket pitch – not one pitch – not one – I mean – (*he tries to stop himself again*). Stop talking to yourself – why do you always talk to yourself – torture yourself – that's all you're doing – torturing yourself –

PRISON GUARD: (*voice O/S*) Are you alright in there Lewis?

LEWIS: Yes – yes – I'm – er – I'm ok – yes.

PRISON GUARD: (*voice O/S*) Just checking – there'll be a check every hour at least for today – the first twenty four hours – same for every new prisoner here at Dovegate – ok?

(*Lewis doesn't answer*)

PRISON GUARD: (*voice O/S*) Did you hear me Lewis?

LEWIS: I heard you.

OTHER MAN: (*O/S*) As long as you know.

(There is the sound of the shutter being closed and Lewis visibly shrinks and curls himself up in a foetal like position on the bed with his head away from the audience)

Blackout

SCENE 2

The next day – Dovegate Prison – the Lights come up and Lewis is now sitting on the lower bunk rubbing his head. The Other Man is on the top bunk apparently asleep. Lewis is not looking at him when he speaks and yet he may be addressing him. It is equally possible that he is speaking to himself.

LEWIS: I mean – I knew the theory – Christ – everyone knows the theory – everyone – but that's all it is – if it's not you – if you've not been banged up – it's theory – words: – 'prison' – 'loss of freedom'. Words – and they mean nothing – not a thing – not if it's not happened to you – that's all they are – words: – 'prison' – 'loss' – 'freedom' – empty words – sounds any two year old could make – and no more understanding than a two year old – not if you've not been here – stuck here. 'I'll just nip to the the pub'. 'No.' 'The shop on the corner.' 'No.' 'Next door'. 'Out in the garden.' 'Stand on the drive.' 'Open the front door.' 'The back door.' 'The window.' 'No – no – no – no – and – no.' No negotiation – first in time in your life – no negotiation. (*Parodying a child persuading his mother*) 'Please mum – let me go – I won't be late – I promise.' 'Alright then son – just this once.' No! Not 'this once' – no way – never in fact – and there's nothing you can say – not a word – nor do – not a

11

single thing – can change the fact – the word
– the non–negotiable word – it's like it's
chained to everything – that unyielding –
uncompromising word – 'No' – chained and
padlocked to every breath you take – every
thought or hope or wish – 'No – no – no –no.'
(*Stopping himself*) No! Don't say any more –
no more – you know what you're like –

OTHER MAN: Exactly – good – try not to work yourself up.

LEWIS: (*Chris now begins to rub and slap his head as if
trying to silence something inside it*) Just take
it easy.

OTHER MAN: (*soothing*) It's still early days.

LEWIS: Stay calm.

OTHER MAN: You can get through this.

LEWIS: (*suddenly becoming agitated again*) Fuck it!

OTHER MAN: You hear me.

LEWIS: Fuck it – fuck it – fuck it – fuck it.

(*Lewis rubs his head*)

OTHER MAN: You're rubbing your head again.

LEWIS: I can't.

OTHER MAN: Hey come on Chris –

LEWIS: I can't stay calm – how do you stay calm –
I'm sick of hearing it – of saying it – 'stay
calm' – 'keep yourself busy' – (*beat*) – doing
what? What is there to do? I mean – seriously
– what?

OTHER MAN: Lots of things.

LEWIS: There's nothing to do. I mean – how do you get through when you've nothing to do.

OTHER MAN: You find a way –

(*There is a pause during which Lewis becomes aware of The Other Man*)

LEWIS: Sorry – I wasn't – I didn't – (*beat*) – you said something.

OTHER MAN: You find a way – one that suits you – your way.

LEWIS: Are you in with the Chaplaincy or something?

OTHER MAN: And you will – believe me – you will – you'll find a way.

LEWIS: Yes – well – I don't have a way – maybe I lost it – maybe I never had one.

OTHER MAN: You did.

LEWIS: Where is it now then – come on? Tell me if you know so much. (*With mocking irony. He looks around the room*) Oh – I know – perhaps it's in here somewhere – (*he looks under the bed*) – under the bed maybe – (*beat*) – no – no – of course – I know where it'll be – (*he looks in the toilet*) – down the toilet – (*Beat*) – with the rest of my fucking life.

OTHER MAN: Hey – come one – don't wind yourself up.

LEWIS: That's something else they keep telling me: 'calm down', 'stay cool', 'stay positive' – 'Stay positive!' That's the biggest joke of all and where are they now eh – solicitors,

13

	barristers – everyone who was supposed to be on my side – where are they all now?
OTHER MAN:	This isn't going to help Chris.
LEWIS:	They're back in their big 'fuck off' offices – screwing over some other poor bastard.
OTHER MAN:	They did their best.
LEWIS:	Then why the fuck am I here?
OTHER MAN:	Yes – yes indeed – that's the question.
LEWIS:	And?
(*Pause*)	
LEWIS:	(*more emphatic*) And?
(*Beat*)	
LEWIS:	See! You don't have an answer – (*he sneers*) – same as the rest of them –
OTHER MAN:	Hold on a second –
LEWIS:	None of you have an answer.
OTHER MAN:	Are you including me in this?
LEWIS:	Of course not.
OTHER MAN:	Who then?
LEWIS:	Like I say – it's not one person – it's the whole thing – the system – all of it – and what chance have I got – has anyone got when the system's – you know – (*beat*) – when it's how it is?
OTHER MAN:	And how is it?

LEWIS: Everyone pretending – the Police, the lawyers – pretending it's all fair – maybe even believing it – but once they've got you – once you're in the system – it's like you're automatically on the other side – they're right – you're wrong – and nothing you can do to change it – nothing.

(*Pause as The Other Man ponders what has been said*)

OTHER MAN: What if you did what you were accused of? What if you were guilty?

LEWIS: It wasn't my fault – ok.

OTHER MAN: So you say – but just for a moment – if it was – what would you say then about being sent to prison – sent here –

LEWIS: The same.

OTHER MAN: Even if you were guilty?

LEWIS: It's no way to treat anybody.

OTHER MAN: So no–one deserves this – is that what you're saying – rapists, murderers, terrorists –

LEWIS: You're twisting what I'm saying.

OTHER MAN: Who does deserve it then?

LEWIS: Not me – ok – that's all I know – I don't care about the rest –

OTHER MAN: But you want them to care about you.

LEWIS: Look – I didn't ask you for this – ok – so if you don't mind –

(*Beat*)

OTHER MAN:	Tell me something – was it worth it – six and a half years of your life? I mean let's take your valuation shall we – the sums are pretty simple – £50000 divided by six and a half is just over £7500 a year – spread among how many?
LEWIS:	What do you mean?
OTHER MAN:	You're not the only one punished here – not the only one paying the price.
LEWIS:	And you think I don't know that?
OTHER MAN:	(*with sarcasm*) Oh yeah – I'm sure you took them all into account when you did the calculation – when you asked yourself whether £50000 was worth the price you and all the others affected might have to pay.
LEWIS:	I don't want any more of this.
OTHER MAN:	No come on – we've got to finish the sum. How much would you and your family get for your six plus years? (*Rhetorical question*) Now how many are there? There's mum, brothers, sisters, nephews, nieces, close friends who've stood by you – not too many of those fortunately. (*Beat*) I reckon it comes to 15 in total – give or take the odd one – so quick calculation – that's £500 each. What a great little earner! What a terrific day's work it was – that day you flew in from St Lucia.
(*Pause*)	
LEWIS:	That's enough, ok – enough. I don't need any more of this.

OTHER MAN: When did you last stop and think – I mean – deliberately – consciously make a decision to put time aside – put everything else on hold and find a quiet place – private – no disturbance – and use the time and that space you'd set aside to think.

LEWIS: I can't stop thinking – that's the trouble.

OTHER MAN: 'Churning' isn't thinking.

LEWIS: Churning?

OTHER MAN: When your mind's like a washing machine – the drum spinning – full to the brim with stuff – all spinning round and round so you can't focus on any one thing for more than a split second – the more you churn the more entwined – the more knotted all those thoughts get – till they're all a whirring blur and you can't distinguish one from the other. (*Beat*) Recognise that?

LEWIS: Yes.

OTHER MAN: So come on then – when did you last give yourself time and space to focus on just one thing – one thought – one idea – from beginning to end – problem to solution – the whole thing – nothing else entangled in it. When was it?

LEWIS: If you're so smart – what are you doing in here?

OTHER MAN: (*ignoring the question and becoming more emphatic*) When?

LEWIS: No – come on – tell me –

OTHER MAN:	No – you tell me – when – when did you last think – I mean *really* think.

(*A pause as The Other Man puts pressure on Lewis to answer*)

LEWIS:	Sorry to disappoint but it's not me — that kind of thinking – concentration – focus – not something I'm any good at – in fact there's not much I am any good at.
OTHER MAN:	What about cricket?
LEWIS:	What about it?
OTHER MAN:	It was *your* life.
LEWIS:	Not any more it's not.
OTHER MAN:	You played for England.
LEWIS:	That counts for nothing – not now – not here – no way
OTHER MAN:	'Nothing', 'not', 'not'. 'no'.
LEWIS:	Sorry?
OTHER MAN:	Four negatives – in what – twelve words – can't be any more than twelve – maybe less.
LEWIS:	So?
OTHER MAN:	You're still churning all that negative crap round.
LEWIS:	It's how I feel – ok – it's the way things are.
OTHER MAN:	It's the way you *see* how they are
LEWIS:	Same difference.
OTHER MAN:	No – no it's not.

LEWIS: Are you trying to be a shrink or something – is that what you're doing – 'cos I'm not crazy if that's what you reckon. I wish I was and then I wouldn't know what was going on here but sorry to disappoint you mate – I know exactly what's happening and I don't want to talk about it – (*beat*) – I'm tired – ok – more than tired – (*tapping his head*) – exhausted in here – that's what I am – and I don't want to listen to any more of your shit – 'cos that's all it is – it's shit – and I'm not listening.

Blackout

SCENE 3

The Other Man as Unnamed Accomplice

The action now moves back in time to August 2008 – a bar somewhere in London. The lights come up to reveal The Other Man as Unnamed Accomplice sitting down stage left with his back to The Audience so that his face is unseen throughout the exchange. Lewis enters.

OTHER MAN: (*getting up to greet him but remaining turned away from the audience*) Chris, mate – good to see you – sit down – have a drink. (*Pause*) Have a drink mate. What can I get you?

LEWIS: I'm alright thanks.

(*Lewis sits opposite him so that he is clearly visible to the audience*)

OTHER MAN: So – mate – how's it going?

LEWIS: Not great.

OTHER MAN: I heard.

LEWIS:	That's the way it goes.
OTHER MAN:	So – anything planned?
LEWIS:	Not really – no – a bit of coaching maybe – sign on – who knows?
OTHER MAN:	I've been there, mate – it's a real bummer.
LEWIS:	I'm looking – you know – but nothing yet.
OTHER MAN:	Not easy – not with the recession and all that.
LEWIS:	No.
OTHER MAN:	What about the club – what about Surrey?
LEWIS:	What about them?
OTHER MAN:	They must know someone – have some contacts – you know – find you something.
LEWIS:	You're joking.
OTHER MAN:	Why not?
LEWIS:	That's not how it works – not in cricket – once you're gone, you're history; they all want to cosy up when your star's rising – the moment it starts to fall – (*he makes the action of blowing into his closed hand then opening it to reveal it's empty*) – all gone – all of them – nowhere to be seen.
OTHER MAN:	Yeah – well – to hell with them – that's what I say – to hell with the whole system.
LEWIS:	They didn't even pay me when I got injured.
OTHER MAN:	No way!

LEWIS:	They signed me on a match basis, see – if you don't play you don't get a penny – nothing – and you can't do anything else 'cos you're under contract.
OTHER MAN:	That is really shit.
LEWIS:	They've got you by the balls.
OTHER MAN:	So – no money then.
LEWIS:	(*defensively*) I'm not asking for a loan.
OTHER MAN:	No – no – no – no – not what I mean, mate.
LEWIS:	Ok.
OTHER MAN:	But I do know people.
LEWIS:	(*understanding the drift*) Right.
OTHER MAN:	And it's good money – and – well – you know what I'm saying.
LEWIS:	Yes – yes – I know what you're saying.
OTHER MAN:	And you won't need a P45.
LEWIS:	And what am I likely to… you know – I mean –
OTHER MAN:	How much?
LEWIS:	Yes.
OTHER MAN:	How much do you need?
LEWIS:	I don't know.
OTHER MAN:	Well let's put it another way – how much have you got?
LEWIS:	Nothing – not a penny.

OTHER MAN: Ok then – how does fifty grand sound?

SCENE 4

The action returns to Dovegate Prison as in Scene 2. During the blackout there is the sound of a bell ringing followed by the sounds of lockdown for the night. The lights come up to reveal Lewis lying on the bed in a foetal position asleep in the middle of a nightmare. The Other Man is apparently asleep on the top bunk

LEWIS: (*in the middle of a nightmare in an increasing state of panic*) Alright mum – yes mum – yes – yes – I'll be alright – thank you – I will – I'll be fine – honestly mum – I will – (*beat*) – yes – yes – I'm eating – they're feeding me – and – and – (*beat*) – thank you – thank you mum – that's kind – but you can't – they won't let you – not food – they won't let you bring any food in – not food – no – but I am eating – and I promise – I promise mum – I promise – I promise

(*He sits bolt upright hyperventilating and starts knotting his sheets together in the form of a noose. He checks that The Other Man is still asleep and then attaches the bed sheets to a fastening on the ceiling, puts the noose around his neck and stands on a chair. Lewis pauses indecisively and The Other Man sits up*)

OTHER MAN: What's stopping you?

(*Lewis stands frozen*)

LEWIS: (*more emphatic*) I don't know.

OTHER MAN: Well maybe you should know.

LEWIS: It's got nothing to do with you – it's none of your business.

OTHER MAN: You've just made it my business.

LEWIS: I don't care – you can't stop me – not if I really want to.

OTHER MAN: Probably true.

LEWIS: No–one can – no–one can be watching all the time – no–one – not all the time.

(*Pause*)

OTHER MAN: How tall are you?

Lewis: (*puzzled*) Sorry?

OTHER MAN: How tall are you?

LEWIS: What are you on about?

OTHER MAN: I reckon you'll need a coffin of let's say six foot five by two foot six – and here you are complaining about spending six and a half years in a ten by six room and your solution is to rot for eternity in well under half that space.

LEWIS: I don't care.

OTHER MAN: Come down – then we can talk.

LEWIS: I don't want to.

OTHER MAN: Yes you do.

LEWIS: How do you know what I want?

OTHER MAN: Just come down.

(*There is a pause as The Other Man faces Lewis down who eventually comes down off the chair and realising the enormity of what he has attempted breaks down. The Other Man comforts him*)

LEWIS:	This dream – every night – the same dream – I can't stop it – it doesn't matter what I do. I can't stop it – I can't stop her coming into my mind – my mum – her first visit after I've been arrested and I'm on remand and I can see it in her eyes – the agony – and all she can say is: (*Lewis speaks as his mum*) – 'are you alright Chris – are you ok son? Are they treating you ok? You're looking thin – too thin. Are you eating – 'cos you need to eat – you need to keep your strength up – you don't want to be looking all scrawny – not when – when – when – you know?' (*He speaks as himself*) And she can't say it – what we both know is coming: 'trial – judge – jury' – she can't say the words – they're too big – too momentous to say – so she carries on: 'you need to look your best – not all scrawny – 'cos Mark noticed – the same as me – when he came to see you – he said you were looking thin – so you make sure you. You hear me?' (*Speaking as himself*) And I want her to stop – I want her to go – my own mum – I want her to go so I don't have to see the pain in those eyes. (*Beat*) And it's the eyes – every night I dream them and wake up like this –
OTHER MAN:	You're going to be fine.
LEWIS:	No – no – I think my heart's about to burst – it's all over the place.
OTHER MAN:	Everything's going to be ok. I promise you.
LEWIS:	I'm sorry.
OTHER MAN:	No need to be.

LEWIS:	(*indicating his head*) All this stuff in here – I can't handle it – I don't know how.
OTHER MAN:	Perhaps you know more than you think you do.
LEWIS:	I've got no qualifications – none – not one – no GCSE'S – no A Levels – nothing like that – never had a proper job – I know nothing about anything.
OTHER MAN:	You know about negatives. That was eight I counted.
LEWIS:	I've told you before – that's me – it's how I see things.
OTHER MAN:	And that's it is it?
LEWIS:	What do you mean?
OTHER MAN:	There's nothing you can do about it – about how you are – is that what you're saying – you can't change? (*Pause*) What about when you were playing cricket – didn't you ever look for ways to improve – make things better – your technique. I mean – you played for England – you must have shared ideas with other players – sought advice from coaches – tried new things – you must have.
LEWIS:	I don't know what you think you're trying to achieve with all this bollocks – but I sure as hell didn't ask for it and I don't want it. I don't need it.
OTHER MAN:	They were right about you then.
LEWIS:	Who were?

OTHER MAN:	The cricket pundits – the media.
LEWIS:	Don't talk to me about the media –
OTHER MAN:	(*quoting from the media*) 'Never one to learn from his mistakes'.
LEWIS:	Been doing your homework have you?
OTHER MAN:	'Rarely willing to take advice'.
LEWIS:	Yeah well – the guy who wrote that – well – he had it in for me from the start.
OTHER MAN:	So it's not true then.
LEWIS:	No – no it's not. I took advice from people I respected.
OTHER MAN:	Such as.
LEWIS:	You'd be surprised.
OTHER MAN:	Go on then.
(*Pause*)	
OTHER MAN:	Go on – surprise me!
LEWIS:	Ok – if I must – Viv Richards – there – is that good enough for you?
OTHER MAN:	And what did he say?
LEWIS:	I don't remember.
OTHER MAN:	Nonsense.
LEWIS:	It was twenty years ago. Do you remember what was said to you twenty years ago?

OTHER MAN: I would if it was Viv Richards – he was the best player in the World – of course I'd remember.

LEWIS: Well I don't.

OTHER MAN: (*Emphatically*) What did he say?

LEWIS: I've told you!

OTHER MAN: You've told me nothing.

(*A long pause as The Other Man stares out Lewis who eventually gives in*)

LEWIS: Alright – ok well – he said some nice things.

OTHER MAN: Like what?

LEWIS: It was after a match – second or third time I'd played against him. He said I'd done alright.

OTHER MAN: It was more than that – what exactly did he say?

LEWIS: It doesn't make any difference – not now anyway.

OTHER MAN: Why not?

LEWIS: (*getting visibly upset*) It just doesn't – (*he opens up briefly*) – it upsets me – ok – I don't like to think about it.

OTHER MAN: About that moment in particular?

LEWIS: Any of it.

OTHER MAN: Your playing days.

LEWIS: If you like.

OTHER MAN:	It upsets you.
LEWIS:	What do you think – especially things like – like – (*he closes down again*)…
OTHER MAN:	(*finishing his sentence for him*) That time with Viv Richards.

(*Pause as Lewis does not answer*)

OTHER MAN:	What did he say – come on – spit it out – tell me what he said?
LEWIS:	He was kind – that's all – he didn't have to talk to me – I wasn't a teammate – and I'd got him out – twice in the match. He had every reason to be pissed off but he wasn't – he was nice.
OTHER MAN:	(*with real emphasis*) What did he say?
LEWIS:	It was about something he'd noticed I was doing when I was batting – that after the bowler had delivered the ball and it was dead I'd kept looking at him – watching the bowler walk back to his mark – that all my focus had been on the bowler – trying to work out what the bowler was going to do rather than looking away between deliveries, clearing my head. 'Taking a stroll to the beach' he called it – 'refreshing your mind'.
OTHER MAN:	And you listened.
LEWIS:	Of course I listened.
OTHER MAN:	And?
LEWIS:	It worked – his advice – what he said – it did – pretty well in fact – I got a hundred – a big

	hundred – the next match – against Essex it was – 189 not out – smashed them to all parts. So yeah – I listened.
OTHER MAN:	And it made a difference.
LEWIS:	But Christ – I mean – what would he think now? – 'what a waste of time that was!'. I'll bet he wishes he hadn't bothered – and you can't blame him – it's what I deserve.
OTHER MAN:	Ah! And why's that?
LEWIS:	Why's what?
OTHER MAN:	(*quoting him back*) 'It's what I deserve'.
LEWIS:	Just a manner of speaking.
OTHER MAN:	No – no it's more than that.
LEWIS:	(*shrugging his shoulders*) I don't know what you mean.
OTHER MAN:	Why can't you face up to what you've done?
LEWIS:	What do you think this is – locked up in here – if this isn't paying for what I've done I don't know what is.
OTHER MAN:	That's not what I said – 'paying' for what you've done is one thing –
LEWIS:	It's six and a half years of my life – and that's only if I get parole.
OTHER MAN:	'Facing' up to it – is an entirely different matter.
LEWIS:	That's what I've done.

OTHER MAN:	No – no – you haven't – you've lied about it – to everyone – including yourself.
LEWIS:	I'm not a liar.
OTHER MAN:	No?
LEWIS:	No.
OTHER MAN:	What about The Oval in 1996 – the match against Pakistan?
LEWIS:	Christ!
OTHER MAN:	What?
LEWIS:	All this stuff – what people have written – and dates – matches – games I've played in – you knowing all this stuff –
OTHER MAN:	It's nothing you can't find in the papers.
LEWIS:	Only if you're looking for it.
OTHER MAN:	You're just being evasive.
LEWIS:	What's that supposed to mean?
OTHER MAN:	You don't want to talk about that match – the one against Pakistan – the lie you told.
LEWIS:	It wasn't a lie.
OTHER MAN:	What was it then?
LEWIS:	An excuse – that's all that was – an excuse.
OTHER MAN:	What's the difference?
LEWIS:	Anyone would have done the same – you would have – my arse was on the line.

OTHER MAN: Like when they found that cocaine in your bag at Gatwick Airport and you tried and to wriggle your way out of it.

LEWIS: I thought we were talking about that day at The Oval.

OTHER MAN: It all comes down to the same thing.

LEWIS: No – no – it doesn't – what happened at The Oval was no big deal – the whole thing was blown out of all proportion. I'd overslept – that was all. It was a cricket match for fuck sake.

OTHER MAN: An international cricket match.

LEWIS: Hardly World War Three.

OTHER MAN: You were a professional cricketer – thousands of people paid good money to watch – it wasn't just a Sunday afternoon knock about in the park.

LEWIS: Alright – ok – I was a bit late.

OTHER MAN: A bit late!

LEWIS: It wasn't intentional.

OTHER MAN: (*parody*) 'It wasn't intentional' – 'I didn't mean to do it' – as if that makes it ok – makes it like you're not responsible. You missed the entire team training session on the morning of a critical Test Match

LEWIS: Ok – alright – so I fucked up.

OTHER MAN: And lied about it.

LEWIS: So I missed a training session. It's not a hanging offence.

OTHER MAN: If it wasn't serious – why did you lie about why you were late?

LEWIS: Is this – a court or something – I've just been through all the stress of a trial – and I don't want another.

OTHER MAN: And the jury didn't believe you any more than the England selectors believed your pathetic excuses at The Oval. (*He parodies Lewis making excuses*) 'I was late because I had a puncture and I couldn't ring 'cos my phone had no battery.'

LEWIS: And I paid for it big time – they dropped me – same as I'm paying for it now.

OTHER MAN: That's not the point.

LEWIS: It was the excuse they'd been looking for – the selectors and Ray Illingworth – the big 'God–Almighty–I'm–In–Charge–And–The–Rest–Are–Shit–Cricket–Supremo' – I knew what he thought of me – (*Lewis offers a cruel parody of Ray Illingworth*) 'There's no place for Chris Lewis in any England side while I'm in charge – He's not a team player and never has been – he doesn't fit in – prefers his own company. Ask any of the lads – Thorpey, Nasser, Corky – ask any of them – they'll tell you. He's not one of the boys. Never goes out for a drink with them. No good for team spirit – drop him – that's what I say – drop him.' (*Beat as he speaks himself*) And I never played for England again – wasn't that punishment enough?

OTHER MAN:	What did you learn from it though – that's the question – and what have you learnt from being sent here?
LEWIS:	Proves the point then doesn't it?
OTHER MAN:	What point?
LEWIS:	Prison is a waste of time.
OTHER MAN:	No – no – all it proves is that you blame everyone else for anything that goes wrong.
LEWIS:	Not true.
OTHER MAN:	Always looking for excuses.
LEWIS:	I'm not.
OTHER MAN:	Got anyone else to blame for anything else have you – for all the other 'fuck ups' in your life?

(*Throughout what follows The Other Man is ironic and provocative as he plays Devil's Advocate*)

OTHER MAN:	What about the media – treat you the same as everyone else did they?
LEWIS:	They didn't take me seriously.
OTHER MAN:	Why not?
LEWIS:	They just didn't like me – I don't know why – I mean – listen – there was the time I got sunstroke – just before the Test Match in Antigua it was – and the papers had a field day – The Sun especially – 'The Prat Without The Hat' – that was the headline – I mean – maybe the guy who wrote it – maybe he thought it was funny – 'a black man getting

sunstroke! – maybe they all did. I'll bet they had a right laugh. All I'd done was shave my head – for charity it was – but that never got a mention in the papers – that I'd done it for charity – they never wrote that – all they wrote was that I'd gone out in the sun without a hat and got sunstroke – like it was one big joke. But what if it had been one of the fair skinned guys – would that have made the headlines? 'White Man Gets Sunstroke!' I mean – please!

OTHER MAN: So you reckon they wrote the story because you were black?

LEWIS: All I'm asking is why it was always me the press guys took the piss out of – why me?

OTHER MAN: (*more emphatic*) Because you're black?

LEWIS: You tell me – I don't know – would it have been the same if I wasn't – the tone – the ridicule? You tell me.

(*Pause*)

OTHER MAN: Anything else?

LEWIS: What do you mean?

OTHER MAN: (*Still being provocative and ironic*) Anything or anyone else to blame – while we're on the subject – any other excuses – you'd like to offer?

LEWIS: For what?

OTHER MAN: For your life –

LEWIS: What about your life?

OTHER MAN: (*continuing*) For the way things are – being in here –

LEWIS: Why can't we talk about your life?

OTHER MAN: Who's to blame – eh?

LEWIS: Are you listening?

OTHER MAN: Your parents – is all this fault? Is that what you think?

LEWIS: I want to talk about your life.

OTHER MAN: Or just your dad.

(*Lewis is blown off course by the mention of his dad*)

LEWIS: (*Defensively*) Nothing wrong with my dad.

OTHER MAN: Apart from the fact that he walked out as soon as you were born.

LEWIS: He had his reasons.

OTHER MAN: Which were?

LEWIS: He had his own life to lead –

OTHER MAN: And to the hell with everyone else – is that it? He was a priest for God's sake.

LEWIS: (*correcting The Other Man*) A Baptist Minister.

OTHER MAN: A preacher.

LEWIS: If you like.

OTHER MAN: (*offering an ironic parody*) 'Hallelujah! The Lord be praised.'

LEWIS: He had his mission – a big following – a huge congregation.

OTHER MAN: More important than his own wife and children.

LEWIS: It was the Caribbean – that's how it was – lots of kids didn't have their dads around – I was no different. I didn't feel any different.

OTHER MAN: Maybe not in the Caribbean but this is England.

LEWIS: I never felt I was missing anything – here or there. I don't blame him for anything – others can judge if they want – but I like him. He has a nice energy. He may not have been like a dad to me – a conventional dad – but he's been pretty cool. I mean – when I was thirteen – and he was a minister, remember – a man of the cloth – when I was thirteen he said to me: 'It's time you think for yourself, son – time you decide what you believe and whether you go to church or not.' How many Baptist preachers do that? (*Beat*) But I know what you're doing here – all these questions about blame – I know what you're up to – you want me to point the finger like in the stereotype – play the victim – 'I'm just a poor little black boy with no dad – and everyone's against me – what chance in life have I got?' Well – no – sorry – that's not how it was – it wasn't like that – and none of this – being in here I mean – 'cos that's what you're digging for – how I ended up in here – but none of it's to do with my dad – nor my childhood – nothing like that.

SCENE 5

The Other Man speaking as The Customs Official.

The action moves back in time to December 2008 at Gatwick Airport. As the lights come up beneath the dominant sound of airport noise is the faint sound of a heart beat which gradually increases in pace and volume as Lewis enters the Nothing to Declare zone in customs. He pushes an airport trolley on which there is a large Puma kit bag. He carries a Prada bag and walks steadily towards the exit. Far stage right in front of a table is The Other Man as The Customs Official. He has his back to the audience so that his face remains unseen throughout the exchange.

OTHER MAN: (*stopping Lewis as he is about to pass*) Excuse me, sir, may I check your luggage?

LEWIS: I haven't got anything to declare.

OTHER MAN: Nevertheless, sir – (*indicating to Lewis to put his bag on the table*) – if you don't mind.

(*Lewis puts his bag on the table*)

OTHER MAN: Would you open it for me please sir?

(*Lewis opens the bag*)

OTHER MAN: And did you pack your own bag, sir?

LEWIS: Yes – yes I did.

(*The Other Man as The Customs Official now searches the bag and takes some cans apparently containing fruit juice*)

OTHER MAN: And what are these, sir?

LEWIS: They're cans – fruit juice.

(*The Customs Official scrutinises the cartons and then shakes them*)

LEWIS:	Orange juice in fact.
OTHER MAN:	(*continuing to examine*) I see.
LEWIS:	From St Lucia – you know – for my nephews.
OTHER MAN:	Right – well if you don't mind waiting here a minute sir.
LEWIS:	Is there a problem?
OTHER MAN:	I'm just going to have a closer look – a quick x ray –
LEWIS:	X-ray?
OTHER MAN:	It shouldn't take long, sir – if you just wait here.

SCENE 6

The action returns to Dovegate Prison as in Scene 4. The lights come up to reveal Lewis and The Other Man in the cell

LEWIS:	Why do you bother?
OTHER MAN:	With what?
LEWIS:	Me – talking to me – you know – (*trying to find the right word*) – talking.
OTHER MAN:	Who else is there?
LEWIS:	I'm serious.
OTHER MAN:	You're not worth it – is that it?
LEWIS:	Probably – I don't know – look – (*Beat*) – I did what I did – ok.
OTHER MAN:	Ah! You admit it.

LEWIS: No point in denying it – not now – I mean – here I am – a prisoner – guilty as charged – yes I admit it. I've got what I deserve – and I feel shit about it.

OTHER MAN: Everyone does from time to time.

LEWIS: Yeah – well – for me it's pretty much all the time.

OTHER MAN: Maybe because you don't handle it too well.

(*Lewis shrugs and does not respond*)

OTHER MAN: Ok – alright – apart from this – you know – prison – what's the worst thing – that's happened to you?

LEWIS: I don't know.

OTHER MAN: Yes you do.

LEWIS: You tell me then.

OTHER MAN: What about The World Cup Final?

(*Lewis' reaction makes it clear The Other Man has hit a raw nerve*)

OTHER MAN: I'm right then.

LEWIS: Make you feel good does it – dragging up every – every disastrous cock–up you can find?

OTHER MAN: Why was it so disastrous?

LEWIS: Jesus! It was the World Cup Final mate – the pinnacle of my career – playing in the World Cup Final – how many people get that chance? And even better – we're in trouble at

144 for 5 when I walk out to bat at Melbourne in front of a packed crowd.

OTHER MAN: The situation when heroes are born – when someone seizes the moment – shifts the momentum – turns all expectation on its head.

LEWIS: Exactly! (*Speaking in the third person*) And what does Lewis do? The first ball from Wasim Akram knocks his off stump clean out of the ground – first ball – out first ball in his one and only World Cup Final – what a waste of space.

OTHER MAN: Why do you speak in the third person?

LEWIS: It makes easier I guess.

OTHER MAN: Ok – no problem – so what then?

LEWIS: What do you mean 'what then'?

OTHER MAN: After his off stump has been knocked out of the ground. What does Lewis do then?

LEWIS: He has to trudge all the way back to the pavilion.

OTHER MAN: And how far was that exactly?

LEWIS: 100 metres – 110 maybe – he doesn't count the steps.

OTHER MAN: No of course – but that walk back – how does he feel?

LEWIS: (*with heavy sarcasm*) He feels fucking wonderful! What do you think?

OTHER MAN: I'm being serious.

LEWIS:	He wants the ground to swallow him up. I mean – there were 90,000 people in the ground and God knows how many watching on TV – millions around the world – all looking at him – and there he is shuffling back – totally humiliated.
OTHER MAN:	Trying to get off the ground as quickly as he can.
LEWIS:	But nowhere quick enough 'cos it feels to him like an eternity.
OTHER MAN:	And what if he's making that same walk with a hundred to his name?
LEWIS:	He isn't – he's out first ball.
OTHER MAN:	You're a right pain in the arse sometimes – (*beat*) – what if he had?
LEWIS:	I don't know.
OTHER MAN:	Yes you do.
LEWIS:	How the hell do you know what I know?
OTHER MAN:	You've done it – eleven times in fact – that's how many centuries you've made in first class cricket – eleven times you've made that walk back to the pavilion with a hundred to your name – so you know exactly how it feels.

(*Beat*)

OTHER MAN:	Go on – describe it to me.
LEWIS:	I can't.

OTHER MAN: No such word – just give it a go – and this time – *you* relive it – no 'third' person – be yourself.

(*Pause*)

LEWIS: (*reliving and re–enacting the moment as he describes it*) Well – I'm out – doesn't matter how – 'cos I've got a hundred and I don't care – and then there's this split second of silence – a moment's stillness before the crowd registers – before I take my first step towards the pavilion – and then – it's like it's simultaneous – I move and the noise erupts – and I raise my bat to them – acknowledge the applause – and now I'm into my stride – walking – head up and unstrapping my helmet with my left hand and pointing my bat like a baton to each corner of the ground in turn with my right hand – like I'm conducting an orchestra – each wave bringing more clapping – more cheering – and as I near the pavilion steps it's rising to a crescendo – and up I go and in through the pavilion door – disappearing from view as the noise fades – back into the obscurity of the dressing room. And it's over – done in a flash – like it was a 10 yard dash.

OTHER MAN: There you are. It's the same walk – whether you're out first ball or you've got a hundred – it's the same walk – the same distance – it takes the same time – it's only how it feels that's different.

LEWIS: So?

OTHER MAN: It's a matter of perception – your frame of mind and how you see things because of it – like how you described getting a hundred – like conducting an orchestra – feeling in control – not controlled by events.

LEWIS: Yeah – well it doesn't apply in here.

OTHER MAN: Why not?

LEWIS: I've no say in anything – it's all regulated – the time I eat, sleep, take exercise, have visitors – shut down for the night – everything.

OTHER MAN: Those things – yes – yes – of course – but not how you think – how you feel – that's still down to you – glass half full or half empty – I mean – you can only plan for the future if you believe there is one.

LEWIS: I've never made a plan in my life.

OTHER MAN: I bet you have. (*Beat*) What about bowling – what about when you came up with a strategy for a particular batsman? You must have done that.

LEWIS: It didn't always work.

OTHER MAN: So you gave up then. Is that it? If the first plan didn't work you packed up and went home.

LEWIS: Of course – I tried something else.

OTHER MAN: So you had your own framework – a set of principles.

LEWIS: Yes – yes I did. The most important thing is to have an overall objective – I mean – the aim was always to get the batsman out and then break it down into action points of how and then – when you're putting into practice – not to think too far ahead.

OTHER MAN: Ball by ball.

LEWIS: Yes – and get the batsman used to a pattern.

OTHER MAN: And then?

LEWIS: Introduce a variation.

OTHER MAN: Think of an example.

LEWIS: Javed Miandad in the Lords Test in 1992.

(*He now re–enacts his over*) The first four balls of the over – (*he makes the muscular movement of bowling four successive balls*) – one – two – three – four – all fired in on a length from wide of the crease – all aimed at middle and off – no room to free up his arms – each one racking up the pressure to score off the next one – and then – the variation – the fifth ball – from close in to the stumps – (*he re–enacts the muscular movement of bowling again*) – pitching off stump and shaping away – and he flashes his bat at it – (*Lewis relives the commentary*) 'And he's out – Javed Miandad is out in his first over – caught Russell bowled Lewis nought.'

OTHER MAN: There you are – see –

LEWIS:	It worked like a charm
OTHER MAN:	You do know how to plan.
LEWIS:	Alright – ok – so what do you want me to do?
OTHER MAN:	Give it a go – make a plan – so come on what's the first principle?
LEWIS:	Decide on the overall objective.
OTHER MAN:	Which is?
LEWIS:	Get out as soon as possible – maximum parole – out on licence.
OTHER MAN:	Second principle.
LEWIS:	Break it down into actions points
OTHER MAN:	Action Point One.
LEWIS:	What do you reckon?
OTHER MAN:	Your plan not mine.
LEWIS:	The Annual Prisoner Review system.
OTHER MAN:	What about it?
LEWIS:	I can start preparing – it's a year ahead but if I prepare now – I'll be –
BOTH:	(*speaking together*) Ready to apply.
LEWIS:	Apply to become a Category C prisoner – more freedom – new prison –
OTHER MAN:	Closer to home.
LEWIS:	If possible – yes – that'd be good.
OTHER MAN:	Action Point Two!

LEWIS:	Apply for a prison job.
OTHER MAN:	And?
LEWIS:	Do it well – be reliable – thorough – cooperative.
OTHER MAN:	Excellent!
LEWIS:	Preferably one in the gym.
OTHER MAN:	More opportunity to use the equipment yourself.
LEWIS:	Keep myself fit.
OTHER MAN:	Action Point Three.

(*Pause as Lewis tries to think*)

OTHER MAN:	(*prompting Lewis*) What's going to convince the Review Board that you're serious about rehabilitation?
LEWIS:	If I do courses.
OTHER MAN:	Exactly!
LEWIS:	Computing.
OTHER MAN:	Cooking and bricklaying.
LEWIS:	Psychology –
OTHER MAN:	Everything you can get on. Action Point Four:
LEWIS:	As soon as possible after getting Category C status start preparing an application to become Category D – and move to an Open Prison.

OTHER MAN: Action Point Five:

LEWIS: Get parole – out on licence – freedom – end of plan.

(*Lewis is visibly lifted by the creation of the plan*)

OTHER MAN: Good – (*handing him a pen and some paper*) Write it down – the plan – you need to write down what you've decided and tick things off as you go.

LEWIS: (*as he writes*) It's the first plan I've ever had – real plan – proper plan – apart from the cricketing stuff – you know – 'cos that's never been me – plans – rules and stuff –

OTHER MAN: Bit of a rebel then – is that how you saw yourself?

(*Pause*)

    Well?

LEWIS: No – no – not a rebel – not really – not like a real one –

OTHER MAN: Why not?

LEWIS: 'Cos they kind of believe in stuff – at least that's how I see it – a real rebel knows why he's rebelling – knows what he's fighting for – what he's angry about –

OTHER MAN: And you?

LEWIS: Me? Shit! No idea – none – I was just angry – don't even know what about – (*beat*) – angry and aimless –

SCENE 7

The Other Man as Solicitor

The action moves back in time to March 2009 – Lewis is on remand awaiting trial. He is meeting with his solicitor. As the lights come up Lewis is sitting stage right opposite his Solicitor who is played by The Other Man who has his back to audience so that his face remains unseen throughout.

OTHER MAN: I'm going to need a bit more than that I'm afraid Chris.

LEWIS: (*speaking direct to the audience*) Four weeks I've been in here – four weeks – and I don't care what he says even if he is a solicitor.

But I didn't know.

OTHER MAN: Just saying that you didn't know is not going to be a realistic defence I'm afraid.

LEWIS: (*still talking to the audience*) I can see where it's heading already.

OTHER MAN: In law you are responsible for whatever you bring through customs – no–one else –

LEWIS: I (*still talking to the audience*) And I'm not pleading guilty – no way.

OTHER MAN: And we have to prove those cans were planted without your knowledge – and you've told me already that you carried them willingly.

LEWIS: Because I was asked – I thought he was a friend.

OTHER MAN: Ok – I mean – there's nothing wrong with carrying something for someone else but you have to know what it is and it has to be something that is legal to bring through customs.

LEWIS: I didn't know what was in those cartons – all I could see was the labels – how was I supposed to know that stuff was concealed in them – how – you couldn't tell – not by looking at them – you couldn't.

OTHER MAN: Fine – fine – that's a legitimate line of defence –

LEWIS: Good.

OTHER MAN: But your friend –

LEWIS: Like I say – he's not my friend.

OTHER MAN: Whatever he is or isn't – the reality is he's blaming you.

LEWIS: He's lying.

OTHER MAN: And that's the problem. The jury are going to see two men 'slagging each other off' for want of a better phrase and I'm sorry to have to tell you Chris – in cases like this – in my experience – they won't believe either of you.

LEWIS: So what do you suggest?

OTHER MAN: If you plead guilty –

LEWIS: No way.

OTHER MAN: Hold on – let me finish – if you plead guilty the maximum sentence for this particular offence is ten years.

LEWIS: I know but...

OTHER MAN:	And it's unlikely – given it's your first offence of any kind – that you'll get ten years.
LEWIS:	But I don't want to go to prison.
OTHER MAN:	My guess is seven years.
LEWIS:	No.
OTHER MAN:	And with parole –
LEWIS:	No!
OTHER MAN:	You'd be out on licence in three and a half years.
LEWIS:	You're not listening.
OTHER MAN:	I know it's hard.
LEWIS:	No you don't – you've no idea what it's like in here – none – none at all.
OTHER MAN:	I know but –
LEWIS:	I can't do any more time – not beyond the trial – no way – it's been bad enough these last four months – since bail was refused – it's only the thought of the trial – the possibility – you know – the jury – the verdict – that they'll find me not guilty
OTHER MAN:	Yes they might but –
LEWIS:	That's all that keeps me going,
OTHER MAN:	But on the other hand.
LEWIS:	I'm not pleading guilty.
OTHER MAN:	But if it goes the other way – if the jury don't believe you…

LEWIS:	You said they might
OTHER MAN:	It's a balance of risks – and in my experience – in a case like this – a case like yours – it's not worth taking.
LEWIS:	You're supposed to be on my side.
OTHER MAN:	I am – which is why I'm saying what I am – if you plead not guilty – big risk.
LEWIS:	But I might get off.
OTHER MAN:	And you might not –
LEWIS:	It's all I've got to cling to.
OTHER MAN:	Yes, but given the circumstances –
LEWIS:	You mean because I'm black and it's drugs –
OTHER MAN:	Because you can't prove that your version is true – and on the balance of probabilities you'll be found guilty and having pleaded not guilty the tariff is fifteen years and not ten –
LEWIS:	I don't care.
OTHER MAN:	You don't have to decide now.
LEWIS:	I have decided.
OTHER MAN:	Yes – but – there's still time to change your mind. There's six weeks before the trial
LEWIS:	I couldn't do another six minutes if I didn't have some kind of hope. I don't care how small – I can't face it – not without that – I can't – I know I can't – and if I plead guilty – well – that's it – all hope gone – so I'm not – I won't – I won't plead guilty not when

there's a chance – I won't – and you won't
persuade me – 'cos I won't.

SCENE 8

*The action returns to Dovegate Prison as in Scene 6. The lights
come up and Lewis is outside his cell. He is on the phone watched
by The Other Man*

LEWIS: Listen Mark – I've got to be quick. (*Pause*) No
– we've been on lockdown here mate – all
week – it's why I haven't phoned. This is
actually the first time I've been out of my cell
since yesterday afternoon. (*Pause*) Yes –
because of the snow – it's been pretty heavy
up this way and more on its way apparently
so God knows when we'll get back to normal.
(*Pause*) Twenty three hours. (*Pause*) Every
day for four days. (*Pause*) Not enough staff –
they can't get in through the snow – that's
what they say anyway. (*Beat*) Still – not your
problem mate – and it's not why I've called.
(*Pause*) It's about Gran – what to get her for
Christmas. (*Pause*) No – no – and I want it to
stay that way – you promise me now Mark –
promise me – no matter what – you tell Jason
not to tell her ok. (*Pause*) I'm sure he won't
but tell him anyway and tell him to get her
something really nice – I was thinking
perfume – she likes smellies – she's always
liked smellies – so yes – tell him to get her
some nice perfume and not to forget a card –
get her a nice card and if you could transfer
the money I'll pay you back mate. Is that ok?
I'd sort it myself but I can't ring Guyana
from here – well I can but – you know – I only

have a few minutes. (*Pause*) You're a star
mate – thanks. (*Pause*) Yeah – I'm fine – I'm
doing fine – but listen – I am going to have to
go. (*Beat*) Yes and remember to tell Jason she
mustn't know – I don't want her knowing –
no way. (*Pause*) No – no – there's been
nothing in the papers recently – all died down
after the trial – so there won't be anything in
Guyana – not in the papers – there won't –
not that Gran's ever read the papers. (*Pause*)
Yeah – thanks Mark – and don't forget to tell
Jason to get a card. (Pause) He can sign it for
me – she won't know – (*Pause*) one with
flowers on – (*beat*) – roses on – yes – she likes
roses – yeah – I remember she used to love
roses. (*Beat*) Ok mate – thanks – and say hi to
Jason.

(*Lewis puts the phone down and there is a ritual as he lines up and
goes back to the cell followed by The Other Man. Once inside the cell
we hear the sound of the door being locked. Lewis goes to the window
and looks out*)

LEWIS: It's snowing again.

OTHER MAN: You haven't told her.

LEWIS: Shit! Shit! Shit! Shit!

OTHER MAN: Do you hear me?

LEWIS: It'll be lockdown again tomorrow – you see if
                 it's not.

OTHER MAN: (*with slow emphasis*) You haven't told your
                 Gran that you're in prison

LEWIS:	How can I for Christ's sake – she's in Guyana and I'm here? Besides it's not my place to tell her.
OTHER MAN:	Making excuses again are we?
LEWIS:	She's an old woman – she's well into her eighties...
OTHER MAN:	With the same rights as everyone else.
LEWIS:	And she's frail – she's in a home – she had a fall – a couple of falls – I mean – the shock could kill her. That's what mum thinks and it's her call not mine. She's her mum.
OTHER MAN:	Isn't that a bit convenient?
LEWIS:	Maybe it is – yes – maybe it suits both of us – all of us that she doesn't know.
OTHER MAN:	But she has no say in the matter.
LEWIS:	Don't think she doesn't matter to me.
OTHER MAN:	That's not what I'm saying.
LEWIS:	(*throughout the speech he gets more impassioned and upset*) 'Cos she does – ok? She pretty much brought me up back in Guyana – I loved her like she was my mum – and she was – more like a mum than a Gran – especially when mum – my proper mum – came to England – over a year I lived with Gran – more like two years – and I've seen what being sent to prison has done to my mum – the hurt in her eyes – and why would I do to that Gran as well – not when there's no need – 'cos Gran loves me as much as I love her – and I'd spend the rest of my life in here if it

54

meant she wouldn't find out– if that's what it took to stop her knowing – I would – and if that's selfish – if that's running away – not facing up to what I've done – then fuck it – Gran's worth a million times more than parole – she is.

OTHER MAN: Hey come on – calm down – it's alright. It's going to be ok.

LEWIS: I don't want you thinking it was just about me –

OTHER MAN: I was only playing devil's advocate.

LEWIS: (*continuing*) It wasn't about saving my own skin – not this time it wasn't.

OTHER MAN: It's alright – it's ok.

LEWIS: I don't want you thinking that.

OTHER MAN: I don't.

(*Pause*)

LEWIS: It's funny though.

OTHER MAN: What is?

LEWIS: Gran – just thinking about her makes me smile – and there's this one morning – always makes me smile to think of it. I must have been ten 'cos mum had come to England.

Lewis now relives the moment with The Other Man.

The Other Man playing Lewis as a 10 year old

Lewis playing his Granny

OTHER MAN: I can't go to school today Gran – I'm feeling really sick.

LEWIS: You know something Chris – you must be the sickest ten year old in Guyana.

OTHER MAN: But my stomach really does hurt gran.

LEWIS: There always seems to be something – stomach ache, headache, earache – every part of your body takes its turn for a day's aching.

OTHER MAN: It's real this time gran – honest – I'm really bad.

LEWIS: Not too bad to play cricket this evening with all your friends.

OTHER MAN: I couldn't play even if I wanted to.

LEWIS: Why not?

OTHER MAN: Our bat's broken – one of us has got to make a new bat. The one I made the other day only lasted one game.

LEWIS: How many's that you've bust.

OTHER MAN: Only 'cos those old fence slats from down the road are rotten.

LEWIS: I know what you're thinking Christopher Lewis and the answer is no.

OTHER MAN: I'll only take one gran.

LEWIS: That's what you said last time – my fence has got more gaps than slats.

OTHER MAN: But I promised – I promised the boys I'd make a new bat out of some wood that's not full of woodworm and you always say a promise is a promise.

LEWIS: And my fence slats are my fence slats!

OTHER MAN: Please!

LEWIS: (*with amused resignation*) What am I going to do with you?

OTHER MAN: I don't know.

LEWIS: And what's your mum going to say about missing all this school.

OTHER MAN: Don't tell her gran – please don't tell her.

LEWIS: Well – there's time for me to change my mind – she won't be back from England for another six months or more – so like I say – there's time for you to mend your ways – start going to school.

OTHER MAN: I will gran – honestly, I will.

LEWIS: Get yourself off to school.

OTHER MAN: I'll go tomorrow.

LEWIS Today!

OTHER MAN: If you let me go tomorrow, I'll never be sick again.

LEWIS: You promise.

OTHER MAN: As long as you'll let me have one of the fence slats.

LEWIS: You'll be the death of me Christopher Lewis.

(*Lewis reverts to being himself. He starts to rub his head*)

OTHER MAN: You're rubbing your head again.

LEWIS: It's the uncertainty – I can't bear the uncertainty – not knowing what I'm doing and what I'll be doing next – 'cos I need to know and then tick it off – when the day's over – after it's gone to plan – I can tick it off – and then the week – that's how I can cope – it's how I stay in control – I don't want to lose control.

OTHER MAN: You won't – in a couple of days – maybe even by morning – the snow will be gone and everything will be back as it was.

LEWIS: What about now though? That's the problem – now – how am I going to cope with the routine all to cock –

OTHER MAN: (*offering a particularly cruel account of Lewis's past*) 'When the going gets tough you can always rely on Chris Lewis to throw the towel in. Any pressure and he jacks it in – always been the same.'

(*Lewis does not respond*)

OTHER MAN: 'The only Test Century Chris Lewis ever got was in Chenai against India when the game was already pretty much over and England were on the verge of losing – and that pretty much sums him up – (*beat*) – a loser.'

LEWIS: (*carrying on with his cruel parody*) 'Great natural talent but lazy – lazy – a lazy bastard who threw it all away – a lazy bastard who always looked for the easy way out – no fight – no backbone – no spirit – a waste of space.'

OTHER MAN:	Struck a chord have we?
LEWIS:	I'll show you – you wait – you'll see.
OTHER MAN:	Show me what?
LEWIS:	That you're wrong – I'm going to prove you wrong.
OTHER MAN:	By lying on the bed with your head under a pillow?
LEWIS:	By getting away from here once my Category C status is approved – away from you – so I won't have to listen to you any more – so you carry on if you want – say what you like – yeah – why not – get it all out – every bit of shit you've got stored away – say it now – 'cos I won't be around to hear it for too much longer.

SCENE 9

June 2010 – Hemel Hempstead – The Mount Prison. The lights come up to reveal Lewis standing outside his cell. He is on the telephone. The Other Man is in the cell apparently asleep on the top bunk. He is under a blanket and is facing away from the audience

LEWIS:	Mark – how are you? (*Pause*) And mum? (*Pause*) No – I'm here – (*beat*) yes – Hemel Hempstead – The Mount Prison – I arrived last night. (*Pause*) Yes really relieved – what with all the red tape and delays and everything I began to think it'd never happen – but like I say – I'm here now – (*Pause*) Much better – more freedom – easier for you and mum – so much closer – (*Pause*) Lots more – lots – and I've already enrolled on a

59

psychology course. (*Pause*). Hey – that's
great – and you'll bring mum with you –
(*Pause*) Excellent – can't wait – great news –
see you then. (*Beat*) Love you too – (*beat*) –
miss you. (*Pause*) Yes – same time next week.

(*Lewis puts the phone down and rubs his head anxiously. He
returns to his new prison cell followed by The Other Man. Lewis
paces the cell and talks to himself unaware of The Other Man who
watches*)

OTHER MAN: You're upset.

LEWIS: You!

OTHER MAN: You're rubbing your head again.

LEWIS: Why are you here?

OTHER MAN: What's worrying you?

LEWIS: How did you get here?

OTHER MAN: It was the phone call – wasn't it?

LEWIS: But here – this prison – Hemel Hempstead –
I don't understand.

OTHER MAN: I came the same way you did.

(*Lewis shakes his head with angry bewilderment*)

LEWIS: I don't get it. (*Beat*) Are you reporting back
on me or something?

OTHER MAN: This isn't about me.

LEWIS: (*continuing*) Is that it – is that what's going
on?

OTHER MAN: I can see you're upset.

LEWIS: Too right I am.

OTHER MAN: It's the telephone call.

LEWIS: It's you!

OTHER MAN: It's when you ring home.

LEWIS: That's total rubbish.

OTHER MAN: It's the same every time.

LEWIS: You don't know what you're talking about.

OTHER MAN: I see what I see.

LEWIS: I can't wait to ring home.

OTHER MAN: Anticipation is one thing –

LEWIS: I count the hours.

OTHER MAN: When you actually ring –

LEWIS: Literally count them –

OTHER MAN: – When you speak to them – hear their voices – that's when it catches you –

LEWIS: You don't know what it does or doesn't do.

OTHER MAN: It overwhelms you. You can't pin it down. It's not them – they couldn't try harder – 'how are you son?' 'How's it going bro?' 'Look after yourself Chris – remember we love you.' And that makes it worse 'cos they don't deserve it –

LEWIS: Alright, alright – ok – I know

OTHER MAN: (*apparently changing the subject*) Why don't you listen to music anymore?

LEWIS: You're not listening.

OTHER MAN: Why no music anymore?

LEWIS: Things change.

OTHER MAN: You've gone off it, then.

LEWIS: I don't care one way or the other.

OTHER MAN: Let's play some of the old favourites then.

LEWIS: No thank you.

OTHER MAN: Barry White – *Practice What You Preach* – I've seen that on your playlist.

LEWIS: No.

OTHER MAN: D' Angelo's version of *Higher* –

LEWIS: Please.

OTHER MAN: Or the Lauren Hill number: *Sweetest Thing* or *I Forgot to be Your Lover* by Jaheim.

LEWIS: I can't – honestly – no.

OTHER MAN: This then.

(*He turns on a CD player and the sound of I wish I Didn't Miss You by Angie Stone is heard*)

LEWIS: (*with real fervour*) For God's sake turn it off.

(*The Other Man stops the music and Lewis is clearly upset and is rubbing his head*)

LEWIS: I can't listen to that stuff – not any more I can't.

OTHER MAN: (*continuing*) You've got to do more than just eat, shit and breathe –

62

LEWIS: I'm doing alright – thanks.

OTHER MAN: That's not what you said just now.

LEWIS: I was wrong – I'm fine.

OTHER MAN: Like some of the 'lifers' in here – they're doing 'alright' – I mean – their hearts still pump blood around their bodies – but you've seen them – nothing behind the eyes – dead from the neck up.

LEWIS: I'm nothing like that.

OTHER MAN: No?

LEWIS: Nothing! And coming here – getting here – Cat C – more freedom – it'll be different –

OTHER MAN: But it isn't is it?

LEWIS: It's just early days – that's all it is – and once I'm in the routine – once I'm back to the plan –

OTHER MAN: It's a good plan – as long as you don't shut yourself down inside – shut life and living out.

LEWIS: That's the reality of prison.

OTHER MAN: No mate – where this is concerned you're not just the prisoner – you're the prison and the prison warder as well and you're locking away everything you've lived for – everything that's given you joy – cricket , music –

LEWIS: It's too raw.

OTHER MAN: Don't wipe your past out – 'cos all you'll be left with is what goes on in here – that'll be it – your whole life. Why apply for parole if all you've got left is this – you might as well serve the whole sentence and then repeat the whole process – do it again – re–offend – get the full fifteen year tariff next time – 'cos that's what lies ahead – a lifetime in here.

LEWIS: Why do you think I'm doing all the courses?

OTHER MAN: Rehabilitation isn't just about *doing*.

LEWIS: Just let me be for once will you.

OTHER MAN: So you can stay as you are – is that what you want – same old pain in the arse Chris Lewis who pisses all his teammates off and never stops to ask himself why – never stops to think – never stops to reflect. Someone once said – I can't remember who – 'Life is for each man a solitary cell whose walls are mirrors' – and it's true.

LEWIS: I don't know what you're talking about.

OTHER MAN: It's about looking at yourself – really looking – not turning away if you don't like what you see – facing up to yourself – like looking in the mirror – seeing who you are – what you've become – the good and the bad – recognising what's good – affirming it – taking it with you.

SCENE 10

The Other Man as Mark

The action goes back in time to December 2009 – two weeks after Lewis' arrest. He is on remand. He is sitting at a table with his head bowed.

The Other Man as Mark enters. Lewis glances and rises but keeps his head bowed.

LEWIS: How's everyone else?

OTHER MAN: Fine.

LEWIS: Vanessa?

OTHER MAN: Everyone's fine – Candace, Mikael, Liam – all of us – all good – and we all send – you know – all of us –

LEWIS: Thanks – and send the same back.

OTHER MAN: Of course

(*There is a pause as Mark watches Lewis rub his head*)

OTHER MAN: So you're doing ok?

LEWIS: Yeah – yeah – I'm – I'm – I'm ok – yeah – doing ok.

OTHER MAN: And the hearing?

LEWIS: Yeah – yeah – the hearing.

OTHER MAN: To get bail – yeah?

LEWIS: A couple of weeks – after Christmas most likely – I think that's what they say.

OTHER MAN: You're not sure?

(*Pause*)

OTHER MAN: And have you got a solicitor?

LEWIS: Not yet – no – no – but listen – er – um – I will – but – how's mum?

OTHER MAN: Like I say – she's fine – mum's good – she's doing ok.

LEWIS: 'Cos the papers – the press – you know – it'll upset her – the media – about the arrest – 'cos I'm out of touch in here – I mean – has there been much – 'cos in here – keeping up with the news – with what's being said – well – you miss stuff.

OTHER MAN: (*clearing his throat before answering – uncomfortable at having to lie*) Of course you do – yeah – well – no – there's not been much – hardly anything – not that I've seen.

LEWIS: Are you sure?

OTHER MAN: Of course – yeah – but – but about this solicitor – you know – for the hearing – you need to get a solicitor – a good one.

LEWIS: Yeah – yeah – I will – but listen – what about the TV – the News – you know – anything on the News.

OTHER MAN: Not that I've seen.

LEWIS: 'Cos in here – you know – it's hard to keep track.

OTHER MAN: Like I say – I haven't seen much.

(*Pause*)

LEWIS: And you're looking after mum. – yeah?

OTHER MAN: We all are.

LEWIS: Good.

OTHER MAN: We won't let you down, bro.

(There is a pause as Lewis struck by the irony of The Other Man as Mark's comment struggles once again to control his emotions)

LEWIS: Well you make good and sure you tell her I'm ok – tell them all I'm ok. I want them to know I'm ok. You promise me – now – yeah?

OTHER MAN: Promise

LEWIS: Good.

OTHER MAN: And you promise you're going to sort out this solicitor for the hearing – a couple of weeks you say.

LEWIS: Just after Christmas most likely.

OTHER MAN: You make sure you do it – yeah?

LEWIS: *(attempting humour)* Hey! I'm supposed to be the big brother here.

OTHER MAN: 'Cos we want you out of this place – you need to get bail.

LEWIS: I'm working on it.

OTHER MAN: So you need someone good.

LEWIS: It'll be fine – you'll see – it'll all be fine.

SCENE 11

The action returns to The Mount Prison as in Scene 9. The lights come up and Lewis is outside the prison cell with a bucket and mop cleaning the floor of the gym. He has his ear plugs in and is listening to music

OTHER MAN: *(pointing out an area of the floor)* You've missed that bit over there.

(Lewis can't hear him because of his ear plugs and The Other Man taps him on the shoulder to attract his attention)

LEWIS: Sorry – couldn't hear.

OTHER MAN: I said – you've missed that bit over there.

LEWIS I did that first. It's just that it's dried.

OTHER MAN: It doesn't look like you've done it

LEWIS: Ok – give me time.

OTHER MAN: The judge has already done that

(Lewis laughs and goes over to the area pointed out and mops it)

LEWIS: There! Is that any better?

OTHER MAN: Much.

(Lewis carries on working)

OTHER MAN: I wish I had a camera – I could put you up on Facebook – 'Chris Lewis actually working' – imagine the shock!

LEWIS: They'll think you've must have superimposed my head on someone else's body.

(They both laugh)

OTHER MAN: Can I ask you something?

LEWIS: Fire away.

OTHER MAN: What was it about you that attracted all this stuff?

LEWIS: I used to think it was just because they didn't like me.

OTHER MAN: And now?

LEWIS: Now I *know* they didn't like me. (*There is a beat before he laughs*) Seriously though – it's true – apart from my family – and a couple of mates – who's been to see me – ex teammates, selectors, administrators – who?

OTHER MAN: And would you have gone to see any of them if the situation was reversed?

LEWIS: No way! I've got nothing in common with any of them – that's the point – no one's fault – but that's how it was – they made no effort and I have to confess nor did I.

OTHER MAN: A confession!

LEWIS: If you like – yes – yes – I confess – I was flash – not with words – I never shot my mouth off – with me it was things – clobber – I let them do the bragging – I had a whole boutique in Manchester close down one afternoon while they packed up all the gear I bought and took it back to my hotel – shirts, trousers, hats – half the shop – but that was nothing – not compared to my biggest 'cash splash' – absolutely nothing – 'cos this time I'm walking past a Mercedes showroom – and through the window I see this brand new white and chrome Mercedes convertible – and spur of the moment – no thinking – I'm in there – slapping forty grand down on the man's desk – (*Relives the moment*) half an hour later off the forecourt cruises Lewis – hood down – windows down – left hand on the wheel – right elbow resting on door – music pumping – (*he makes the sound of the music*) – 'boom cha cha boom cha cha boom cha cha boom' – on course for the cricket ground – and in through the gates he revs – crashing down the gears – clutch half in – throttle full – a hairpin tyre–screaming right into the pavilion car park – and then – finally – still racking up the rev counter – with a muscle bracing screech of brakes he's there – engine purring beneath the sign: 'Nottinghamshire County Cricket Club – Reserved for Chairman Only'. As if to say:

(*As if making an announcement*) 'Here I am everybody – look at me – a black, immigrant kid with a few quid in his back pocket – what are you gonna do now then – now the boot's on the other foot? (*A pause as if waiting for an answer but not getting one*) Well – I'll tell you – you can all go fuck yourselves!' (*He reverts to the present*) And that's what pissed them off – especially the county boys – the ones who were never going to play for England – never going to make any money out of the game – who could only afford second hand Minis. I mean – thinking back – no wonder – after the spot fixing business kicked off – no wonder they ostracised me.

OTHER MAN: That was hardly your fault.

LEWIS: Making excuses is supposed to be my line.

OTHER MAN: But it wasn't all your fault – the spot fixing business.

LEWIS: No – all I'd done was inform the Police after I'd been approached by this Indian businessman – but my name got leaked to the News of The World together with allegations that three England players had previously

70

been mixed up in a betting scam – and that was it – I was the man who'd ratted on his mates.

OTHER MAN: Which you hadn't.

LEWIS: The result was the same though – ostracised by teammates – playing contract terminated – and apart from a disastrous come back with Surrey – career over – 32 years old – no source of income – no qualifications – no prospect of employment – every negative you can think of.

OTHER MAN: And angry.

LEWIS: So angry I couldn't see what it was I was angry with – it becomes everything – yes – all-consuming anger –

(*The Other Man reminds Lewis of his cleaning duties*)

OTHER MAN: Have you finished yet?

LEWIS: Still that far corner to do – that's all – then I'm done.

OTHER MAN: It looks good – much better.

LEWIS: I don't mind cleaning as it happens – don't much fancy it full time – you know – making a career of it – I wouldn't fancy that.

OTHER MAN: Still time to prepare yourself for whatever it is you do want to do.

LEWIS: I'm under no illusions.

OTHER MAN: Good – 'cos it won't be easy.

LEWIS: I know.

OTHER MAN: So you realise what people are going to say –
those who've read your story in the tabloids
or seen you on the news – taxpayers – the
calculations they are going to make: the cost
of your bricklayers course, your plasterer's
course, psychology and God knows what else.
You know what they'll say.

LEWIS: (*parodying the views*) 'A waste of taxpayers
money.'

(*The Other Man and Lewis parody the 'lock 'em up and throw away
the key' attitude*)

OTHER MAN: 'Why should hardened criminals enjoy the
benefit of free education while innocent law
abiding university students the length and
breadth of the land rack up tens of thousands
of pounds in debt paying for their courses?'

LEWIS: (*continuing the parody*) 'People like that
shouldn't be allowed to do courses in the first
place.'

OTHER MAN: (*continuing the parody*) 'Shouldn't be allowed
out of their cells.'

LEWIS: (*continuing the parody*) 'Lock 'em and throw
away the key – that's what I say.'

OTHER MAN: (*continuing the parody*) 'Especially that Chris
Lewis.'

LEWIS: (*continuing the parody*) 'Couldn't agree more!
Had it all and chucked it all away.'

OTHER MAN: 'And the only reason the two faced arsehole's
enrolled on all those courses is because his
review for Category D status is coming up.'

LEWIS: (*continuing the parody*) 'Who's he trying to kid! All he wants is a tick in the "I'm a good boy" box so he can move to one of those cushy open prisons.'

(*They revert to speaking as themselves*)

OTHER MAN: Are they right? I mean – how do you convince them otherwise – how do you prove you're genuine?

LEWIS: I don't know – but I guess if you feel you've got to prove it – tell everyone – make a big show of it – then maybe you're not. People are bound to reserve judgement – take their time and see – so yeah – I'll be watched – there'll be people watching – waiting for me to fuck up.

OTHER MAN: And some hoping you do.

SCENE 12

September 2013 – Hollesley Open Prison Ipswich. The lights come up and Lewis is in the prison cell packing. The Other Man watches before speaking

OTHER MAN: So here you are at last!

LEWIS: Yes.

OTHER MAN: Hollesley Open Prison and just eighteen months left to serve.

LEWIS: Yes.

OTHER MAN: And you're packing.

LEWIS: Yes.

OTHER MAN: Your first home visit.

(*Pause as Lewis does not respond*)

OTHER MAN: A whole weekend at home – you should be happy.

(*Another pause as Lewis does not answer*)

OTHER MAN: So what's the problem?

LEWIS: I'm just a bit worried about the journey.

OTHER MAN: The journey?

LEWIS: The train.

OTHER MAN: You've been on a train before.

LEWIS: Not for five years.

OTHER MAN: And?

LEWIS: It's bound to have changed.

OTHER MAN: How?

LEWIS: Automated tickets – pinless card payments and all that. It's all new – I've never used those.

OTHER MAN: You won't have to pay for anything – you'll be given your ticket before you leave. You know that – they told you.

LEWIS: Yeah but –

OTHER MAN: No buts – it's simple – nothing to worry about

LEWIS: Easily said.

OTHER MAN: You get on at Ipswich and off at St Pancras. Mark will be there to meet you.

LEWIS:	I know – but –
OTHER MAN:	What did I say?
LEWIS:	No buts.
OTHER MAN:	Right!
LEWIS:	Yeah but –
OTHER MAN:	(*correcting him*) Come on!
LEWIS:	I can't help it.
OTHER MAN:	Yes you can.

(*Long pause*)

LEWIS:	I'm scared.
OTHER MAN:	Of course you are.
LEWIS:	And cars – I mean – there are bound to be more cars on the road.
OTHER MAN:	Bound to be.
LEWIS:	Lots more.
OTHER MAN:	You're going by train.
LEWIS:	I'll still have to cross roads.
OTHER MAN:	(*being deliberately provocative*) Oh well – in which case you'd better not go then – you'd better tell the prison authorities to cancel your home visit.
LEWIS:	No!
OTHER MAN:	Then stop worrying – see it as a challenge – I mean – you've managed on your own in a cell all this time.

LEWIS:	That's different.
OTHER MAN:	In what way?
LEWIS:	Like a relief – having somewhere to myself – a space to think things through – without – you know –
OTHER MAN:	Without interruption.
LEWIS:	I know it was meant to be for my own safety – not knowing how other prisoners might react to me and all that – but being on my own – that's not been a challenge – not like this – I mean – I'm nervous – more than nervous – I'm terrified
OTHER MAN:	(*with irony*) Because of the traffic!
LEWIS:	I want to go – of course I do.
OTHER MAN:	What's stopping you?
LEWIS:	I don't know.
OTHER MAN:	Yes you do.
(*Pause*)	
LEWIS:	It's all I've thought about.
OTHER MAN:	I know.
LEWIS:	Literally nothing else – going home's the only thing – you know – trying to visualise it – the moment – the welcome – mum – Mark – the whole family: (*He acts it out as he speaks as if responding to different members of the family*) 'Welcome home, son.' 'Great to see you brother.' 'So good to have you home, Chris.'

(*He pauses*) I mean – what if – you know – what if – (*he stops himself*)

OTHER MAN: Say it – come on – spit it out.

LEWIS: The last five years – they've got on with it – got on with their lives.

OTHER MAN: Without you –

LEWIS: There are new nieces and nephews I've never met – you know – the family's changed – they've all moved on.

OTHER MAN: And so have you.

LEWIS: Exactly – that's the point – everyone's moved on – so why – you know – why would they – after everything that's gone on – all the shame – the pain that I put them through – (*beat*) – oh Christ!

OTHER MAN: Just say it

LEWIS: Why would they want me home?

(*Pause*)

OTHER MAN: You love them, right?

LEWIS: Yeah – of course – of course I do.

OTHER MAN: No, of course about it.

LEWIS: I do – more than anything. I know I do.

OTHER MAN: How – how do you know?

LEWIS: What sort of question is that?

OTHER MAN: The kind that needs an answer – so come on – say it –

LEWIS: How do you know you're breathing? You just do – you don't think about it.

OTHER MAN: Well perhaps you should.

LEWIS: It's not my style.

OTHER MAN: There's no–one listening remember – no–one to judge you or laugh at you – no–one – just you – so – one more time. How do you know you love them? Do you even know what love is?

LEWIS: (*adamant*) Of course I do.

OTHER MAN: How can you be sure?

LEWIS: Because I still feel it – whenever I think about it – when Mark was born – (*he acts out the moment*) – when mum placed this little baby boy in my arms – ever so gently so I knew he was precious. (*Repeating the words his mum had said*) 'Meet your new brother' – and that instant – here he is – in my arms – and just me holding him – (talking to an imaginary baby) – 'Hello Mark – hello little fellah'. (*He resumes his narrative*) And my face is as close as this to his – (*speaking to the baby again*) – 'I'm Chris – I'm your big brother – yes I am – your big brother.' (*He resumes his narrative*) And I can hear him breathing – feel his breath – and that's it – the first time in my life – just a boy – thirteen years old – and I've never felt anything like it – and that's love – and nothing you or anyone else can say or do will ever change that – never.

(*There is the sound of the prison tannoy*)

TANNOY V/O: Prisoner Lewis – calling Prisoner Lewis – the bus for Ipswich Station will be leaving from outside the main gates in ten minutes. Please report to reception immediately.

(*Lewis gets his things together and then pauses as if finding the resolve to leave*)

OTHER MAN: It's the same for them you know.

LEWIS: What do you mean?

OTHER MAN: Your mum – Mark – your family – It's the same for them – how they feel about you – nothing can change that either.

SCENE 13

A few days later at Hollesley Open Prison. The lights come up on Lewis who now sits on his bed with his head between his hands. There is a lengthy silence before The Other Man speaks

OTHER MAN: Are you going to sit like that all day?

(*Pause*)

Don't pretend you can't hear me – 'cos I know you can and you're not going to do this – not with just over a year to go – you're not – no way – I won't let you.

(*Pause*)

For Christ's sake – you've got your next home visit to look forward to.

LEWIS: Not for another twenty eight days.

OTHER MAN: That'll soon pass.

LEWIS:	It feels like twenty eight years.
OTHER MAN:	Don't be ridiculous.
LEWIS:	I'm telling you – these home visits – four I've done – it's like I'm breathing freedom – breathing it in so I can smell it – almost taste it – but then I'm back here – outside the gates – lining up to come back in – and it's gone – like it never was – and I've twenty eight days before I can breathe again.
OTHER MAN:	And you will – soon enough.
LEWIS:	(*touching his head*) I've moved on in here – that's the problem – and each day drags like a month did back in Dovegate.
OTHER MAN:	But you're not in Dovegate – you're here – Ipswich – it's an open prison.
LEWIS:	I know but –
OTHER MAN:	You can't let this wear you down – not with just 18 months to your release and it's going to be tough enough then.
LEWIS:	I know.
OTHER MAN:	And you're going to have to be strong – 'cos you know what people are going to say:

(*The Other Man now parodies the voice of Public Opinion*)

| OTHER MAN: | Six and a half years is that all he served? What about the people whose lives are made a total misery by these drug dealing bastards. And not just the users. |
| | What about the poor parents. I mean – imagine watching your kids' lives go down the |

pan while some arsehole lines his pockets at
their expense. I've got no sympathy – and if
it means taking these people off the streets for
good then so be it – give them life – 'cos that's
what they take – lives.'

(*The parody ends*)

LEWIS: They're entitled to their opinion – I mean –
you can't stop people thinking like that.

OTHER MAN: And are they right?

LEWIS: I think people deserve a second chance.

OTHER MAN: And what about the victims – they don't
always get a second chance.

(*There is a pause as Lewis does not respond*)

OTHER MAN: Nothing to say?

LEWIS: Not really no – I mean – why would I have
anything to say?

OTHER MAN: You tell me.

LEWIS: There weren't any victims – not in my case
there weren't.

OTHER MAN: No?

LEWIS: Apart from my family – and I know what I've
done to them so you don't have to say any
more on that score – I know – there's not a
day goes by when I don't think about what
I've done to them.

OTHER MAN: I wasn't thinking about them.

LEWIS: Who then?

(There is a pause as The Other Man does not respond and Lewis tries to puzzle out what he means)

LEWIS: Come on – tell me – what victims – I've no idea who you mean.

OTHER MAN: Exactly!

LEWIS: Exactly what? Tell me what you mean.

OTHER MAN: Not this time no – no – this time it's up to you to work it out.

SCENE 14

The action moves back in time to May 2009. The lights come up and Lewis who is on trial standing in the dock at Croydon Crown Court. The Voice of The Judge and The Voice of The Foreman of The Jury are recorded

LEWIS: *(speaking directly to the audience)* I know what they've decided – but that's not it.

JUDGE V/O: Foreman of the Jury – have you reached a verdict?

LEWIS: *(speaking directly to the audience)* That's not what I'm worried about.

(There is a pause to allow imaginary time for an answer to be given)

JUDGE V/O: And that verdict is?

FOREMAN V/O: Guilty.

LEWIS: *(speaking directly to the audience)* How long – that's all that's worrying me.

OTHER MAN: *(as The Judge)* Clairmont Christopher Lewis – You have been found guilty of attempting to smuggle seven pounds of cocaine into the United Kingdom.

LEWIS: (*direct to the audience*) I know The Judge is talking to me – I'm looking straight at him – at his lips moving – but the words he's saying – no – they must be somewhere else – or I must be. How long – that's all I want to know – where doesn't matter – I don't care where – but not too long – please – please –

JUDGE V/O: This court frequently has to deal with drug smugglers and drug runners. Normally they show considerable naivety and poverty because they come from poor countries. Even so, the majority of those who are guilty have the courage to face up to what they did and take the punishment. You showed neither of these qualities. In a cowardly attempt to evade justice, you sought to blame your accomplice for a crime you obviously jointly committed. You made it to the top of your profession.

LEWIS: (*as if to himself*) Please – not too long.

JUDGE V/O: But your drug smuggling was calculated greed and you knowingly and willingly engaged in major organised crime. Under the circumstances I am sentencing you to thirteen years.

LEWIS: (*to himself*) 13 years – shit – that's 156 months, 676 weeks, 4750 days. (*beat*) Don't think about it – you mustn't think about it.

JUDGE V/O: Take him down.

SCENE 15

The scene returns to Hollesley Prison. The lights come up and Lewis and The Other Man are standing outside the prison

LEWIS: I don't want to go back in through the gates yet.

OTHER MAN: You've got ten minutes left – Open Prison it may be but it's still a prison

LEWIS: I just want to have a moment.

OTHER MAN: A curfew is a curfew – you know the rules and if you're not back inside those gates....

LEWIS: I'll be back. I just need a moment – you know – a few minutes – to get myself – (*he pauses*) – I mean today's been – (*he sighs to a halt*) – I can't say I didn't know – I did – the sort of things that happen – 'cos she warned me – Sarah who runs runs the place – when I volunteered – she warned me – the kinds of thing I might come across – working at the centre – but I thought – cooking – you know – working as a cook – doing the lunch – not involved in any of their problems – not directly – 'cos there are people there trained to deal with the homeless – paid to deal with them – and I'm just a volunteer – so what do I know – how can I help – I mean – I can't help – I'm not trained – I'd as likely do more harm than good – so I've stayed in the kitchen – doing the whatever – lasagne, spag bol – all the stuff I did on the cookery course at Dovegate – and it's not like today's my first day – it's been six months – that's how long I've been going there – every day – so I know the kind of people – and I shouldn't say that

84

– I shouldn't talk about them like they're all
of a kind – I shouldn't but I do – everyone
does – like all they're after is money for booze
or anything else that'll get them off their
faces. But what you said about victims – who
my victims might be – well – today – I – I –
well – let me tell you : I'm at the centre – I'm
doing my job – cooking spaghetti and a
bloody great pan of bolognese is bubbling
away beside me – and I'm just about to serve
– forty or more queuing up – and then – thud
– and I look out through the serving hatch
and someone's lying on the floor – as close as
I am to you. And I know him from his cap –
he comes to the centre every day and he
always wears this blue New York Yankees cap
– and he always calls me 'banana man'.
(*Parodying the Man*) 'Hey Banana Man
what's cooking today?' But there he is – lying
on his back writhing – and he's like foaming –
he's frothing from his mouth and making this
low bubbling noise. (*Lewis makes a low
bubbling noise*). And none of the others
queuing take any notice – like it's normal –
except for Smithy – the ex para guy – who
steps over him and shouts at me – 'when's
that fucking spaghetti coming'. Half an hour
later – it's like it never happened – Sarah's
come in and given him mouth to mouth and
the paramedics have been and gone – and
lunch is finished and it's like he's been cleared
away with the plates.

OTHER MAN: It really is nearly curfew time.

LEWIS: Just listen will you – 'cos I've got to get my
head round this before I go back in there. It

was 'Spice' that did it – that's what Sarah said it was – and what hit me – what I've been thinking is – what if – you know – (*beat*) – you know what I mean.

OTHER MAN: What if you hadn't got caught that day at Gatwick?

LEWIS: Yes – I mean – I watched a man die – and I've cooked lunch for him most days for six months – and I don't even know his name – and that's the point – like you say – if I hadn't have got caught – it could have been anyone – I'd never have known. (*He starts to get upset*) I'd never have known who they were – and that's the point – I didn't care – it never entered my head – you know – who they might be – it never entered my head because I didn't care – I didn't care – never thought about it – about them – who they might be – I never thought about the consequences for them – 'cos in my mind they didn't exist – (*Beat*) – like the man today – 'Robbie' – that was his name apparently – I still don't know his second name – no–one did – not at the centre – no–one – he didn't exist – not really – not enough to care – enough to ask him his name – he was just 'one of them' – that's all he was – 'one of them'.

SCENE 16

A few weeks later at Hollesley Open Prison. The lights come up and Lewis and The Other Man sit side by side on the bed. They have identical suitcases by their feet

TANNOY V/O: Prisoner Lewis – calling Prisoner Lewis – report to reception.

(*Lewis and The Other Man rise together in response*)

OTHER MAN: This is it then.

LEWIS: Yes.

OTHER MAN: So what's keeping us?

LEWIS: Thinking –

OTHER MAN: Ah! A big step forward.

LEWIS: I've tried to imagine it for six and a half years – you know – this instant – this very moment – I've tried visualising it – picking up my case and walking to reception – taking the step from one side of the gate to the other – prisoner to free man in one short stride – like that's all there is to it – that's what I've always thought – that it would be so simple –

OTHER MAN: The moment of release.

LEWIS: But not escape – 'cos now it's about to happen – it's clear – release and escape –

BOTH: (*speaking together*) Not the same thing.

LEWIS: Not the same thing at all – because walking out of here – getting released – it's not like escaping anything – how can it be – 'cos it all has to come too –

OTHER MAN: All of it.

LEWIS: Everything we've done – learned – forgotten even – it's coming too – all of it.

(*The Other Man nods in response*)

OTHER MAN: Have we got everything?

LEWIS: I think so.

OTHER MAN: Good – in which case –

LEWIS: Yes –

OTHER MAN: We'd best be going.

(*There is a brief pause before Lewis and The Other Man pick up their suitcases and leave the cell together*)

Blackout

THE END